Forest Resource Policy in Latin America

Edited by Kari Keipi

Published by the Inter-American Development Bank
Distributed by The Johns Hopkins University Press

Washington, D.C.
1999

To order this book, contact:
IDB Bookstore
1300 New York Ave, NW
Washington, D.C. 20577
Tel: (202) 623-1753 / (202) 623-1390
Fax: (202) 623-1709

Cataloging-in-Publication data provided by the
Inter-American Development Bank
Felipe Herrera Library

    Forest resource policy in Latin America / Kari Keipi, editor.
       p. cm.
       Includes bibliographical references.
       ISBN: 1-886938-34-2
    1. Forest policy – Latin America. 2. Sustainable forestry – Latin America. 3. Deforestation
– Latin America. 4. Forest conservation—Latin America. I. Keipi, Kari. II. Inter-American
Development Bank.

    333.7516/098 F7161   99-71560

Preface

About a quarter of the world's forests and over half of its tropical forests are located in Latin America. Forests cover half of the region's land, and the per capita forested area is the highest in the world. In addition, Latin America boasts many forest ecosystems and a tremendously rich ecological diversity. As a result, natural resource policies vary from country to country.

Some nations favor the conversion of natural forests to other uses and the establishment of forest plantations. Others place a higher priority on the environmental value of the forests and favor conservation. And still other nations argue that the main opportunity for conserving natural forests lies in recognizing and paying for the environmental services that they provide. Yet, in many countries, the main role of forests (be they natural or manmade) is to provide products to fill the basic needs of the local population and generate income through the production of marketable commodities.

In this volume, forest policy specialists look at better ways to manage and conserve forest resources in the region. They assess the economic and social impacts of alternative macroeconomic and sector policies on forests, and discuss financing mechanisms for sustainable use and management, including incentives for forest management. The authors also provide a description of the stakeholders, highlighting land tenure issues and the rights of indigenous groups, and provide an analysis of alternative forest policies. The future direction of sustainable forest development in Latin America will be affected by whether present opportunities are recognized and taken advantage of, as well as by the types of decisions that are made.

Waldemar W. Wirsig
Manager
Sustainable Development Department

Acknowledgments

Many people have contributed to the preparation of this book. The editor wishes to thank especially those authors who not only wrote their own chapters, but also reviewed the draft text. More than forty people participated in the preparation process. Comments on various sections of the document came from international agencies, private sector companies, nongovernmental organizations and universities involved in forest resource policy issues in the region. Peer reviewers included Arnoldo Contreras of the World Council for Forestry and Sustainable Development; Joshua Dickinson of Tropical Research and Development Inc.; Hans Gregersen of the University of Minnesota; Hans-Harald Jahn of the European Investment Bank; David Kaimowitz of the Centre for International Forest Research; Suzie Kerr and Stefanie Kirschoff of the University of Maryland; Cormac O'Carroll of Jaakko Poyry Ltd.; Manuel Paveri of the United Nations Food and Agriculture Organization; Glenn Prickett and John Reid of Conservation International; Jeffrey McNeely and Martha Rojas of the International Union for the Conservation of Nature; and Nigel Sizer of World Resources Institute.

The following IDB staff members also reviewed the report: Sergio Ardila, Michael Collins, Arthur Darling, Anne Deruyttere, Ruben Echeverría, Hector Malarin, Mario Nicklitschek, Gil Nolet, Jonathan Renshaw, Steven Stone, Raul Tuazon and William Vaughan. Special thanks go to Walter Arensberg, who oversaw the preparation of the book. The work would not have been possible without the faithful support in research, translation and document production of Maria Antola, Ligia Espinosa, Ana María Ibáñez, Graciela Testa and John Williams. Finally, editor Eva Greene was instrumental in bringing this publication to completion. Sincere thanks are extended to all of these coworkers, from outside and within the Inter-American Development Bank, who participated in a shared effort to analyze and provide future directions for forest resource policies in Latin America.

Abbreviations and Acronyms

ACT	Amazon Cooperation Treaty
AIDESEP	Inter-Ethnic Association for The Development of the Peruvian Jungle
BOLFOR	Bolivia Sustainable Forest Management Project
BTRTF	Brazilian Tropical Rainforest Trust Fund
CANAFOR	National Forestry Council of Costa Rica
CATIE	Center for Research and Learning in Tropical Agronomy
CBD	Convention on Biological Diversity
CCAB-AP	Regional Council on Forests and Protected Areas
CCF	Costa Rican Forestry Council
CCT	Tropical Sciences Center (Costa Rica)
CDF	Centro de Desarrollo Forestal (Bolivia)
CDS	Commission for Sustainable Development
CERFLOR	Certificate of Origin of Forest Raw Material (Brazil)
CETUR	Corporación Ecuatoriana de Turismo (Ecuadorian Tourism Corporation)
CGIAR	Consultative Group for International Agricultural Research
CI	Conservation International
CIAT	International Center for Tropical Agriculture
CIDESA	Fundación de Capacitación e Inversión para el Desarrollo Socio-Ambiental (Foundation for Training and Investment for Socio-Environmental Development)
CIFOR	Center for International Forest Research
CITES	Convention on International Trade of Endangered Species
CNF	National Forestry Council (Bolivia)
CNF	Cámara Nacional Forestal (Peru)
CNPT	National Center for the Sustainable Development of Traditional Populations (Brazil)
CNS	National Council of Rubber Tappers (Brazil)
CO_2	carbon dioxide
COFYAL	Cooperativa Forestal Yanesha Limitada (Yanesha Forestry Cooperative Limited)
COHDEFOR	Honduran Corporation for Forest Development
COICA	Indigenous Coordination Association of the Amazon
CONAF	Corporación Nacional Forestal y de Recursos Renovables (Chile)
CONAIE	Confederación de Nacionalidades Indigenas del Ecuador
CORMA	National Timber Corporation of Chile
CSA	Canadian Standards Association
CSRMP	Central Selva Resource Management Project
DNS	Debt-for Nature Swaps
ECE	Economic Commission for Europe
ECLAC	Economic Commission for Latin America and the Caribbean
EPAT/MUCIA	Environmental and Natural Resources Policy and Training Project / Midwest Universities Consortium for International Activities
EU	European Union
FAG	Forest Advisors Group
FAO	United Nations Food and Agriculture Organization
FOB	free on board
FPCN	Fundación Peruana para la Conservación de la Naturaleza (Peruvian Foundation for the Conservation of Nature)
FSC	Forest Stewardship Council
FSR	forest sector reforms
FUNAI	National Indian Foundation (Brazil)
FUNDECOR	Foundation for the Development of the Central Volcanic Range (Costa Rica)
FUNTAC	Foundation for Technology of the State of Acre (Brazil)
GATT	General Agreement on Trade and Tariffs
GDI	German Development Institute
GDP	gross domestic product
GEF	Global Environmental Facility

GSP	Generalized System of Preferences
GTZ	Gesellschaft für Technische Zusammenarbeit (Agency for Technical Assistance)
ha	hectare
IBAMA	Brazilian Institute for Environment and Renewable Natural Resources
ICDP	Integrated Conservation and Development Project
ICRAF	International Centre for Research in Agroforestry
ICT	Instituto Costarricense de Turismo (Costa Rican Tourism Institute)
IDB (BID)	Inter-American Development Bank (Banco Interamericano de Desarrollo)
IFAD	International Fund for Agricultural Development
IFPRI	International Food Policy Research Institute
IICA	Inter-American Institute for Agricultural Cooperation
ILO	International Labor Organization
IMAFLORA	Instituto de Manejo e Certificação Florestal e Agrícola (Brazil)
IMAZON	Instituto do Homem e Meio Ambiente da Amazônia (Institute for Man and the Environment of the Amazon)
INBio	Instituto Nacional de Biodiversidad (Costa Rica's National Institute of Biodiversity)
INEFAN	Instituto Ecuatoriano Forestal, de Áreas Naturales, y de Vida Silvestre (Ecuadorian Institute of Forestry, Natural Areas, and Wildlife)
INRA	National Institute of Agrarian Reform (Nicaragua)
ISO	International Standardization Organization
ISTF	International Society of Tropical Foresters
ITTA	International Tropical Timber Agreement
ITTO	International Tropical Timber Organization
IUCN	International Union for the Conservation of Nature (now the World Conservation Union)
LAC	Latin America and the Caribbean
LAFN	Latin America Forest Network
m^3	cubic meter
MACA	Ministry of Peasant Affairs and Agriculture (Bolivia)
MARA	Ministry of Agriculture and Agricultural Reform (Brazil)
MBR	Maya Biosphere Reserve
MFN	most favored nation
NAFTA	North American Free Trade Agreement
NBER	National Bureau of Economic Research
NGO	nongovernmental organization
NPV	net present value
NTFP	nontimber forest product
NWFP	nonwood forest product
OECD	Organisation for Economic Cooperation and Development
ONF	National Office of Forests (France / French Guyana)
ONIC	National Indigenous Peoples Organization of Colombia
OTA	Office of Technology Assessment (U.S.)
PRODEIN	National Indigenous Development Program (Colombia)
PSE	producer subsidy equivalent
SBS	Sociedade Brasileira de Silvicultura
SO_2	sulphur dioxide
SPN	Servicio de Parques Nacionales (National Park Service, Costa Rica)
SPNG	Servicio del Parque Nacional Galápagos (Galápagos National Park Service)
SRP	Subsecretaría de Recursos Pesqueros (Subsecretariat of Fishery Resources, Ecuador)
TCA	Tratado de Cooperación Amazónica
TFAP	Tropical Forestry Action Plan
TSC	Tropical Science Center
UNCED	United Nations Conference on Environment and Development
UNCTAD	United Nations Conference on Trade and Development
UNDP	United Nations Development Program

USAID	United States Agency for International Development
USD	United States dollar
WCED	World Commission on Environment and Development
WCFSD	World Commission on Forestry and Sustainable Development
WRI	World Resources Institute
WTO	World Trade Organization
WWF	Worldwide Fund for Nature / World Wildlife Fund

Contents

Introduction

CHAPTER 1

Kari Keipi

Perhaps only the world's oceans rival forests in importance as a life-supporting mechanism for the planet. Forests play a vital role in sustaining the biodiversity of natural ecosystems and in regulating the world's climate system. Latin America has one of the largest and most diverse remaining forest areas on Earth and, as such, is a region of contrasts and paradoxes. On the one hand, there are abundant natural resources including forests, rich mineral deposits, and bountiful inland water and coastal resources. On the other, the same natural resources that form the basis for the region's wealth are being rapidly destroyed, a process that contributes to the persistently high levels of poverty in rural areas.

Latin America's rapid forest deterioration has important economic and environmental consequences. In a period when the region is focusing on social development, resource degradation is leading to increasing rural poverty. The alarm over forest resource degradation in Latin America has led to intensified activity in the forestry sector. If the forests of Latin America are to be managed sustainably, and areas of particular environmental value conserved, policy changes at the national and international level must take place. Thus the principal objective of this book is to provide ideas and provoke discussion on how to achieve more effective management and investments in Latin American forests.

Close scrutiny of the causes of forest degradation and deforestation in the region suggests policy failure as one of the main culprits. Policies affecting forests have failed for several reasons, including the relative overvaluation of other competing land use options. The drive for short-term political gains has frequently caused this overvaluation, placing forests at a disadvantage. In addition, most countries have not taken advantage of the benefits of the public good aspects of forest resources. Other primary reasons for poor forest practices have been inadequate participation of affected groups in decisionmaking and the poorly analyzed effects of public policies on natural resources (Contreras-Hermosilla 1995). Operational weaknesses in public institutions have also contributed to policy failure; and recent privatization and trade liberalization efforts may have resulted in the unsustainable forest development of the region.

The State of Latin American Forests Today

The forests of Latin America and the Caribbean have global importance due to their size: one-fourth of the world's total forests and half of all tropical forests lie in the region. It contains more trees, shrubs, and other plants than any other continent—about 85,000 species. This corresponds to some 31 percent of the world total of 270,000 species (FAO 1995a). It is estimated that approximately 20 percent of forest habitats have already been lost in South America. In other parts of the region, the loss has been even greater: such is the case of Mexico, which has lost between 60 and 70 percent of its forest habitats.

Table 1.1 Forest Area and Deforestation Rate, 1990

(In thousands of hectares)

Subregion	Natural forested area	Area deforested annually	Annual deforestation (% of total)
Central America and Mexico	68,000	1,112	1.63
Caribbean[a]	47,000	122	0.26
South America	854,700	6,244	0.73
Total	969,700	7,478	0.77

[a] Includes Suriname, Guyana, and French Guiana.

Source: World Resources Institute (WRI), 1994.

Most protected areas in Latin America and the Caribbean are located in forests. The region has a total of 230 million hectares of national protected areas; some 98 million ha are in internationally established biosphere reserves and world heritage sites. In fact, these national protected areas correspond to 11 percent of the region's total land area, but their management could be greatly improved.[1]

Considerably more than a third of the total area of the region is classed as forest. The rate of its deforestation corresponds to the world average: some 7.5 million ha, or 0.8 percent of the forests, disappear each year. Central America and Mexico have the highest rates of forest clearing, with 1.6 percent of their remaining forests being destroyed annually (see Table 1.1). This rate is higher than that of continental Southeast Asia (1.5 percent) which has the world's second highest regional deforestation rate. The reason that Central America and Mexico have "high" rates, while the Amazon area has "low" rates, is largely because the Amazon forests are so huge that even major deforestation represents only a small percentage of the total remaining forest area.[2]

Deforestation is broadly defined as the conversion of forest land to other uses. Conversion to agricultural use includes colonization and shifting cultivation by small farmers. When wealthy farmers convert forest land, it is typically put into livestock production and is often related to land speculation. Still another form of agricultural conversion is for large-scale industrial plantations and clandestine drug cultivation, although these are lesser causes of deforestation. Further incursions are made by mining and infrastructure development in forest frontier areas, resulting in increased access to the forest and its conversion to agricultural use by colonists and land speculators.

Commercial logging and firewood collection are almost never direct causes of deforestation in Latin America. Over the long term, however, they can seriously degrade forest resources. As with infrastructure and mining projects, the actual logging impacts may not be severe, but they allow access to forest resources by colonists and land speculators. The same is true of developments that enable the exploitation of oil and mineral deposits or potential sources of hydroelectric power (reservoir construction). The result is gradual land fragmentation and uncontrolled development in these areas, especially when they do not form part of any overall regional or land use planning scheme.

---

[1] First Latin American Congress on Parks and Other Protected Areas. 1997. Santa Marta Declaration: Guide to Action. Minambiente, Bogotá.

[2] WRI (1994). A record level of deforestation of 2.9 million hectares was reported in the Brazilian Amazon for 1995. Although the figure fell sharply in 1996, the trend remains worrying (*The Economist*, February 1997).

There are many causes of deforestation in Latin America, and the particular impact of each is difficult to measure. On the one hand, the most commonly mentioned factors—population growth and poverty—both affect deforestation rates, but in complex ways. Their impact is most evident in areas of increasing settlement pressures from marginalized sectors of the population and where rural wages are low. On the other hand, increasing land values foment speculation and deforestation by wealthy investors. Economic studies show that rising agricultural and timber prices have a positive correlation with deforestation rates. In contrast to these trends, the existence of land markets and tenure security improve the interest for long-term investments by farmers. However, these investments may not be directed to forest management. Combined factors (such as rising agricultural prices in tandem with tenure security) may also increase the propensity to change land use from forest to agriculture (Kaimowitz and Angelsen 1997).

On a larger scale, it is generally hard to find any clear-cut relationship between deforestation and macroeconomic variables and policies. However, a number of the policy reforms included in current economic liberalization and adjustment efforts may increase the pressure on forests. In this context, a key role is frequently played by logging companies and road builders when they open up previously inaccessible forest areas.

Frequently, the various factors mentioned above, either on their own or in combination, form part of an interlinked, mutually reinforcing process of destruction of the region's forests and natural resources. This process is becoming increasingly uncontrollable, in large part due to the special circumstances of these mostly peripheral regions and to a lack of proper government administration. In this context, underlying structural conditions—such as unbalanced or unregulated land ownership, contradictory laws, or tax incentive schemes—may have a further detrimental effect on forests. The situation may be further exacerbated by shortcomings or abuses of power in the area of state planning, administration, and control.[3]

Box 1.1 shows the major types of deforestation/forest degradation and their causal factors. Although there is extensive deforestation throughout the region, there are ways to decrease it or counterbalance it. Deforestation can be countered either by protecting existing forests or by compensating for their loss through establishing new forests. The latter can be accomplished through promoting natural tree regeneration or through creating new plantation forests. Very little research is available on the natural regeneration capability of different forest types in the region. However, natural regeneration would be an inexpensive way to reproduce trees, since both the seeds and seedling development would be a free product of the existing forest. Nevertheless, plantations are normally preferred in the region (even though they are more expensive to establish) because their wood and other products are usually much more valuable than most of the products extracted from natural forests.

Regional estimates of the area in plantation forests vary from 8 million to 11.1 million ha.[4] Thus, the total planted area corresponds to approximately only 1 percent of the area of natural forests, or the deforestation rate of a single year in the region. While most of the fuelwood, nonwood products, and environmental benefits come from natural forests, over half of the industrial timber is produced in plantations.

---

[3] *Tropical Forest Conservation and German Development Cooperation: Experiences, Contributions, Perspectives.* 1997. Bonn: BMZ.

[4] According to the FAO, plantations cover some 8 million ha in tropical Latin America and the Caribbean, while the World Resources Institute (1994) estimates that there are 8.6 million ha of forest plantations in the region. The temperate zone of the region has some 2.5 million ha of plantations (FAO 1995b).

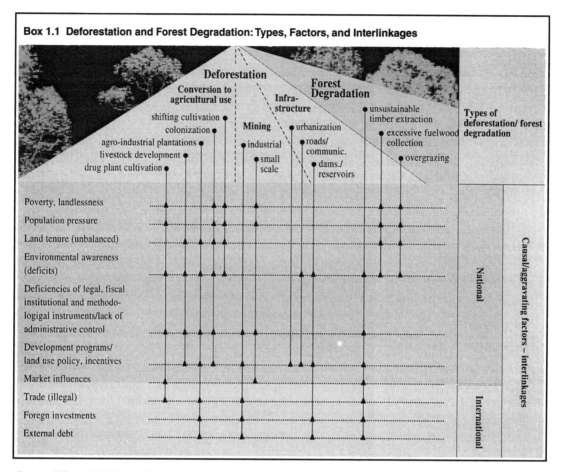

Box 1.1 Deforestation and Forest Degradation: Types, Factors, and Interlinkages

Source: Volmer (1993). Used by permission of publisher.

The largest plantations are in Brazil, with some 7 million ha, 4.1 million of which are industrially utilizable manmade forests. Chile has 1.6 million ha of reforested areas, practically all for industrial purposes. Argentina has 0.7 million ha; Venezuela, 0.5 million ha; Cuba, 0.4 million ha; and Peru, 0.3 million ha. Colombia, Mexico, and Uruguay include some 0.2 million ha each. In every other country of Latin America and the Caribbean, the reforested area is less than 100,000 ha. Estimates of the current yearly reforestation rate vary from 386,000 (FAO 1995a) to 520,000 ha (WRI 1994).

Plantations account for most of the economic potential of forests in many countries. Practically all of them have been established on abandoned or low-yield agricultural lands where erosion was prevalent. The overwhelming majority of plantations have been established with fast-growing exotic species in the *Eucalyptus* and *Pinus* genera, although research is also finding fast-growing native species that are increasingly used on plantations. Only in exceptional cases has prime agricultural soil, or land with existing natural forest, been used for tree plantations. This has happened lately in Chile, where industrial plantations are highly profitable and are encouraged by government incentives. Although the majority of existing plantations are industrial in nature, agroforestry and social forestry (in which communities grow trees for their own nonproduction needs, e.g., firewood) are widely practiced in the region. These plantations are yielding important benefits to local communities and have improved environmental conditions.

To date, investment in the sustainable development of forest resources in Latin America has been restricted to plantations and experimental projects in natural forest management. These projects require increased research and funding if they are to be of immediate benefit to the region's countries. Forest use decisions made by the present generation will have long-term effects, and they should not adversely affect the welfare of future generations.

The region's governments could take several measures to diminish deforestation. First, they could adopt policies and implement institutional and infrastructural supports that would make sustainable forest use financially competitive with alternative uses such as agriculture and ranching. Second, trade policies, export bans, and the use of tariffs have kept many forestry operations from becoming competitive in international markets, and should be revised. Third, forest concessions that have traditionally been doled out with relaxed standards for environmental impacts, replanting, and best management practices need to be redesigned. Finally, a lack of land tenure security has contributed significantly to a short-term, open-access approach to resource use and exploitation with serious negative impacts on sustainability, and governments must actively address this issue.

Forest Potential and Policy Adjustments

Latin America's forests preserve essential economic, environmental, and ecological resources. They encompass opportunities for sustained timber and nontimber forest product extraction, fuelwood production, ecotourism, bioprospecting, and other uses. With these products and commercial opportunities come prospects for employment and income-generating activities to raise the standard of living for the region's poor. The forests also provide regional and local environmental services in the form of water quality protection, erosion control to prevent soil loss, and hillside stabilization—services that, if not provided, would cost local and national governments substantial sums in mitigation and health care costs. In addition, national parks, reserves, and undisturbed forests provide habitat for one of the most numerous and diverse assemblages of species in the world. A major portion of the world's flora, fauna, and natural ecosystems exists only in the forests of Latin America and the Caribbean.

However, forest preservation, management, and rehabilitation come at a cost. The opportunity cost for developing and safeguarding these forest resources must come at the expense of other land uses. Frontier agriculture, ranching, colonization, and mining are relatively short-term, profit-seeking activities whose long-term damages to the land and society often appear unjustifiable. These activities are all too often destructive when they occur in an unregulated and haphazard manner.

Such deforestation does not always translate into the expected benefits of the new land use due to unsustainable production patterns. The conversion often results in a sacrifice not only of renewable economic resources such as timber and fuelwood, but it also includes the loss of such life-giving environmental amenities as watershed and soil protection, biodiversity, and carbon sequestration. There may be great disparities between the sustainable economic and environmental potentials of the region on the one hand, and the current economic yield and rate of resource degradation on the other.

Sustainable or not, however, these activities produce income and employment for both the poor and the well-to-do. Thus, sustainable forest management practices must be competitive in the types of economic opportunities they provide in order to be an acceptable alternative to other land uses. The challenges, then, are twofold: *first*, to develop and support sustainable, forest-based economic activities that are solvent and competitive with other land uses; and *second*, to eliminate the current biases against forest-based activities and in favor of other sectors, as well as incorporate the cost of negative consequences of unsustainable forest land uses into the operating budgets of those activities.

Forestry can be a very profitable business in Latin America. The increasing flows of international investments in the forestry sector of the region indicate this. In looking at the profit issue, the question of time horizon is of utmost importance in promoting sustainable forest management. The time frames for sustainable forest practices are often longer than for other types of investments, and affect their relative profitability compared with other land uses. Yet the returns on this type of investment accrue much more broadly than solely to the private investor's pocket book. As explained above, the returns also accumulate in the form of ecological and environmental benefits to local, regional, and global societies.

When forestry generates positive externalities, the investors may end up paying for benefits that accrue to a free-riding society. Thus, as it sometimes stands now, investors may face relatively low financial returns compared with other investments because of the longer investment periods, and have to maintain a certain degree of altruism as they watch a portion of those returns go to society. Therefore, even though the region's forests are a threatened and valuable resource, their wise use and conservation is not only a private-sector priority. It should also be a priority for the area's governments to create an economic and financial climate that is favorable for private investment in forestry. In certain cases with very high externalities but marginal private profitability, government plans for compensating the providers of environmental services may be justified when considering the benefits they provide to society.

While many types of investment strategies involve the public sector, the international community, and various public-private partnerships, this volume focuses on ways to encourage private sector investment in the prudent utilization and conservation of forests. Roles of the public sector, nongovernmental organizations (NGOs), and the international community are examined here mainly in the context of financing and policy development.

Policy support is an important mechanism for encouraging sustainable forestry investment. Specific forest-related policies such as trade liberalization, structural or monetary incentives, and land tenure security can be used to directly promote or inhibit certain types of forest use practices. Just as important though, are policies that affect domestic and export markets, the macroeconomy in general, and political stability—all of which need to be dependable and predictable for a long-term investment such as a managed forestry operation.

Regional and International Mandates

Three international conventions relate directly or indirectly to the need for a better use of the world's forest resources. The Framework Convention on Climate Change, the Convention on Biological Diversity (CBD), and the Convention to Combat Desertification all emphasize the importance of forests in preserving a healthy planet and providing opportunity for future generations. The Convention on Climate Change outlines the obligation of developed countries to increase the financing of actions that will improve the climate in the global common interest, while the two other agreements emphasize the concept of sustainability as well as managing and conserving resources that lie within national boundaries.

In addition to the global conventions mentioned above, there are several regional agreements relevant to forests such as the Convention on Nature Protection and Wildlife Preservation in the Western Hemisphere (1940), signed by 18 countries in Latin America and the Caribbean. The Amazon Cooperation Treaty (1978) promotes a comprehensive management of the Amazon and its tributaries. Its implementing entity is the Amazon Cooperative Council which consists of high level representatives from eight countries. The Central American Convention for the Protection of the Environment (1989) calls for cooperation in sustainable development. The objective of the Central American Convention for Biodiversity and the Protection of Wild Areas (1992) is the conservation of biological resources in the subregion. The Central American Commission on Environment and Development is in charge of developing strategies that support both conventions. These agreements have reiterated the need for a number of improvements in the sector, such as improving financing through entities like the Global Environmental Facility, creating financial instruments and funding mechanisms at the local and national level, increasing domestic public and private sector investments in ecological conservation, and sustainable natural resource management.

Thus, the principal nations of the world have clearly given a mandate for global, regional, and local efforts to improve the state of the world's forests. Recognizing the problems inherent in the forest sector, they have enumerated goals and objectives and developed strategies to combat those problems. However, in practice, the countries of the region have scarcely applied the policies, action plans, and programs that have been proposed on the basis of the noble ideals set forth in the conventions.

Contents of the Volume

Forest Resource Policy in Latin America represents the thoughts and creative ideas of a score of experts who have dedicated their professional careers to deciphering, analyzing, and improving the ways forests and forest products are exploited, shared, and preserved. Their conclusions and suggestions are based on diverse experiences in the field and on synthesizing innovative ideas. Each chapter deals with different situations and issues, and together they offer a comprehensive picture of the present circumstances and direction of forest management in Latin America.

The authors carefully analyze the macroeconomic conditions, political climates, and local realities responsible for the condition of forests and forest management in the region today. In addition, they trace various schools of thought to illustrate why certain policies, investment strategies, and development tactics have been in effect, and where their evolution is leading. The chapters employ a wide array of case studies that include localized efforts, national investment strategies, and international treaties. The follow-up analyses explain many of the reasons for past successes and failures, and should improve the chance of success for future efforts.

In Chapter 2, **Jan Laarman** reviews government policies affecting forests, setting a framework for analyzing the tradeoffs of different policy options discussed throughout the book. Laarman explores not only forest policies affecting the sector and competing land uses, but also extrasectoral policies in the areas of macroeconomics and trade. He lists the public goods and externalities that are not necessarily promoted by strengthening the private sector and liberalizing markets. He recommends that countries monitor the impact of reduced public spending on the capacity of forestry agencies to carry out their mandates. Foreign participation in forest investments should be made compatible with national socioeconomic and environmental objectives. Laarman concludes with suggestions for improving various policies so as to stimulate responsible private investment in the region's forest lands, while also providing for biodiversity preservation.

Ramón López, in Chapter 3, proposes policy instruments and financing mechanisms to promote the sustainable use of forest resources. He urges an intensified but focused exploitation of natural resources in certain areas combined with the genuine protection of forests elsewhere. Scattered and undefined international efforts have coupled with contradictory domestic policies to make both of these objectives unreachable thus far. The chapter discusses features of an international agreement to protect most of the remaining forest. It shows that, just considering the value of carbon sequestration, preserving the tropical forest is an extremely profitable enterprise for the world. If the value of preserving biodiversity is also included, the net benefits for the world are even greater. The author offers a variety of policy instruments and then outlines a financial mechanism to help solve the problems. He puts extra emphasis on the possibilities for global compensation of environmental services provided by Latin American forests.

Olli Haltia and Kari Keipi analyze the advantages and drawbacks of various means of financial incentives for forest investments in Chapter 4. They note that almost all Latin American countries are providing direct or indirect support to private sector forest investments. Capital market imperfections, as well as the long period of maturity for these investments, have resulted in high capital costs and the lack of liquidity for forest management projects. However, the use of incentives may be justified to compensate the forest owner due to possible environmental externalities. The authors conclude that if incentives are used, they should be cost-effective, temporary, and directed locally if possible. Rent-seeking behavior should be minimized and may be achieved by auctioning at least part of the funds. Indirect incentives through, for example, financing extension and research, may be more effective than direct incentives.

Marc Dourojeanni, surveying the future of Latin America's natural forests in Chapter 5, contends that natural forests in Latin America are for the most part *not* being managed. One main reason for this is the low financial profitability of tropical forest management to forest landowners. Two possible ways to slow down deforestation are by paying for the environmental services provided by forests and by producing highly priced, environmentally acceptable "green products." However, it may take time to establish the adequate conditions needed to implement these means. Dourojeanni argues that, in the meanwhile, the best measure may be to establish and better manage the protected areas in the region. For industrial purposes, plantation forestry offers great prospects. For community forestry, agroforestry techniques and managing secondary natural forests are more promising.

In Chapter 6, **Ronnie de Camino** analyzes the role of particular social and economic actors in the forest sector and the impact of existing policies in the region. Participation of the stakeholders in decisionmaking is key to sustainable forest development. In the past, utilization of forest resources has focused on extracting wood and nontimber forest products. This chapter identifies some promising experiences with sustainable management for these products. Little attention has been given to the potential of environmental services: it will be necessary to create policies and instruments that permit key actors to capture income from these services.

Carlos Felipe Jaramillo and Thomas Kelly address the complex and interrelated issues of deforestation and property rights in Chapter 7. They conclude that land tenure security alone will not halt deforestation in the region—a combination of reforms and policy changes is needed. Reforms related directly to land ownership should include issuing individual property rights for settled agricultural areas in order to stimulate agricultural intensification and diminish pressure on the forest frontier. Governments should eliminate the practice of requiring proof of land clearing in order to obtain legal title or credit and end colonization efforts in areas without agricultural potential. The authors also suggest that formal property rights to forests by indigenous and traditional communities should be strengthened, logging concession rights should be granted in favor of local forest dwellers, and restricted private property rights should be established over forest areas that cannot be adequately safeguarded under public ownership.

Julio Tresierra outlines the rights of indigenous groups over natural resources in Chapter 8, stating that indigenous communities have clearly lacked adequate ownership and user rights of natural resources in the tropical forests of Latin America. This is despite recent positive developments in indigenous legislation in some countries. Laws are often contradictory, and the application of national policies is unfavorable to indigenous groups. Specific actions are needed in land use regulation and titling, and in supporting investment programs in the communities. These programs need to take into consideration the cultural traditions and structures of decision making, both in the project design and execution and in the financing conditions. Training should be an important component in these programs, especially in strengthening negotiation skills and technical capabilities.

Jared Hardner and Richard Rice challenge the current practices of forest concessions in Latin America in Chapter 9 and identify important constraints to sustainable forest management. They examine the limitations relating to economic viability, institutional capacity, technical knowledge, and unobserved cultural and social norms by forest dwellers. Their recommendations are presented in four general areas: work with and not against financial forces, replace costly command and control mechanisms with periodic performance audits, promote the participation of affected interest groups, and increase the technical knowledge on tropical forest management. They also propose an area tax instead of the often complex and ineffective current revenue systems between the concessionaires and the state.

Markku Simula analyzes trade's potential role in contributing to sustainable forest management in Chapter 10. "Environmental friendliness" is starting to be used as a marketing component for various forest products. Certification of forest management and ecolabeling of products also offer interesting possibilities for the future. However, avoiding adverse impacts to small-scale producers who may not be able to bear the high initial costs of certification, should also be an objective of its effective implementation. Market liberalization and structural adjustments have led to trade expansion with several negative effects on forests. These effects could be mitigated by complementary policy provisions. The author also notes that the use of subsidies in forest production may cause trade disputes. He states that log export bans and export taxes have a tendency to lead to inefficiency and that ecotaxes on forest products have been ill-conceived.

The final chapter concerns future directions for policies and financing. Given the central premise that forests have economic value, a balance can be struck between their preservation and their contributions to short-term economic development. The chapter suggests ways to improve national and international policies and to promote a range of forest uses, and emphasizes the need to increase investment. Finally, it identifies areas for future research in evaluating forests on the basis of the many goods and services they provide. The private and public sectors should jointly develop criteria for sustainable forest management. Such criteria would not only encourage husbandry of resources, but might also facilitate green certification and the marketing of environmentally benign products. Additional work is needed to establish innovative financial mechanisms, both for investments in production of marketable goods and in providing environmental services at the country and global levels.

CHAPTER 2

Government Policies Affecting Forests

Jan G. Laarman

Introduction

Numerous policy issues affect the extent, distribution, and condition of forests in Latin America. This chapter identifies the principal issues that confront government policymakers, donor agencies, and interest groups in the region. The analysis offered here expands upon existing policy taxonomies and assessments, including Repetto and Gillis (1988), Ascher and Healy (1990), Grainger (1993), and Abt Associates (1992).

Forest management policies are only one element in the framework. On lands of low agronomic productivity and in remote locations, most forests are a residual land use. As a consequence, policies related to agricultural development and land tenure can have potentially negative consequences for forests. Mineral exploration, hydroelectric reservoirs, highway projects, and urban expansion also have impacts on forest conversion. Finally, macroeconomic policies affect forests through their impact on investment, public spending, foreign trade, and other economic variables that have consequences for land use.

Thus, forests and forestry are generally affected by external factors. This explains why evaluations of "forestry sector" policies are inadequate and often misleading. Instead, an assessment of forest policy must consider a complex web of intersectoral and cross-cutting relationships. Previous policy work on forests (Repetto and Gillis 1988) has established this fact.

In discussions of sustainability, some words have extraordinary power. "Deforestation," for example, is a negative or even derisive term, implying unquestioned loss or sacrifice. The term "forest conversion" is more neutral, implying change or transformation. In several forested subregions of Latin America, some amount of forest conversion is considered a legitimate and desirable goal, especially from a regional and local perspective. A dynamic and growing society cannot be expected to live with a static land use pattern. "Forest degradation" implies destruction, even though some species of birds and wildlife respond favorably to various kinds of forest disturbances (forest alteration). "Sustainability" is not a useful term until we know more about what it implies (see Johnson and Cabarle 1993).

Appropriate natural resources policies seek to identify and manage tradeoffs among economic, social, and conservation considerations (de Camino and Müller 1993). The mix of economic policies for forest management and other land uses should be guided by strategies that raise national income. Moreover, the goods, services, and values derived from forests should increasingly be distributed to indigenous peoples, low-income populations, women and children, and other socially disadvantaged groups. Finally, policies for the protection and management of natural resources should make the country at least as well off in the future as in the present.

These are not the criteria that governed traditional forestry in previous decades. Their complexity and tradeoffs pose considerable difficulties for the development of suitable policy frameworks and indicators. Moreover, the pursuit of multiple complex objectives is problematic: "Few things are more difficult for policymakers to do than to pursue multiple objectives simultaneously" (Ascher and Healy 1990).

A Changing Policy Agenda for Forests

According to Clawson (1975), the central policy question about forests is almost always: Forests for whom and for what? The answer is complex, because forests supply a wide range of products and services, many of which are not marketed and, therefore, are not priced. Moreover, many are public goods or result as externalities of other activities. Finally, forested land has alternative uses for cropping, grazing, mineral production, infrastructure, and urbanization. Hence the central policy question is answered differently by timber industries, livestock and agricultural producers, petroleum and mining companies, indigenous peoples, environmental groups, and others. The competing claims on Latin America's forests are many and politically volatile.

Historically, many of Latin America's forests were treated as "empty lands" to be penetrated and colonized (Nelson 1973). Although this legacy persists, often without justification, new voices call attention to the overlooked or ignored value of forests. In virtually every country, environmental and social activists are expressing a revised set of priorities for forest protection and management. Their ideas emphasize forest sustainability, the rights of indigenous peoples to forested homelands, and forests as suppliers of critical ecological and environmental services. Traditional pressures to open and settle forests now coexist, usually uncomfortably, with this newer collection of answers to the question of "forests for whom and for what."

For the most part, governments have addressed these competing claims on forests by attempting to increase controls and expand regulations within centralized agencies. This explains regulated timber concessions on public lands, mandatory reforestation requirements, and government controls on trade in forest products.

Most of the public authority to oversee forests and forestry rests with public forest administrations (PFAs). Depending on the country, PFAs could be forestry agencies or directorates, departments within ministries of agriculture, or divisions within environment and natural resource agencies. As with other public bureaucracies in the region, the performance of Latin America's PFAs has suffered from two sorts of failures. "Failure by commission" refers to government production and control of goods and services that private enterprises are able to supply more efficiently (Krueger 1990). Various PFAs have traditionally engaged in activities such as seedling production and distribution, afforestation and reforestation, wood processing, or export marketing, that overlap with private activity.[1] The opposite policy error, "failure by omission," occurs when governments do not provide adequate legal and institutional frameworks (e.g., property rights), public infrastructure, or public goods (e.g., information services). Many PFAs have been unable to enforce the terms of forest concessions, publish reliable forestry statistics and analyses, or offer an attractive investment climate for long-term forest management. These

---

[1] To resolve fiscal and efficiency problems resulting from state ownership of the means of production, various government-owned enterprises in Latin America were privatized in recent years (Sánchez and Corona 1993). Yet privatization and deregulation have extended well beyond industry to also include agriculture and forestry. Honduras, Nicaragua, and Peru offer prime examples, as will be discussed.

failures are generally more difficult to correct than the often simpler matter of withdrawing government participation in and control of production.

The changing institutional context for forests increasingly acknowledges these issues (Morell and Paveri 1994). The revised agenda features changing objectives, organizational structure, and policy means. For example, the previous focus on industrial timber is now joined by two types of pressures. One is for management of natural forests through approaches consistent with environmental protection. The other is forest and tree management by peasant and indigenous communities (social forestry), often focused on nonindustrial objectives and nontimber outputs.

Additionally, pressures for decentralized and participatory policymaking have been building steadily in several countries. Many critics want the PFAs transformed from closed, centralized bureaucracies to open, responsive organizations in touch with local problems. This implies greater decentralization. More consultations and partnerships between PFAs and grassroots social, environmental, and business groups are also desired. Contacts among these groups are presently few and often antagonistic.

Finally, the current ideological trend is towards privatization of production, with governments acting as facilitator rather than producer. Yet because forests (particularly natural forests) provide important externalities and public goods, forest ownership and management cannot be left entirely to the will of the private owner. The division and control of forests and forest industries between private and public hands is understandably one of the most controversial of all policy issues for forests.

Institutional Constraints

Because much of the impetus for change did not originate within the PFAs, the transition from the old to the new agenda cannot move far or fast until policy shifts are internalized. Forest policy commands attention precisely because of contrasting hope and skepticism over whether the PFAs will succeed in internalizing the new prescriptions. Several years ago, Llaurado and Speidel (1981) identified numerous administrative obstacles in the way of PFA effectiveness. Many of these obstacles persist (Box 2.1).

Many PFAs continue to experience inadequate institutional capacity, often despite years of efforts to strengthen them. Most have been the object of frequent and sweeping reorganizations, partly in response to changing ideas of the correct relationship of forestry to agriculture, the environment, and other natural resources (wildlife, watershed management, and others). In summary, the identification of leading policy issues affecting forests must simultaneously consider how governments will implement them.

Management of Forests

The distribution of Latin America's forests is highly uneven between and within countries. They span an enormous variation in elevation and climate, from sea level to the Andean highlands, and from thorny woodlands to rain forests. The range of climatic conditions, soil types, and past and present human impacts account for the vast diversity of forests. Imposed on this mosaic of flora and fauna are varying cultural, economic, and political responses to the question of "forests for whom and for what." Yet despite this heterogeneity, forest policy concerns are common to many settings.

In most Latin American countries, forests are largely or even exclusively in state ownership (de jure property rights). In many of these forests, indigenous groups and other local residents earn all or part of their livelihood through the exercise of customary use

> **Box 2.1 Obstacles to the Effectiveness of PFAs**
>
> ***Staffing Problems.*** PFA directors and staff are isolated from top executive and legislative decisionmakers, and from key ministries in charge of finance, budgeting, and economic planning. The data available on forest inventories, production, and environmental indicators are insufficient, and there is low capacity to collect and manage information. Not enough PFA staff possess education and skills in the resource management disciplines, management sciences, and social sciences. They are overloaded with ineffective regulatory duties and excessive paperwork, and the poor conditions of their employment (low salaries, small operational budgets, negative image of forestry) contribute to low morale among the staff.
>
> ***Inadequate Policies.*** Forestry laws, regulations, and mission statements are often unrealistic and not accompanied by operational plans and budgets. Powerful and influential special interests (companies dealing in wood products, petroleum and mining, and agribusiness) can often control policy issues. PFA policies sometimes conflict with policies in other units of government (land colonization, agriculture, minerals and petroleum, roads and public works, energy). In general, the PFAs place too much emphasis on implementing reforestation and other government projects, rather than building a national policy consensus and facilitating the activities and goals of its various constituencies (stakeholders).

rights (*de facto* property rights). The PFAs are under considerable pressure to define and coordinate policies to protect and manage state forests for economic development (that is, to serve as a source of new jobs and income) and environmental services (genetic resources, carbon storage, watershed protection, wildlife habitat, and many others). At the same time, the PFAs are expected to establish a policy framework that more broadly protects customary use rights and the sociocultural values of local populations.

Regarding the production objective, the government has three alternatives. First, forest resources (logs, nontimber products, ecotourism sites, etc.) may be used by the government itself in parastatal operations.[2] Second, the government may issue forest concessions (see Chapter 10) while retaining ownership of the land, but allowing specified individuals the right (or privilege) to obtain specified forest resources through utilization contracts (FAO 1971). Third, it may transfer property rights to forests and their resources to private or communal owners through sales or grants. This analysis will deal with public and private ownership issues and public assistance for private forests.

Public and Private Ownership

Since the early 1980s, the trend toward reducing the size of the public sector in favor of private ownership and management has recast the development strategies and policy assumptions of past decades. Privatization is widely seen as the main strategy to reduce government participation and control. The most important forms of privatization for the purposes of the present study are the sale or transfer of government assets to private interests, liberalization of regulatory controls over the activities of private enterprises, and competitive tendering of services to private contractors.

---

[2]   Protected areas are a central theme of Chapter 5.

Box 2.2 Government Divestiture in Honduras

Honduras established a public forest administration (COHDEFOR) in 1974, and gave it a manu-facturing role as well as a virtual monopoly over marketing and exports. COHDEFOR's manu-facturing losses have been large. In 1990, its public companies (Corfino, Casisa, Fiafsa, Locomapa, Semsa, and Promagua) lost 50 million lempiras (about US$11.1 million), charged against accounts receivable. In addition that year, they lost another 19 million lempiras charged against the asset value of investments. By 1991, the accumulated losses of CORFINO alone were 122 million lempiras. Debt servicing may be about 4 million lempiras per year. These figures may understate the real situation: the auditor refused to approve COHDEFOR's finan-cial statements because of inadequate data and inappropriate accounting methods. As of 1992, these public companies ceased to operate and have been sold or closed.

Source: IDB internal documents.

PFAs typically are expected to meet extra-enterprise objectives, even if these ob-jectives lessen financial and economic performance. Ramanadham (1991) enumerates several extra-enterprise objectives, including some that are critical for forests and forest industries. The most important are environmental protection, favoring of socially merito-rious groups in forest concessions, PFA employment, and retaining central control over the type and amount of foreign investment in natural resources. In this framework, some national objectives are traded off against others because social efficiencies are more en-compassing than financial ones.

Forest Industries. State-owned forest industries which have been closed or divested in-clude Demerara Woods in Guyana, Celulosa Arauco y Constitución in Chile, and CORFINO and five other companies in Honduras. Additionally, the governments of Guyana and Honduras have disbanded the marketing boards for the export of wood products. The Honduran experience is a classic illustration of divestiture to cut unresolvable financial losses (Box 2.2). This contrasts with Arauco in Chile, which was sold primarily to generate revenue. Not researched is the number, size, and financial condition of state-owned forest products companies, tree nurseries, and other enterprises that continue to operate in Latin America.

The analytical framework for policy discussions of privatization options should rigorously take into account the precise nature of privatization, exposure to market forces, incentives for managerial performance, and whether or not owner control will be directed toward financial objectives (Ramanadham 1991). These are briefly discussed below.

Precise Purposes of Privatization. This is a fundamental question. Policymakers should clearly understand the reasons for undertaking privatization. Such purposes could include the following: to raise revenues, reduce fiscal losses, avoid political embarrass-ment, reduce government payrolls, create ideological symbols, resolve a labor dispute, or increase exports.

Exposure to Market Forces. Will privatization stimulate market competition, or merely shift ownership of a monopoly enterprise from the public to the private sector?

Incentives for Managerial Performance. What are the determinants of higher managerial performance after an enterprise is privatized? Two areas to be examined are higher compensation, and freedom from government controls. Yet even private companies will be regulated, and some governments pay compensation incentives similar to those paid by private companies.

Owner Control Directed Towards Financial Objectives. Will privatization be of the kind in which owners keep management alert to profitable operation? A focus on financial returns is not necessarily paramount if an enterprise's managers and workers are among its principal owners.

Because of the foregoing, most studies conclude that the form of ownership is insufficient to explain financial or economic efficiency. Market structure (competition) and managerial freedom (discretion in decisionmaking) are at least as important (Hartley and Parker 1991). On this point, the forest products industries should be no different from others.

Forest Ownership. A very large share of Latin America's forests, particularly its natural forests, are nominally state-owned (*de jure* basis). This is consistent with the pattern of forest ownership in most of the world. Public ownership of forests is generally justified on the basis of the failure of markets to achieve social efficiency in forest allocation and production. With few exceptions, markets do not effectively allocate or lead to investment in the production of biological diversity, carbon fixation, wildlife habitat, watershed protection, opportunities for science and education, and other unpriced forest outputs (Loomis 1993). Moreover, many of these goods and services are generated as spillovers, or positive and negative externalities not incident upon forest owners (Hyde and Newman 1991).

In the absence of other incentives or controls, the actions of private holders are governed by profit motives. The private holder of a forested tract has reasons to guard it against encroachment from the outside, and may be more effective at policing than the public sector. However, this is not the same as acting in the public interest. In responding to market signals, the private owner rationally maximizes the net present value of the asset. Where future financial returns from the forest are unprofitable or uncertain, deforestation without investment in future forest management may ensue. In addition, such a situation could result in practices that control only private costs, ignoring public costs. From the private owner's perspective, the principal factor in forest management is profitability rather than property rights.

Some political conservatives argue that market failure is not a satisfactory justification for government ownership and management (Baden and Stroup 1981; Anderson and Leal 1991). The arguments for transferring forests from public to private owners are several. Researchers have noted the difficulties that government agencies face in carrying out the analytical tasks required, the existence of perverse incentives, and unlimited special interests, as well as cross-country experiences and issues of multiple use.

Impossible Analytical Tasks. Even if nonmarket values and social (distributive) weights could be fully identified and quantified, it cannot be assumed that a PFA or other public agency can effectively use the information for decisionmaking. Even the world's most sophisticated and expensive models to quantify forest tradeoffs have been found inadequate (for a critique of the United States' FORPLAN model, see O'Toole 1988).

Perverse Incentives. PFAs, like other bureaucracies, are vulnerable to political interference, patronage, and ambiguous and contradictory objectives (Cook and Kirkpatrick 1988).

Unlimited Special Interests. Forest products companies, environmental NGOs, social NGOs, peasant associations, indigenous groups, and international agencies are among the special interests that place expectations and demands on PFAs. These expectations and demands are unlimited and often internally inconsistent. Collective action to address conflicts is not always in the interest of the PFA. Instead, individuals who control public agencies manipulate competing claims in order to appropriate favors for themselves. Wealthy and powerful interests have the advantage in the competition for attention. Thus, public control of contested resources such as state-owned forests does not reduce social inequities, but actually reinforces them (Brett 1988).

Cross-Country Experiences. Worldwide data on public and private forests should be reviewed for lessons on actual performance. New Zealand recently sold off extensive state forest holdings, mainly plantations, premised on the superior efficiency of private management (Kirkland 1988). In Latin America, there are examples of the successful private operation of a variety of nature reserves, ecotourism sites, and forests for science and education (Alderman 1990; Castner 1990). Deforestation and forest degradation in boreal regions (Barr and Braden 1988) and the tropics (Stewart 1985) have been linked to state ownership. There is thus considerable support for the argument that private ownership is not necessarily predatory, nor public ownership always protective.

Multiple Use Through Dominant Uses. True multiple-use forest management on every hectare is virtually impossible from a technical standpoint. Instead, public forests usually are zoned into production and protection areas of various classes and sizes. In theory, the same result may be achieved, with greater potential for enforcement of property rights, if forests are transferred to a mix of private and communal owners. The new owners need not be solely private timber companies, but may also comprise indigenous groups, peasant associations, environmental NGOs, and other entities. Within the privatization framework, the PFA retains responsibility for a permanent forest estate scaled down to a size compatible with its management capacity. Other forest lands are transferred to private and communal owners in phased steps backed by land use mapping, forest inventories, social surveys, and other supporting information.

These arguments, however, do not address all the issues. Practical questions on forest privatization are complex (Box 2.3), beginning with defining which forests to divest, and for what reason(s). The criteria for considering the mix of forest buyers and grantees are contentious because PFAs may try to favor or exclude groups because of foreign capital, ethnicity, and other reasons. The timing and sequence of divestiture, and the valuation and pricing of forest assets, can be expected to attract political attention. Finally, a government must have a sound policy and workable strategy to compensate individuals and groups who perceive that they incur losses because of privatization.

Forest privatization has substantial budgetary implications; its economic benefits are mainly distant and uncertain rather than immediate and concrete; and it may entail significant political costs. Private ownership is unable to produce the socially desired amount of nonmarket goods and services from forests except through the government's regulatory and fiscal interventions (Loomis 1993), but these interventions are sadly ineffective in Latin America (e.g., Guess 1991; Gottfried et al. 1994). Hence forest privatization policy should not be rushed, and should focus continuously on the question, "forests for whom and for what?"

Public Assistance for Private Forests

Private forests in Latin America encompass industrial plantations, and farm and community trees on private, *ejidal,* and communal lands. Latin America's industrial tree plantations include some of the world's most productive planted forests (Zobel et al. 1987). Trees

Box 2.3 Forest Privatization in Honduras

The circumstances of forest privatization in Honduras illustrate a number of practical issues. In 1974, the Honduran government nationalized forests on private lands (freehold title), which make up an estimated half of the country's pine forests and a tenth of its broadleaf forests. In 1992, the Agricultural Modernization and Development Law reinstated private property rights in these forests. The objective is to allow private landowners to obtain higher prices for their forest commodities, and to allow and encourage them to practice forest management. For the communal groups living in or near the forests, the overriding issue is retaining customary tenure or obtaining formal tenure in the face of privatization.

The new policy raises several issues, including the following:

- Compensating or assimilating persons formerly engaged in resin collection and pitsawing on private lands;
- Winning the support of displaced persons and other community groups by increasing their opportunities to earn income from forests on public lands;
- Preventing land grabbing that exploits the poor cadastral system (property records) and unclear landownership;
- Granting land titles to all forest occupants on public lands, if that should become necessary to head off social unrest;
- Controlling the public costs of relocating forest occupants;
- Implementing forest management plans to induce private forest owners to retain forest cover; and
- Controlling the negative environmental impacts of forest harvesting with incentives and sanctions.

Sources: IDB internal documents; Stanley (1991).

on farms and on communal lands furnish a wide range of market and nonmarket goods and services (Tschinkel 1987).

Government policy on private forestry is currently in transition. In part, this reflects considerable criticism of past efforts. Several Latin American governments have granted large financial subsidies to industrial plantations, but often without a satisfactory *ex ante* or *ex post* (prior or subsequent) accounting of benefits and costs. Government assistance for farm and community forestry has been far less generous, but is similarly short on program evaluation. Various NGOs, environmental groups, and biologists urge greater attention to planting with native species. They also endorse government assistance for natural forest management, not just tree planting. Finally, governments can easily over-regulate private forests, and possible corrections are needed in this area.

Industrial and Farm Forestry. Progress in plantation forestry in various Latin American countries has been considerable, especially since the late 1960s (see IDB 1995c). For the region as a whole, tree planting (by area and expenditure) is dominated by medium and large private companies. However, private tree planting requires the indirect, and often direct, policy support of public authorities. Several governments have provided subsidies for reforestation in the form of tax incentives, cost reimbursements, and other mechanisms. Subsidized private reforestation has been considered in virtually all countries in the region (see Chapter 4).

Indeed, the reforestation and afforestation of large areas in Latin America has been made possible by the availability of public financial incentives. Government subsidies for planting trees make sense if they benefit others as well as the landowners receiving the subsidies. Examples of such benefits are improved water quality through sedimentation control, the preservation or expansion of wildlife habitat, improved subsistence gathering for non-landowners, improved air quality, and the provision of amenities and aesthetic benefits. Some of these are public goods (nonrival in consumption). In addition, the plantations serve as a source of new employment. The provision of plantation-related employment is possibly an external economy if social gains from this extend beyond private wages and salaries.

In the orthodox framework of market imperfections, each of these contributions may qualify as a positive externality under the right circumstances. Yet they must be demonstrated to exist in each case, not merely assumed just because spillovers are plausible. Critics argue that forest plantations often decrease rather than increase environmental amenities (Sargent and Bass 1992), implying that governments should tax rather than subsidize them. Moreover, social efficiency requires that public payments to landowners not simply substitute for private capital that would otherwise be invested. The substitution question has been examined in North America (Mills 1976), but apparently not in Latin America.

In Brazil and in Costa Rica, numerous reforestation projects have been motivated more by tax considerations than by future long-term return on investment. Consequently, the public objectives of subsidization have been compromised by suboptimal planting practices, unfavorable plantation locations, and other technical deficiencies (Gottfried et al. 1994). Early studies indicate that private financial returns from these programs are exceptionally attractive, even if social returns (i.e., over the sum of public and private inputs) are not (Beattie and Ferreira 1978; Berger 1980). In comparison, some observers believe that Chile's public-private cost sharing has been successful from both the private and social perspective (McGaughey and Gregersen 1983; Amacher et al. 1994).

Given these results, governments are advised to prudently consider whether and how to subsidize tree planting. To date, key questions remain unanswered, including the following:

- Which government programs to subsidize tree planting are supported with acceptable information regarding types and quantities of positive externalities? Is this confirmed by field studies?
- Who are the recipients of these external benefits? More specifically, can it be shown that they flow to relatively disadvantaged populations living in or near the areas where tree planting occurs?
- What is the evidence for and against positive environmental amenities from planted trees in different contexts? This must be approached through various case studies, related to such factors as tree species being planted, type and condition of vegetative cover prior to planting, and size and configuration of planted areas.

Only limited analysis is available to address these issues. Initiatives to provide new or continuing public subsidies for private afforestation and reforestation should be supported by a rigorous study of financial, economic, social (equity), and environmental benefits and costs.

Large and medium companies have historically received most of the available public financial assistance for reforestation. Yet hundreds of community-based reforestation projects on farms and communal lands are taking place throughout the region (FAO 1992b). Many if not most of these projects receive no financial or technical support from the government.

Native Species and Natural Forests. Policies on species choices for tree planting are highly controversial. Most afforestation and reforestation in Latin America comprises industrial plantings of pine, eucalyptus, gmelina, and other timber species grown primarily in plantations. Foresters in Chile and other countries have been criticized for planting radiata pine over large areas without diversifying to other species, and for removing native forests to make room for plantations (Castilleja 1993).[3] Yet removal of natural forests is the exception (Evans 1992), and the IDB has been very careful to avoid this when financing plantations (Keipi 1991).

Field trials with planted native species are beginning to generate useful data on survival and early growth compared to traditional plantation timbers (Butterfield and Fisher 1994). In light of these reports and field demonstrations, Latin American PFAs are now in a position to re-examine assumptions and policies regarding species choices for reforestation and other tree planting.

To date, government programs for both industrial and farm forestry have been largely synonymous with planted trees. However, this has not gone unquestioned (Johnson and Cabarle 1993). Chile has passed a specific Law of Native Forests, which would help subsidize the costs of managing natural forests (Wünder 1994). Costa Rica recently established financial subsidies for natural forest management, subject to caveats on security of land title. However, observers question whether subsidies can be sustainable in light of budget constraints, and whether forest management will continue if subsidies are removed (Gottfried et al. 1994).

Regulatory Setting. Like other Latin American government agencies, PFAs rely heavily on command and control management. Forest laws and regulations tend to be highly prescriptive. Excessive regulation hinders the ability of forest operations to adapt to local circumstances, thus sacrificing growth prospects (employment and income), and adding to transactions costs (bureaucratic red tape).

The regulation of private forests poses questions similar to those for forest concessions on state-owned lands. Property rights in "private" forests are divided among state, individual, and communal claimants. Governments are charged with defining whether there is a divergence between private and social net benefits in the way forests on private lands are managed or not managed. If there is evidence of divergence, then the intervention costs of changing private (or communal) practices must be weighed against the estimated environmental and social benefits to be obtained.

The appropriate conceptual framework, then, is to minimize the sum of transactions costs (time and money for government effort and for landowner response) plus damage costs (environmental and equity problems of purely private action). Increased forest regulation is normally expected to reduce environmental and social costs, but it also drives up the transactions costs for governments and landowners (for inspections, legal

---

[3] Critics also point to Jari Florestal as an example of large-scale clearing of native forests to make room for block plantations (Fearnside 1989).

costs, compliance costs, and the like). Considering the minimum sum of damages plus transactions costs, a certain amount of forest mismanagement need not be corrected in order to arrive at a social optimum.

Government over-regulation of private forest management has two consequences. When regulations are followed, as in Europe, they lead to excessive investment in forests: i.e., beyond the margin of social efficiency (Turner and Wibe 1992). When regulations are not followed, as in many parts of Latin America, they lead to avoidance, fraud, and injustice.

On the matter of reviewing PFA regulations on private forest management, analysis must begin with the goals that regulation is to achieve in relation to the costs that it will impose. This should be grounded in well-defined notions of what to measure, and why. In the absence of this social cost-benefit framework, regulatory policy is not necessarily better than a *laissez faire* approach. On the contrary, regulatory policy can easily generate negative net benefits.

Opening the administrative process to public review and comment may enhance the transparency and impartiality of plan approval (or rejection). The same type of oversight may be useful in processes to sanction violators of forest regulations. Without effective public oversight, forest owners have incentives to engage in covert bargaining with the PFA. The context is not much different than for concession holders on government lands. If forests are privatized but heavily regulated, the social and environmental implications of public versus private ownership may be small or even irrelevant.

Land Policy and Infrastructure Development

Pressures on Latin America's forests stemming from agricultural policies and infrastructure projects are described in a large body of reports, articles, and books too numerous to cite here. The demand to convert forests to other uses is explained by the skewed distribution of arable lands, together with a chronic landlessness reinforced by the macroeconomic stresses of the 1980s. A second explanation is competing claims over forest lands as open-access resources. Tenure insecurity discourages permanent investment in any particular property, thus perpetuating the expansion of low-input agriculture. In many countries, such expansion is fostered by an open land frontier that encourages land speculation. In traditional Latin American law, lands are claimed by clearing them of trees. Each of these aspects is negative for retaining forest cover.

Government interventions in agriculture have both direct and indirect consequences for forests. Subsidies and price supports for products such as beef, bananas, coffee, and citrus fruits increase the demand for new lands to produce them. Additionally, credit programs and extension services have been developed mainly for livestock and cropping, and only much less so for forest management and agroforestry. Yet the production biases for agriculture are countered by other (mainly market) biases against it, particularly in macroeconomic and trade policies (Bautista and Valdes 1993). Removal of production biases which favor agriculture should generally reduce the demand for forest clearing, while removal of market biases against agriculture could be expected to have the opposite effect.

Forests are residual land frontiers increasingly opened by roads, mining, petroleum exploration, and hydroelectric and resettlement projects (Schneider 1993a). These projects often complement each other, and also link synergistically with logging and expansion of agriculture. Due to these interactions, causality in land use change is difficult to define and isolate. However, several analyses conclude that the aggregate impact of agricultural policies and infrastructural development is far more significant for forest conversion than mismanaged policies within forestry itself (e.g., see Leonard 1987 for Central America; Mahar 1989 for Brazil).

Zoning and Project Impact Assessment

Governments can apply several instruments to guide land use decisions and the siting and design of projects. Regionally, land use planning and master planning are important tools for the formulation of strategies as to which activities should be encouraged or discouraged in specific geographic zones (Dourojeanni 1990). Sometimes land use planning can be framed in terms of regional carrying capacity (Daly 1990). Within this regional scheme, the probable impacts of specific projects are assessed (*ex ante*) using cost-benefit, social impact, and environmental impact analysis. These tools are not costless, and moreover, all are to some extent philosophically inconsistent with the current trend toward government deregulation.

In principle, governments want their policy and technical approaches for land use zoning and project assessment to be suitable for large and small activities. The first category includes major roads, plantation agribusinesses, mining and petroleum projects, hydroelectric projects, and directed resettlement projects. Policies to guide the siting and design of big projects have multiplier implications for in-migration by colonists, construction workers, transport workers, retail shops, and other service suppliers.[4] The second category refers to peasant colonizers, small-scale miners (such as Brazil's *garimpeiros*), and other largely spontaneous movements of persons into forested areas. Governments have few policy strategies to address this second category of incursions other than through policies on population planning, macroeconomic management, and other indirect means.

For much of Latin America, efforts to continue opening land frontiers are virtually inevitable. Moving people into frontier zones has been politically attractive as an alternative to land reform, as a symbol of economic development, and as a means to establish national presence in remote regions. Despite the recent rise of environmentalism, these political advantages will not disappear quickly. Ideally, governments should focus on reforming and intensifying agriculture rather than colonizing forests for new lands. In reality both are taking place. Therefore, if policies cannot stop frontier expansion, they should at least seek to accommodate it at least cost.

Past exercises to plan integrated regional development, such as those financed by the Organization of American States (OAS 1984; 1987), offer a number of lessons. OAS experience shows that regional planning must be compatible with the national system of project generation. It has to be an integral activity within the ministries and agencies that define priority policies and projects. In addition, it must be goal-oriented rather than a collection of unfocused data. Effective regional planning proceeds from overviews of large areas to more detailed investigations of limited areas having the greatest potential for the successful implementation of specific projects. Such planning requires broad-based popular and political support, which has to be built into the process of plan preparation and debate. When final documents are being submitted, it is too late to win advocates.

---

[4]   Thus Brazil's President Castelo Branco (1964-67) foresaw that "growth poles" could be established in frontier areas through tax breaks, land concessions, credits and loans, road-building, and other government interventions (Hecht and Cockburn 1990). Subsequent critics of the Transamazon Highway, Polonoroeste, Grande Carajas, Jari Florestal, and the Tucuruí and Balbina dams have not doubted that human settlement can be increased in "underdeveloped" areas. However, they question the net benefit or cost of such projects in financial, economic, social, political, and environmental terms, and the appropriate mix of policies to guide frontier development in the future.

Box 2.4 Planning for Land Settlement: Nicaragua, Honduras, and Panama

In the 1970s, the government of **Nicaragua** undertook to settle farmers into 4 million hectares in the Atlantic zone, more than 25 percent of the country. The planning team overestimated the availability of arable land, underestimated the resident population, and recommended the wrong crops. Although intended to promote ecologically sustainable production, the project was notable for its ambitious goals and its lack of concern for technical limitations.

The government of **Honduras** has attempted to design new communities and promote certain crops (cotton, banana, oil palm) in agroindustrial cooperatives in several river valleys. This attracted many more migrants than anticipated, swelling the area's population and threatening the watersheds.

The master plan for the Darién isthmus of **Panama** designates a strip of land along the Inter-American Highway that is to be carefully managed. Provisions include road frontage, maximum size of holdings, and controls over land use. Plan implementation was paralyzed for many years by the government's institutional fragmentation over issues of legal authority. As a result, farmers simply appropriated lands and took advantage of government disarray to illegally cut and sell timber. On several occasions government agencies formally discussed lack of coordination on Darién, without success. A sustainable development program for Darién has now been launched with the help of the IDB. The program was formulated with the participation of the affected communities, the private sector, involved government agencies, and the international community.

Sources: Jones (1989); IDB internal documents.

Several states in Amazonian Brazil recently approved zoning legislation, and efforts to conduct land use planning are underway in the area known as Legal Amazonia. Brazil recently used this framework to designate numerous extractive and indigenous reserves, forest research areas, and forest production areas (for timber harvest). The IDB and other multilateral banks are increasingly insisting upon the existence of regional land use plans as a precondition for financing highways and settlement projects (ACT/IDB/UNDP 1992).

In a World Bank publication, Mahar (1989) argues that the success or failure of land use zoning will depend on the technical quality of the plans, the strength and depth of political support for the concept, and the existence of a policy framework consistent with rational land use. The key policy issues are the legal and regulatory aspects that define the scope of planning analysis, determine planning costs, and impose sanctions for noncompliance and violations. It should be noted that proposals for agro-ecological zoning of the Brazilian Amazon date from the 1970s, but early versions failed to win political support because of their strong preservationist tone.

Regional planning based on land use capability is impossible to oppose in principle. However, examples of planning for land settlement in Central America and Panama illustrate the fertile ground for unintended negative consequences (Box 2.4). Governments, colonists, and developers tend to fall back into familiar and routine patterns of land settlement in the general chaos and high expectations created by the access to new resources. Publicly endorsed land use plans are overlooked as the social, legal, and political conditions of the past reproduce themselves in the frontier zones (Jones 1989).

This tendency to avoid innovation is reinforced by the scarcity of funds, errors in planning and administration, and utopian visions that ignore technical feasibility. The unsurprising conclusion is that land use planning is only as good as the technical, financial, administrative, and policy support behind it. Until improvements are realized in each of these dimensions, land use planning could have negative consequences if it raises expectations that cannot be met (political and social costs), or imposes "solutions" inconsistent with reality (financial and economic costs).

Project analysis for roads, especially penetration roads, demands far greater attention now than in the past. Road projects have allowed millions of settlers into Amazonia (Moran 1989b). The expansion of roads is also a policy concern in Central America, particularly in Panama (Leonard 1987). Road expansion or improvement (paving) may add to population growth in remote areas, accelerating forest alteration and conversion. Yet in the long run, roads help improve rural-urban terms of trade, raising rural incomes and decreasing pressures on forested frontiers.

Predicting project impacts becomes technically difficult and politically sensitive when projects are very large. Big projects produce supra-marginal impacts, are redesigned frequently, and generate large but generally unpredictable secondary impacts. The huge Jari Florestal investment in Amazonia is a good example: Jari's technical design, enterprise mix, and operating procedures were modified many times through 25 years of learning and adaptation (McNabb et al. 1994). It is doubtful that *ex ante* analysis could have foreseen either the problems the company would encounter, or the adjustments it made in the face of them. Box 2.5 presents other examples to illustrate what are often political obstacles confronting *ex ante* project analysis, particularly if the projects include foreign participation.

Therefore, an important step forward would be to reform legal and administrative frameworks to make them favorable to project analysis as a decisionmaking tool. The process of implementing and reviewing project analysis has to be opened to the NGOs, industries, news media, academia, and the general public as a means of educating them. Not incidentally, this helps diminish the potential for corruption. Public participation will not necessarily resolve conflicts, but at least it reduces the volatile repercussions of closed negotiations between top government officials and company executives.

Land Tenure

Land tenure refers to the multiple social rules and understandings about who has access and rights to different parcels of land and the resources on them. These rules and understandings help determine incentives and disincentives for maintaining or removing forests and trees. This is the subject of extensive policy inquiry (Fortmann and Riddell 1985; Bromley 1989; Thiesenhusen 1991).

The policy measures to make land tenure serve forest protection and management are reasonably clear. They are discussed in further detail by Jaramillo and Kelly in Chapter 7. The political costs of tenure reform, following centuries of conservative land policy in Latin America, may be high. A principal strategy to conserve forests is to reduce the open-access character of public lands. If governments cannot enforce property rights in forested frontiers, then the forests should be transferred from public to alternative (communal and private) hands. This policy should be complemented by agrarian reform in settled areas to assimilate rural residents. This dual strategy has been distinctly unpopular with governments. The first policy reduces the "safety valve" option of political administrations, affronts PFAs by ceding away the public forest estate, and risks short-run

Box 2.5 Impacts of Development Projects on Forests

Coca-Cola in Belize. In 1985, the Coca-Cola Company purchased 82,000 hectares of forests in Belize to grow oranges for a subsidiary operation. Coca-Cola regarded the lands as transitional forest between subtropical moist and tropical dry forest, and claimed the lands had been logged for more than 100 years. It intended to plant citrus trees on only 10,000 to 12,000 hectares. Environmental groups denounced the project and urged a boycott, even though Coca-Cola insisted it was not going to clear tropical rain forest. Coca-Cola canceled the project to protect its image. Ironically, it sold the bulk of its holdings to a Belizean logging company and a group of Mennonites, who are reported to have cleared significant portions for farming. *Question:* Would initial project analysis have been able to predict what would happen with and without the Coca-Cola project?

Geest in Costa Rica. Geest is a British company cited by Costa Rica's Ministry of Natural Resources and Mines (MIRENEM) in 1992 for illegally cutting trees along creeks and streams to create a banana plantation. Although it has been widely ignored for years, Costa Rican law prohibits tree cutting within 100 meters of stream banks. Geest claimed that it did not violate the law because the water was in a depression and not flowing. However, MIRENEM prevailed, in part because of the political climate created by NGOs hostile to banana companies. *Question:* Would an *ex ante* environmental impact assessment (EIA) of the Geest operation have been able to anticipate that a dispute would arise over the definition of a stream?

Grande Carajas in Brazil. Several billion dollars have been invested in the mining, smelting, and railroad operations in the Grande Carajas project in the Amazon forest. The state-owned CVRD, which manages the project, conducted baseline studies of the climate, flora, and fauna of areas proposed for mining before operations began. It spent US$54 million on land reclamation, protected areas, erosion control, and other environmental activities. However, this was insufficient to offset criticism of the company's forest cutting to provide fuel for its ore smelters, as well as of the violent social conflicts that resulted from large migration into the area. *Question:* Is project analysis possible for a project of this magnitude, and who provides the oversight on EIA for a government enterprise?

Source: MacKerron and Cogan (1993).

deforestation. The second policy confronts the power of large landowners, and creates uncertainty regarding agricultural production.

Most tenure reforms have been cautious and experimental. Yet there are several policy directions which push but do not break the limits of political acceptability. These include the following:

- Reviewing government policies on methods of obtaining land titles, and the granting of informal land rights to squatters;
- Demarcating and granting formal protection to indigenous reserves and homelands, as well as peasant forestry communities;
- Examining feasibility analysis in relation to frontier colonization; and
- Working to design and apply land taxes that tax forested lands less heavily than other lands.

Land Titling. Several problems surround current government policies regarding informal land claims. First, the eviction of *campesino* families from public lands risks adverse political reaction in societies that view squatting as the poor family's hope for a better future. Secondly, while some private landowners may feel threatened by encroachment on their property, other private interests conspire with squatters to acquire new lands, mainly from the public estate. This second group can be expected to oppose, generally unofficially, proposals that would eliminate informal land claims. Finally, it can become very expensive for governments to expel and resettle squatters, and this could further strain public budgets. Even though the activities of squatters have adverse implications for forests, the typical response of governments in the past—that is, to do nothing—is readily understandable in light of the financial and political costs of action. In some countries, pressure from environmentalists and indigenous communities may be changing this.

Land Colonization. Latin American governments have pursued land colonization policies for years; the modern era of colonization in the region spans the last four or five decades. These policies were controversial long before the environmental era that began in the 1970s (Loomis 1938).

Directed colonization has been costly and prone to a high incidence of failure because it has been used to serve objectives other than agricultural production. In a detailed study undertaken about twenty years ago, Nelson (1973) observed that land colonization projects were selected (1) without regard to alternative sites or designs, (2) as side effects of other projects such as highway construction, (3) because of national security considerations to settle remote zones, (4) to use "unoccupied" tracts of public lands, and (5) because completed resource surveys were available for the particular area.

Land Taxes. In rural economies, land is the most significant form of wealth and the source of most income. To date, taxation has been underutilized as a means of influencing land use and possibly also land ownership. In most of Latin America, land taxes are low, eroded by inflation, and not enforced. Yet in principle, proponents of imposing significant land taxes (Dorner 1992; Strasma and Celis 1992) contend that they would encourage landowners to use their land productively, or sell or lease it to others who will. In theory, this helps dampen land speculation and control the size of land holdings. Moreover, a land tax could be differentiated to tax croplands and pastures more heavily than forested lands. Given a sufficiently large tax gradient by land use (or potential use), a differentiated structure may help discourage further forest clearing. This is precisely the opposite of past policies that taxed "idle" forested lands more heavily than others.

With few exceptions, Latin American governments have not employed land taxation as a policy tool (Shearer et al. 1990). To apply land taxes effectively implies considerable public expenditure to improve land titling, registration, and valuation methods. More importantly, land taxes are opposed by both large and small landowners. As noted by Dorner (1992), land taxation has no political constituency, especially when compared with other types of tenure reforms (e.g., land redistribution). An exception may be local governments to the extent they are allowed to assess and collect property taxes without interference from central governments.

Agricultural Markets

Agriculture and livestock displace forests by competing for the existing land. Conversely, forests are favored by policies, technologies, and market trends that reduce the demand for cropping and grazing land. From this simple proposition flow several complex ideas about the interactions between agriculture and forests.

Bias in Favor of Agriculture. From the perspective of traditional agriculture ministries, forested lands are free goods to be brought under cropping and grazing when the profit margin permits. Thus, Latin American governments have promoted agricultural and live-stock output at the producer level through tax breaks, subsidized inputs (credit, fertilizers, equipment, fuel, crop storage facilities), and programs of technical assistance, media support, and the like. Also favoring agricultural producers are policies that keep rural labor prices low; improve roads, electricity, and other infrastructure in the countryside; and restrict imports of agricultural products.

Bias Against Agriculture. Although governments subsidize agricultural production, other policies often discriminate against it. Such is the effect of domestic price controls on milk, meat, and basic foodstuffs, and direct and indirect taxes (for instance, through overvalued exchange rates). Also harmful to agriculture are badly managed parastatal companies and excessive regulatory burdens on the sector. Moreover, Latin America's development strategy through the 1970s favored the Prebisch doctrine of self-sufficient industrial growth at the expense of agriculture (Stewart and Gibson 1994).

Biases for and against agriculture yield inconclusive consequences for the demand for land, particularly when considering interactions with other macroeconomic policies, tenure policies, and policies on forest management and protection. On the one hand, stagnation in agriculture increases pressure on forests as landless and unemployed *campesinos* migrate to frontier zones (and the cities) in search of work. On the other hand, agricultural booms threaten forests since high producer incomes increase incentives for placing more land under cultivation.

This poses an empirical puzzle, since studies more often relate forest area to agricultural technologies (output per hectare) than to sectoral growth (change in number of hectares as determined by profitability). For example, sufficient work has been done in Mexico to suggest how productivity per hectare can be raised in cattle ranching and maize cultivation, suggesting that forest conversion can be slowed. However, productivity comparisons have not translated well into implications for land use. Cattle ranching has expanded extensively by an amount that could not have been anticipated, while productivity gains in maize farming have been held back by less than full adoption of recommended techniques (Gómez-Pompa et al. 1993).

Various substitutions and changes may add even more complications. Market agriculture competes with subsistence (*colono*) agriculture in terms of inputs (supply of land and labor) and outputs (types and prices of products). Government policies influence this composition. Within agricultural markets, a shifting mix of export products and domestic food crops can change the demand for land. Likewise, the production of nontraditional products (flowers, melons, nuts, spices) may replace traditional plantation crops and basic food crops. These complexities imply a need for caution in relating agricultural policies to the area and condition of forests.

Livestock Production. Beginning in the 1960s, several Latin American governments extended generous policy support for cattle production. Hecht (1992) and Kaimowitz (1992) contend that the removal of credit subsidies and price distortions has been insufficient to halt the continued expansion of pastures in forested areas. Producers have not chosen to

Box 2.6 Effects of Agricultural Policy Changes on Forests: Honduras

The IDB has supported efforts to eliminate controls on retail food prices, reduce government intervention in grain marketing and rural finance, devalue the lempira, and phase out export taxes. The effect of these policies on selected agricultural subsectors are described below.

Traditional Export Crops. The devaluation of the currency and removal of export taxes should favor traditional plantation crops such as bananas, coffee, sugar, cotton, and tobacco. Traditional crops occupy comparatively large areas in Honduras, possibly implying new pressures on the forest frontier. However, the supply response may be constrained by world commodity prices, trade policy in the industrialized countries, and other factors.

Nontraditional Export Crops. Honduran nontraditional exports comprise shrimp, lobster, pineapple, and melon. Key provisions of the Agricultural Modernization and Development Law allow land rental and joint ventures intended to accelerate investment and expand production capacity. Activities such as shrimp farming can have negative consequences on mangrove forests. According to the Tropical Conservation Newsbureau (San José, Costa Rica), a major controversy is whether shrimp farming is hurting mangroves and fishing in the Gulf of Fonseca.

Basic Grains. The basic grains consist mainly of maize, along with lesser quantities of sorghum, rice, and beans. Devaluation of the lempira reduced the quantity of maize imports and increased demand for domestic production. Prices have risen at the consumer level, with an expected shift in real incomes from urban consumers to rural producers. The impact on forests is unclear, since farming of basic grains only occupies 15 percent of cultivated land.

Livestock. Cattle ranching and exports in the 1990s are well below levels of the 1970s and early 1980s. Low world market prices for beef and contraband exports of cattle have resulted in some domestic shortages. In addition, domestic consumption of meat is shifting away from beef towards chicken. However, the government of Honduras has embarked on a policy to rebuild the cattle herd. This should make consumption of beef relatively more attractive once more. Given the land-intensive character of cattle production, the consequences for forests are potentially significant.

Source: IDB internal documents for descriptive narrative; author's interpretation of consequences for forests.

engage in cattle ranching as a productive activity, but rather to speculate in land and establish a hedge against inflation and taxation. As a result, the creation of pastures has remained attractive even when raising cattle becomes unprofitable. This may explain why the elasticity of supply of livestock products with respect to prices and subsidies is higher in settled zones than in frontier zones (Kaimowitz 1992). To the extent that forest clearing is driven by land acquisition rather than cattle production, policy prescriptions are to be found in tenure, road construction, land use zoning, and similar strategies. In this case, the emphasis on getting the prices right is not the most appropriate one.

Agricultural Revitalization. Latin America's past policies to promote industrialization through import substitution at the expense of agriculture may partly account for the region's debt crisis and structural imbalances. Thus, it is not surprising that current assistance for stabilization and adjustment is associated with attempts to rediscover agriculture's po-

Box 2.7 Effects of Agricultural Policy Changes on Forests: Nicaragua

Institutional Framework. The planning, coordination, and policymaking capabilities of the Ministry of Agriculture and Livestock (MAG), the National Agrarian Institute (INRA), and the Ministry of Environment and Natural Resources (MARENA) are to be strengthened. In principle, institutional strengthening will help control the expansion of agriculture into new areas.

Technology Generation and Transfer. An important element in the generation and transfer of technology is the creation of private bodies for research and technology transfer in coffee, cotton, and livestock to replace inefficient public agencies. Concurrently, the government will develop an entity for agricultural extension to serve small and medium landowners. Conceivably, short-run supply will increase on the existing pastures and cropland, and long-run increases in agricultural income will stimulate the demand for new lands. However, supply responses are highly speculative in view of tenure problems, world commodity prices, and other possible constraints.

Land Tenure. IDB financial assistance supports legislation to consolidate and guarantee land property rights, measures to title lands and compensate displaced land owners, and instruments to establish criteria for land ownership and agrarian reform. On the whole, tenure reform should be one of the most positive elements for forest protection.

Trade and Prices. In order to stimulate Nicaragua's agricultural exports, tariffs on agricultural inputs are being reduced and agricultural exporters are being exempted from certain taxes. In addition, foodstuffs received from foreign donors are being sold at prices approximating market opportunity costs, so as not to drive out domestic producers. Restrictions on the export of timber, beans, and live cattle are being gradually lifted. These measures should help raise agricultural income, subject to social and macroeconomic constraints on supply response. The impact for forests is likely positive in the short run, but less certain in the long run if it results in an increase in domestic agricultural production.

Rural Finance. After years of virtually costless credit, access to financing is presently constrained by the requirements of economic stabilization. Reforms call for a thorough restructuring of the National Development Bank, including incentive mechanisms for increasing financial services to small farmers. As long as credit remains difficult to obtain, agricultural producers will be constrained from investing and applying intensive technologies. Thus, improved credit availability will raise short-run agricultural output and potentially expand the long-run demand for new land.

Source: IDB internal documents for descriptive narrative; author's interpretation of consequences for forests.

tential for national economic growth. While agricultural reforms are far from complete, agricultural output has generally outperformed GDP growth since 1980 for the region as a whole (Goldin and van der Mensbrugghe 1992).

Boxes 2.6, 2.7, and 2.8 illustrate selected agricultural policy reforms in Honduras, Nicaragua, and Peru and their impact on forests. As suggested by these illustrations, the analysis of the impact of agricultural revitalization on forests is difficult in a partial equilibrium framework because the long-run elasticity of agricultural supply is affected by dynamic and induced effects in land markets, labor markets, and production technologies.

Box 2.8 Effects of Agricultural Policy Changes on Forests: Peru

Peru's proposed changes in agricultural sector policy comprise nine elements. For forests, the most important of these elements are institutional strengthening of the Natural Resources Institute (INRENA), deregulation of land transfers, privatization of agricultural research and technology transfer, and transfer of property rights in water and forests to private entities. The policy proposals for water markets and land markets may have considerable consequence for forests in the Amazon frontier, even if most water and land transfers take place in the coast and in the highlands.

Water Markets. A proposed water law would grant transferable water rights to current users, who would pay an annual fee to the government. Short-run effects may include an overall reduction in water consumption, along with sales of water rights to those best positioned to acquire them. To the extent that small users are displaced, the policy has the potential to increase migration to forests and cities.

Land Markets. Pending legislation will liberalize current laws which restrict land sales among private owners, and will expedite land titling and registration. This may have the effect of allocating land to its highest productivity use. Agricultural output would rise, but the impact on employment will depend on the technologies used on the new consolidated holdings. A policy risk is that smallholders who sell their lands may move to the forested frontier.

Source: IDB internal documents for descriptive narrative; author's interpretation of consequences for forests.

Macroeconomic and Trade Policies

Forests and associated natural resources are not a direct focus of macroeconomic or even sectoral reforms, so it is logical that impacts on forests are neither all positive nor all negative. Past macroeconomic imbalances in countries like Nicaragua and Peru have been so debilitating that policy changes for forest management (that is, within the sector) are relatively inconsequential for influencing the behavior and decisions of private agents (concession holders, forest industries, farmers).

In Nicaragua's forestry program, de Vylder (1992) has found a pronounced but unfounded optimistic bias that is detached from the reality of macroeconomic distress. In Peru, rural production very closely tracks macroeconomic performance, so that the post-1987 collapse of the country's economy had immediate recessionary consequences for rural producers (Hopkins 1991). In contrast, Chile's efforts to depreciate the currency and liberalize direct foreign investment help account for rapid export growth, including exports of products from pine plantations (Sanfuentes 1987). In sum, macroeconomic conditions determine sectoral performance possibilities through rising or falling aggregate demand and supply.

The impact of macroeconomic and trade policies on forest protection and management are mainly indirect and diffuse. This section examines the partial consequences of inflation, interest rates, public spending, investment, and trade.

Monetary and Fiscal Policies

On balance, the crisis of the 1980s was probably unfavorable for forest management, because forest management requires continuous long-term investment. Where inflation is high or out of control, short-term defensive and speculative action can be expected to take precedence over long-term commitments of capital. Moreover, Agosin and Ffrench-Davis (1993) contend that instability in exchange and interest rates stimulates profit-taking over production, and sends mixed signals to decisionmakers regarding the allocation of resources. If forestry taxes and fees paid by forest concessionaires, forest products industries, and others were indexed to inflation, the incentive to liquidate the standing capital in forests would be dampened. However, because forestry taxes and fees in Latin America have always been modest, any profit-taking behavior should be ascribed to reasons more important than inflation.

An unstable domestic currency normally results in an increase in the demand for dollars and other hard currencies. This might prompt increased forest cutting to raise export revenues. However, the export response is easily limited by production constraints in faltering domestic economies, and by weak external demand.[5]

Another effect of high or hyperinflation is the tendency of central banks to maintain high real interest rates to prevent sudden new surges in inflation (Batista 1993). High interest rates discourage investment in forest management because the payback period is typically decades into the future. Instead, private capital can be expected to flow away from real property into short-term and liquid financial instruments. The significance of this for forest plantations is unclear. Investments in natural forests have been constrained for other reasons (tenure insecurity) unaffected by high interest rates. Except for perhaps the largest companies, commercial credit has not been a major input in Latin American forestry (McGaughey and Gregersen 1988).

More important, perhaps, are policies to hold down the size of government by reducing subsidies, payrolls, and government programs. If past production subsidies greatly favored agriculture over forests (Stewart and Gibson 1994), then current pressures to cut subsidies should reduce the demand for land in cropping and livestock. That is, a proportionate withdrawal of government from rural production hurts private profitability in agriculture more than in forestry. In practice, this result is far from certain because subsidy programs are never scaled back uniformly, but only in proportion to the weakness of the private interests which seek them.

Payroll reductions in the public sector may be lessening the ability of governments to manage forests. For example, the staff of Peru's Ministry of Agriculture was reduced to less than 4,000 in 1993 from 45,000 prior to 1990. Similarly, the number of permanent employees in COHDEFOR (Honduras) is being reduced by half, and employment uncertainty has slowed or stopped work in the forest districts.

The impact of reducing civil service employment may not necessarily be negative. Critics consistently challenge the effectiveness of PFAs, meaning that a reduction in their size may have negligible effects on forests. Countries like New Zealand drastically cut their PFA payrolls, while sectoral output rose dramatically (Brown and Valentine 1994; Trummel 1994). To the extent that the PFAs are staffed by persons whose employment resulted from political patronage, their work does not affect forest protection and man-

---

[5] Demand weakness may have been exacerbated in recent years by a reluctance to buy tropical woods among "green" consumers in many industrialized countries. This is less important for plantation-grown products, which comprise a large share of regional exports.

agement because they tend to be redundant employees. Their dismissal is a welfare problem, but not a production problem. Redundancy is a useful hypothesis, but fails if the demoralization effect (as noted above for Honduras) is large and pervasive.

Investment and Trade

Like other protected industries, many of Latin America's plywood plants, sawmills, and other wood-processing establishments are highly inefficient by world standards. According to estimates by Stewart and Gibson (1994) for three countries (Costa Rica, Ecuador, and Bolivia), domestic log processing does not add economic value, but rather subtracts it. The three countries lose economic surplus by processing logs rather than purchasing imported products and exporting logs. These conclusions are, to some extent, weakened by sparse data, and by positive social (employment) objectives served by domestic processing.

Nevertheless, if the figures by Stewart and Gibson are approximately correct, they indicate that reluctance to open markets to external competition results in the inefficient use of forest raw materials. Employment is provided, but at a high social cost per job. Equity suffers when inefficient domestic processing increases the prices paid by domestic consumers. Stewart and Gibson, therefore, assert that the policy tends to be regressive. This, however, overlooks the fact that many producers are microentrepreneurs (Prestmon and Laarman 1989). Also, the consumers of domestic wood products include wealthy and middle-class homeowners and businesses, meaning that the equity question is far from resolved.

In the short run, the removal of import barriers lessens forest cutting if increased imports of finished or semi-finished products substitute for domestic processing of logs. This favors consumers, but displaces processing workers. Often, import liberalization generates a demand for new processing technology to compete with the inflow of imports (Agosin and Ffrench-Davis 1993). New technology may utilize logs more efficiently than existing mills, but often also implies an increase in the capacity to process logs. Thus the opening of a previously protected wood products market to world competition can result in several types of adjustments, some of which have negative implications for forests.

Removal of export barriers, including bans on the export of logs, is at least as complicated because it has both immediate and long-term effects on forest cutting and investments. This may be the case in Ecuador, where policy changes have permitted the export of eucalyptus logs. Landowners in the highlands have responded quickly to the export opportunity. However, domestic sawmills that use eucalyptus logs now face higher prices as increased competition reduces their supply. Whether an increase in the price of eucalyptus logs will stimulate increased investment in eucalyptus plantations is uncertain, as other factors may act in the opposite direction.

Environmentalists favor a certification process to ensure that forest-based exports are from "sustainable sources." As a result, several certification programs have been put in place since 1990 (see Chapter 10, by Simula). To date, these programs, covering only 2 percent to 3 percent of the traded volume, are too small to affect mainstream trade in tropical timbers (Johnson and Cabarle 1993). Certification programs operate mainly between certifying agents and individual producer companies, largely bypassing governments. Thus from the viewpoint of national governments, policy implications are unclear. In the future, it is conceivable that governments that liberalize forest-based exports will be pressured into setting up environmental certification programs. To the extent that certification requires time and money, it can be construed as imposing another impedi-

Box 2.9 Rejected Foreign Investments in Forest Industries: Honduras and Nicaragua

Stone Container Corporation in Honduras. In 1991, Stone announced plans to harvest an area of pine forest in the Mosquitia region. The company claimed that it planned to reforest at a level that would more than replace its harvest. However, Honduran environmental groups complained that the terms of reforestation were not in the contract with the Honduran government. Also, even though no broadleaved forests (rainforests) were in Stone's harvesting plan, the environmental groups contended that broadleaved forests would be harmed by cutting in the nearby pine forests. In 1992, Stone and the Honduran government suspended their agreement, even though Stone asserted that it would have provided an estimated 3,000 jobs and US$20 million in revenues to the Honduran economy.

Equipe Enterprises in Nicaragua. In 1992, this Taiwanese company was close to signing a 20-year timber concession with the Nicaraguan government. The proposal was opposed by environmental and human rights groups, who claimed that it would displace thousands of people from the Sumo and Miskito indigenous groups and damage the forests of the country's northeastern coast. Equipe was to build and operate processing plants in Nicaragua that would have generated an estimated 5,000 jobs and an investment of US$100 million. The company was also committed to reforest 200,000 hectares of degraded pineland. The transaction was stopped not on the basis of project analysis, but because the U.S. State Department believed that former Sandinista military officers would benefit from it. Reportedly, the State Department held back a loan until the "environmental dispute" could be resolved. Other critics charged that the Nicaraguan government was under pressure to grant the agreement in exchange for debt relief from Taiwan.

Source: MacKerron and Cogan (1993).

ment to trade. However, certification of forest-based exports appears to conform with international trade law so long as certification is voluntary (Office of Technology Assessment [OTA] 1992).

Foreign investment represents an important source of capital, new jobs, and access to export markets. Large forest products companies, many of them wholly or partly foreign in origin, have been shown to be good forest managers because of their long-term need for raw materials and their economies of scale (Blake and Driscoll 1976; FAO 1986). Yet as suggested in Box 2.9, foreign investment remains problematic.

Conclusions: Elements of a Policy Framework

To sort out the complicated policy matrix for forests requires a return to fundamentals. Forests, especially natural forests, are generally considered a residual land use of comparatively low commercial value. While public forest authorities (PFAs) make policies for forests, other public and private agents do not. Yet nonsectoral policies and activities can have a dominant impact on forests (Repetto and Gillis 1988; Abt Associates 1992; de Camino and Barcena 1994). Consequently, forest boundaries contract and expand in unplanned and unintended ways because of policies and activities exogenous to public forestry administrations.

Forests are an open-access resources for two reasons. First, many governments have been too weak or too unwilling to establish and enforce workable property rights. As a result, forests are "empty lands" to be taken and used. Second, because forests provide numerous goods and services on a given parcel of land, there are multiple and conflicting claims. Few governments have been able to settle the "for whom and for what" issue in an unambiguous manner, and indeed some may have concluded that it is politically unwise to attempt to do so.

Ordinarily, the public goods dimension of forests should justify strong government intervention. Yet public policy in much of Latin America has been moving toward deregulation. The policy fit between economic liberalization and mixed public-private forest resources is debatable, and contending arguments on the subject are more speculative than factual. The unfortunate choice at the moment has, on one side, public management which in principle protects nonmarket values, but is often deficient in terms of its managerial abilities. On the other side is private management which acts in response to focused objectives and goals, even if they are not always in the public interest.

Policy Challenges

The setting just described translates into an exceptionally difficult one for protecting and managing forests. Given the current relation of low-income populations to extensive areas of forest, multilateral banks, NGOs, and developing country governments will contend with deforestation for a prolonged period because of dynamics already in motion (Schneider 1995). No policy prescription, however dramatic, will quickly end net forest displacement. Those people and organizations directing the course of development will have to define what amounts to "intelligent deforestation," or policies that minimize opportunity costs and achieve the highest possible land use from some amount of forest conversion. Governments cannot openly use this terminology because it will provoke sharp reactions. Instead, public authorities will continue to propose programs to stop deforestation, even as forest clearing advances. This duality seems unavoidable in forested but relatively low-income countries such as Honduras, Nicaragua, and Peru.

Forests have public goods and externality aspects that are not necessarily promoted by strengthening private enterprise and liberalizing markets. A prominent role for government intervention is philosophically and pragmatically appropriate, even if current public capacity to protect and manage forests is generally weak. The challenge is to test and ultimately implement interventions superior to failed "command and control" laws and regulations, but not to discard the principles of intervention.

Forest conversion, especially on land frontiers, is driven by policies and actions outside of the forestry sector. Much deforestation is a side effect of nonforestry activity. Consequently, policy approaches have to rely on cross-sectoral and cross-agency efforts if they are to have a chance of being effective. This makes the managerial and institutional aspects of forestry strategies far more difficult to achieve than if policy changes could be confined to one or two specific agencies. Our understanding of the tradeoffs between distributional and environmental consequences is incomplete and unreliable because strong philosophical positions (environmental vs. developmental interests) often stand in the way of dispassionate analysis.

Long-term responses to policies relating to regeneration and growth of natural forests are difficult to predict. Concerning forest development, the use of quantitative models to analyze policy tradeoffs is severely limited. Reed (1992) reports on the attempted use of input-output models, less restrictive general equilibrium models, and approaches based on more limited macroeconomic models to link macroeconomies (of Mexico, Thailand, and Côte d'Ivoire) with the environment. These efforts proved difficult due to lack of data. Even more importantly, the models could not be made to address the links of interest. In the end, the modeling team had to be satisfied with simple partial analysis models to answer specific questions.

Some previous examinations linking policies and forests have concluded with "do everything" recommendations: extend the duration of concessions; price forest goods and services on the basis of residual value (land, rent); re-examine strategies for protected areas; conduct social and environmental impact assessments of infrastructure projects; reform land tenure; remove agricultural subsidies; stabilize inflation and interest rates; and liberalize investment and trade. Of course, policies must be internally consistent, and the impact of one policy may depend upon the implementation of others.

Forest Planning and Monitoring. Governments should make sure that investments in data gathering on forests are guided by important policy questions, not by information gathering for its own sake. Perhaps the most prominent question is the definition and delineation of a permanent public forest estate. Inevitable controversies will arise about criteria, methods, and prices for allocating lands to protected areas, peasant lands and indigenous reserves, commodity production, and other uses. These issues can hardly be avoided, even if governments prefer not to face them.

A related objective is building participatory strategies into the efforts, such as by expanding upon the work of indigenous and peasant communities to map homelands and forest uses. Another objective is institutional strengthening with respect to field inventories, data management, decision analysis, cross-agency cooperation, and public outreach. A government's success or failure in these tasks is a test of its competence for larger responsibilities on forests.

Intersectoral Coordination on Forests. As noted, many irrational activities that affect forests are due to absent or faulty coordination among different government agencies and programs. Countries need to develop and improve intersectoral public-private coordinating bodies on forests. These agencies should provide a main forum where real and potential land use conflicts are heard and addressed.

The appropriate model for this has to be debated within the institutional context of each country. One possible example is Ecuador, where INEFAN (the public forestry administration) has established a Directorio, comprising INEFAN's executive director plus one representative each from the Ministry of Agriculture, the Ministry of Energy and Mines, the Armed Forces, the Corporation for Tourism, an NGO representing the environment, and an NGO representing the wood products industries. This panel communicates viewpoints on trends and events which affect the country's forests, anticipates impending issues, and advises INEFAN on policy directions. The size and structure of these coordinating bodies will vary from one country to another, but their functions are likely to be broadly similar.

Land and Forest Tenure. Land tenure security is insufficient in itself to encourage tree planting and forest management. Nothing prevents land users who have secure property rights from behaving in ways that impose social costs on others. At the same time, countries cannot ignore the property rights approach in relation to forests. There are four specific policy areas that would benefit from reform.

Guidelines on privatizing forests. Trends and developments in Latin America's recent experiments with forest privatization (for example, in Honduras) should be monitored and evaluated. Based on this information countries could adopt intelligent guidelines for forest privatization. For example, the theory of collective goods suggests a stronger case for privatizing plantations than natural forests. Within each category, additional decision structure is warranted. Thus lands not designated for a permanent forest estate can be privatized. Whether planted or natural, ownership of forests in critical watersheds should be public in most circumstances. These are examples of the types of criteria which need development and debate (see also Chapters 5 and 6).

Granting land titles in cases where forest clearing is considered a land improvement. This outdated policy needs to be recognized and repealed.

Expediting land titles in settled areas, opposing them in frontier zones. This is the political question of determining where land titles are to be given. In general, the countries should not title land inside forest borders except where directed colonization is backed by reliable impact assessments. Concurrently, the countries should make every effort to strengthen titling in settled and semi-settled areas (see Chapter 7).

Strengthening indigenous land claims. Many of these are *de facto* claims over large forest areas. Strengthening the recognition of indigenous land claims would allow retaining significant forest tracts under sustainable treatment (Chapter 8).

Fiscal Measures for Agriculture and Forests. Subsidies and taxes in most of Latin America have discriminated against forests in favor of grazing, cropping, and other nonforest development. This implies that fiscal measures can be modified to correct the bias. However, fiscal reform is a highly challenging policy area for achieving socially optimal land uses.

Government subsidies for tree planting on private lands do not necessarily reduce deforestation (see Peuker 1992 for Costa Rica). However, subsidies may be justified as a self-financing investment (Amacher et al. 1994 for Chile), or as providing positive externalities (Gregersen et al. 1987 for watershed projects). Countries should determine, through expanded cost-benefit analysis, whether subsidies are warranted in each case. Critics of subsidies for industrial timber plantations want government support shifted to native species, natural forests, and smallholders. This can be good or bad policy, depending on answers to the same issues noted above (see Chapter 4).

The removal of agricultural subsidies from frontier zones offers a potentially powerful intervention to slow forest conversion. This refers to reducing tax breaks, credit, subsidized inputs, and extension services. At the same time, the strengthening of agricultural subsidies in settled areas (for instance, in populated highlands) may help raise output and employment on existing farms and ranches. The strategy is relatively unambiguous for land use, but faces the constraint that government officials have pursued the opposite policy for as long as anyone can remember. Governments should reformulate the biogeographical zones and agripastoral activities that determine eligibility for subsidies

Finally, the land tax needs to be re-evaluated. Although politically unpopular, land taxes have potentially important implications for land uses, as discussed earlier. The tax structure in principle favors forest conservation if croplands and pastures are taxed more heavily than forests; if newly cleared lands are taxed more heavily than long-established ones; and so on. However, the land tax is unlikely to work well without internally complementary policies on tenure, land use planning, agricultural subsidies, and granting the tax collected to local authorities for improved implementation.

Macroeconomy, Trade, and Investment Issues. Latin America's policy adjustment process has had a mixed impact on forests. This refers principally to the consequences of currency devaluation, fiscal restraint, and liberalized trade and investment. Forests are not a focus of macroeconomic or even sectoral reforms. Nevertheless, economic conditions determine what happens in forests through numerous indirect influences.

It can be argued that macroeconomic distress puts pressure on forested frontiers to accommodate the overflow of marginalized persons, although this has not been systematically documented. If this hypothesis is correct, then policy measures that result in macroeconomic stabilization, *ceteris paribus,* have to be judged as helpful for forests.

At the same time, a few specific policy areas deserve close attention for potentially adverse effects. International organizations and lending institutions should monitor the impact of reductions in government spending on the capacity of PFAs to carry out their mission. Additionally, they should encourage public interest groups to monitor the impacts of liberalized trade on the scale and environmental aspects of forest harvesting. Lastly, governments should reform laws and incentives to make foreign participation in the forestry sector consistent with national socioeconomic and environmental objectives.

Prospects for Policy Changes

As observed by de Camino and Barcena (1994), efforts to change policies affecting forests proceed from a weak starting point. There are few uncontested policy successes regarding Latin American forestry: most experience is with policy weaknesses. This does not bode well for assisting policy teams to identify proven approaches.

Utopian ideas and grand goals often dominate the rhetoric about saving forests. Many political figures and government officials are devoting considerable time to "sustainable development" without knowing what it means in operational terms. They are reluctant or politically unable to abandon abstractions and embrace specifics.

Policy recommendations are being put forward in forms that are insufficiently flexible for the reality of particular countries. Proposals to stop all logging in tropical primary forests perhaps fit into this category. More broadly, the policy environment for forestry and forests is characterized by a number of North-South differences in perspectives and values. Various high-level international efforts have been disappointing, some pessimism has been expressed about many national exercises with the Tropical Forestry Action Program, and understandable confusion exists about newer initiatives (national environmental action plans, biodiversity strategies, and others).

Measures to make policy changes on forests more self-financing are mainly in the discussion stage. Strategies to finance forest protection and management are improving, but are still immature and untested (Spears 1994). Moreover, even if the perfect policy package could be designed for forests and forestry, the ability of governments to implement these policies lags far behind.

While the above limitations are serious, there are examples of positive developments in the region that have yet to be thoroughly evaluated. Just as Repetto (1985) used gap analysis to suggest "the global possible," a similar exercise may prove useful for examining policies in relation to forests. Who are the leaders in policy achievements, and what factors explain their successes? Possible illustrations are protected areas in Costa Rica, industrial forestry in Chile and Brazil, and community forestry in Mexico.

The basis for these accomplishments dates to before 1970, and they were the work of visionary individuals. However, the policy programs and adjustments which carried these efforts forward are imperfectly understood. Also not widely known are the mistakes and costs, and how policies had to be reformulated as lessons were learned. A study of positive experiences calls attention to comparative advantages and minimum requirements, with implications for assessing success in policy-based lending.

CHAPTER 3

Policy and Financing Instruments for Sustainable Use of Forests

Ramón López

About 800 million hectares of natural tropical forest are estimated to remain in Latin America, more than 60 percent of the world's remaining tropical forests. In 1992, the United Nations Food and Agriculture Organization (FAO) estimated that the world lost about 15.4 million hectares of tropical forests per year during the 1980s, compared with losses of only 11.3 million hectares per year for the previous decade. That is, tropical deforestation is not only very significant, but accelerating.

Annual forest losses in Latin America during the 1980s were estimated at about 7.5 million hectares, almost 50 percent of the world's total loss of tropical forests. More recently, deforestation has been accelerating in several countries. A substantial increase in timber prices between 1991 and 1994, as well as the recovery of grain and other agricultural commodity prices, may have contributed to this. For example, Dourojeanni reports that some 39,900 forest fires were detected in 1995 in the Brazilian Amazon (Chapter 5). In the first half of 1998, fires destroyed large areas of forest in Roraima, Brazil, Central America and Mexico—causing health hazards to millions of people and resulting in immense losses of biodiversity. Selective logging of valuable species, mainly mahogany, has led to their virtual disappearance from Bolivian forests (Kaimowitz 1995a). Additionally, road construction into forested areas has exceeded the levels prevailing in the 1970s and some of these roads are cutting through the last remaining patches of virgin forests (see Chapter 5).

Much of the destruction of the region's tropical forests has been the byproduct of efforts to promote economic development. Some forest destruction, however, has questionable effects on economic growth. Deforestation causes wasteful forest loss in areas where soils are particularly poor, and thus inadequate to support agriculture or other activities even for short periods. And deforestation in steep areas and watersheds is likely to cause flooding and soil erosion.

Deforestation: National versus Global Interests

Consequences of Deforestation for Latin America

Not all deforestation is wasteful. Using certain tropical areas for lumber, agriculture, minerals or oil can provide positive net returns, to the extent that the loss of trees does not cause serious domestic negative externalities. From a purely domestic perspective, forest policy should promote forest conversion to agriculture and other activities in areas that allow for positive rates of return after considering all local externalities. From the perspective of individual countries, there is an optimal degree of deforestation, which, given the current high stock of forests in most of tropical South America, is probably far from being reached.

Contrary to common belief, the conversion of forests to agriculture and cattle production in tropical areas has yielded adequate rates of return, even when the calculation of profitability excludes government subsidies. A recent study by Schneider (1993a), using a large volume of empirical evidence of settlement and colonization projects in the Amazon, concludes that ". . . in economic terms, agriculture in the Amazon is doing relatively well; incomes and asset accumulation by colonists in the Amazon appear high relative to similar indicators elsewhere in Brazil. . . ."[1] A study by Mattos, Uhl, and Gonçalvez (1992) found that ranching in the Eastern Amazon is economically viable under a variety of circumstances. In fact, they found that ranchers, particularly holders of medium and large tracts, are currently investing in improving degraded pastures and obtaining sizable profits from doing so. Furthermore, a detailed analysis of five settlement projects in the Brazilian Amazon by Ozorio de Almeida (1992) provides evidence that crop yields are increasing and real land prices are rising. Other studies, in particular FAO/ UNDP/ MARA (1992) and Jones et al. (1992), provide evidence consistent with these findings. In particular, they show that incomes in Amazon settlements are generally high, allowing for significant rates of capital accumulation, and that soil fertility has not declined.

This empirical evidence covers settlement projects that have remained active during the last two or three decades. To generalize for Amazon settlements from these cases is risky, however, due to sample selectivity biases. The settlement projects that have survived for long periods are by definition those that were implemented in areas suitable for agriculture. But how many settlement projects have been completely abandoned because they were not economically feasible?[2] An unbiased assessment of the Amazon's agricultural potential can only be obtained by analyzing both surviving and nonsurviving settlements. Nonetheless, the existing empirical evidence suggests that profitable agriculture is feasible in many areas of the Amazon, and that at least part of the deforestation can result in economic improvements.

When the global externalities of Latin America's tropical forests are considered (carbon sequestration and biodiversity reserve), the optimal level of tropical forests is much greater. Global welfare maximization might even require a forest area larger than currently exists. By contrast, welfare maximization for individual Latin American countries may imply natural forest areas only modestly larger than those in North America or other developed countries, where less than 10 percent of the original natural forests remain.[3] This could imply providing public incentives for protecting ecosystems that clearly generate positive domestic externalities, including preservation of river basins, watersheds, other water sources, recreation areas, and forest areas to prevent soil losses.

One must differentiate, however, between cutting trees for land conversion and the sustainable management of forests. In principle, sustainable exploitation of natural forests could bridge part of the gap between global and national interests. Where feasible and profitable, sustainable forest management could increase national income and at the

---

[1] Schneider does indicate that turnover remains high and the abandonment of plots is still reported. He shows, however, that the most likely causes for this are differences in the opportunity costs and discount rates between early settlers and newcomers, as well as certain government interventions, and not the agronomic limitations of the soil.

[2] Schneider does include abandonment in his analysis, but this refers only to abandonment within projects that, on the whole, have survived.

[3] Given the fragility of tropical soils, natural biomass is more important in tropical areas than in temperate areas. Thus, one could expect that the individual country's interest would call for somewhat greater forest areas in the tropics than in temperate regions.

same time preserve large forest areas for carbon sequestration. Unfortunately, sustainable natural forest management appears difficult to achieve.

Despite its vast resources, Latin America's production of timber and forest goods is low and inefficient. Total production of industrial timber in 1990 was about 90 million cubic meters of industrial roundwoods, compared to 140 million in Asia (excluding India and China), even though tropical South America has almost three times as much forest area as Asia (World Resources Institute 1994). Moreover, in various cases, the value added of the wood processing industry is negative (Stewart and Gibson 1994).

Mexico and most Central American countries have reduced their forests to levels so low that, continuing the practice is no longer in their national interest. Other countries (including Brazil, Bolivia, and Peru) with large remaining forested areas are likely to continue to increase national income by cutting natural forests in the "right" places, i.e., in relatively flat areas, places with reasonably good soil qualities, or areas particularly rich in oil, minerals, or highly priced wood. For these countries, the question is not whether, but where, to cut. Their national interests require protecting those ecosystems whose destruction could cause substantial negative domestic externalities, or where alternative uses of forested lands cause little economic benefit.

Compensation for the Global Benefits of Latin American Forests

In effect, the national interests of most heavily forested countries of South America are not compatible with global interests. Because forests belong to countries, however, tropical countries should be compensated for preserving a larger forest area than is dictated by national interest. The policy framework will vary, depending on whether global welfare is maximized or only the country's interest is served. In the latter case, policies and investment should be devised to avoid wasteful deforestation and to promote "rational" exploitation and conversion of the natural forests. To serve global interests, even certain exploitation and forest conversion that increase net income would have to be avoided. There is considerable potential for trade in carbon emissions between the North and South, rather than aid from the North.[4] By this we do not mean foreign aid for the benefit of particular countries, but rather, mutually beneficial cooperation between the North and the South.

Figure 3.1 illustrates the benefits and costs of forest conservation. The horizontal axis measures the remaining forest areas before any settlement, with F-bar being the land area originally covered with forest, or the maximum forest area. The vertical axis measures the forest land (rental) value. The schedule NN represents the net marginal value product of the alternative uses of the forest lands (i.e., agriculture, logging, etc.). The schedule D^W shows the marginal value product of the standing tropical forest for the whole world, and D^L shows the marginal value of the standing forest for countries where the forest is located. The NN curve is upward-sloping, reflecting the increasing opportunity cost of conserving a forest area. The downward sloping of the D^W and D^L schedules reflect the increasing cost of deforestation for both the world and the landlord countries as the forest gets depleted. As the position of the demand schedule D^W naturally depends on the availability of forest in the world, the analysis is conditional on a fixed level of forest outside Latin America.

---

[4] The fact that about 25 percent of all carbon emissions are associated with tropical deforestation (World Resources Institute 1994) suggests that the scope for lowering carbon emissions by reducing deforestation is indeed very significant.

Figure 3.1 Value of Tropical Forest

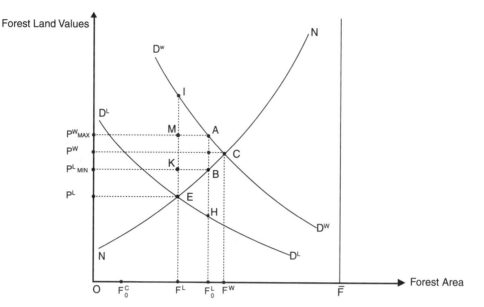

The D^L schedule includes all benefits from standing forests for the landlord countries, including protection against slides, floods, and soil degradation, and the valuation of their biodiversity and carbon sequestration capacity. The D^W schedule is the summation of the D^L schedule and benefits for the world that the standing forests provide (primarily the avoidance of global climatic changes and the value of biological reserves). The convex curve reflects the fact that the marginal value of standing forests increases rapidly as forest stocks decline.

Welfare of the whole world would be maximized at point C where the stock of forest is F^W and the forest's marginal value is P^W. By contrast, the welfare of landlord countries is maximized at point E, at a forest level of F^L and a rental value of the forested land of P^L. Deforestation takes time and investments and, thus, the landlord countries may not yet be at the point of welfare maximization. Suppose that the current level of the forest remaining is between F^L and F^W as is the likely case in most tropical South American countries where there is still a large area covered with forests. If the world does not compensate the landlords, deforestation would continue at least to level F^L with large losses to the world (indeed it could go beyond F^L if the domestic externalities are not internalized). If the loss of natural forests is more or less irreversible (biodiversity losses, for example, are likely to be irreversible), the best the world can do is to minimize further losses by stopping deforestation at level F_0^L.

In principle, the world can easily compensate the landlord countries to stop further deforestation, because world marginal gains are P_{max}^W and marginal opportunity cost of the landlord countries is only P_{min}^L. The actual compensation at the margin will be somewhere between these two prices, depending on the negotiating capacity of landlord countries vis-à-vis the rest of the world. Because landlord countries also obtain benefits from the standing forest (represented by schedule D^L), the rest of the world would only have to pay BH as a minimum and AH as a maximum. Indeed, the minimum total compensation in order to stop deforestation at F_0^L would be the area EBH and the maximum possible total compensation would be the area IEHA. Most important, even if the rest of the world pays the marginal price P_{max}^W per hectare for all the excess (potential) deforestation $(F_0^L - F^L)$, the rest of the world would still have a net gain of IMA.[5]

Forests at a level between the world optimum and the individual country optimum, such as point F_0^L in Figure 3.1, probably depict the situation that prevails in most tropical South America. The situation in Central America and Mexico is perhaps better approximated by a point such as F_0^C in Figure 3.1, that is, where current forest levels are below even the individual country optimum.

This distinction matters, because the most common forms of international involvement (technical assistance, policy advice, and concessionary loan projects to decrease deforestation) are likely to be more effective and encounter true cooperation from the national governments in cases illustrated by F_0^C than in those represented by F_0^L in Figure 3.1.[6] In the latter case governments are not likely to cooperate and many international initiatives could be diluted.

Without a comprehensive program to reduce or eliminate deforestation, projects to protect specific sites are likely to be ineffective. That is, a government might agree to receive aid to protect specific sites, but allow more deforestation elsewhere.[7] Therefore, international policy advice, technical assistance, and sporadic concessionary loan projects to halt deforestation are likely to be most effective in countries with extreme past forest losses, but less effective in countries that could benefit from greater deforestation.[8] International support in its present form would be better invested in Central America and Mexico than in the still highly forested countries of South America.[9] In South America, international support should be limited mostly to protection of ecosystems that provide

---

[5] In fact, studies have shown that the value of Amazonian forested lands for agriculture or logging is less than its value for carbon sequestration (Schneider 1993b). But, of course, this large carbon sequestration value is obtained by considering the benefits for the whole world. If only the Amazon countries' benefits of carbon sequestration are considered, the agriculture and logging value is probably greater.

[6] Given the current world concern about tropical forest losses, national governments are not likely to publicly recognize that their true objective is to exploit their forest resources more intensively. Greater forest exploitation in countries that still have massive forest areas is not only economically beneficial for the countries' economies, but also politically expedient. Forest colonization is often an important way of relieving social pressures stemming out of excessive land concentration and poverty. Additionally, forest development can be used to attract foreign capital and establish national sovereignty (López 1992). The expansion of roads and infrastructure into forested areas (with or without international assistance) in many countries of tropical South America is consistent with this hypothesis. Massive forest concessions currently being negotiated in various countries in the region is another indication of the true objectives of the country governments (Dourojeanni 1995). The willingness of governments to actively promote forest loss has been recognized in the literature: "... Most of the policies leading to forest loss and degradation are well intended, *but others have been adopted with full knowledge of the destructive consequences*" (Johnson and Cabarle 1993, emphasis added by the author).

[7] Foreign assistance might still be effective in preserving certain unique localized ecosystems which might be particularly important to protect for special characteristics that are not found elsewhere. That is, foreign assistance to the still highly forested countries of South America can be effective when it is targeted to the protection of sites that do not have good substitutes.

[8] It is important, however, to focus international assistance on either protecting remaining natural forests or on degraded areas where their restoration is not too difficult or expensive. Some areas may, indeed, be so degraded that their restoration would be extremely expensive.

[9] It might be argued that there is too little forest remaining in Central America and the Caribbean to have any significant impact on carbon sequestration. Although deforestation has been very intense, five Central American countries have about 17 million hectares of natural forest remaining (Kaimowitz 1995b). Moreover, there are large areas of secondary forests that can still be preserved. Additionally, there are certain unique ecosystems in Central America that are worth protecting for the benefit of the region and the world.

domestic positive externalities (including watershed protection) or that are virtually unique. The only other way to reduce deforestation significantly in most of South America would be through a comprehensive international agreement that incorporates the national governments in the conservation objective through an adequate compensation mechanism.

Current methods of deforestation in Latin America involve too much waste of potentially valuable timber due to the heavy reliance on fire to clear forest lands. One reason for this may be insufficient roads and other infrastructure in remote areas to make logging profitable. If agriculture is less intensive in transportation than timber, then the lack of adequate transportation would give forest burning for agriculture an advantage over logging.

Since forest burnings are a major source of carbon dioxide emissions that contribute to the global greenhouse effect, a change in the method of deforestation toward more timber extraction and less forest burning would also benefit the world. Although most of the wood extracted will eventually be released into the atmosphere as CO_2 (and thus increase carbon emissions), there is an important difference. Forest burning causes a massive emission of carbon gases over a very short time period, while if the wood is extracted for industrial uses, the emissions are spread over a long period of time. Because the world ecosystem has a limited carbon clearing capacity per unit of time, and new carbon-reducing techniques are being developed, gradual emissions of carbon are a less serious source of greenhouse gases than concentrated emissions.

Thus, there may be room for cooperation in promoting this shift without any need for significant compensation. That is, even within the current narrow mechanisms of North-South cooperation, it is possible to achieve important gains for both Latin America and the world. This would require focusing international assistance more sharply on reducing forest burning, rather than projects that are not economically feasible or lack ecological uniqueness.

Mechanisms and Financing to Reduce Deforestation

A comprehensive international agreement would have to encompass the vast majority of the forested lands in order to avoid the "substitution" leakage. It will need to focus on land allocation and on a system of compensation and monitoring of deforestation. Land use can be classified into four categories: (i) Areas designed for conservation of natural forests; (ii) areas designed for benign exploitation of natural forests including ecotourism, biodiversity prospecting, nontimber forest products, and sustainable natural forest management for wood production; (iii) areas for industrial forest exploitation and reforestation with commercial species; and (iv) areas for intensive exploitation including agriculture, mining, and oil exploration.

An international agreement would be directed mostly to increasing the land allocated to categories (i) and (ii). But natural forest management for productive purposes has been largely a failure, as many empirical studies document (see Chapter 5); thus, most efforts should be directed to increasing conservation. There are more than 70 protected areas in the Amazon Basin, covering 4.5 percent of its area. Many of the protected areas are threatened by encroachment and pressures from commercial interests who want to exploit their resources.

A cornerstone of an international agreement would have to involve a dramatic expansion of the protected areas. The idea is to include most forest areas that can be reasonably protected, excluding only those that are already in settled areas or that are highly threatened given existing population and development pressures. Given that, as argued before, the piecemeal approach does not work, it is essential that the protection programs encompass a very sizeable portion of the forested lands. The larger the protected areas relative to the total forest, the less important the substitution effect.

A sufficiently large compensation fund could assure a real commitment from national and local governments. The fund would be devoted to investments in already settled areas and to rural poverty programs to reduce pressure on national parks. Some would go toward improving the physical protection of national parks, particularly in establishing an efficient system of park rangers.[10] Subject only to broad guidelines on the use of the international fund, national and local governments should decide for themselves how the money should be allocated to protect the national parks. The countries would receive an annual payment on the basis of the natural areas which they commit to protect. The annual payment would be conditional on the preservation of the agreed areas, which can be closely monitored using remote sensing and other techniques.

To finance a scheme like this, Dourojeanni and others have proposed a worldwide carbon tax (see Chapter 5). The rationale is that forest preservation would result in the carbon sequestration needed to mitigate the climatic effects of carbon emissions. Financing this initiative could also involve expanding the "joint implementation" provision of the Convention on Climate Change signed in Rio de Janeiro. This allows firms in the North to enter into direct agreements with developing countries to develop experimental carbon-offset schemes. That is, firms could choose either to restrict their carbon emissions or to fund carbon sequestration projects in the South, usually by promoting less deforestation or greater reforestation. Some U.S. utility companies have entered into agreements with Costa Rica to develop carbon sequestration projects.

An important advantage of the joint implementation system is that it works in a decentralized manner and does not necessarily require the establishment of another bureaucratic body. Also, the fact that no direct new tax is involved is a feature that could make the scheme easier to accept politically, particularly in the United States. The firms that provide the funding retain some control over its use, an additional factor that could increase the acceptability of the scheme. Finally, the joint implementation procedure was approved at the Rio Convention, which suggests that most countries in the North and South would be prone to implement it. Discussions about "clean development mechanisms" have continued within the framework of the Convention on Climate Change. Notwithstanding these advances, it is likely that joint implementation or clean development mechanisms may be insufficient to permit the massive transfer of resources required to ensure the protection of most remaining tropical forests.

The South's acceptance of a forest protection scheme would be critical. The North can afford to pay the South more than their opportunity costs for most forested lands, so both can gain by allowing carbon trade through forest protection. Still, the economic benefits may not be sufficient to entice the South to accept an international agreement. Many governments may regard such an agreement as a loss of sovereignty over their territories; however, these concerns could be reduced by early integration of national,

---

[10] The need for park police to enforce national park protection is rarely mentioned in the literature. However, effective national park protection requires both reductions in the incentives to encroach and exploit national park resources and the physical protection of the parks. No matter what you do to decrease incentives, there will always be people interested in obtaining easy profits by exploiting the resources of the national parks. In the absence of adequate enforcement, most efforts to decrease encroachment incentives are likely to be lost.

state, and local governments (as well as community organizations and local NGOs) into cost and benefit analysis, planning additional areas to be protected, allocation of funds, and monitoring and enforcement of the measures to protect forests.[11]

Regarding the cost of protecting a large portion of Latin America's remaining tropical forests, the opportunity cost is difficult to estimate. But recent estimates of the land values of settlements in the Amazon can give an idea of the orders of magnitude involved. The average land value in eight large Amazonian settlements estimated by Ozorio de Almeida (1992) and reproduced by Schneider (1993a) in 1991 was $219 per ha (all dollar amounts refer to US dollars) or about $245 in 1995 dollars. Since this includes the value of investments attached to the land, as well as the value of part of the public infrastructure required to bring the land into production, the actual value of the undeveloped forest land for agriculture must be much less. Thus, the $245 per ha represents an absolute upper bound for the opportunity cost of land.

The lowest observed average land value among the eight settlements was about $70 per hectare in 1995 dollars. Since this value applies to the least developed and most remote settlement, we may use it as a better estimator of the opportunity cost of undeveloped forest. Schneider (1993b) provides a range of estimates of the value of forest land in agriculture for various Amazon regions. He found that these values fluctuated between $2.50 and $300 per hectare.[12] Our $70 falls well within this range.

An opportunity cost of $70 per ha implies a rental annual value of about $7 to $14 per ha if we assume a discount rate in the 10 percent to 20 percent range (and an infinite time horizon). Apart from the opportunity cost of the land, one also has to include the cost of physically protecting and managing the national parks.[13] Assuming annual management cost of $2 to $3 per ha, the total annual cost per ha of forest land protected would range between $9 and $17. This would imply that compensation ranging between $6.5 billion and $10 billion per year could promote the conservation of 650 million ha, which is perhaps as much as 80 percent of Latin America's tropical forests.

According to estimates by Goldemberg (1990), a tax equivalent to only $1 per barrel of oil or $6 per ton of coal-equivalent would generate $50 billion annually. Thus, preserving a vast proportion of the remaining natural forest in Latin America would require a tax equivalent to less than 20 cents per barrel of oil (or $1.2 per ton of coal-equivalent). This would amount to a value added tax on carbon of about 1 percent. Another way of putting in perspective this cost is to consider that world GNP in 1994 was about $30 trillion. Thus, the total forest protection bill would amount to less than 0.03 percent of total world income.[14]

---

[11] An interesting example is the case of Suriname, where a recent study by Sizer and Rice (1995) clearly demonstrated that the benefits of providing logging concessions to certain logging firms are far less than what the country could obtain from international sources interested in protecting the forests or in promoting sustainable exploitations. In fact, the IDB has participated in designing an assistance package that could compensate Suriname for protecting those forests.

[12] These values, however, include the value of investments attached to the land as well as part of the public infrastructure value that is capitalized in the price of land.

[13] It is possible that investment in forested areas may provide rates of return to capital above the market rates, that is, that a disequilibrium situation may prevail in which the rates of return to capital invested in formerly forested areas are higher than elsewhere in the economy. Compensation should, thus, also allow for this additional opportunity cost.

[14] Because such a transfer would benefit both the North and the South, it is not appropriate to compare it to current levels of foreign aid.

Schneider (1993b), using various estimates based on measures of the marginal world damage from global warming per ton of carbon, found that the cost per ton of carbon saved (i.e., not released into the atmosphere) varies between $1.80 and $66. The implicit cost in enacted carbon taxes, mostly in Northern European countries, ranges from $6 to $45 per ton of carbon saved. Multiplying the cost per ton of carbon by the carbon content per hectare of Amazon forest, he found that the value of carbon sequestration per hectare of the Amazon fluctuated between $198 and $803 when the marginal world damage cost estimates were used. It ranged between $671 and $4,950 when the implicit cost of carbon in the European tax scheme was used. Consequently, it appears that there is ample room for mutually beneficial trade in carbon emissions between the North and the South. The minimum price that the Amazon countries would require to avoid conversion of forest lands ($70 per hectare) is less than 40 percent of even the lowest estimates of the marginal benefits of the forest that the North would be willing to pay ($198 per hectare).

Using Figure 3.1, we can obtain a lower bound measure of the net benefits for the world of an agreement that would place 650 million hectares of South American forest under permanent protection.[15] Assuming the lowest carbon sequestration estimated value per hectare, P_{max}^w = $200, P_{min}^L = $70 and F_0^L = 650 million hectares. Also, suppose that in the absence of an international agreement, the South would continue reducing its forest cover until only about 20 percent of the original forest remains, i.e., deforestation would cease at about 200 million hectares, that is, F^L = 200 million hectares in Figure 3.1. The total benefit for the world of implementing an international agreement that stops deforestation at 650 million hectares is equal to the area IABE. Since we do not know the slopes of the D^w and N curves, we cannot determine the size of this area. However, it is minimized if both D^w and N are flat. That is, the minimum gain out of the agreement is the area AMKB, where KB = 450 million hectares and AM = P_{max}^w – P_{min}^L = $130. Therefore, the minimum net global benefit of the agreement, considering only the carbon sequestration value of the Amazon, would be about $58.5 billion. This is the absolute minimum for two reasons: First, we are using the lowest carbon sequestration value per hectare of Amazon land and second, we are assuming that both the demand for carbon sequestration and the supply of forest land are infinitely elastic, clearly a highly unrealistic, conservative assumption.

Table 3.1 provides a range of estimates for net world gains of stopping deforestation in the Amazon (leaving about 650 million hectares covered with forest), under alternative assumptions. The D^w demand schedule is likely to be steep, that is, as the forest is reduced its marginal value increases very rapidly. Hence, assuming conservatively that the elasticity of demand for forests is equal to one, the value per hectare of carbon sequestration increases as we move from F_0^L to F^L, that is from $200 to $655 per hectare. In this case, the area IMA is equal to almost $67 billion and the total net gain for the world increases to $125 billion. If the value per hectare of forest is estimated using the lowest implicit cost in enacted carbon taxes, $671 per hectare, the net benefit of an international agreement reaches about $692 billion. The most plausible values in Table 3.1 are those given by the middle scenario, with unit elastic supply and demand curves. This yields a net gain of about $713 billion, corresponding to the total present value of the cumulative

---

[15] The 650 million hectares figure is used as an illustration of the potential benefits of the agreement. More detailed studies would be required to establish the optimal forest areas to be protected.

Table 3.1 Carbon Sequestration Benefits of an International Agreement
(In U.S. dollars)

	CARBON SEQUESTRATION VALUE PER HECTARE		
	Lower bound	Midpoint	Upper bound
ALTERNATIVE SCENARIOS	$200	$671	$4,950
Infinitely elastic world demand and supply schedules for forests	$58.5 billion	$270 billion	$2.2 trillion
Unit elasticity in world demand for forest; infinitely elastic supply	$125.5 billion	$692 billion	$3.8 trillion
Unit elasticity in world demand and supply schedules	$146 billion	$713 billion	$3.89 trillion

Note: The following assumptions are made:
(1)   The agreement would protect 650 million ha of tropical forest in Latin America (mostly in the Amazon).
(2)   In the absence of an agreement, the closed forest area in the Amazon would decline to 200 million ha.
(3)   The lower bound carbon sequestration value per ha corresponds to the lowest estimate of global warming costs available. The mid-point level corresponds to the lowest implicit value in the carbon taxes enacted in Europe, and the upper bound corresponds to the maximum implicit value of such taxes.

benefits for the world. Using a 10 percent discount rate implies a net annual benefit of about $70 billion, or approximately 0.2 percent of world GNP.

Policy Reforms and International Markets

Structural Adjustment and the Forest Sector

Most Latin American countries have undertaken far-reaching policy reforms since the late 1980s. Adjustment has led to significant changes in the structure of incentives, with important consequences for the forest sector. The agricultural sector, which historically has been discriminated against in favor of industry, has benefited from these policy shifts. As Krueger, Schiff and Valdés showed in 1990, economic distortion such as overvalued exchange rates and import restrictions acted as a burdensome tax on agricultural producers in most countries. At the same time, the agricultural sector was, in part, compensated by special tax treatment, credits and input subsidies.

The net effect, however, was a large tax that significantly reduced agricultural incentives. This can be measured using the producer subsidy equivalent (PSE), a comprehensive indicator of intervention that gauges both price intervention and nonprice transfers to producers.[16] According to Valdés (1995), the PSE for agriculture between 1985 and

---

[16] Governments intervene in a variety of ways in an attempt to assist agricultural producers. Although price interventions represent an important form of assistance, nonprice measures could be important as well. The producer subsidy equivalent (PSE) can be defined as compensation to farmers for the loss of income resulting from the removal of domestic agricultural policy measures at a given level of production. Specifically, it is the sum of net output market support, input subsidies, marketing/transport/storage subsidies, deficiency payments, and nonprice transfers (research, extension, irrigation). Expressed as a sum, the PSE is an absolute aggregate monetary figure and can be calculated both for individual commodities or as an overall sector PSE. However, to make the PSE comparable across commodities and countries, the aggregate PSE should be expressed as a ratio. It is a ratio of policy transfers compared to the total value of domestic production (valued at domestic prices).

1990 averaged –3.4 percent of the value of agricultural production in Brazil, –22.5 percent in the Dominican Republic, –18.1 percent in Ecuador, and –42.2 percent in Paraguay. These figures mean that the effect of economic distortions overshadowed the compensating effect of subsidies by a wide margin. Moreover, the producer subsidy equivalent for Brazilian agricultural importables was –20.5 percent of the value of agricultural imports during the period, and that for agricultural exportables from the Dominican Republic, Ecuador, and Paraguay was –48 percent, –46 percent, and –42 percent, respectively, of the value of agricultural exports.[17] These data are most significant for cattle production because beef was an importable commodity in Brazil between 1985 and 1990, while it was an exportable commodity in the other countries. Among all the tropical countries analyzed by Valdés, only Colombia showed a positive producer subsidy equivalent measure.

The role of tax allowances and subsidized credit for cattle ranching was often considered a major source of deforestation during the 1970s and 1980s (Binswanger 1991). But, since the net effect of policy intervention was to tax agriculture, including the beef sector, one has to conclude that the overall incentive policy intervention did not promote more deforestation through agriculture and cattle production incentives.[18] That is, if the tax allowances and credit subsidies were only a partial compensation for the negative effects on the profitability of the sector due to overvalued exchange rates, export taxes, and large import protection to the industrial sector, one can hardly argue that the incentive policies were promoting the expansion of the cattle industry and, thus, were causing further deforestation.

By the same token, the removal of most of these policy distortions is likely to increase rather than reduce the competitiveness of agriculture and in particular the cattle industry. The elimination of tax allowances, credit and other input subsidies that, in fact, took place in Brazil and most other countries in the region, was accompanied by a reduction in trade protection to the industrial sector, the elimination of export taxes and restrictions affecting agriculture and other primary exports, a deep devaluation, and exchange rate liberalization. Since the beef sector is eminently tradable, the more realistic exchange rate is likely to cause a positive impact on the competitiveness of the cattle industry.[19]

Also, removing the extremely high levels of industrial protection allows agriculture to compete more effectively for the allocation of capital and other resources. Thus, the net effect of eliminating price distortions is to increase the competitiveness of agriculture (including the cattle sector) and, therefore, to increase the profitability of not only agricultural intensification, but also of expanding the agricultural frontier into forest areas.

In fact, in many countries in the region, the elimination of exchange rate distortions and the reduction of protection to the industrial sector was not accompanied by a comparable reduction of nominal protection to the agricultural importable sector. Hence,

---

[17] Importable and exportable goods are subsets of tradable goods. In the case of importable goods, the cost, insurance, and freight charges must be less than their local cost. For exportable goods, the free-on-board cost must be higher than the local costs of production.

[18] It is true that cattle production in the Amazon received some special incentives over and above the tax allowances and credit subsidies that production elsewhere received. The exchange rate and trade policy distortions in Brazil and other Amazonian countries were, however, so deeply discriminatory against agriculture, including the cattle industry, that it is hard to imagine that the special Amazon subsidies provided enough compensation.

[19] After the first real devaluation, the real exchange rate started to gradually appreciate in several Latin American countries, because of market forces (rather than government intervention) resulting in large capital inflows between 1991 and 1994 (López 1995).

the net effect of government intervention has been not only to eliminate the anti-agricultural bias, but also to create positive net incentives for import substitution in agricultural products. This important change is likely to make the Latin American economies even more dependent on primary sectors with a consequent relative contraction of the industrial sector.[20]

The structural adjustment process has also led to important reforms that directly affect the forest sector. In the process of reducing trade restrictions, export taxes and prohibitions affecting raw and semiprocessed logs have been eliminated in several countries. Bolivia, for example, eliminated all restrictions on exports of timber as part of the effort to increase nontraditional exports (Kaimowitz 1995a). Nicaragua and several other countries are now in the process of eliminating restrictions on timber exports (see Chapter 2). At the same time, several countries have reduced the protection of the wood processing sector by eliminating quantitative import restrictions on processed products. In the past, these policies contributed to the inefficiencies of the wood processing sector and some authors have argued that, by depressing domestic timber values, also contributed to deforestation and to the generation of disincentives to forest plantation (Kishor and Constantino 1993; Stewart and Gibson 1995).

Forest plantations cover a minuscule fraction of the forested land in Latin America, not only because of low timber prices, but also because there are plenty of forests that can be exploited at little private cost. The problem is that given the lack of enforcement of forest regulations and the lack of collection of royalties and stumpage fees from timber extraction in public lands, the incentives to private plantations are minimal even if timber prices are good. Private plantation timber production requires costly investments and, therefore, can hardly compete with timber extracted from open-access or semi–open-access forest lands where the only effective cost is the cost of extraction and transportation. High timber prices in the presence of vast, effectively open-access public lands are more likely to result in greater timber extraction from public lands than more private tree plantations.[21]

Thus, the liberalization of the timber trade is likely to cause even greater incentives to cut trees in public forest reserves. There is empirical corroboration for this. In fact, Cropper and Griffiths (1994), using aggregate data, found that timber prices and deforestation are positively correlated in Latin America. The evidence from Chile points in the same direction. Although Chile has had no restrictions on raw timber exports for many years, the development of private tree plantations has required the use of heavy subsidies, despite the fact that in Chile, unlike most countries in South America, the availability of open access or semi–open-access forest lands is quite limited and concentrated in relatively isolated areas.

An important issue is the sequencing of the policy reforms. Before completely liberalizing timber trade it is important to introduce reforms in the management and enforcement of regulations affecting public forest lands. As indicated, regulations affecting logging concessions are not enforced and concessions typically last a very short time.

---

[20] In most countries of the region this phenomenon is not yet detectable, mainly because of the relatively short time that has elapsed since the reforms. In Chile, however, a country that initiated the reforms much earlier, available statistics show the primary sectors (agriculture, mining, fisheries, and forestry) growing at a rate 25 percent faster than the economy as a whole, and a significant decline in the contribution of the industrial sector to total output (López 1995).

[21] On the other hand, higher timber prices allow logging activities to compete better with agriculture for the use of forest lands. This could have the effect of reducing forest conversion to agriculture.

This provides all the incentive to maximize timber extraction regardless of the environmental consequences. Moreover, royalties and stumpage fees, that theoretically should be large enough to capture rents out of exploiting public lands, are not effectively used. In reality, the collection of royalties and stumpage fees corresponds to only a small fraction of the true forest rents. Thus, if the idea were to reduce deforestation and really promote forest plantations, before liberalizing trade in timber products, it would be necessary to reform the system of management of public lands and concessions. Additionally, greater physical protection of forest reserves and national parks should be implemented to avoid illegal forms of deforestation which are likely to increase in a liberalized policy environment.

For countries not interested in slowing deforestation, liberalizing the timber trade without implementing the above complementary measures may, however, be rational. The elimination of the discriminatory policies against the logging industry associated with traditional trade policies is likely to increase deforestation, but at the same time, reduce forest burning as a mechanism for land clearing. The reason for this is that as timber products become more valuable, greater efforts would be devoted to wood extraction rather than the cheaper forest burning alternative. Since, as we indicated before, excessive forest burning is a major problem for many countries, the change in the pattern of deforestation resulting from the liberalization of timber trade is probably consistent with the national interest.[22]

In general, structural adjustment, as implemented in most of Latin America, is likely to result in increased deforestation. Policies that improve production incentives for the primary sectors have not necessarily been accompanied by policies to ameliorate distortions in the use of forests. Protection of national parks, the enforcement of forest regulations, and charging stumpage fees are examples of measures that have not been taken in parallel with structural reforms.[23]

The Role of International Commodity Prices

In the late 1980s and early 1990s, the new policy environment was accompanied by a considerable deterioration in the international prices of meat and many other agricultural commodities that, in large part, offset the improved profitability of agriculture and the cattle sector brought about by the new policies. The real international price of beef has declined steadily since the early 1980s. In 1994, beef prices were less than half their 1970 level and about 60 percent of the price prevailing in 1980. Similarly, real prices for most commodities that are important to Latin America and that compete for land with forests have tended to decline significantly. The decline in cereal prices was particularly important because cereals are the second most land-intensive agricultural output, after cattle production. Declining international prices for agricultural commodities and beef mitigated the effects of the structural reforms on forests, resulting in less deforestation than would have occurred otherwise. However, agricultural commodity prices are beginning to show clear signs of revival. For instance, the international prices for bananas, maize, rice, and wheat prices have moved up in recent years. Even beef prices have shown signs of a modest recovery since their trough in July 1995.

---

[22] Of course deforestation through burning and logging are both negative for the rest of the world from the point of view of biodiversity losses.

[23] López (1994a), in a more general conceptual framework, showed that trade and other economic reforms that decrease macroeconomic and trade distortions are likely to reduce natural resource stocks in a context of open or semi–open-access resources.

There are indications that the recent upswing in prices reflects more than just temporary fluctuations or weather-related problems. It appears that the fast economic growth that several highly populated developing countries have been experiencing (mainly China, Indonesia, and India) is beginning to affect the demand for agricultural commodities and meat products. Accordingly, an eventual new agricultural commodity boom combined with recent free market reforms, could lead to an acceleration of deforestation in Latin America in the near future, particularly if complementary sectoral reforms are not implemented soon.

Slow regional economic growth in the 1980s and early 1990s has also tempered the pace of deforestation, as few public funds were available for building roads and other infrastructure into forest areas. Slow growth also reduced the availability of private funds, implying fewer investments in forest areas and a lower demand for land. However, growth has resumed in most of the large countries in the region. The effects of this revival in growth is already beginning to be felt in many places such as the Amazon, where forest burning has increased significantly.

Looking ahead, three factors are likely to lead to greater forest loss. First, a liberalized policy framework seems to have eliminated most of the historical anti-agricultural bias and is in the process of also eliminating anti-timber biases. Second, international agricultural commodity prices seem to be rising. And third, economic growth is accelerating. Even more importantly, free market policies may now allow for a rapid and complete transmission of international price booms into the domestic economy. This is in sharp contrast with the historical patterns where domestic distortions hindered the full transmissions of international changes.

The improvement in economic performance due to the combination of higher commodity prices and more rapid use of forest resources may benefit the region's forested nations in the short run. However, the consequences for the rest of the world are likely to be negative. Countries with abundant forest resources are likely to benefit even if one considers the potential long-run cost of forest conversion and tree cutting.

Policies and Financing Mechanisms for an Efficient Forest Sector

In this section we discuss a policy framework to promote the effective conservation of protected areas, efficient and sustainable exploitation of areas designated for industrial forestry and agroforestry, and efficient reforestation of selected degraded lands. It is assumed that the land allocation goal has been already determined and that the policy objective is to accomplish the allocation goal and obtain the largest economic benefit for a country. If an international agreement as the one previously described is reached, the structure of land allocation is going to be completely different than without such an agreement. If an international agreement is implemented, the largest efforts would have to be directed to protecting areas targeted for conservation, while in the absence of an international accord the problem of conservation and protection is likely to be restricted to a much smaller geographic area. In this case, the major task is to focus on how to develop the vast forest areas that are going to be designated for agroforestry, timber extraction and conversion to agriculture, generating the highest returns and minimizing negative domestic environmental losses.

Regardless of the extent of international involvement, the countries in the region need to develop a land allocation blueprint for public lands, specifying clear goals for their utilization. At the same time, regulatory and policy mechanisms need to be designed in a manner consistent with land utilization goals. General policy, management, and investment requirements to meet these objectives are discussed below. An analysis of the financing mechanism to cover the costs of these measures also follows.

National Parks and Protected Areas

Although deforestation in Latin America is caused more by large commercial interests than poor peasants, most threats to national parks come from the poor. National parks cover only a small fraction of the forested lands so that deforestation within their boundaries constitutes a minor portion of total deforestation. While illegal encroachment by poor peasants practicing slash-and-burn cultivation and by small illegal loggers is a problem for the preservation of parks, the implied deforestation is small relative to the loss of forest outside national parks.[24] The most serious risks are faced by parks that are close to heavily populated areas.

The selection of the site for a national park should take into consideration the feasibility of effectively protecting it. For this reason, new national parks should not include areas that are already densely populated. Additionally, for parks with an increasing resident population, the options are either to retrench and reduce the size of the park to new boundaries that can be protected, or to provide incentives to the local population to voluntarily relocate. In any case, whatever option is chosen, local communities should be actively involved so that they can understand the value of forests and the rationale for establishing the park. They should also participate in the process of planning and protecting the new boundaries, and in the planning of the voluntary resettlement, if that is the option chosen.

The relocation of poor people out of a national park and/or the reduction of the pressure of the poor on the park boundaries need significant positive incentives. Land, housing, and basic services need to be provided. The provision of agricultural land to the rural poor may require the enactment of a land reform that improves the unequal distribution of good agricultural land prevailing in most of the region. Government assistance in the form of agricultural extension, schooling, credit, and other services should be made available outside the protected areas to entice local residents to stay outside the park boundaries.

Perhaps the largest financial cost of effectively protecting national parks is the provision of these services as well as the cost of land redistribution to large numbers of poor people. But, in addition to reducing the incentives for the rural poor to settle in national parks, national parks must be protected physically. A clear demarcation of park boundaries is essential, as well as ample information to the public about such boundaries. A sufficient number of park rangers is needed to patrol the parks. Provision should also be made for hiring the administrative and professional staff to monitor the national parks. The physical protection of the national parks implies significant operational costs that require financing.

Management of Forest Reserves and Other Public Lands

One of the most serious problems facing public forest lands is their semi–open-access status and the lack of government enforcement of regulations. Given current administrative, institutional and financial capabilities, governments in the region are simply unable

---

[24] Indeed, large commercial interests are often too "visible" to illegally encroach on national parks although they have also caused damages in isolated incidents. Also, land speculation is much less likely in national parks.

to control the use of forests in public lands. The almost complete absence of government control and misdirected incentives concerning the establishment of private property rights over public lands have given rise to a chaotic process of land speculation, where forest burning is the main mechanism for land clearing. This has led to large timber losses as well as serious environmental consequences. The failure of the government to enforce concession conditions, low or almost nonexistent stumpage fees and royalties, and the legitimization of land encroachment (after "proper development" of the land), have led to the underdevelopment of forest plantations. The fact that public natural forests are almost freely available (legally to those with sufficient clout in the government and illegally to almost everyone else), makes it very difficult for tree plantations to compete with the exploitation of public lands. The lack of enforcement of concession agreements and short concession periods, are invitations to predatory behavior in public forests.

The key measures proposed concern improving government enforcement capabilities and accepting that, even if they do improve, it is not likely that they will be sufficient to allow for the effective control and enforcement of regulations in all existing public lands. As result, rather than permitting the continuation of the process of alienation of public lands currently in existence, it would be better to allow for an orderly and transparent process of land privatization. A previous report for the IDB (López 1994b) suggested a scheme for privatizing public lands giving priority to lands that are closer to populated areas and to forests that are less unique in terms of biodiversity, and are located in environmentally stable areas. That article proposed three types of lands for privatization: First, lands to be sold only in large tracts to responsible enterprises, including NGOs, under restricted conditions, to be exploited only for agroforestry, nontimber products, ecotourism, and other forms of relatively benign exploitation; second, lands that can be utilized for timber extraction but that cannot be burned; and third, lands to be sold without restrictions on their future use or method of clearing.

In order to ensure the transparency of the privatization process, the report suggested the use of an auction mechanism and appropriate public information campaigns. The government would retain a forest reserve that it can realistically manage or for which it can administer a concession. Various countries in the region are already seriously considering such a privatization process.

In the forest that the government ultimately retains, concessions should be transparently allocated through an open bidding mechanism. Concessions should be long term so that firms have the incentives to really manage the forest. This probably requires concession lengths of 25 to 40 years. Stumpage and royalty fees should capture most of the economic rents and an effective collection system should be established.

The management of the remaining public lands should be given to the state or local government, allowing them to retain a significant part of the revenues collected. This should provide incentives to local governments to enforce regulations in order to ensure a more or less steady flow of financial resources out of the concessions. Also, part of the revenues should be earmarked to peasant organizations, charities, and local NGOs, so that private sector organizations can develop a stake in controlling local government actions, to diminish corruption and other nontransparent practices.

The construction of roads and other infrastructure into forest areas should be carefully planned, beyond usual environmental assessments of projects. Roads should only be constructed in areas that appear profitable to develop, that is, in areas where deforestation is not likely to cause serious local environmental problems, where there is an ample supply of timber, or where the land can profitably support agriculture.

Improving Forest Utilization and Establishing Domestic Financing

Land speculation should be reduced through special policies aimed at that purpose. A closely related goal should be to diminish the incentives to the anarchic sequence of land occupation, forest burning, and land rights that has prevailed. Furthermore, incentives should be market-oriented.

A straightforward mechanism to reduce land speculation and excessive forest burning is to tax the speculators. In fact, some countries in the region have legislation concerning taxation of capital gains on land, but these taxes are rarely collected. In Brazil, for example, there is a 25 percent federal capital gains tax on land sales (Moran 1993); yet the government lacks the ability to collect it. The best way of assuring tax collection is to leave it in the hands of the local governments, with the incentive that they can retain part of the revenues. As with the royalties and stumpage fees, a study should be prepared to estimate the potential revenues of such a tax. Local private sector organizations should be entitled to a certain fixed percentage of potential tax revenues. This should help maintain the accountability of local governments and force them to collect the taxes.

Lack of a land tax or the inability to collect the tax leads to unequal distribution of land and to land speculation. Land is valued as a tax shelter. This makes it attractive to speculators and other investors, raising the price of land well above the present value of net farm revenues. It also reduces access to land by poor peasants. A land tax that exempts forested areas from taxation would also diminish incentives to clearing excessively large areas of land and burning forests. Indeed, it would allow the tax shelter role to continue but applies it only to the forested land. As with the capital gains tax on land, the regular land tax should be collected by local governments, and revenues should be distributed between the local government, local private organizations, and the national government. Local private organizations would receive a fixed percentage of potential revenues.

Despite their efficiency and equity advantages, land taxes are politically difficult to implement. However, as the enactment of legislation to liberalize imports and privatize state-owned enterprises shows, the fact that land taxes have been difficult to implement in the past does not mean it would be impossible to do so in the future. In particular, public information campaigns to adequately explain the proposed legislation, and the government's commitment to the measures would make their implementation politically more palatable. A larger capital gains tax on land sales can be instituted in the meantime. This tax is more likely to be accepted since it does not tax the land itself, but only the appreciation of its real value.

The complete elimination of export restrictions on timber and other raw wood products, in the absence of complementary policies, is risky. It could create a large demand for natural timber that, if not matched by higher stumpage fees or royalties and greater controls, could lead to the massive extraction of timber products from the almost open-access public lands. Since land privatization and the implementation of the measures discussed would take some time, it might be advisable to consider replacing timber export controls with a temporary export tax. The export tax should yield revenues that can be used to finance the many initiatives previously discussed. In any case, before putting this tax into effect, a careful empirical analysis should be carried out to quantify its effect on deforestation.

To avoid reducing incentives to planting trees and sustainable timber extraction, the export tax should be clearly presented as temporary. A fixed schedule indicating a gradual reduction of the tax rate should be made public and strictly followed. Since forest investments are long term, a temporary export tax with a credible withdrawal schedule, should not only be innocuous to forest plantation, but should cause a reduction in deforestation in the short run as people find it more profitable to delay cutting the trees until the tax is phased out.

The wood processing industry could potentially make an important contribution to the region's economies in terms of both income and employment. Moreover, the fact that Latin America has significant comparative advantages in the production of timber, can lead to similar advantages in wood processing because the large transportation costs of raw timber creates a wedge between the domestic price of raw timber and international prices. Additionally, the wood processing sector is relatively labor intensive and its expansion can play an important role in increasing rural employment and reducing poverty. For these reasons, it appears convenient to provide some support to the wood processing industry. The sector can suffer a severe compression as trade protection is reduced. Diminishing import duties will lower prices of finished goods, and the removal of export restrictions will raise raw material prices, creating a profit squeeze. Technical assistance and the provision of unsubsidized credit, particularly to small- and medium-sized wood processors, can smooth the transition of the industry from a highly protected environment to a free market one. Assuring the provision of unsubsidized credit to small- and medium-sized firms is important because, given the imperfections of credit markets, these firms are likely to suffer liquidity shortage as profit margins decline.

Another issue of importance is property rights and their enforcement. Lack of definition of property rights and tenure insecurity limit long-term investment, particularly investments in land, including tree planting. Perhaps even more important is the inadequate protection from squatter encroachment on private forested lands. This forces landlords to cut trees to show that the land is being used and discourage squatters.[25] An important policy implication is that governments should provide the necessary institutions to facilitate legalization of land titles and should consistently enforce property rights and protect private lands from squatters. This should go a long way toward discouraging deforestation as a means to securing property rights. Additionally, land reform laws should consider forests an appropriate use of the land and eliminate the existence of forests as a cause for expropriation of the property.

Reforestation of certain degraded lands can result in positive local externalities, which is a justification used to subsidize reforestation in degraded land. The subsidies are justified under relatively strict conditions (see the analysis in Chapter 4); the case for plantation incentives arises only when the private net returns are lower, but the returns including externalities are greater than the returns to alternative land uses.

The concept of charging user fees for the use of natural resources has been very difficult to implement in the past. Given the increasing consensus on the expanding role of markets in Latin America, it is likely that user cost charges can now be implemented in many areas. In particular, national parks should be allowed to charge fees for entry and other services. The goal is that user charges cover a significant part of the maintenance costs of national parks. Additionally, large beneficiaries from protecting major watersheds, such as electric utilities, should be charged special fees to cover the costs of protection. Colombia provides a good example of the feasibility of this initiative (López 1994b).

An important feature of these policies is that, apart from promoting economic efficiency, many of them also may result in large financial flows to fund the programs and

---

[25] A recent World Bank (1995a) study for Guatemala clearly documents the use of deforestation to establish property rights not because of any legal requirement to develop the land, but simply to reduce encroachment.

investments proposed in the foregoing. A land tax, a capital gains tax on land, and stumpage fees and royalties could make a sizable contribution to financing national park protection as well as improving public institutions and the capacity of local and national governments to conduct forest policies and programs.

The privatization of forest lands at market prices can also raise revenues. For example, the privatization of 20 percent of the Amazon may yield $9 billion to $10 billion assuming that land is sold at an average of $60–$70 per hectare. Assuming a 10 percent net rate of return, this could yield $900 million to $1 billion, which could cover a large portion of the additional annual funds needed to improve the staffing of forest departments and the management of public lands. Total foreign aid for environmental projects (not only to the forest sector)—including bilateral aid, the Global Environmental Facility, the Montreal Protocol, Debt for Nature Swaps, the Brazil Rain Forest project, and private sector contributions—were estimated at about $460 million per year in the mid-1990s. This figure is almost twice as large as the total annual concessional environmental contributions that Latin America receives from the industrial economies (López 1994b).

At least part of the financial resources raised using the measures suggested in this section should be earmarked to promoting and protecting national parks and, more generally, to promoting the sustainable development of forests. On the other hand, it is inevitable that part of these financial resources will be allocated to other purposes. The important thing is to develop explicit criteria to assign a significant portion of them to the forest sector.

Community Funding to Correct Local Externalities

Several of the negative local externalities of deforestation and forest degradation are felt on the availability and quality of water. Local populations normally understand the connection between deforestation of certain key areas and soil erosion, and the increasing scarcity and deteriorating quality of water for consumption and for productive purposes that they experience.[26]

The clear understanding and concerns of many local communities about this problem suggests the potential for financial contributions by the affected communities to protect, maintain, and renovate forests that directly affect water sources and reservoirs. Funds can be collected by community organizations with the assistance of local governments through water and energy tariff surcharges for the protection of the forests in the water sources. Further, in the cases where the protective forests are privately owned, it is possible to promote forest buy-back schemes, through which local communities are able to control the forests that are vital for their water supplies.

The same concepts can be applied to local forest-related externalities that are not related to water. An interesting example is the Baboon Sanctuary for local primates in Belize (World Bank 1994a). Local residents decided to join efforts and money to invest in the protection of local forests where howler monkeys live. The investment paid off, as the residents obtained large benefits from ecotourism revenues.

International Financing Sources

The Global Environmental Facility (GEF) is one of the most important mechanisms used to direct the financial contributions of the North to promote environmental sustainability

---

[26] The importance of these issues is illustrated in the case of Nicaragua (IDB 1996b). In other Latin American countries, water issues are also of prime importance, as indicated in the World Bank Development Report (1992).

in the South, by combating deforestation, land degradation, and desertification. In 1994, total ongoing GEF investment projects around the world amounted to about $1.3 billion, of which Latin America and the Caribbean received $160 million. Only a relatively minor fraction of these funds went to projects that have a direct effect on forests. The fact that financing projects to reduce deforestation and land degradation are now an integral part of GEF activities implies that financial flows for these purposes are likely to increase significantly in the near future.

The Brazilian Tropical Rainforest Trust Fund (BTRTF), established in 1991 by the Group of Seven, is another mechanism to channel international funding to Latin American forests. A fund of $250 million was set to implement projects to conserve biological diversity, strengthen forest management institutions and related projects. Over the last few years, the annual proceeds of the BTRTF have fluctuated between $15 million and $20 million (Figueroa 1995).

Debt-for-Nature Swaps (DNS) allow countries in the South to convert part of their external foreign debt into obligations in domestic currency to be used in promoting environmental sustainability. DNS have been used in a limited way in Latin America; by 1995, some 15 agreements had generated about $68 million in conservation funds over a five-year period. A large proportion of these funds have been used for wildlife conservation and for the protection of national parks. The largest beneficiaries have been Costa Rica, Brazil, Bolivia and Ecuador.

In addition to official financing, significant sums are contributed by the private sector of the industrialized countries. It is estimated that annual private contributions from the North for sustainable natural resources management in the South ranges between $25 million and $35 million (López 1994b). A large portion of these go directly or indirectly to the forest sector. Apart from traditional contributions via NGOs, there are other international contributions from the for-profit private sector. Among those, the most promising is the joint implementation mechanism. It permits international carbon trade by allowing firms to obtain carbon credit by contributing to forest protection. Given that the reductions in carbon emissions in the United States and several other developed countries are, so far, purely voluntary, this mechanism has been used to a limited degree. The most important joint implementation agreements have involved U.S. electric utilities and the Norwegian government in Costa Rica.

The total annual concessional financing of the forest sector from the various international sources is unlikely to be much above $150 million. To put this into perspective, gross estimates of required expenditures in Latin American forests to bring about sustainability should be considered. Our own estimates of the annual expenditures that would be required to cover just the opportunity cost of a large portion of Latin America's tropical forests are in the $6.5 billion to $10 billion range. Of course, this assumes that most of these forested lands could be converted into other uses in the near future. In fact, many of them are currently inaccessible and for the time being, are not threatened. A study by the Amazon Commission on Development and the Environment (1994), estimates that the total cost of protecting ecosystems in Amazonia is about $10 billion per year.

These figures indicate that international funding to support sustainable forest in Latin America is minimal compared to the needs. The North will have to accept a much greater financial responsibility to effectively promote forest protection and sustainability in the South. The joint implementation mechanism has great potential to increase the financial flows of the private sector in the North. But this requires that the agreed-upon carbon reduction objectives be effectively implemented, so that reductions in carbon emissions become compulsory for each country, and an effective trading mechanism is established to use forests as a carbon sink.

Public and Private Sector Roles in Forest Financing

An important role of the public sector is to identify and exploit potential sources of financial revenues (taxes, fees for public services, royalties) that promote economic efficiency. The use of policies that are, in addition, equitable is another important criterion in this respect. Most of the policies discussed above are beneficial under these criteria. They provide financial resources that can, at least in part, be used to promote sustainable development; they promote economic efficiency by leading to a more proper valuation of forest resources; they are equitable by forcing mostly large and medium-sized producers to reduce the rents they obtained from national resources.

The proper use of the revenues raised in this way is an important task of the public sector. The financial resources should be used in the most decentralized way possible, providing ample support to local governments, private NGOs with a proven record of promoting sustainability, and to other community organizations. The public sector should use part of the revenues to provide effective protection to the national parks and other protected areas. Similarly, a portion of the revenues should be used to allow national and local government agencies to monitor changes in forest resources and enforce the implementation of existing forest regulations.

Private financing of forests depends very much on the incentive framework. For instance, if rents from logging public forests are eliminated through increased royalties or other means, incentives for private investment in reforestation projects will increase, at least in certain areas. Similarly, if private industries are forced to pay the full market value of the wood extracted from public lands to produce charcoal, they will have greater incentives to produce wood in private lands.

In many instances, private firms can make large contributions to protecting natural forests and related ecosystems if this will improve their public image, thus contributing to their long-run profitability. Private financing of forests for public relations purpose also requires the right incentives. For example, the government may make such expenditures tax deductible. Promoting public recognition of these contributions in a manner that enhances the reputation of the corporations involved is another way of attracting private financing in forestry.

National and international NGOs also play an important role in raising funds to finance forest initiatives. The state should facilitate NGO initiatives by developing a clear legal framework and promoting joint ventures with for-profit firms and local community organizations. Finally, as already discussed, local populations are frequently willing to make financial contributions to protect forests that generate positive externalities that benefit them. Governments should support local communities in these efforts and, at the same time, provide the legal means to facilitate these types of actions.

Equity Issues

Several of the existing public forest policies discussed have negative connotations not only from the point of view of economic efficiency but also from that of social equity. Forest concession systems, user fees, capital gains and land taxes, and credit policies generally favor the wealthy, lead to unsustainable forest practices, and create obstacles to raising revenues to finance sustainable forest development.

The lack of transparency of the public lands concession system contributes to corruption and the allocation of land to wealthy and politically powerful groups, depriving access to land to the rural poor. In many cases, forest concessions have a negative effect on forest dwellers (mostly poor native groups), as their lands are given in concession to large commercial interests. The proposed changes to the system of forest concession, increasing transparency, and fully incorporating local populations into the decisionmaking process regarding the allocation of land and monitoring of concession conditions should reduce rents to large forest interests and permit greater benefits from forest resources to accrue to local dwellers.

The proposed greater emphasis on collecting user fees, including stumpage fees and royalties for the right to exploit public forests, should provide the financial resources to compensate local populations for any indirect losses caused by the exploitation of forest resources. One proposal was to allow a portion of the revenues raised to remain with local governments and community organizations as an incentive to promote enforcement of the collection of fees. Such a measure would protect forest resources, increase economic efficiency, and improve income distribution.

The lack of taxation of capital gains and collection of land taxes clearly benefit land speculators and large landowners. An effective system of tax collection for speculative capital gains and of land taxes, as proposed here, will raise economic efficiency, protect the environment, and improve social equity. Part of the revenues raised by these taxes can be used to finance education and other social programs for the benefit of the rural poor.

Public credit programs in many countries are heavily biased in favor of large producers. In many instances, subsidized financing is used to convert forests into pastures for livestock and to expand production of land-intensive crops (Heath and Binswanger 1996). Most of these activities do not demand much labor, causing the displacement of the local population into more marginal lands and greater poverty. The elimination of credit subsidies will also have a positive impact on economic activity, social equity, and the environment.

Some of the recommendations provided in the previous sections, however, do not necessarily improve social equity. Policies to increase protection of private land holdings against squatters may affect the ability of poor people to acquire land. These obviously favor the largest land properties (which are the ones most vulnerable to encroachment by squatters), leading to a worsening of income distribution at least in the short run. On the other hand, improving land rights for small farmers and increased protection of forest lands owned by native communities are consistent with improved social equity.

Suggestions for Policy Support and Program Financing

The Latin American countries should lead the development of an international framework to promote trade in carbon emissions at a scale that can make a real difference in reducing deforestation. This is by far the most important action that arises from this study. International organizations, as well as individual countries, should promote international institutions that facilitate the expansion of initiatives such as the joint implementation (or clean development) mechanism and the GEF. By so doing the potential gains from trade in carbon emissions may be fully realized. This can only be achieved by setting carbon emission quotas by country with the specific condition that such quotas can be freely traded both nationally and internationally.

Much research is needed to establish an operational framework for international trade in carbon emissions. It is important to value the opportunity cost of forest lands at a fairly detailed level by region; it is also urgent to determine the forest areas that would qualify for joint implementation agreements and, also, to determine the most effective means to allow for transfers of financial and technological resources to the South. Additionally, it is critical to establish the systematic monitoring of forests designated for conservation or for sustainable management as well as of reforestation efforts. It is also important to understand the impact of tropical timber export restrictions on the rates of deforestation and reforestation. These are just examples of high priority research that is needed.

The successful implementation of structural adjustment in most countries has shown that pressure from multilateral banks is important in convincing governments to enact policies that raise economic efficiency. In particular, (a) the enactment of measures that contribute to improving efficiency, (b) raising financial resources that can be used to promote forest sustainability, and (c) increasing social equity should be avidly pursued. Capital gains taxes on land and other land taxes, adequate user fees for environmental services, and the diligent collection of stumpage fees and royalties are policies that, if adequately designed, can lead to gains in the three fronts mentioned. Multilateral institutions should decidedly promote these policies and assist governments in implementing them. Earmarking of part of the revenue raised should be encouraged for local investment, strengthening of policy design, implementation, and monitoring capacities of local institutions.

Concomitantly, the involvement of local governments, communities and private sector organizations should be promoted in the collection of revenues and in monitoring and enforcement. Projects implemented by local agencies, including local governments, NGOs, and the private sector should have a high priority. Particular emphasis should be placed on local initiatives to internalize forest-related externalities. Finally, the countries should continue supporting projects that improve land demarcation as well as legalization and enforcement of land property rights. The provision of legal land rights and enforcement against illegal occupation or expropriation is important to reduce the use of deforestation as a means to protect land rights.

Conclusion

In many respects, the forest sector in Latin America is caught in the worst of two worlds. Tropical forests are being lost very rapidly in an anarchic process of forest burning. Moreover, the forest sector is highly inefficient. It produces only marginal economic benefits to the region and large gains to the world as a whole in terms of carbon sequestration and biodiversity.

Industrialized countries are reluctant to commit resources to forest protection in a decisive way and content themselves with token contributions. The scattered projects that they support, by and large, are ineffective to reduce forest losses because they lack scope and are misguided. At the same time, the Latin American countries are not able to develop a program to exploit forest resources more intensively in order to increase the sector's economic contribution. The forest policies of Latin American governments are contradictory. They are unable to openly recognize that their objective is to exploit forest resources for the economic benefit of their nations. At the same time that they enact legislation to "protect" forests they invest heavily in expanding roads and other infrastructure into forest areas and implement policies that promote a more intensive exploitation of forests. There is increasing recognition that this situation cannot continue, particularly given the successful completion of structural adjustment in most countries. The forest sector in Latin America is at a crossroads. The time has come to make an unequivocal decision regarding policy aims.

This chapter has discussed the main features of an international agreement to protect most of the remaining forests. We have shown that, considering the value of carbon sequestration alone, preserving tropical forests is an extremely profitable enterprise for the world, generating net annual benefits (after fully compensating the countries of Latin America for opportunity costs) of about 0.2 percent of world GNP or about $70 billion. If the value of preserving biodiversity is also included, the net benefits for the world are likely to be much greater.

Financing Forest Investment: The Issue of Incentives

CHAPTER 4

Olli Haltia and Kari Keipi

Introduction

Almost all Latin American countries are providing direct or indirect support for private forestry investments. The justification for this practice varies from country to country. Increasing use of direct financial incentives is the result of successful experiences like that of Chile, where forest plantations helped stimulate vigorous growth in the forest industry. This has raised the value of forest exports to the level of agricultural exports. In some other countries, incentives have been justified on social or environmental grounds. However, there is a strong counterargument that improving other policies that positively affect investment decisions and the profitability of forestry (due to higher demand for forest products and services) may render some incentives unnecessary (IDB 1995c).

The need to sustain the world's forests and to manage them for future generations is based on an appreciation of the growing demands for their goods and services. The worldwide projections of the UN Food and Agriculture Organization (FAO) indicate that between now and the year 2010, the total land under crops will increase to 850 million hectares, with most new expansion taking place in Latin America and Sub-Saharan Africa. A sizeable amount of this land is currently forested and will be cleared for agriculture (FAO 1993). Between 1990 and 2010, consumption of wood products is expected to continue growing, at annual rates ranging from 1.2 percent for fuelwood and charcoal, to 3 percent for paper and 4.3 percent for panel products. Demand for nonwood forest products essential for rural societies (such as medicinal plants), recreation, and environmental benefits will continue to grow. Forest gene pools will remain of crucial importance, especially for agriculture and medicine. These trends indicate that forests will experience increasing pressures for multiple and often conflicting uses. It will be necessary to protect and manage existing forests and create additional forest resources to meet growing demand (UN 1995).

Latin America and the Caribbean have about one quarter of the world's existing forests. Natural forests cover about 970 million hectares, of which 115 million are in Central America, Mexico, and the Caribbean, and 855 million are in South America. Approximately 52 million hectares of temperate forests are situated in Argentina, Chile, and Uruguay, and in high elevation areas of the tropical countries of the region (WRI 1994).

Estimates of the area in plantation forests in the region vary from 8 million to 11.1 million ha.[1] Thus, the total planted area corresponds to approximately only 1 percent of the natural forest areas, or the annual deforestation rate in the region: some 7.5 million ha (FAO 1995a). While most of the fuelwood, nonwood products, and environmental ben-

---

[1] The World Resources Institute estimates that the region's forest plantations cover 8.6 million ha. About one-fourth of these plantations, 2.5 million ha, are in the region's temperate zone (WRI 1994; FAO 1995a).

efits come from natural forests, an ever-growing portion of industrial timber is produced in plantations (FAO 1995b).

Rationale of Government Incentives for Forestry

Substantial change has occurred in the way the forest sector and forest investments are viewed in an economy. The following section offers a perspective on this changing framework, as a background for the discussion of forest incentives.

Economics of Forest Development

The economic rationale for forest investments (and incentives) can be traced to Keynesian ideas. While Keynesians stressed the task of expansionary fiscal policy in combating unemployment, early development economists argued for some form of public investment planning. Investments would mobilize the underemployed for the purpose of industrialization, and should be allocated in accordance with a pattern of balanced growth. Therefore, several sectors should be stimulated by investments simultaneously to retain the balance between supply and demand and to reach the highest rate of economic growth (Scitovsky 1954).

Hirschman (1958) agreed that investments were the right way to stimulate the economy, but he questioned how they should be allocated. What was needed were "pacing devices" and "pressure mechanisms." Hirschman argued for unbalanced growth, i.e., concentrating investments on only one or a few sectors. This would guarantee the utilization of economies of scale (Streeten 1959), while intermediate linkages between sectors would ensure that investments would spread throughout the economy.

The theory of unbalanced growth, as introduced by Hirschman (1958), rests on the concept of a "key sector." Concentrating investments in a key sector with high backward and forward linkages would result in the highest possible stimulus to the economy through a multiplier effect. Westoby (1962) initially suggested that the forest sector would be an especially appealing vehicle for industrialization and development. The forward linkages of forestry may be considerable if the sector integrates vertically to processing industries, such as pulp and paper and other high-value products.[2]

In 1978, at the Eighth World Forestry Congress in Jakarta, Westoby expressed frustration concerning the poor impact of foreign aid on the forest sector and economic development. His original optimism, based on linkages and other positive effects of the forest sector, had now turned to pessimism, fed by unsuccessful forest projects in the developing world during the previous two decades. He declared that "forestry projects had little or nothing to do with . . . a significant and many-sided contribution to overall economic and social development . . . [but] had everything to do with the fact that many of the rich, industrialized countries needed, and needed badly, new wood material resources; and their forest industries, their equipment manufacturers, together with miscellaneous agents and operators, scented golden opportunities for profit in those underdeveloped countries with forest resources. This was the dominant consideration which determined the location, shape and direction of forestry and forest industry development projects" (Westoby 1978).

---

[2] From the beginning Westoby's linkage approach was closely related to staple theory. This theory emphasizes the export role of resource-based products in the economic growth of countries with abundant resources but lack capital.

Instead of large export-oriented pulp and paper mill projects, Westoby was now suggesting a smaller scale agriculture-supportive forestry, which would not exclude forest industries. The main target of forest-based development would be to respond to local people's needs and to support the rural economy. Small rural industries would become an integral part of agriculture-supportive forestry, producing fuelwood, charcoal, poles, stakes, fencing, building materials, and simple furniture—that is, forest products that would satisfy most basic domestic demand (see, e.g., Arnold 1992).

Douglas (1983) challenges Westoby's claim that rich countries are better off than developing countries because forest product exports flow from the latter to former. Douglas concludes: "Better control of natural resources in wood-rich lesser developed countries (LDCs) would undoubtedly be to their economic advantage, and there are good theoretical and practical reasons for LDCs to trade in forest products with other countries to mutual advantage. Our argument is merely that this should be kept in some perspective. Wood-short LDCs, in particular, should pay most attention to their own specific needs when determining resources policy" (Douglas 1983). Thus, Douglas does not share Westoby's doubts about the mutual benefits of using forest resources, and takes the conventional development economics position relying on the results of international trade theory (cf., Riihinen 1981).

Nevertheless, since Westoby's 1978 paper, rural development issues have played a central role in strategies for forest-based development. For example, the principle of people's participation has been applied in the FAO's Tropical Forestry Action Plan. While Westoby's approach in practice often implied "top-down" planning, now it is suggested that "top-down" should be merged with a "bottom-up" approach—emphasizing the goals of rural communities while also taking national targets into account (Simula 1991).

Vincent and Binkley (1992) find economic and sector-specific policy failures a main reason for the problems experienced in forest sector management: "[I]f the right policies are followed, forest-based industrialization can provide an important source of employment and income and can promote conservation by enabling forests to outcompete alternative land uses." Correct policies can only be formulated based on well-defined principles of efficiency that should serve as guidance in organizing the forest sector. Vincent and Binkley no longer question whether the forest sector can promote development, but how the forest sector should be organized to eliminate possible inefficiencies. On the other hand, they note that macroeconomic stability is of crucial importance for forest-based development, due to the relatively long time period required for investments to reach maturity. Therefore, government's most important role is to create stable conditions where market driven forest-based development can take place.

There is general agreement that the market system should determine prices for forest products. Competitive pricing would eliminate inefficiencies in processing industries, signal "optimal size" of forest stocks and result in appropriate allocation of raw material and products to exports and domestic industries. The development of downstream industries should be guided by the principle of comparative advantage, and therefore government tasks would include promoting free trade. Forest policy planning should also take into consideration the environmental externalities that markets may not incorporate.

Reasons for Using Incentives

In light of earlier theories, it is interesting to notice changes in the investment practices and the application of incentives. The prevailing systems of incentives have their rationale in the economic philosophies reviewed above. Some Latin American incentive systems were designed in the 1960s and 1970s, while others are more recent. Due to the changed rationale and different histories of incentive systems in different countries, the motivations for afforestation subsidies vary considerably (Beattie 1995; McGaughey and Gregersen 1988; Southgate 1995b). The following are some of the reasons given to justify afforestation subsidies:

(i)   Modifying the social bias against forestry investments among farmers, who have traditionally considered forests detrimental to agricultural development;

(ii)   Increasing the rates of return on investments that may have relatively low private profitability but offer externality benefits for society as a whole;

(iii)   Reducing risk and uncertainty that arise particularly from the long return time of afforestation investments;

(iv)   Reducing cash flow problems during the often long periods required to recover planting and operational costs through harvest income;

(v)   Establishing a critical mass of plantations needed for initial building of competitive forest industries; or

(vi)   Acceleration ("jump starting") of initial development of plantations, either for industrial or social forestry purposes.

Traditional development arguments for subsidies have included import substitution or promoting exportable production. However, the validity of this rationale depends on the competitive advantage of the forest sector with respect to forest production in other countries, or relative to activities in other sectors in the same country. On the other hand, plantation subsidies can be justified socially, on the basis of employment generation and reduction of rural poverty. But this raises obvious questions about the labor intensity of plantations versus alternative investments in rural areas. Therefore, an analysis has to be carried out on the effectiveness of forest investments compared to other sectors.

Forest investments may generate important environmental externalities. Government incentives for converting land to forest uses may be considered payment for the production of public environmental benefits. They compensate the investor for revenue forgone by not engaging in a more lucrative private land use. However, guidance may be needed to make ecologically sound forest investments: for example, mixed plantations may be preferred to monocultures in some areas, while in others it may not matter.

It is possible to consider forest incentives as a self-financing investment in the sense that the income generated over time may greatly exceed the subsidy, and if that income is taxed, a government may at least partly recover its contribution. In Chile, the subsidies have reportedly been profitable to the state (Beattie 1995).

Incentives and government subsidies are highly controversial. Vaughan (1995) quotes two different views. The old conventional wisdom is reflected in the study by McGaughey and Gregersen (1983): "Debate over the various arguments about subsidies for forestry investments is not as critical as the recognition that subsidization is already widely accepted and practiced by Latin American governments. Subsidies have become a politically legitimate and accepted tool for promoting investment in forestry and forest industries."

The new conventional wisdom does not advocate subsidies as corrective measures to offset distortions existing elsewhere in the economy; rather it proposes the direct elimination of those distortions. Stewart and Gibson (1995) make a strong case, recommending: (i) removal of export bans on forest products and tariff and nontariff barriers to international trade in all products; (ii) elimination of export subsidies; and (iii) removal of all forest product consumption taxes other than the general sales tax. They argue that once these reforms are in place, direct incentives for forestry are not necessary; therefore, subsidy programs for afforestation and forest management should be eliminated. In a study of environmental fund usage, the OECD (1995) concludes that financing through subsidies cannot act as a substitute for proper policies and institutional framework.

Promotion of Forest Plantations

The roles of the public and private sector have undergone major changes in Latin America during recent years. Many countries, such as Brazil and Uruguay, have eliminated or reduced the use of forestry subsidies. This transition has been part of a general economic policy, but not specific to forestry. In planning such new policies, it is essential to identify conditions in which forest management or tree plantation investments may prosper. Constantino (1995) cites the following key factors in forest land development in Chile:

- Political and macroeconomic stability;
- Trade liberalization and open foreign investment;
- Stable property rights for land with and without trees;
- Credible government with adequate institutional capacity to enforce laws and administer possible incentive schemes; and
- Good natural growing conditions, availability of proper technologies and basic infrastructure (roads, electricity, ports) to support investment decisions.

In Brazil and Chile, the availability of adequate incentives was a minor factor contributing to forest industry growth once a critical initial mass of plantations was established (Beattie 1995). For example, Wunder (1994) claims that subsidies had only a secondary impact in promoting plantations in Chile. Factors such as low production costs and a favorable general economic environment have been more important. Today many Chilean forest companies choose not to access incentives in order to avoid major government controls related to long-term tying of the land to forestry and restrictions on the management and harvesting of the plantations. Similarly, Brazil, which has been using incentives longer than Chile, has discontinued much of its forest incentive program.

Yet in other countries, new subsidies are being proposed. For example, in Colombia, Ecuador and Paraguay, the Chilean case has been taken as a model, although the justification for the use of incentives may be different. In Colombia the rationale has been largely environmental. In Ecuador the traditional subsidy arguments prevail, as far as getting the wood products sector off the ground, generating jobs and increasing forest products exports. In Paraguay the incentives are a response to a high deforestation rate and the interest in industrial development. However, a lack of comparative advantage may limit the effectiveness of the government incentive programs in these countries (see Southgate 1995b). On the other hand, subsidies may not be necessary if the activity is already financially attractive or if policy measures other than financial incentives are more effective in promoting afforestation.

Private and Public Benefits

This section reviews the factors that critically affect forest investment decisions from the private and public decisionmakers' point of view. The owner of forest lands can expect financial returns from future sales of timber, fruits, latex and other marketable products. The projected profitability, the risks involved, the opportunity costs of land in other uses, and the availability of financing are the most important factors affecting the investment decision. In Latin America, the predominant alternative land use to forestry is cattle ranching. Lack of liquidity during the long gestation period for forest plantations is a major disadvantage compared to cattle ranching.

Opportunity Cost of Land

In considering forest investments, the question of optimal land use arises. Suppose a country faces the problem of whether to convert agricultural land to forestry use or to continue with agriculture. The welfare of the country is now assumed to be a function of market and nonmarket benefits from agricultural and forestry land uses. The country aims at maximizing welfare, taking into consideration that agricultural and forestry land uses are inversely related (i.e., increase in afforestation implies smaller areas of agricultural production). However, adjustments in world market prices could change the relative private profitability of agriculture and forestry.

Solving the welfare maximization problem yields a useful cost-benefit rule for land conversion: it makes sense to convert agricultural land to forestry use if the social opportunity cost of agricultural land is smaller than or equal to the marginal value of land in forestry production, minus the associated costs of conversion. *Forestation is justified if the discounted net benefits exceed the discounted net benefits of the next best use of land.*

Cost of Capital and Risk

Capital market imperfections and high rates of inflation in Latin America have depressed investments in forestry in the past. Inflation rates reached 1,000 percent in the 1980s in Argentina and Brazil, 100 percent in Mexico, and 25 percent in Chile and Colombia. High inflation has increased the borrow-lend interest differential (Fernández 1995), as expected inflation has been embodied in the expected value of monetary assets. Structural adjustments in the region slowed inflation to the following rates in 1995: Argentina, 3.4; Brazil, 84.4; Mexico, 35; Chile, 8.2; and Colombia, 21. Nevertheless, the real interest rates in many countries have remained relatively high (IDB 1996a).

Capital market imperfections in Latin America have been partly due to government intervention and regulation of capital markets. As a result, capital market liberalization has been an important policy in recent Latin American economic reforms. For example, in Chile, several restrictions have been removed from capital flows, including reserve requirements imposed on external borrowing, and regulations on the overseas issues of stocks and bonds made by Chilean companies. Access to the foreign exchange market was improved by allowing investors to obtain and pay back foreign debt, to make investments abroad, and to purchase hard currency for portfolio management (Eyzaguirre 1993). In Colombia, restrictions on foreign investments and profit remittance have been largely eliminated and the private sector has been allowed to borrow from abroad (Martinez 1993). Argentina and Mexico have also adopted fairly liberal policies, especially for attracting foreign capital. Brazil has not yet moved towards a comprehensive approach in deregulating its capital account, however (Fernández 1995). These developments suggest that future forest investments in Latin America are likely to be less hampered by lack of capital (cf. Scott and Litchfield 1994). Although the struggle against inflation is likely to continue, there is no doubt that financial reforms have already decreased inflation and improved the availability of capital (see Bulmer-Thomas 1991, 1992).

Forestry investments with a long gestation period are especially vulnerable to high real interest rates. The smaller the cost of capital, the greater would be the private profitability of an investment. The cost of capital of a forest investment can be reduced by lowering the cost of debt or risks. Cost of debt can be decreased by eliminating part of the debt (for example, through cofinancing without getting into debt). Other strategies may include, for example, implementing suitable tax regimes that decrease the cost of debt through tax breaks or credits. The cost of capital can also be reduced by minimizing systemic risk. Systemic risk, or nondiversifiable risk, is measured by the so-called "*beta* value" and is affected by macroeconomic factors such as the rate of national economic growth and the volatility of exchange rates. The *beta* value is also increased by such forestry factors as the probability of forest fires. The *beta* value of forest investments can be reduced by creating stable political and macroeconomic conditions to which forest investments, in particular, are sensitive due to their long-term nature. For example, establishing and securing property rights reduces systemic risk: the current existence of property rights in Chile has been mentioned as a major driving force for forest investments, while lack of property rights has been blamed for stagnation in the forest sector of Costa Rica. Finally, the availability of extension services and technical assistance can also improve information and reduce risk.

Liquidity

The long gestation period of forest investments also affects liquidity. In principle, a forest owner with a current need for cash might sell the property outright, liquidate the timber at its current commercial value, or borrow from capital markets using the forest property as collateral. Each of the alternatives is optimal only under special conditions. The first option is optimal if the value of the asset is set equal to discounted future net cash flow. The second option is only optimal if the growth rate of the value of forest stock is equal to the market rate of interest (i.e., trees have reached financial maturity). Additionally, borrowing capital (option 3) is difficult in most Latin American countries, especially if the stand of trees is of marginally marketable size. Thus, for a young forest, practically the only feasible liquidation option is to sell the land.

In terms of liquidity, forest investments only become comparable to other investment opportunities if an instrument is introduced that allows timber revenue to be cashed out before the end of the rotation period. For example, Rinehart (1992) has suggested a forest loan program based on an expectation of the future value of the forest (unlike a conventional loan which is based on an estimate of current value). Such a loan would probably be considered nonconventional and a guarantor may be required to ensure a secondary market for the loan. For the administration of such a credit line, availability of a service for forest valuations and forest management would be crucial.

Empirical Analysis of Financial Feasibility

The following section includes simple empirical case studies that compare the profitability of forest investments to agriculture (i.e., cattle ranching). Profitability is measured by net present value over various discount rates. Results are presented in Table 4.1 for Brazil, Chile and Costa Rica.

Assumptions and Data

(i)   Cattle ranching is considered in the analysis as the best alternative land use for forestry.[3]

(ii) In Brazil and Chile the investor buys treeless land and must decide whether to allocate the land for forestry use or cattle ranching.

(iii) The length of the rotation (period of one generation of planted forest) as well as the timing of intermediate harvests, protection and management activities depend on the species.

(iv) At the end of the rotation period the land has to be replanted.

(v)   In the case of Costa Rica, all commercial species of the natural forest are harvested (see Kishor and Constantino 1993). The area will be reforested and managed with native species.

(vi) Cattle are assumed to yield revenues from meat four years after birth in Brazil and Chile, and after two years in Costa Rica due to productivity and market conditions.

The site-specific features of the applied forest and cattle ranching models are as follows. The data for Brazil were collected from southern and southeastern areas of the country during 1995 (Scatolin 1995). For Chile the models describe conditions in Regions VIII and X. Eucalyptus and pine are the most common species used in plantations in these countries. In Costa Rica, the results are specific for *Cordia alliadora*, a native species; the data were derived from Kishor and Constantino (1993). Prevailing prices for wood products and meat were used. This simplified analysis does not include agroforestry systems or other agricultural or forest products.

Results. The results shown in Table 4.1 suggest that in Brazil forestry yields greater benefits than cattle raising, especially in the case of *Eucalyptus grandis*. The plantations of *Pinus taeda* compared with cattle ranching would generate positive private benefits only at interest rates below 12 percent. Forestry in Chile would yield positive returns under all discount rate scenarios. In Costa Rica, plantation forestry is profitable at discount rates below 12 percent, while cattle ranching would yield higher private benefits than managed natural forests over all discount rates examined.

Hence, a rational decisionmaker would prefer forest investments to cattle, with a discount rate of 8 percent or less, in all cases examined, apart from managed natural forest in Costa Rica. However, investor decisions may be distorted by imperfect capital markets. If the availability of credit is restricted, the relative position of forestry is likely to weaken.

Restrictions on the availability of capital may affect the forest investor more than the extensive cattle rancher due to the larger investments needed to initiate the forest operation. The limits to capital have the same effect as a higher interest rate (cf., Kuuluvainen

---

[3] Unused, deforested or degraded agricultural lands are available in Brazil and Chile, but in Costa Rica, land is a scarcer commodity. For example, it has been estimated that in the state of Paraná in southern Brazil, at least 20 percent of the land is not being used.

Table 4.1 Net Private Benefits from Forestry Investments Compared to Cattle Ranching, 1993

(*In US$/ha*)

Discount rate (percent)	Brazil[a]		Chile[a]		Costa Rica[b]	
	Eucalyptus grandis	Pinus taeda	Eucalyptus globulus	Pinus radiata	Cordia alliadora	Managed natural forestry
20	20	-272	322	173	-763	-378
15	151	-217	512	246	-454	-415
12	274	-101	705	405	61	-438
8	522	297	1,133	1,065	1,904	-465
4	928	1,380	1,932	3,364	8,942	-456
2	1,223	2,484	2,582	6,186		

Note: The formula used is $F^{PRI} = \Sigma_t \, \alpha^t (B_{F,t} - C_{F,t}) - \Sigma_t \, \alpha^t (B_{R,t} - C_{R,t})$.

F^{PRI} is the difference between private net benefits in forestry and cattle ranching;

α^t is discounting factor;

$B_{F,t}$, $B_{R,t}$ denote benefits from forestry (F) and cattle ranching (R), respectively at time t;

$C_{F,t}$, $C_{R,t}$ denote costs for forestry (F) and cattle ranching (R) at time t.

Source: (a) Authors' calculations; (b) Derived from Kishor and Constantino (1993).

1989). Table 4.1 suggests that if the virtual (credit-rationed) discount rate is 12 percent, compared to a market discount rate of 8 percent, private benefits from cattle ranching in Brazil become greater than benefits from *Pinus taeda* plantations. Correspondingly, if credit rationing implies a discount rate of over 12 percent, net benefits from planting *Cordia alliadora* in Costa Rica become negative. In the first example of pine plantations in Brazil, rationing would decrease the positive difference in net benefits of forestry over ranching by US$ 398 per hectare. In the second reforestation example using *Cordia alliadora* in Costa Rica, rationing decreases the positive difference in net benefits of forestry over ranching by a striking $1,843 per hectare.

Externalities

Without intervention, banks will look at market benefits but will not necessarily allocate funds to those projects for which the social returns are highest (Stiglitz 1993). For forest investments, the social returns differ from private returns because of externalities. These externalities can be classified as ecological value, recreation use value, and option and bequest values.

Because private enterprises do not receive all the forest's benefits, land use tends to be distorted. More than the socially optimal amount of land is often allocated to agricultural and livestock activities. Furthermore, when competition for land suitable for forest exists, there may be excessive transformation of native forests into plantations using exotic fast-growing species with higher private returns. This may not be socially optimal because native forests usually produce higher social benefits than plantations, especially in the form of biodiversity, and option and bequest values (see Kanowski et al. 1992, Sargent and Bass 1992). The distortion becomes even greater if governments allow plantation incentives to be used for areas currently with tree cover.

The ecological benefits of tree plantations include positive hydrological and soil quality impacts. In cases where a variety of species is used, biodiversity benefits may also exist. Plantations are most likely to have recreational use value as green space within or near urban areas. Carbon sequestration is another important benefit (although it accrues globally, while hydrological, soil, and recreational benefits are local or regional by nature). Countries tend to be more willing to cofinance forestry investments that generate positive externalities at the national and local levels. They are less willing to finance programs with mainly global benefits (Constantino 1995; see also Chapter 2).

On the basis of these observations, Niklitschek (1995) proposes that if subsidies are used, they should be directed primarily to the protection and management of native forests where the benefits are most significant. Incentives may be used to convert deforested lands to plantations. However, in this case regions should be selected where positive externalities are most significant. When incentives are used they can be considered as payments for environmental services (positive externalities) produced by forest landowners or plantation investors.

Analysis of the Impact of Environmental Externalities

The environmental values of forests are generally nonmarket benefits; therefore market prices do not usually exist. The analysis that follows examines the significance of carbon sequestration and hydrological benefits in social returns from forest investments.

Trees take carbon dioxide from the atmosphere and convert it into organic matter. Depending on the use of wood, the fixed carbon is eventually released in the form of CO_2 in varying degrees. For example, burning wood would result in a sudden emission of carbon, whereas wood used in construction would "lock up" carbon for a relatively long period, since natural degradation occurs slowly.

Data and Method of Analysis. Environmental externalities were incorporated into the analysis by obtaining rough estimates for environmental output volumes, both for carbon sequestration and hydrological impacts. Corresponding prices were based on the literature and a model of carbon sequestration (Pearce 1994). The environmental values accruing to society were discounted using a social discount rate of 8 percent (cf. Kishor and Constantino 1993, Niskanen et al. 1993).[4]

Based on the estimated total carbon sequestration and hydrological benefits, the net present value for each species used in the analysis was as follows:

Species	Eucalyptus grandis	Eucalyptus globulus	Pinus taeda	Pinus radiata	Cordia alliadora	Managed natural forest
US$/ha	385	451	474	510	550	750

---

[4] Lawrence (1991) has demonstrated that rates of time preference vary widely among economic agents (i.e., different decisionmakers). These variations affecting the discount rate are independent of the assumed social discount rate of 8 percent. The social discount rate is held constant in the comparisons below, while the private discount rate applied to marketed inputs and outputs is allowed to vary (see Stiglitz 1994). Note that the applied approach is formulated to answer the question, "Would incentives based on externalities affect the behavior of private land users?"

Table 4.2 Net Private and External Environmental Benefits from Forestry Investments Compared to Cattle Ranching, 1993

(*In US$/ha*)

Discount rate (percent)	Brazil[a]		Chile[a]		Costa Rica[b]	
	Eucalyptus grandis	*Pinus taeda*	*Eucalyptus globulus*	*Pinus radiata*	*Cordia alliadora*	*Managed natural forestry*
20	405	202	773	683	-213	372
15	536	257	963	756	-96	335
12	659	373	1,156	915	611	312
8	907	771	1,584	1,575	2,454	294
4	1,313	1,854	2,383	3,874	9,492	285
2	1,608	2,958	3,033	6,696		

Note: The formula is $F^{SOC} = \Sigma_t(\alpha_P^t(B_{F,t} - C_{F,t}) + \alpha_S^t B_{EF,t}) - \Sigma_t\alpha_P^t(B_{R,t} - C_{R,t})$.

F^{SOC} is the difference between the sum of private and social net benefits in forests, and private net benefits in cattle ranching;

α_P^t is a private discounting factor (cf. Lawrence 1991);

α_S^t is a social discounting factor (cf. Kishor and Constantino 1993);

$B_{F,t}$, $B_{R,t}$ denote market benefits from forestry and cattle ranching, respectively, at time t;

$B_{EF,t}$ denotes non-market benefits from forestry at time t;

$C_{F,t}$, $C_{R,t}$ denote costs for forestry (F) and cattle ranching (R), at time t.

Sources: (a) Authors' calculations; (b) Authors' calculations, partly derived from Kishor and Constantino (1993).

Results. Environmental externalities may be a significant reason for the use of incentives, as Table 4.2 shows. First, *Pinus taeda* planting in Brazil is preferable to cattle ranching not only at low discount rates, but also at rates of 12 percent or higher. Here, incentives equal to the value of the environmental externality ($474/ha) would result in correct social ranking between forestry and cattle ranching over all examined rates.

Second, it should be noted that if soil type and other factors allow a free choice of tree species, *Eucalyptus grandis* should be preferred to *Pinus taeda* in Brazil at a discount rate of 8 percent or higher, as was the case in the analysis of private profitability. The fact that eucalyptus may have negative externalities in terms of soil quality and fertility has not been taken into account due to lack of data (see Sargent and Bass 1992).

Third, taking environmental externalities into account ($750/ha) in Costa Rica would make managed natural forest the preferred option over cattle ranching and plantation forestry with *Cordia alliadora* at a discount rate of 15 percent or higher (see also Kishor and Constantino 1993).

Finally, the calculations suggest that incentives would not be justified in Chile based on environmental externalities. Positive environmental externalities increase the attractiveness of plantation forestry, which in this case was found preferable to extensive cattle ranching based on purely private benefits (Table 4.1).

Criteria and Selection of Incentives

Economic Justification

Based on the financial analysis of forestation investment to the land owner, three basic cases can be identified with regard to justification of incentives (Table 4.3). First, incentives are not justified if forestry yields higher private profitability than alternative land

Table 4.3 The Case for Incentives

Situation [a]	Action
1. Private forest investment is more profitable than the next best use of land ($F^{pri} > 0$).	No incentives. If the calculated investment opportunity is not realized, macroeconomic factors, capital market imperfections, misguided sectoral policies or institutional arrangements should be rectified.
2. Forest investment is not profitable in socioeconomic terms ($F^{soc} < 0$).	No incentives.
3. Forest investment is profitable only in socio-economic terms ($F^{pri} < 0$, $F^{soc} > 0$).	Incentives possibly justified. They should be: *Effective:* This means just enough incentive to offset the marginal net benefit of alternative land use, in order to induce forestation. *Efficient:* As the marginal productivity of forest investments differs among land holders, apply auctions to allocate subsidy funds. *Cost-effective:* There may be alternatives to forestation to internalize the externality. Use the least expensive method.

a. See definitions in Tables 4.1 and 4.2.

uses ($F^{pri} > 0$). If the investment opportunity provided by tree planting under these conditions is not realized, the reasons may lie in macroeconomic factors, capital market imperfections, or misguided sectoral policies or institutional arrangements. The negative impact of these factors may be eliminated by reforms rather than by incentives (Stewart and Gibson 1995).

Second, incentives are not justified if the net present values of forest investments, including externalities, are lower than returns obtained from alternative land uses ($F^{soc} < 0$). This may be due to the fact that externalities of forestry are positive but small (compared to private losses) or that they are negative. A combination of the first and the second case ($F^{pri} > 0$ and $F^{soc} < 0$) would call for taxation or a negative incentive for afforestation.

Finally, the case for incentives arises when the private net returns are lower, but the returns including externalities are greater than the returns from alternative land uses ($F^{pri} < 0$ and $F^{soc} > 0$). Here incentives should be designed to alter the land-use pattern in a direction considered socially more desirable. The formulation and scale of possible incentives should also be guided by *efficiency and cost-effectiveness*.

With limited funds available for incentives the government should maximize the area under plantation. A convenient solution could be an *auction* arranged such that landowners and investors submit bids for the number of hectares they wish to forest, and the compensation they solicit to do so. The ranking of the bids, according to payment per hectare, would provide a cost-minimizing subsidy allocation.

Types of Incentives

Given that under specific circumstances incentives may be justified in economic terms, how do we define various types of incentives? Gregersen (1984) defines incentive mechanisms narrowly as "public subsidies given in various forms to the private sector to encourage socially desirable actions by private entities."

Direct monetary subsidizing is not the only way to encourage forest investments, however. McGaughey and Gregersen (1988) classify market information, extension and education, and research as indirect incentives. Structural adjustments such as securing property rights and eliminating capital market imperfections also encourage forest investments; these objectives should be approached by eliminating certain distortions, rather than through monetary incentives.

The socially desirable allocation of forest investments can be a vague concept. It normally incorporates some income-generating goals for low-income groups and environmental benefits. The argument is, as discussed earlier, that society often benefits more from forest investments than does the private entity undertaking the investment (McGaughey and Gregersen 1988). In general the issue is not the existence of externalities, but their measurement and magnitude.

Hueth (1995) reports on research by David Kaimowitz in 1992, according to which direct subsidies for forestry investments in 18 watershed management projects in Central America included direct input financing, food for work, wage payments, directed credit, and special prizes for competition. However, Kaimowitz did not find any evidence detailing the effectiveness of the alternative forms of incentives.

Fiscal subsidies have been widely criticized since they may ignore the fundamental purpose of the incentive, which should be afforestation and the generation of productive and environmental benefits. Fiscal subsidies are often established with inadequate technical considerations (poor species and site selection, etc.). The recipient of a tax incentive is often more interested in short-term tax relief than future benefits from the trees once they mature. Therefore, these subsidies are often ineffective for stimulating tree planting. Moreover, tax-based incentives may not be equitable. They are often used by large industrial landowners who may not need the incentive. Small land holders may not benefit from them because they are not informed or because they do not pay income or property taxes (e.g., Levingston 1983, Ugalde and Gregersen 1987).

Subsidized credit is not a proper incentive mechanism, because it leads to decapitalization of the financial institution giving the loan. Directed credit also has its problems, as it may be difficult to administer. Although loan guarantees and government supported insurance for plantations have been proposed, they are hard to establish in practice. Finally, Hueth (1995) criticizes using food for work as a subsidy, because it can cause distortions in local markets as well as perverse incentives that discourage food production.

Due to the failure of other mechanisms, the most common direct incentive has been government cofinancing of inputs such as seedlings, and the provision of extension services. The indirect incentives of research and access to market information may also provide good ways for governments to support private forest investment efforts (see McGaughey and Gregersen 1988; Southgate 1995b).

Argentina is currently using auction procedures to lower the government's costs of forestation incentives. Nicaragua and other countries are contemplating following suit. This mechanism may work well with large and medium-sized landowners, but may be more difficult to implement with small farmers with fewer skills to prepare forestation bids. However, its incorporation would improve transparency and competition, thus creating a base for efficiency. Hueth (1995) proposes a similar procedure for its use in watershed management programs.

According to the conclusions of a workshop organized by the IDB, financial incentives should be targeted and temporary. "Targeted" means that producers should only be offered enough money to cover their marginal cost adoption. This may be implemented through an auction system. "Temporary" means that subsidies should be paid during a well-defined period to prevent any relationship of ongoing dependency between the beneficiary and the government (IDB 1995c).

Public Participation

Gray and Jenkins (1982) proposed a set of requirements for policy evaluation that may be applied to the analysis of incentive policies. *Political preconditions* require that the incentive mechanisms must have the support of high government officials; this is obtained especially when forestation produces important national benefits. *Organizational preconditions* indicate that a policy should be administered efficiently both at national and local levels, and must be incorporated in the decisionmaking cycles and budgeting processes.

Cultural and social factors need to be taken into account when considering the appropriateness of a grant financing approach (McGaughey and Gregersen 1988). As an example, in some countries food security may have more public support and higher priority than forest incentives. The policies on incentive mechanisms should be subject to *consultations* with the relevant groups. This is gradually becoming a standard principle in Latin America since democracies became prevalent in the 1980s. Among the international donor agencies, for example, the Inter-American Development Bank subjected its forest policy to consultation (IDB 1992). It also has an information disclosure policy requiring that environmental impact study results and other documents of IDB-financed investment projects be made available for public scrutiny in the target countries.

The general objective for forestry is to manage existing resources and establish new forests so that different local, national and global requirements for forest uses can be met now and in the future. Establishing favorable conditions for private investments is not an easy task: it calls for strategies on different levels and requires flexible incentive mechanisms. Therefore, it may not be advisable to incorporate incentive mechanisms in forest laws, but through decrees or administrative and budgetary measures that can be designed as temporary, adapted to changing situations and directed locally if necessary.

Latin American and Caribbean countries are providing incentives to forest investments that yield important benefits on local and national levels. They are not necessarily ready to create them for investments with primarily global benefits. Incentives for projects with global benefits should probably be a task for the international community which can provide appropriate financing through mechanisms such as the Global Environmental Facility (see also Chapter 3).

Government Incentives for Forestry Investments

The roles played by public and private sectors have experienced major changes in Latin America and the Caribbean during recent years. In addition to progress in establishing democracy, the countries have reevaluated the responsibilities of the public sector, moving it toward an increasingly normative role. Private investments are preferred, and government subsidies are not considered to be the primary tool for achieving economic development. However, if incentives are part of a country's policy, they should not be relegated to lip service, as has often been the case in Latin American legislation. Instead, they should be real and effective, directed to the indicated purpose (McGaughey and Gregersen 1988).

The most effective vehicles for obtaining significant levels of forest investment are probably the macroeconomic, political and institutional reforms whose principal goal is to create a thriving private sector without the support of subsidies. At the same time, there is increasing environmental awareness in the region. Forestry investments bring potential social benefits in rural areas with high poverty rates and environmental degradation. Forestation programs may provide important positive ecological and social externalities.

The justification for incentives has to be made through applied economic analysis based on beneficial externalities (IDB 1995c). In addition to improving the general economic environment for private investments, the indirect incentives (research support, training, extension, and possibly providing market information) may be areas where governments can make cost-effective contributions to promote private forestation programs.

If direct financial incentives are used, they should be cost-effective and targeted: that is, producers should be offered money to cover the marginal cost of adoption that compensates for the opportunity cost. This may be achieved by auctioning at least part of the incentives available. Rent-seeking behavior should be minimized, and the maximum number of hectares should be forested within available budgets (Hueth 1995). Targeting may or may not include low-income groups. The cost-effectiveness of forestation programs in reducing rural poverty should be evaluated relative to other sustainable development programs (Vaughan 1995).[5]

Some countries with comparative advantages in forestation may use incentives as a policy tool to accelerate the rate at which plantations are established. Whether governments can control the pressures to extend subsidies to sectors without such advantages is unclear. For example, Chile, with the most successful incentive scheme in Latin America, is having difficulties making a transition away from subsidies, even though the subsidies served their purpose by providing an initial stimulus for plantation investment (Beattie 1995, Constantino 1995).

Possible government participation in financing forest investments on private lands should be based on assessed market and nonmarket benefits (IDB 1995c). Cost-recovery mechanisms must be contemplated if such participation is established. These mechanisms would ideally be indirect, based on taxes and fees. Direct recovery through benefit-sharing mechanisms (such as timber harvest) may not be feasible due to the often long gestation periods of forestry investments. Changing public sector administrations and regulations may pose a risk to private investors and diminish their willingness to establish long-term investment partnerships with the government.

To summarize, the use of incentives for forestry may be justified as compensation for positive externalities or payment for environmental services that need to be identified and, if possible, quantified. Incentives will only be effective if the externalities are significant enough to warrant a change in the land use pattern driven by the private sector. Incentives only need to be as big as the difference between the private net benefit from the owner's best land use and the net benefit from forestry use.

---

[5] This chapter has not considered income distribution patterns as a justification for forestry incentives. However, skewed income distribution, poor food security, and low forest coverage are often closely related to subsistence farming. Therefore, income distribution is likely to affect forest investment level.

The scale for intervention and formulation of possible incentives must be carried out only after alternative mechanisms have been studied, such as evaluating the cost-effectiveness of reducing carbon in the atmosphere through industrial emission controls. Finally, forestry intervention may take forms other than those of direct financial incentives. As indicated earlier, low levels of forest investment, especially by small farmers, may be caused by imperfect information about forestation possibilities and technology. Preferably, this distortion should be tackled through technology transfer programs justified by their social profitability.

<table>
<tr><td>CHAPTER
5</td><td># The Future of Latin America's Natural Forests</td></tr>
</table>

The Future of Latin America's Natural Forests

<table>
<tr><td>**CHAPTER**
5</td><td></td></tr>
</table>

Marc J. Dourojeanni

Latin America has the highest level of deforestation in the world: 7.5 million hectares per year, versus 4.1 million in Africa and 3.8 million in Asia. Brazil alone is losing at least a million hectares every year, about one percent of its natural forests. In terms of country size, however, Brazil's situation is better than that of El Salvador, Haiti and Jamaica (with more than 3 percent loss a year), or Ecuador, Nicaragua, Honduras and Guatemala (with more than 2 percent loss a year) (WRI 1994).

The causes of deforestation in Latin America have remained basically the same for the past 50 years. Deep social inequities are at the root of deforestation. Poverty and lack of opportunities for social improvement launch millions of poor against the newly opened wildlands. Poor farmers remain ignorant due to a restricted educational system. Additional causes are biased and inefficient judiciary systems; primitive public institutions and lack of law enforcement; profiteering; and institutionalized corruption (see Chapter 1).

Failure of Natural Forest Management for Wood Production

In Latin America, forestry is a young profession.[1] Forest management has been mostly absent from natural forests, but successful in plantation forestry, especially in Chile, Brazil and Venezuela.[2] In fact, forest management of mixed tropical natural forests hardly exists (Dourojeanni 1987a). Many efforts have been attempted, and sooner or later most failed. In a recent review by Kirmse et al. (1993), 23 forest management projects are listed in the region. Yet these management initiatives seem to have been abandoned after one or two decades. The oldest efforts were developed by the colonial powers in Trinidad and Tobago and Suriname, and those ended soon after independence. More ambitious projects were those in the Tapajós, Von Humboldt, Iparia and Ticoporo national forests in Brazil, Peru and Venezuela—all of them with technical cooperation from the FAO, the U.S. Agency for International Development (USAID), or other sources. Today, all but one are abandoned, and some have been completely cleared or degraded. The single exception is a fragment of the Ticoporo National Forest, in Venezuela.[3]

---

[1] The older Latin American forestry schools were founded in the 1950s, but most were established in the mid-1960s or later (see Dourojeanni 1986).

[2] Forest management is defined here as sustained production of forest goods. The World Bank adopted the following definition for sustainable forest management: "the controlled utilization of the resource to produce wood and nonwood benefits into perpetuity, with the basic objectives of long-term maintenance of forest cover and appropriate reservation of areas for biodiversity protection and other ecological purposes" (see Johnson and Cabarle 1993).

[3] The Ticoporo National Forest was established in 1956 with 270,000 ha. By 1972, its area was reduced to 170,000 ha. Out of four units established in 1970 with private sector participation, only one of 40,775 ha (CONTACA) is still forested and under operation. The CONTACA sector is the most enduring example of successful forest management in Latin America (Plonczak 1993).

Other efforts were entirely private, such as Luconyope, in the Peruvian province of Tingo María, Cartón de Colombia, in the Chocó region, and Jari Florestal, in the Brazilian state of Pará. The first two are currently abandoned and the third is making questionable progress in natural forest management. Other efforts have been developed in indigenous or communal land, such as the Yanesha project in Peru, and the Quintana Roo and Sierra Madre projects in Mexico. They also had heavy support from USAID, the German Development Agency (GTZ), the World Bank, and NGOs. The Quintana Roo project initiated in 1982–83 is ongoing and can be considered a partial success (Janka and Lobato 1995). There are also a few joint ventures with governments and the private sector, such as the Chimanes project recently established in the Beni department of Bolivia.

Interestingly enough, none of the aborted projects failed due to technical problems or lack of scientific information (although none of these forests had been managed long enough to test the technical viability and sustainability of the management plan). There were other causes: (i) lack of economic profitability; (ii) social and political pressures by the landless to use the land for agriculture or by loggers to exploit the forest without control; (iii) poor administrative management, especially in state-run forests; and (iv) shortage of funding and political support.

Ongoing forest management projects are too new to tell their future. There is little indication that they will fare better than previous efforts, except where they are research-centered and have a secure funding source, such as the Risquetou/Organabo project in French Guiana, funded by the Bureau National des Forêts. Management of forests owned by local or indigenous communities may be more successful because they are less susceptible to invasion by shifting cultivators.

Has forest management for nonwood products been any more successful than management for wood production? The fashionable concept of harvesting nontimber forest products (NTFPs) has led to the establishment of extractive reserves, especially in Brazil where there are more than 2.4 million ha of state and federal extractive reserves. Many people expected that forest dwellers who had some external technical support would develop a model for sustainable forest management. For several reasons, this has not been the case. One report on two NTFP extraction systems in Petén, Guatemala, and in West Kalimantan, Indonesia, concluded that extractive reserves are far from panaceas (Salafsky et al. 1992). Southgate reached a similar conclusion for reserves near Iquitos, Peru and other countries (Southgate 1997). Organizational difficulties were a major destabilizing factor in Brazil.

One can argue that there is not a single extractive reserve being sustainably managed, although generally these areas are better protected than forests without use restrictions. Nonetheless, low profitability is still the main reason for the limited success of extractive reserves. For the most part, harvesting of latex, Brazil nuts and hundreds of fruits, resins, gums, oils and other forest products have always provided a standard of living below the poverty line. Thus, the forest dwellers are usually obliged to move to "garimpo" mining, agriculture or logging. Currently, development of sustainable forestry inside extractive reserves is being considered as a way to make them more profitable.

Relative Success of Forest Management for Conservation

While initiatives in forest management for wood production tend to fail, the management of protected areas established in the natural forests of Latin America have been more successful and have provided the region with an impressive system of protected forest ecosystems.[4] While many national forests are no longer forested, a large number of national parks, biological reserves and other categories of strictly protected areas are still intact. Private forests for timber production are abandoned, while private reserves for ecotourism or pure conservation are flourishing—in May 1996, 86 private reserves covering 709,000 ha were recognized by the IBAMA in Brazil, and more are proposed.

In the Amazon basin, 74 strictly protected areas (International Union for the Conservation of Nature [IUCN] categories I to IV) covering 32.2 million ha, or 4.5 percent of the basin, were established before 1990 (Rojas and Castano 1991). At least half of these areas have been protected for longer than 20 years; over 20 percent have been under protection for more than 30 years; and 30 percent have an approved management plan or have had some basic field research, mapping, biota inventories and social studies. Ten of these protected areas are larger than 1 million ha, and three are larger than 2 million ha (Pacaya-Samiria in Peru and Pico da Neblina and Jaú in Brazil). Despite the threats to forested protected areas, not a single protected forest area in Latin America has been entirely deforested. This relative success is even more remarkable in that during the last 50 years the protected areas of Latin America have been under the control of government forest services. These agencies have normally given priority to investment, staffing and annual operating budget for wood production and silviculture.

This success story is partly due to the fact that protected areas are not required to be profitable in conventional economic terms. Management for conservation purposes concentrates on ecosystem and biodiversity conservation, research, and public recreation and environmental education. A new activity receiving more attention in protected areas is the promotion of ecotourism. Although economics is not the principal measure of results in conservation management, several national parks located in forest areas have been economic successes, such as Iguazú in Argentina and Brazil. Staff motivation and commitment, the reduced influence of corruption, international and local support, and clearer objectives are also important in explaining the difference from management for production.

Signs of Progress

The state of the world's forests has become the subject of international debate. Public outcry over deforestation—indirectly promoted by the World Bank's development projects in Rondonia, Brazil, and Kalimantan, Indonesia—was undoubtedly the determining factor in the establishment of strong environmental departments in the World Bank and other multilateral financial institutions.[5] Since 1988, when President Barber Conable of the World Bank decided to establish environmental conditionalities for all projects, the environmental sector of international development banks became the fastest-growing unit in terms of staffing, budget and lending volume.[6] However, the benefit for tropical forests has been questionable, as there has been an avoidance of investment in tropical areas,

---

[4] According to the World Conservation Monitoring Center, there are 706 protected areas (IUCN categories I to V), covering 230.2 million ha in South America alone. Of these, 391 are totally protected areas (IUCN categories I to III) and cover 67.5 million ha.

[5] Both projects, while not intending to cause deforestation or intrude in indigenous land, were instrumental in creating an unprecedented rate of deforestation through migration, logging, mining and urban development in nearly pristine areas.

[6] The World Bank's staffing for environment and environment-related matters grew several times between 1988 and 1994. In the Inter-American Development Bank, the number of staff working in environment also has increased significantly since 1990. The IDB's environmental lending grew from $485 million in 1990 to $1,186 million in 1994. After a contraction in 1995 and 1996, it reached $862 million in 1997.

rather than a concerted effort to improve tropical natural forest management. For example, during the first half of the 1990s, under pressure from donor countries and NGOs,
the revised forest policy of the World Bank specifically prohibited investments in the utilization of primary natural forests.

Rhetorical Progress

The caution of the banks was caused in part by NGO pressure regarding tropical forests
and nourished by the confusion over what was meant by "sustainable forest management." Many nonforesters and a few foresters argued that forest management in tropical
natural forests is simply not feasible (Goodland et al. 1990). Others began to elaborate a
set of "sustainability" indicators, initially so complex that, had they been applied under
existing social and economic conditions, forest management would have been economically unfeasible.[7] The criteria and indicators more appropriate for tropical humid forests
are those in the Tarapoto proposal for the Amazon Basin Treaty (Carazo 1997).

   Confusion also arose from the jargon that came out of events like the 1972 and
1992 UN conferences on development and environment. Terms like "national parks" and
"reserves" became "conservation units" and then "protected areas," concepts that may
mean anything from strictly protected areas to agricultural, and even urban, landscapes.
The already diffuse concept of sustainable development became "human sustainable development." With regard to forests, a series of euphemistic names were invented, such as
"social forestry," "parks for people" and "community forestry." These terms redefine with
insignificant variation what was already known, and in some cases give new auspices for
legitimizing unsustainable forestry practices.

   A good example is the message that forests and parks would be better managed by
local and indigenous people than by forest professionals (Poole 1989).[8] The need for local
participation as an element of successful management is undisputed. However, so is the
need for professional staff. UNESCO's "biosphere reserves" sent the message that a protected area may be partially exploited, or even deforested. The questionable "success" of
biosphere reserves in tropical countries arises in part from a curious logic that presumes
compatibility rather than conflict between competitive multiple uses.

   The world's legitimate concern for natural forests has resulted in a number of
bureaucratic expansions, or "epidemics," that, while they focus on important issues, have
caused serious internal resistance to the process of establishing intelligent and functional
policies. A kind of "institutionalitis" can be seen in the establishment of new international
forestry institutions such as the International Centre for Research in Agroforestry (ICRAF),
the International Tropical Timber Organization (ITTO), the Centre for International Forest
Research (CIFOR), and of forest units in many agencies of the United Nations and the
Consultative Group for International Agricultural Research (CGIAR) systems—most of
them clearly competing with FAO's forestry department and other older institutions. Similar
to this is the phenomenon of "commissionitis"—a swelling in the number of collaborative
efforts such as the World Commission on Forest and Sustainable Development, the U.N.
Commission on Sustainable Development (CSD), the CSD Intergovernmental Panel on

---

[7] There are currently at least eight organizations setting criteria and indicators for sustainable forest management. The ITTO, as an example, has drawn up five criteria and 27 indicators at the national level, and six criteria
   and 23 indicators at the forest management unit level (IUCN–WWF 1995). Many of the criteria and indicators are
   extremely difficult to fulfill.

[8] Few published reports question the role of indigenous people as forest protectors. An exception documented by
   Brandt (1992) describes how the Pataxó Indians destroyed the forest of the Monte Pascoal National Park of
   Bahía, Brazil, by selling logs and promoting invasion.

Forests and the Intergovernmental Forum on Forests, the Forest Advisors Group (FAG), the FAO Ministerial Meetings on Forestry, and many more promoted by international NGOs. "Conventionitis" has spawned the Tropical Timber Agreement, the Agenda 21 Chapter on Forests, the Forest Principles, the Convention on International Trade of Endangered Species (CITES), the Biodiversity Convention, the Desertification Convention, and, soon, there may be a forest convention. Finally, "programmitis" has resulted in the creation of the Tropical Forest Action Program, the G7 Pilot Program for the Conservation of Brazilian Tropical Forests, the Conservation and Sustainable Management of Trees project, and others (Sizer 1994).

In conclusion, there is more interest today in forest conservation than ever before. Yet there is also increased confusion in terminology, duplication of effort and competition among agencies. One would expect some positive results from so many efforts. However, there is often little connection between international efforts and the reality in the tropical countries, especially in the forested regions where social and economic inequities are at the root of deforestation. The unsuccessful experiences in the application of the Tropical Forest Action Plan (Winterbottom 1990) and the Biodiversity Convention in Latin America (Dourojeanni 1994), among others, should guide the preparation of new programs or agreements about forests.

Progress in Practice

In terms of tropical forest management, however, there has been concrete progress during the past decade. While international discussion and rhetoric has raised worldwide awareness, on-the-ground progress has also occurred, as research in the fields of environment, forest ecology, environmental economics and social sciences has resulted in new possibilities and new tools to better conserve and manage natural forests. Possibly the most important recent progress in tropical conservation has been made in the field of economic valuation of natural resources and forests (Pearce 1993). Advances in this area have provided new and compelling arguments for making management economically profitable and deforestation less attractive. Scientific research has identified and quantified the importance of environmental services, such as carbon fixation in forest biomass, watershed protection and the potential relevance of biodiversity for human welfare. Pure and applied sciences have also provided new information on tropical soils, water resources, forest sustainability indicators and the ecological importance and management of secondary forests. At the same time, the development of remote sensing techniques is providing better information on the situation of natural resources worldwide, making it more difficult for governments to ignore the facts about forests.

Future Problems for Remaining Forests

It is fascinating to observe that in direct opposition to the worldwide discussion on rescuing forests, mostly promoted by industrialized countries, these same countries are also indirectly facilitating further destruction of natural forests. This contradiction is occurring because of the promotion of the free market economy that encompasses privatization of natural resources, forest exploitation by multinational enterprises and, simultaneously, a reduction in the size of the state (including forest services), which is rarely accompanied by more efficient forestry regulation.

Latin American economic recovery is closely linked to the development of wildlands. In 1995, after several years of a burning slowdown, the Brazilian Amazon experienced burning comparable to the worst historical records. As millions of hectares of fallow forests, grass-lands and old growth forests burned, airports were closed in many Amazonian and Mato Grosso cities, because smoke made flights too dangerous. Remote sensing satellites de-tected forest fires in the Brazilian Amazon, estimating 39,900 fires that caused a dense fog over seven million square kilometers—almost the size of the Amazon Basin itself. In Janu-ary 1998 the government officially announced that deforestation reached 2.9 million ha during 1995, compared to 1.5 million in 1994 (Brasilense and Bento Filho 1998).[9]

The Last Roads in the Forest Frontier

Roads in the forests are neither good nor evil in themselves, but they do facilitate defores-tation. Roads allow legal deforestation in official settlements and farms, unlawful defores-tation for shifting cultivation by the landless and migrating farmers, and increased access to commercial logging, hunting, and fishing. During the so-called lost decade of develop-ment of Latin America in the 1980s, few roads were built or even maintained, as the region faced deep economic crises. In relative terms, this caused a moratorium on forest development.

Today, however, economic recovery is allowing an unprecedented wave of road construction in forest areas. This includes the building and upgrading of international highways, such as the Trans-Amazonica, the Trans-Pantanera and now the Trans-Oce-anic highway, which would link the Brazilian Atlantic Coast with the Peruvian Pacific Coast, crossing the last patches of virgin Amazon in at least two parts. Other roads such as the Marginal de la Selva, in Peru, and the Perimetral Norte of Brazil are also being completed or rehabilitated. The connections between Brazil and Venezuela, Suriname, Guyana and French Guiana are also being improved. In the north of South America, the construction of the Pan-American Highway between Colombia and Panama crossing the Darién forest is also being promoted, while several roads are being built in the Colombian Chocó. In Central America, there are roads planned to link Guatemala's most populated zones to the Petén and to Belize (Dourojeanni 1995). Even the southern forests of Chile are under threat by the Austral Highway and by new roads and related forest development in Tierra del Fuego.

In the past, most roads were built with multilateral financing. Now they are in-creasingly financed by private investors, meaning that building controls are almost nil. Sound development along the roads, environmental impact assessments, indigenous people's rights and deforestation are not the central concerns of the private sector in these investments.

Remaining Natural Forest Area and Deforestation

Many believe that forest destruction in Latin America will stop when a certain minimal area of forest remains intact. That has been the experience in Europe, where forested areas today are actually larger than two centuries ago. This has also been the case in parts of the United States, such as the Appalachian range. But this experience does not seem to apply to Latin America. The rich Atlantic Forest of Brazil has been reduced to less than *three* percent of its original extension, and most of the remaining forest is degraded.

---

[9] Based on earlier estimates of deforestation rates, in July 1996 the Brazilian government had announced a package of forest protection measures, including a two-year moratorium on new permits for the exploitation of mahogany and virola trees.

Massive deforestation allowed the states of southern Brazil initially to become wealthy through logging and agriculture. However, deforestation of the Atlantic Forest continues at a rapid pace, by the poor migrating from other states, by rich farmers expanding their grassland area, as well as by urban developers.

Upper Amazon watersheds show similar trends. The forested area today is restricted to small patches of strictly protected forests that are very difficult to access. But the poor, ignorant, and hungry people still arriving in these valleys that opened to agriculture half a century ago are not deterred by difficult access. They cannot have environmental concerns; their struggle is for food and survival. Many wealthy people, on the other hand, may take good care of their own trees and forests, but see the state-owned forested areas as a means to easy short-term gains through land use changes.

Risks of Privatization

Reducing the role of the state in the management of the economy is a reasonable and desirable goal. Nevertheless, the initial application of privatization may lead to new risks and exploitative excesses such as some being promoted in Latin America (Halle and Steiner 1994; see also Chapter 2). Peru's proposed legislation on water and forests provides a good example: a proposed new water law would establish a free market for water rights, independent from land rights. Thus, farmers may have to compete with other users of the water, such as industry and urban consumers, who can pay much more for water in a country where most productive agriculture is done in the desert coastal zone and in the dry Andean zone. It is expected therefore, that the rising prices of water will displace farmers from the poorest coastal and Andean lands. Simultaneously, a new forestry law may allow the privatization of public forests located in the Amazon Basin. The effect of both laws, combined with new investments in roads, will probably create a new migratory flux of peasants from the coast and the Andes to the Amazon, where loggers will sell or abandon land for cultivation after harvesting the wood.

The Peruvian case is not an isolated one. It is an example of the common governmental rhetoric that speaks of alleviating poverty, improving the environment and even conservation of forests—but then promotes the opening of new lands and the transfer of public commons to a private sector that in Latin America has shown little social or environmental concern.

Reducing the Role of the State

Industrialized countries, among others, are promoting the shrinking of government to reduce costs and increase efficiency. This is a reasonable objective for Latin America, where countries have employed millions of people in government jobs at miserable salaries, who lacked motivation and had scant training, equipment, or work material. In another example from Peru, the Ministry of Agriculture reduced the staff of the combined water, soils, forests, natural resources evaluation, wildlife and parks services from more than 5,000 officers and clerks before 1990 to roughly 600 nationwide. Practically all national forests and most protected areas are abandoned, except where NGOs are helping to keep a presence of rangers. The salaries and working conditions of these officers remain inferior. Under these conditions, it is not reasonable to expect adequate government control and regulation over the privatization of water rights and forests. Privatization can be effective only if the state is efficient in the enforcement of laws and regulations, and in solving conflicts among resource users (Naím 1994).

A Country Case: Suriname

As natural forests in Asia and Africa are depleted, investors become more and more interested in the remaining large patches of natural forest in Latin America. Chile's southern forests were early targets, for the production of wood chips mostly exported to Japan. Various international forestry enterprises are exploiting or planning to exploit the natural forests of the Tierra del Fuego (Villaroel 1994). The government of Suriname has been contacted by forest investment companies that would exploit concessions on 3.5 million ha, or some 30 percent of the country's surface. The areas requested add up to 80 percent of the primary tropical forest remaining in the country and have an important population of maroons and Amerindians. Of course it is expected that, considering the minuscule size of the Surinamese forest service[10] and the poor record of these enterprises, no forest management will be applied. Moreover, the bidders have very little experience in forest management in Latin America. In addition they may be able to practice extensive tax evasion (Sizer and Rice 1995). However, the biggest threat to the forests of Suriname will be the indirect effects of logging roads that can cause deforestation. In the case of Suriname, the construction of highways to facilitate logging rights with Brazil is the issue. These roads may allow settlements by Brazilians in Suriname, both rich and poor, in the same way roads did in Paraguay and Bolivia, with devastating effects on the forests.

Reversing Current Trends

Reversing current trends of forest loss in Latin America without drastic changes in social and economic behavior will be very difficult. The strategy must come from the economic side of the problem, and should consist of four lines of action: (i) developing a market and setting prices for environmental services provided by forests; (ii) increasing the commercial value of natural forests via methods such as certification and green labeling; (iii) forestation; and (iv) expanding forest resource conservation measures such as more and better protected areas, combined with sustainable economic opportunities and private sector investment where possible. To make these measures succeed, adequate policy and institutional support will be required at the international and national levels.

Recognition of Environmental Services Provided by Forests

Natural forest management for wood and nonwood products may not be profitable for the private sector under current social and economic conditions in many regions of Latin America. Additional costs of forest management, due to techniques that provide sustainability, may make it even less profitable in the short run. Therefore, to make sustainable forest management possible it is essential that the environmental services or externalities generated by the forests be accounted for and paid by those who benefit from them. Only then would a forest be carefully managed for the production of goods in order to keep a high level of service generation. These services could be sold to the public in the form of tariffs, as is already the case for water, sewage, energy or recreation.

Many services provided by forests are well known. Today, given the global warming issue (Stone 1992), the newest economic service that a forest and other ecosystems

---

[10] In 1995, the annual budget of the Suriname forest service was $30,000 and included only four professional foresters.

can provide is storage for carbon that would otherwise be in the atmosphere.[11] The value of this service may be calculated on the basis of *carbon sequestration* by unit of forest and by the cost of reducing carbon emissions (Dower and Zimmerman 1992). Several analyses based on available data on carbon sequestration demonstrate that the market value of forested land for agriculture or logging could be less than the value for carbon sequestration (Schneider 1993b). It would be even more profitable if this service were considered in addition to the production of timber and nontraditional forest products.

Therefore, the idea of a *worldwide carbon tax* on users of fossil energy would serve to compensate those who manage or conserve forested areas (Goldemberg 1990), and may prove to be the solution to making natural forest management profitable in the tropics. For example, Goldemberg (1990) estimated that a tax of only US$1 per barrel of oil or $6 per ton of coal-equivalent, would generate $50 billion per year. The collection and distribution of such a tax would be the principal justification of any new "world forest organization." A national carbon tax—such as already exists in Sweden, Norway and the Netherlands—would require a worldwide agreement to standardize implementation. With existing remote sensing technology it would be relatively easy to know exactly how many hectares of forests are cleared or maintained in each patch of land. Even forest degradation could be recorded, and yearly statements could be issued, indicating a country's account balance of forested land. Using these accounts, annual entitlements or payments due could be determined.

Carbon sink or carbon sequestration plantations have been tested in Guatemala and Costa Rica as part of a joint implementation mechanism developed in the 1992 Framework Convention on Climate Change. The idea is that polluters in developed countries may find it cheaper to compensate their carbon dioxide emissions by planting trees or preserving trees somewhere else, especially in tropical countries. In Costa Rica, the CARFIX project already recruited 12,000 hectares belonging to local farmers, where new plantations, forest management and forest protection are being conducted by a local NGO in partnership with the Wachovia Timberland Investment Management, U.S.A. (Reforma 1995). Plantations may not always be necessary, however, as natural regeneration, forest management and forest protection could achieve the same goal.

Carbon sequestration is not the only service provided by forests, of course. Equally important are *conservation of the regional water cycle* (Salati 1989) and *watershed protection* for water quality and quantity, especially for energy, industry and urban consumption. Water provision and water quality in a watershed are services that should be estimable for valuation purposes. In a few areas of Latin America the water and energy tariffs include a percentage reinvested in management of the watershed. Such is the case of coffee growers of Colombia who pay a fee to fund the conservation of local watersheds. Typically water is taken as a free commodity by the water processing and distributing enterprises that charge the final consumer for use, with no money going for watershed management. Notwithstanding, current legal trends show requiring utility companies to reinvest part of their profits in watershed management would be relatively easy to achieve. Any collected monies could then be made available, directly or indirectly, to those who manage their forests or lands following an approved management plan.

Although the *conservation of biodiversity* in natural forests is similar to the case of carbon sequestration, it is substantially more difficult to make people to pay for this

---

[11] Ecosystems other than forests also store carbon: a study of South American savanna grasses indicates that deep-rooted grasses remove up to 2 billion tons of carbon dioxide annually from the atmosphere (CIAT 1994).

service. The Convention on Biological Diversity established complex rules applying to the access to genetic resources, including all the difficulties inherent to patents and intellectual property rights. The U.N. Conference on Environment and Development (UNCED), recommended new and additional financial resources to meet the full incremental costs of implementing the Convention on Biological Diversity. Currently, the Global Environmental Facility (GEF) is serving as the interim financial mechanism. But the GEF has relatively few resources compared to the size of the task; a study for the UNDP (RAFI 1994) estimated "bio-piracy" (bioprospecting without compensation) from developing countries to be worth $5.4 billion a year, while the GEF provides only a few hundred million dollars a year to developing countries for biodiversity conservation. Furthermore, it is coupled with a highly complex procedure for financing and has failed to set adequate priorities for biodiversity conservation (Mittermeier and Bowles 1993). A possible improvement would be a two-part system where first, an average value is arbitrarily assigned to genetic resources of current, mid- and long-term value from each major natural ecosystem. Second, users of products originating from biodiversity prospecting worldwide would pay a fee to be redistributed through mechanisms used for carbon sequestration.

Forests provide many more environmental benefits: some are tangible, such as security against landslides and avalanches. Others are more difficult to measure, such as the value of natural scenery, wildlife refuges, resources for scientific research and existence value (e.g., the value of knowing a tropical forest exists, even though a person may never visit one). The challenge for the future is to estimate and incorporate the value of these services into benefit-cost analyses used to determine optimal forest use.

Ecosystem rehabilitation on degraded lands may provide positive benefits in terms of environmental services and biodiversity conservation. More importantly, perhaps, is that rehabilitation can return degraded land back to a state that is useful for such economic activities as agroforestry and fuelwood production. This option may be highly cost-efficient, as it usually requires modest investments compared to full reforestation with industrial timber species. A good example is being successfully developed in the Guanacaste region of Costa Rica (Janzen 1988). Secondary forests may also be managed to provide products without compromising environmental benefits. This is being demonstrated in Pucallpa and Iquitos, Peru, by joint works of the University of Toronto and the National Agrarian University of La Molina, Peru (Dourojeanni 1987b; Blain 1996).

Increasing the Commercial Value of Natural Forests

In this era of environmental awareness and growing appreciation of natural products, tropical and other hardwoods should have a high value. Mahogany, cedar, and virola in Latin America, or ebony in Africa, are already recognized as such, mainly because they are becoming scarce. But how can prices be increased without distortion? Scarcity of precious wood and market forces are determining factors. For the purposes of paying for sustainable forest management, more is required than allowing species to become rare. Vertical integration of production and processing is a good, albeit classical option. Another possibility is to adopt, through international trade regulatory mechanisms, a *formal policy of pricing selected hardwood species* that may also be associated with the concept of *"green certification."*

Together with this strategy, four conditions would be required, as well as the necessary agreement among countries: (i) increase the number of hardwood species available on the international market, both to improve forest management profitability and to reduce the pressure on the currently traded species; (ii) ensure that an important part of the benefits of the higher prices remains in the hands of the producers who manage the forests; (iii) apply the same criteria to the national and international markets, as most tropical timber currently produced in Latin America is for local or regional consumption; and (iv) make green labeling such a common practice that cutting in forests which are neither managed nor certified will be virtually eliminated.

For the purpose of valuing high quality or rare natural forest products, the concept of "green certification" or "ecolabeling" may be useful (see Chapter 10). The original aim of green certification was not to make certified products more expensive, but to ensure to the buyer that they are produced by environmentally benign processes. The probability that green certification for natural forest products will be accepted by exporting countries is increasing thanks to the barriers and boycotts imposed by European countries,[12] and to the fact that some consumers in industrialized countries are willing to pay more for certified products. For example, Garlipp (1995) reported that 68 percent of U.S. consumers were ready to pay from 1 to 15 percent more for certified timber, and that 33 percent of U.K. consumers were ready to pay up to 13 percent more. The same study revealed that the European consumers were also ready to reduce their imports of tropical timber if not produced in accordance with principles of responsible forest management.

Investments in Forestation

Agroforestry and plantations might possibly reduce the pressure on natural forests by providing cheap timber, fuelwood and other raw materials, thereby allowing other uses for natural forests. Plantations should not be established by deforesting natural forests, however.[13] Forestation is viable where there is a demand for forest products and degraded lands are available for plantations. Alternatively, legislation can require a certain percentage of afforestation to accompany any land clearing. An interesting opportunity is provided in Brazil by a law requiring farmers to keep a percentage of their land as natural forests, especially on river banks, hillsides and other areas not suited for agriculture. This legislation, despite being widely ignored, is applied by some large forest plantation estates to conserve remnants of the original forests. These include, among others, Aracruz Celulose, Amapa Florestal e Celulose, Klabim Paper & Celulose, and Champion of Brazil, and PROFORCA in Venezuela, which are following this practice to conserve a substantial amount of biodiversity. Some enterprises like Veracruz Florestal, in Bahía, Brazil, have also acquired native forest relics for strict conservation.

Agroforestry offers economic opportunities on moderately degraded lands, thus, can preserve a certain amount of forest cover to protect natural biodiversity, among other environmental services. Agricultural and forestry products from these lands provide economic goods that are tradeable in existing local and regional economic markets. Furthermore, the variety of new plants in mixed agroforestry systems may contribute significantly to biodiversity and provide an excellent carbon reservoir as well.

Conservation Through Protected Areas

In the late 1980s, the term "paper parks" was coined to describe protected areas that exist only as a government document, and not as a functioning entity. The term originated

---

[12] Barriers and boycotts are a double-edged sword: while they may facilitate the adoption of ecolabeling, they may also discourage the market from trade in these products, further reducing incentives for sound forest management.

[13] In Chile and Brazil, incentives for plantation forests allowed a substantial clearing of natural forests. One of the better-known cases has been the Jari Florestal, in the state of Pará, Brazil.

from Machlis and Tichnell (1985) who, based on a biased survey and a cursory analysis, concluded that most parks and protected areas would not survive all the threats posed to them. This paved the way for a movement against protected areas, forwarded by a curious alliance of some environmentalists and development experts. As a result, some social scientists were encouraged to propose the transfer of ownership or management of protected areas to local communities. In Peru, for example, the revised national environmental code allows titling of indigenous communities within all categories of protected areas, provided they can prove an area is part of their traditional territory. In Brazil, a proposed protected areas law would allocate 5 percent of existing national parks for the relocation of "traditional populations," even if they have no previous relation to the area, and even if doing so would transform those parks into partial-use reserves. This movement has also discouraged governments from establishing new, strictly protected areas, and international donors from investing in them.

Ahead lies the difficult struggle of revamping national protected area systems by differentiating real protected areas from all cases where protection is only a written objective. Paper parks usually occur because the local population, mostly poor settlers, live inside the park or use the park as an open-access resource. Strictly protected areas with a high area-to-perimeter ratio and minimum nontourist traffic and incursion should be the backbone of conservation.[14] Areas with other varying degrees of protection are useful mainly as complements. Thus, more and better designed protected areas are necessary to conserve the entire set of forest ecosystems and the biodiversity they contain. Particularly, management should become more efficient and of higher quality (Pardo et al. 1994). The strictly protected areas should be considered as security for the conservation of biodiversity, which would be essential in case the efforts to associate development and biodiversity promotion should fail.

Ecotourism is a growing industry that has proved economically viable in numerous cases, and goes hand-in-hand with the concept of protected areas. Nature tourism generated around 7 percent of all international travel expenditures in 1992.[15] Although not exclusively the case, ecotourism is in large part dependent on protected areas, and conversely provides economic incentives that may make protected areas dependent on it. With few exceptions, controlled ecotourism is compatible with even the strictest protection levels. In principle ecotourism could pay for the conservation of forests: either directly, by investing in public or private protected areas, or indirectly, if the national revenues systems are able to tax this hard-to-control industry. This is partly because a major share of ecotourism operations in Latin America is currently in the hands of international businesses.

"Natural condominiums" (Dourojeanni 1996) offer opportunities for the private sector to set aside land for conservation, effectively creating private protected areas. Private natural reserves may become an important complement to national protected area systems in conserving forest ecosystems or establishing biological corridors between them. There are many private reserves in Latin America, especially in Costa Rica, Brazil and Venezuela. Some are purely for conservation, while others are entirely for private initia-

---

[14] Van Schaik et al. (1992) concluded that "...ecologically and economically sustainable development alone will not stop the loss of tropical rain forests caused by fragmentation, exploitation and human activities. ...[W]hile the costs of biodiversity preservation accrue mainly at the local level, the benefits accrue mainly at the regional, national, and especially global level. Therefore, special mechanisms must be devised to fund biodiversity preservation."

[15] The Ecotourism Society and others estimated that ecotourism generated roughly $12 billion worldwide in 1991.

tive. Their creation can either be by agreement with governments or as exclusive private initiatives. Some countries have even provided legal and economic incentives for the establishment and management of private preserves.

The idea of the "natural condominiums" aims to motivate private investment and participation in forest protection. The concept of a condominium normally involves establishing a fund to allow financing for management of protected areas. The owners, as with any condominium, may sell or trade their property, provided that the new owners respect the management plan.

Opportunities for Policy Support

At the *international level*, policy support could come from a worldwide forest convention and the creation of a world forest organization to enforce it. This would make sense only if the principal goals of the convention were to define and manage compensation mechanisms for the environmental services provided by forests and other ecosystems. Existing mechanisms, such as the GEF, have always had a limited impact on conserving the forest heritage of Latin America and the Caribbean. This new organization would not be justified, however, if it ended up competing for funding with the many existing international entities.

At the *national level*, there is an imperative need for better enforcement of conservation policies and forest management. Legislation concerning the matter has generally been satisfactory in most countries, but its implementation is inadequate due to low priority and lack of political will. International policy conventions habitually suffer from weak enforcement mechanisms. During the past decade, most changes in Latin America's national forest policies that affected the situation of natural resources showed a negative trend for forest conservation, due to factors outside the sector. New legislation is eliminating protective barriers for forest use and even facilitating user access to protected areas. For example, a recent revision of the Peruvian Environmental Code allows mining and oil exploration and exploitation in national parks and other protected areas. Other policies include the privatization of public forests, with high probabilities that these forests will be transformed into grassland or agriculture; the dismantling of already weak state forest services; and reduced government investments in university education and research. Additionally, some governments are still looking at the last natural areas to "solve" the problem of poverty, without considering the productive use or the ecology of these areas. For example, the Brazilian Ministry of Agrarian Reform is searching all over the country for "unproductive lands" (which include forests and other natural ecosystems), to hand them over to people without employment (Padua 1996).

Conclusions and Recommendations

Over the past fifty years in Latin America, there is solid evidence that management of natural forests for conservation has been more successful than management for wood production. Protected areas have been able to maintain their forest cover better than other categories of forests in the region. It is also widely acknowledged that protected areas make up the backbone of biodiversity conservation. Therefore, it is worthwhile to strengthen efforts to establish and manage protected areas in tropical forests. This effort is not to be carried out only, or even primarily by governments, but should be increasingly taken over by NGOs and the private sector. Private reserves, nature condominiums, NGO participation in public protected areas management, among other available options, may benefit from activities such as ecotourism, recreation, and management of natural resources that do not diminish the quality of the environmental services provided by these areas.

The failure of projects aiming at natural forest management for production is rarely caused by technical problems or a lack of scientific information. The single dominant cause has been the lack of economic profitability. There are certain unavoidable natural causes for this situation, such as the remote location of most remaining natural forests. However, more significant causes of economic failure of sustainability stem from deficient planning and poor administration of forest enterprises, scarcity of long-term funding, low returns for producers of forest products, competition with tropical timber coming from Africa and Asia, and lack of political will to prevent forest invasion. Just as important, however, is the absence of a public administration to apply equitable and reasonable rules for forest exploitation. The result has been that it is more profitable to practice anarchic logging and forest conversion than forest management.

One of the most likely solutions to improving the valuation of tropical forests is to require society to pay for the environmental services it receives. Carbon sequestration, water provision, water quality protection, and biodiversity conservation are all critical environmental services that need to be developed for their market value.

In reviewing the existing network of international institutions, commissions, agreements and programs, it becomes evident that forests are receiving more attention than ever. Nonetheless, conservation efforts display a great deal of overlap, interagency competition and inefficiency. The author concludes that a world forest convention and the establishment of a world forest organization would make sense *only* if the principal goal were to define and manage the compensation mechanisms for environmental services provided by forests.

The threats to the last primary forests of Latin America have changed little in the past half century. However, the intensity of deforestation has been reinvigorated by the present economic stability of the region. Moreover, the threats are under minimal control, as a consequence of a general adherence to theories espousing the free market economy. New roads and other infrastructure improvements are now being built in forest areas with private funding. At the same time, state controls have been weakened by reductions in the size and responsibilities of state agencies.

In the absence of sound legislation or public monitoring of resource extraction, public forests are being privatized and large international enterprises are starting to operate in the region. Similarly, invasion of indigenous tribal territories and forest conversion have resumed at very high levels. Public and private interest in natural forests could be heightened by charging for forest services, which might spur the region's governments to confront this situation.

Finally, the international institutions should practice what they preach to developing countries—adapting their programs to fit their mandates and specialties, and avoiding costly duplications of effort. The multilateral financial institutions, with their relatively strong influence, should act responsibly by financing the public and private sectors in a way that encourages sustainable forest management. They must place strong emphasis on financing the restructuring of public institutions that manage natural resources to improve institutional quality and efficiency. International development agencies should be proactive on these matters, because otherwise Latin American governments are not likely to make these tasks priorities. Finally, the banks must do more with concessionary funding to improve the quality of long-term management of national protected areas.

CHAPTER 6

Sustainable Management of Natural Forests: Actors and Policies

Ronnie de Camino

Introduction

Natural forests constitute a valuable environmental and economic resource in Latin America. Many of the region's countries possess significant forest resources that should be utilized and managed not only for their development potential, but also for the environmental benefits they generate for the entire global community. Within the framework of sustainable development, there are various options available to reduce deforestation in Latin America. In this chapter, the role of particular social and economic actors in the forest sector is analyzed, as well as the impact of existing policies in the region. The aim is to visualize options for improving forest policies and practices that will, in turn, generate income and ensure sustainability with strong participation by the various actors.

Sustainability

The concept of sustainable development has gained increasing acceptance worldwide as a guiding principle for economic policies. As defined by the Brundtland report, sustainable development "seeks to satisfy the necessities of present generations without compromising the ability of future generations to attain their own development needs." The report describes sustainable development in operational terms as follows: "a process of change in which the exploitation of resources, the flows of investments and technological development, as well as institutional change, work in harmony and improve the current and future potential to satisfy human needs. The concept considers the limits imposed by natural resources, the present state of technology and social organizations, as well as the capacity of the biosphere to absorb the impacts generated by human activity; it also assumes that improvements and advances in both technology and social organizations can open the way for a new era of economic growth" (World Commission on Environment and Development [WCED] 1987).

Therefore, sustainable development would limit the use of forest products and services to activities that (1) occur within the limits of an ecosystem's sustained productive capacity; (2) are economically viable for the stakeholders involved in forest management; (3) allow stakeholders to participate in designing, implementing and evaluating forest policies and programs, as well as sharing in the distribution of associated costs and benefits; and (4) consider the linkages of forestry with sustainable development through other sectors of a country.

External Factors

Reforms within the forest sector should take account of its interrelationships with other sectors. Thus, the formulation of forestry policies should consider agriculture and livestock husbandry, the management of watersheds, coastal zones, biodiversity and energy resources. The same consideration should be given to macroeconomic policies and corresponding legislation that affect the forest sector—namely, fiscal, trade, monetary, infrastructure, transportation and institutional policies (Keipi and Laarman 1995; Gregersen et al. 1994).

While many authors have examined external policies affecting the forest sector (Stewart and Gibson 1995; Gregersen et al. 1994; Pascó-Font 1994; Alfaro 1994; Contreras 1995; IDB/UNDP/ACT 1992), few have adequately analyzed the interrelationships of these often contradicting policies. One recent effort analyzes forestry policies in Central America and the limitations encountered in the sustainable development of forest resources (CCAB-AP 1996).

During the last two decades, development efforts in Latin America have been directed primarily toward ensuring fiscal stability and economic growth. The focus on human development and environmental improvement and protection often seems an afterthought. Nevertheless, if people accept that the goal is to achieve economically, socially and environmentally sustainable development, then it will be necessary to pursue both economic benefits and quality of life improvements at the same time.

Actors' Interests and Objectives

This chapter focuses on those with direct interests in forest resources—whether their interest is to preserve the forest and obtain income from environmental services, or to extract short-term benefits while converting forests to other land uses—and on the role of the government in such activities. The groups are thus classified respectively as conservationists, traditional inhabitants, producers and converters. The number of groups chosen has been limited to simplify discussion. As a result, the actors have been classified into four broad categories. The author understands that a wide range of opinions and viewpoints may exist within a single category and accepts the risks of generalizing about any one group of actors. Because the state has direct interactions with all of these groups, it is discussed in the context of its relations with them rather than as a separate actor competing for resource use. In this sense, the state is obligated to support a range of societal interests in natural resource management, rather than compete with present and future users (World Commission on Forestry and Sustainable Development [WCFSD] 1996a).

Conservationists

Conservationists view the environment as a central factor within the framework of development (Pascó-Font 1994). They have focused their efforts primarily on pressuring governments to establish and maintain protected areas, national parks and buffer zones as a means of protecting intact ecosystems or areas with high biological diversity. Naturalist, aesthetic, scientific, and even economic motivations lead people to take a conservationist stand. The conservationist category represents those groups advocating the conservation of forests in their most pristine state. The principal group consists of national and international non-governmental organizations (NGOs) dedicated to the preservation of flora and fauna (among them IUCN, WWF, The Nature Conservancy, Conservation International and their national analogs). The introduction of sustainable development as a concept has led these organizations to recognize the need for cooperation with groups whose forest use will also protect biodiversity as well as the various functions and services provided by forests.

Traditional Inhabitants

This category includes communities that have traditionally lived in the forest and currently derive their livelihood from forest products without changing the fundamental character of their environment. These groups harvest animals and plants, and carry out subsistence agriculture and animal husbandry. They tend to generate few disruptions to the ecological equilibrium of their environment as a result of low-impact survival strategies, limited population size, or minimal access to technology. These groups have slowly been acquiring user rights to forested areas owned by government throughout Latin America (see Ruiz-Pérez et al. 1992).

To the extent that traditional inhabitants use shared channels of communication, organize themselves, and acquire training, they will be able to defend their common interests and improve their negotiating power. The Maya Forest Action Plan, for example, has unified indigenous communities throughout Guatemala and achieved important concessions from the government (Brenes 1995). Another important example is Brazil's National Council of Rubber Tappers (CNS)—the entity that represents communities living off extractive reserves around the country. Through this organization, communities that derive their livelihood from nontimber forest products have made important gains in the area of forestry and environmental policies. These gains have permitted them to carry out projects that involve developing and processing their products, thus increasing the value of their economic activities (Ruiz-Pérez et al. 1992).

Producers

This group includes timber companies, concession holders, managers of state-owned reserves, forest industries dependent on supplies of round wood, and other local communities and private owners of forested lands that depend on the extraction of wood or the intensive exploitation of forest products. Although all of these groups depend on forest exploitation, there are few examples of firms or land owners that maintain their operations through sustainable forest management.

In many cases, producers have managed to establish associations or lobbying groups to obtain political advantages and to defend industry positions, thus mobilizing powerful economic interests. Good examples of this phenomenon include the National Forestry Council (CNF) of Bolivia, the Costa Rican Forestry Council (CCF), the National Forest Council (CANAFOR) also of Costa Rica, the National Timber Corporation (CORMA) in Chile, and the Forestry Association of Guatemala, among others. Initially, the timber industry became organized with the purpose of promoting legal and regulatory initiatives to favor their interests. They have since expanded their activities to develop markets, promote technology transfer, and advance a few other initiatives that support more sustainable uses of forest resources.

Converters

This group includes cattle ranchers, farmers, builders of dams and other infrastructure, oil and mining companies, and informal miners, as well as public sector agencies responsible for land reform, rural development and colonization programs. All of these groups generate a demand for land that may be best suited to forest cover but will be used for other ends. Converters are not interested in forestry, but wish to transfer the land to other uses such as agriculture, pasture, roads, and housing (among others)—all for economic gain.

Several policies or conditions have been responsible for much of the forest conversion that has occurred. First, public lands are often considered *de facto* open access resources. Second, some policies encourage conversion through perverse incentives, leading to the degradation of forests and soil quality (Cortés-Salas et al. 1995). Third, land titles are granted to settlers and colonizers for land "improvements," i.e., clearing and burning trees to permit farming and animal husbandry. This stimulates farmers to clear land and hold their capital in the form of livestock (Cortés-Salas et al. 1995). Fourth, subsidies to the agricultural sector have promoted deforestation indirectly by reducing the relative value of forest resources compared with agricultural users.

Conflicts and Collaboration among Actors

A basic tenet of sustainable development is that different stakeholders should have the opportunity to participate in negotiations regarding the utilization, designation and distribution of resources. The inclusion of groups affected by policy decisions should lead to planning and management based on mutual interests and responsibilities. To ensure constructive participation, the various groups should identify common objectives on which to reach agreement and consensus; potential or existing conflicts among the different actors; and sources of information or management tools that can support sustainable forestry by all groups.

Recent developments in Latin America suggest that there is already some consensus among actors on the need to design and implement national land use plans to clearly establish the areas to be preserved, those to be dedicated to forest production, and those to be assigned to agriculture and livestock uses (Brenes 1995). The following discussion provides a basic understanding of the principal objectives and conflicts that dominate the agenda of each of the four actor groups. Thus, the focus is on the issues that are likely to unite actors, as well as those that will require the most effort to achieve a consensus.

Conservationists

Conservationists have primarily targeted commercial timber interests as the foremost threat to forest preservation. For example, as a result of the efforts of environmental NGOs, in 1993 the Austrian government approved a regulation limiting tropical timber imports to those sources that manage the resource sustainably. In Honduras, environmentalists blocked the company Stone Forestal from obtaining concessions, and in Costa Rica they exerted enough pressure to stop the same company from developing monoculture plantations of *Gmelina arborea*. More recently, conservationists have substituted boycotts and public pressure, in alliance with other actors.

Cooperation has occurred particularly with indigenous groups who have traditionally enjoyed the support of conservation organizations. Although indigenous groups are more use-oriented than conservationists, these actors have worked together to advance their often complementary objectives. Conservationists have connected local communities with environmentally responsible private firms that utilize forest resources but also manage them (WWF 1991). Conservationists have also supported producer groups of small farmers in order to provide technical assistance in their forest management (see Box 6.1); and they have worked with governments to improve environmental awareness and education.

Traditional Inhabitants

The most consistent source of conflict between traditional forest inhabitants and the other actors is infringements on land tenure due to undefined or unenforced property rights.

Box 6.1 The Power of Alliances

FUNDECOR (Foundation for the Development of the Central Volcanic Range of Costa Rica) is an NGO created to manage the FORESTA Project financed by USAID. The objective of the project is to promote the conservation and sustainable use of the natural and cultural resources in the area. Some of FUNDECOR's achievements include the following:

- Support for an association of 312 land owners that together control 16,000 hectares of forest and are initiating sustainable management of their forest resources.
- Negotiation of prices for producers and efficient organization of local timber marketing.
- Development of innovative financing schemes via the sale of forest products and environmental services.

FUNDECOR is developing a market for timber futures on the basis of management plans, with financing from the International Finance Corporation (associated with the World Bank). It is also linking the sale of carbon sequestration (through accords for Joint Implementation) to the certification of management practices and forest conservation as a way to channel funds to private owners of forests. The program uses the following methods to assist small farmers and producers with forest management:

- Negotiating the certification of cooperative forest management as a way to ensure that it is economically feasible for medium and small producers to participate in sustainable forestry.
- Developing an environmental education and ecotourism program in order to generate support for sustainable forest management, and to generate income for private farmers and land owners.

Source: Alfaro 1996.

Government policies to encourage colonization have created continual conflicts with indigenous groups. The same is true for migrants attracted to tropical forested areas by mining. Commercial farmers and ranchers, whether as individuals or as organized groups, seek to obtain lands that are also claimed by indigenous tribes and other communities. Lastly, there is conflict within this group in cases where different tribes or communities dispute the ownership or rights to land. Similarly, some larger groups have obtained political representation at the expense of smaller, less organized communities.

The potential for cooperation between inhabitants and all the other actors is significant. Timber companies benefit from such collaboration because the communities control the land, supply labor, and have a knowledge of the local environment, while the companies provide capital and knowledge of extractive and processing technologies. Such cooperation is occurring in Nicaragua where some companies have established contracts with Sumu communities to manage hardwood and pine forests. They can create opportunities for an expanded number of economic activities that could raise incomes while maintaining a sustainable and equitable use of forest resources (de Camino 1996).

Producers

Producers' main conflict is with conservationists, whom they see as a serious obstacle to forest resource use because of the public criticism against production some conservationists foment, and the pressures they put on policy makers. With respect to the other actors, producers compete with converters for forested areas, and are increasingly required to acknowledge the territorial rights of indigenous peoples and other rural communities. Such is the case of the forest cooperatives of Quintana Roo, Mexico (Janka and Lobato 1995), where rural communities implement their own forest conservation plans and in the Petén region of Guatemala, where the government is granting a rural community a forest concession on public lands (CATIE 1994).

The principal objective of producers is to obtain sufficient profits from using the forest. They accept the need to change the structure of the forest in order to achieve their objectives. While some producers fight conservationists, others try to incorporate environmental remediation and reclamation measures into their businesses in order to market themselves as "green." Conversely, some property owners and concession holders harvest the forest cover and timber and then abandon these areas, which are then subject to colonization, commercial agriculture, and livestock production.

Converters

Converters, like producers, see conservationists and traditional inhabitants as their principal opponents. The process of land conversion generates conflict with traditional inhabitants, leading often to tragic consequences for the communities involved. There are a few cases, however, when the deforested lands have been returned to their original owners and reconverted to secondary forest (CCT/WRI 1991; Utting 1993). In a typical sequence of events small-scale converters invade government property, or receive land legally from the government but resell it to commercial farmers or ranchers after a few years of cultivation (Schneider 1995).

The fact that converters have only a short-term or transitory interest in forest resources does not mean that they should not participate in the political debate regarding forests. On the contrary, it is important for this group to understand the impact of its activities and to offer alternatives that encourage them to practice sustainable economic activities that do not threaten forest survival.

Moving from Interests to Practices

In many cases, the actors competing for land are not being realistic about their demands on the remaining natural forests. Conservationists seek to protect large areas whose physical and territorial integrity they cannot guarantee in the long run. Forest inhabitants hope to receive large extensions of territory that will permit them to hunt, fish and carry out shifting agriculture, even though they often do not always possess the necessary capacities to exert territorial control over land adjudicated to them. Producers seek to acquire permits and concessions for the exploitation of the best forests, but rather than managing harvested tracts sustainably, wish to move on to exploit other undeveloped areas. And finally, converters push to acquire new areas for cultivation and ranching. They finance improvements to their fields by logging and selling wood from adjacent forested areas.

The effective implementation of land use plans can only be guaranteed through zoning different land uses through a participatory process, identifying permissible activities in these zones, and developing the political, legal and technical tools to manage them. Land use plans should remain flexible enough to allow more than one actor to pursue activities within an area, as long as the interests of principal users are not harmed. In order to avoid conflicts, formal agreements are needed between groups pursuing different activities. It is essential to take into account also illegal utilization of forests (i.e., nonsanctioned squatter and migrant use) and where lands best suited for forestry have been converted to other land uses. Although these areas are not used sustainably, it is unrealistic to reassign them to forest uses when they are controlled by colonists who have no other sources of income (Janka and Lobato 1995). Similarly, where opposing uses are not compatible (for example, indigenous groups competing with converters in the same area) cooperation may not be

Table 6.1 Stakeholder Interests and Policy Responses

Stakeholder and objective	Interests and policy positions	Possible policy responses
Conservationists Ensure that the majority of land areas with forest cover gain some protective status Protect biological corridors connecting ecosystems to allow migration of wildlife and preservation of genetic resources	Conserve primary forests Capture forests' economic value by developing a market for their national environmental services Share costs of maintaining global environmental benefits with the international community	Establishment of national biodiversity strategies and land use plans Development of market mechanisms to capture and distribute economic income from forests' environmental services
Traditionalists Maintain control over traditional lands without outside intervention	Conserve and manage primary forests within indigenous territories and in extractive reserves Expect other actors to focus on raising the productivity of their existing and under-utilized holdings	Enforcement of land management and land use plans Demarcation of traditional lands and extractive reserves, and recognition of indigenous peoples' and extractivist communities' rights
Producers Ensure that areas with most valuable timber species and greatest productive potential are used primarily for harvesting timber	Set aside large tracts of forests exclusively for forest production activities Limit agriculture and ranching to areas where they presently occur Grant new short- and long-term concessions in productive forests Designate incentives to restore degraded forest	Forest programs that accommodate increased production to meet internal and external demand for forest products Classification of forests according to their productive potential and use, and demarcation of areas for forestry activities Policies to support reforestation of areas with degraded land and forest cover
Converters Ensure that forested areas with suitable agricultural soils are designated for farming and livestock production	Growing national and international demand for food requires new areas to come under cultivation and animal husbandry	A national policy that permits conversion of all necessary land to sustainable agriculture and livestock production Rehabilitation of degraded areas to agriculture Improvement of agricultural technologies for intensive use of converted land
Public sector forestry officials Capture the income potential of forests for the government and affected actors Provide associated social benefits and environmental services	Prevent deforestation of remaining primary forests owned by the state, communities and the private sector	A national land-use plan Classification of forests according to their productive and ecological potential Policies that support resource management and permit the state to capture income from the forest Negotiation of the sale of environmental services (biodiversity, carbon sequestration)
Public sector agricultural agents Encourage development of sustainable agriculture and livestock production	Clear forest from remaining areas that are suitable for agricultural production	A national land use plan that considers the conversion of forests to sustainable agriculture and livestock production

Source: Author's analysis.

Table 6.2 Sectoral Policies Favoring Agricultural Production and Forest Clearing

Measures/policies	Effects on agriculture
Agricultural colonization programs (where land titles are linked to land clearing or improvements)	Generate a supply of inexpensive land Improve agricultural land tenure security Make agricultural credits available for mortgages Generate higher prices for deforested land relative to forest land
Fuel subsidies	Reduce the cost of mechanized agriculture Reduce the cost of transporting inputs and agricultural products
Agricultural input subsidies	Reduce direct costs of production Increase agricultural productivity
Investments in roads, irrigation and warehouse infrastructure	Open forested areas to immigration and colonization Increase agricultural productivity, reduce loss of harvested products, and reduce transportation costs
Trade restrictions on food imports	Create a secure market for products even when domestic production is inefficient
Agricultural research projects	Increase productivity and reduce risks
Technical assistance and agricultural extension services (soil sciences, phytopathology, seeds)	Support technology transfer and increase agricultural productivity
Subsidies for agricultural credits	Increase expansion of areas under agricultural cultivation
State-run agricultural markets	Guarantee markets for products Provide guaranteed commodity prices

Source: Author's analysis.

possible and the state may have to intervene on behalf of one or the other. Regardless of which view dominates, all the groups with a stake in natural forests should recognize the need for designing land use plans that accommodate everyone's interests. Table 6.1 summarizes the positions and interests of relevant actors within the context of land use planning and design. Table 6.2 lists sectoral policies favoring agricultural production that may lead to deforestation, especially in forest frontier areas. Table 6.3 describes possible impacts of structural adjustment policies on forest resources.

Towards Sustainable Forest Management

The various actors involved in the debate over forest use all operate within a broader context of political and social policies, at local, national and even international levels. While each group may have its specific interests and goals, all of them affect overall forest use in Latin America.

Table 6.3   Impacts of Stabilization and Structural Adjustment Policies on Forest Resources

Measures/policies	Potential impacts
Dismantling incentives for agricultural and livestock production (elimination of tax breaks, input subsidies)	Reduced incentives for deforestation Lower financial returns from agricultural production relative to those from forestry
Eliminating taxes on exports of forest products	Stimulation of commercial forestry to provide products that are in export demand
Reducing government bureaucracies, lowering subsidies to formerly privileged industrial sectors	Rise in unemployment Increased pressure on natural resources
Cuts in public sector forest agencies without compensatory measures or delegation of responsibilities	Less control of state-owned and privately held forests Destructive exploitation, rather than sustainable management of resources

Source: Author's analysis.

The economic value of products and services offered by forests may lead to a wider adoption of sustainable management. Developing a set of positive policy initiatives to increase the value of forests relative to other land uses would allow the resource base to recover and would generate development opportunities for the future (Dourojeanni 1996; Pascó-Font 1994; Reis 1991; Riihinen 1986; de Camino 1993; IDB 1995a; Centeno 1995; Johnston and Lorraine 1995; Cortés-Salas et al. 1995).

The Economic Value of Forest Benefits and Services

Forests in Latin America are undervalued by both the government and the private sector because a shortage of appropriate information hinders resource use and management. For example, incomplete knowledge on the whereabouts of marketable species could prevent a forest company from harvesting valuable products from a concession stand. Similarly, a government might put a section of forest rich in biodiversity up for commercial bidding, for timber, simply because it was unaware of its biological resources or did not have the manpower to make a species inventory. Even where species inventories and infrastructure exist, the market value of a forest is unlikely to represent its true total economic value. Green labeling of forest products and certification of forest management are potential tools to increase the value of forests and their sustainable management (see Chapter 10 of this book). Forests generate a variety of services at local and global levels that society enjoys, but for which it does not pay. Interest in the long-term preservation of the resource would increase significantly if its total value was determined and if the current nonmarket goods and services were tradeable. Thus, the challenge is to develop a market for, and a societal recognition of, the value of the goods and services provided by intact forests. Some of the nonmarket ecological benefits produced by forests include carbon storage and fixation from the atmosphere, preserving water resources and watersheds, protecting species with pharmaceutical value, and regulating the climate (Pascó-Font 1994).

Examples of calculations of total economic value are well documented (Pearce 1993; During 1993; World Bank 1993c; IICA 1994). Adger et al. (1995) calculate that owners of private forests in Mexico are losing a minimum of $4 billion every year from the

Table 6.4 Estimates of Total Economic Value of Costa Rican Forests
(In US dollar terms)

Item	Value (a) (in $millions)	Value (b) per ha	Value per ha/ yr (with 8% discount)
Market values	403	620	50
Nonmarket values	1,851	1,605	128
Total economic value	2,254	2,225	178

(a) Includes production forests and protected areas; (b) includes only production forests.

Source: World Bank (1993a).

nonmarket components of the forest's total economic value. If traded, these goods would produce an estimated $80 per hectare annually. Förster (1994) estimates that the Noh Bec cooperative that manages a permanently forested area of 19,500 ha in Quintana Roo, Mexico, could generate annual benefits in addition to timber sales of $1.6 million—equal to $7,480 for each of the cooperative's 204 families. Estimates of the total economic value for Costa Rican forests (Table 6.4) show that owners of forested areas (including the state) fail to receive approximately 82 percent of the value of all forests (including protected areas), and 72 percent of the value per hectare from productive forests (World Bank 1993a). Thus, the state, the private sector and local communities could all benefit from expanded market demands for forest goods and services. A good example is provided by the extractivist reserves for nontimber products (see Box 6.2).

Toward Wider Adoption of Sustainable Forest Management

While many countries in Latin America require the submission of management plans for timber activity on private and state forest lands, few have management systems that function effectively. Part of the problem is that public sector forestry agencies, responsible for setting up the norms, pursue goals and objectives that overwhelm their personnel and budgetary capacities, and create bureaucratic requirements they are unable to enforce. This reality is reflected in the high rates of illegal logging.

Although some authors contend that sustainable management of tropical forests in Latin America has failed (Johnson and Cabarle 1993; WRI 1991; Goodland et al. 1990b), one can argue that it has yet to be tested in any systematic way (de Camino and Barcena 1995). A few significant cases suggest strategies for a wider and more systematic adoption of sustainable management practices. Various authors (WWF 1991; Kirmse et al. 1993; Janka and Lobato 1995; de Camino 1996; Arias 1996; and Alfaro 1996) document examples of management at least in a pilot scale. To date, the estimated forest area under actual management represents only 0.3 percent of all dense forests in Latin America. However, experimental projects like Precious Woods (Amazonas, Brazil), Nordvisk (Pará, Brazil) and BARAMA (Guyana) have the potential to double the area under sustainable management. As shown in Table 6.5, these initiatives have emerged from all types of actors: rural communities, private enterprises, NGOs, and governments.

A Conceptual Framework for Reforming Forest Practices

The conditions have not been adequate to generate sustainable and equitable forest management in Latin America. Sustainable development depends on the construction of a framework capable of redirecting forestry policies toward this goal. This new framework assumes

Box 6.2 Extractivist Populations and Nontimber Forest Products

Peters et al. (1989) estimated that nontimber forest products in a hectare of Amazon forest could generate annual revenues of up to $697.79, while timber harvests from that same hectare only generate $1,000 over a 60-year period. These calculations create the impression that it is better to extract only nontimber forest products exclusively and not to harvest wood. In response, bilateral and multilateral organizations have channeled an increasing portion of their assistance to extractivist projects.

It should be clear, however, that if each hectare of Amazon forest were harvested in the manner suggested by Peters and his colleagues, the price for nontimber forest products would approach zero. It is also true that most firms specializing in the development of nontimber products purchase only minimally processed goods at low prices so that they can add value to these products and capture the majority of the products' market value. Ruiz-Pérez et al. (1992) report an enormous disparity between the profits of those who harvest, and those who export, nontimber products from the Petén of Guatemala. Exporters of such products market them for prices several times higher than what they pay harvesters—for palm heart, 7.4 times; for pepper, 3.2 times; and for gum resins, 2.4 times the prices paid to harvesters.

These examples demonstrate that in order to benefit from greater equity of access, extractivist groups must connect themselves to processing activities or carry them out directly, to capture a substantial part of the revenues the products can generate. Yet, even when local value-added processing is successful, the lifetime of a nontimber forest product as a viable market good is limited. This is because manufacturers are often able to cultivate the same product or create synthetic products similar to the nontimber forest products, thus lowering their costs and eliminating the demand for raw materials from the natural forest.

Homa (1993) refers to extractivist activities in the following terms: "It represents a moribund economy that will continue to disappear as the market for these goods grows[.] . . . No housewife is buying bananas, oranges, lettuce, mangos, coffee or cotton of extractivist origin. What will put an end to extractivist activities is not assassinations [referring to Chico Mendes in Brazil], but the market economy. . . . The 'Indian strategy' of living in harmony with nature will also be sold as an ideal option for the Amazon, forgetting the fact that when the indigenous economy comes into contact with the market economy it tends to disintegrate." Given this context, it is unjust to impose external decisions about indigenous lands and permissible activities for them that simply condemn native peoples to ever greater poverty and marginalization based on such simplistic conclusions as are presented in the Peters et al. (1989) article.

Source: Author's analysis.

that: (a) the objectives of individual actors are compatible with sustainable development; and (b) the capacity of forests to accommodate a variety of uses will determine the range of solutions and how the different actors interact. Clearly, reform of the forest sector requires time for experimentation, flexibility and maturation at each stage in the process. Even so, environmental, economic, and social pressures make it urgent to initiate these changes.

Although the challenge is daunting, the path is clear. Countries have to develop the institutional and technical capacities to formulate policy, interact with the various user groups, acquire the necessary scientific and technical knowledge, and integrate the changes they initiate. Because financial and institutional obstacles to the necessary policy reform and implementation persist, countries must work with multilateral and bilateral agencies to achieve their goals. Together they will have to establish priorities, define the pace of reform, and ensure that reform strategies correspond with technical and institutional capacities.

Table 6.5 Experiments in Sustainable Forest Management in Latin America and the Caribbean

Country and Actor	Project	Area (ha)
Bolivia (govt, private sector, NGO)	Chimanes	600,000
Bolivia (govt, private sector)	Santa Cruz MACA	57,000
Brazil (government)	FUNTAC/ANTIMARI	66,000
Brazil (private sector)	Mil Madeiras (Precious Woods)	80,000
Brazil (government)	Tapajos	132,000
Costa Rica (private sector)	Portico S.A.	6,000
Costa Rica (NGO/private sector)	FUNDECOR (CAFMA)	13,000
Costa Rica (private sector)	CAFMA (various organizations)	11,000
Costa Rica (private sector)	Codefor S.A. (CAFMA)	16,000
Colombia (private sector)	Cartón de Colombia	24,000
Dominican Republic (NGO/communities)	Plan Sierra	130,000
French Guiana (government)	ONF	122,500
Mexico (communities)	Pilot Forest Plan, Quintana Roo	400,000
Peru (local communities)	Yanesha	75,000
Trinidad and Tobago (government)	Open Range System	40,000
Trinidad and Tobago (government)	Periodic Block System	10,000
Total		**2,265,500**

Source: Author's analysis.

Necessary Conditions for Change

Stakeholder Participation. Sustainable development requires the participation of all interest groups in formulating and implementing new policies. This implies participation in policy diagnosis, design, evaluation, and implementation. Through participation, not only will the actors involved advance their own interests, but they will have to consider others' interests in order to achieve consensus (see Box 6.3). The government plays a crucial role in this process, with four principal responsibilities. The first is to create candid, straightforward consultation mechanisms that encourage participation of all parties, especially those traditionally excluded from decisionmaking processes (Cortés-Salas et al. 1995). Second, government must recognize and address the legitimacy of diverse objectives, such as obtaining profits, protecting biodiversity and increasing family incomes. Third, state institutions should be redirected to serve a wider spectrum of actors (de Camino 1993). Fourth, government needs to promote coordination and consensus-building among stakeholders.

The government should not regard itself as the main interested party in the development of forestry policy. Rather, it should facilitate agreement among diverse civil society groups. These groups need to take the initiative in looking for joint opportunities that favor mutual interests. The purpose of public consultations prior to decisionmaking is to air similarities and differences and work toward consensus. The availability of reliable and objective information on the topic of debate, the use of conflict resolution methodologies, and the participation of facilitators in the consultation process can all contribute to developing a positive dialogue aimed at achieving agreement (FAG 1995).

Equitable Distribution of Costs and Benefits. Given that equity is one of the objectives of sustainable development, it will be necessary to institute reforms in the distribution of costs and benefits of sustainable forest management. To achieve this, it is necessary to consider the following points.

Box 6.3 Popular Participation in Environmental Law Design

The approval and adoption of Nicaragua's environmental law was the result of an open and participatory process supported by the Nicaraguan Environmental Movement (MAN), a network of nongovernmental organizations unified by the shared desire to protect the environment and the country's natural resources. The consultation process began within some of the MAN chapters that were organized into sectoral and professional fields, followed by a wider consultation effort in different regions of the country. The legislative proposal—which integrates development and environmental objectives—was presented to the Legislative Assembly together with 50,000 signatures of support.

Source: Brenes 1995.

a)   Although a country's forests may be the property of particular actors, the environmental services they supply also benefit society in general. The costs associated with these services should be assumed by those who receive the benefits.

b)   Traditional forest inhabitants should receive a portion of the income generated from third-party economic activity on their land. This requires the recognition of traditional inhabitant property rights, and the subsequent development of appropriate fee or royalty systems.

c)   Private sector industrial forestry interests have the right to capture net income from the difference between their product's sale price and their costs of production. The production costs should internalize the costs of ecological protection and possible social improvements in the territories where they work.

d)   Private owners should receive undistorted benefits from their forests. Otherwise, the resource has little value, and forest conversion becomes attractive.

e)   Exporting countries should consider vertical integration strategies for the production of timber and other products, and participate more actively in their commercialization in order to capture a greater proportion of forest-generated income. To date, 90 percent of the income generated in the market for tropical timber is received by the importers, and only 10 percent by the countries of origin (Centeno 1995; ITTO 1991).

Integrated Policymaking. Changes in forest practices should be based on careful analysis of the policies of other sectors and alternative macroeconomic measures (see Chapter 2; Cortés-Salas et al. 1995; FAG 1995; World Bank 1993c). The groups responsible for these other policies should be consulted, in order to correct, mitigate or avoid the adverse economic, social and environmental impacts they might have in forestry (see Tables 6.2 and 6.3 above).

Principles and Direction of Change

In each country the criteria and the direction of reform in the forest sector will vary depending on the importance of forest resources to the national economy, the pace of resource degradation, and the needs and political power of different actors. Nonetheless, all actors should be working toward the general goal of achieving environmentally, economically, and socially sustainable forest management. The following is a list of principles for consensus-building among actors:

- Design an efficient and straightforward system that recognizes the rights of traditional groups in the forest and regulates access to the resource by others (de Camino 1993).
- Support forest stewardship development programs with the objective of sustainable management involving indigenous communities and other land owners (Pascó-Font 1994).
- Provide necessary technical and economic information to the different actors in order to facilitate their actions in putting sustainable forest management into practice.
- Limit deforestation to land suitable for long-term agriculture and livestock production in municipal land use plans.
- Maximize income from forests' total economic value, including the value of environmental services that generate national and global benefits (Dourojeanni 1996; MacKinnon 1990).
- Adopt measures to mitigate any adverse impacts from macroeconomic and sectoral policies on the development of forests, and design policies that promote sustainable forest management (de Camino 1993).
- Utilize the current and future potential of forest resources to optimize the sector's contribution to national development. Efforts should target internal consumption or exports, depending on each country's possibilities and needs (Pascó-Font 1994; MacKinnon 1990).
- Formulate policies that favor economically competitive value-added processing of the resource. Also, this will allow those with usufruct rights over the forests, its owners and the forestry industry, to receive the appropriate benefits of sustainable resource utilization.

Components of Change
The following section discusses several aspects contributing to possible changes in current forest practices. They include land use and tenure (especially in agricultural frontier zones), forest concession policies, use of incentives, and ways to finance environmental services obtained through forest protection. Each one of these themes has been addressed also in other chapters of this book from other angles but with the common goal of sustainable development. A successful execution of the proposed actions requires the participation of key civil society stakeholders interested in sustainable forestry. However, since each action requires government support, state entities will be in key positions to facilitate the formulation of initial proposals and their implementation.

Land Use and Tenure. Changes in the forest sector require appropriate land use and tenure decisions. It is important to formulate realistic land use plans that recognize the difficulty of reversing already consolidated processes (Janka and Lobato 1995). Land use plans should define criteria for the management of forest areas intended for production and preservation purposes.

Agricultural frontiers pose particular challenges for land management. Land use ordinances should be enforced by the lowest administrative units, taking into account prevailing conditions in their local areas. Otherwise, the adoption of land use zoning requirements and norms restricting forest uses may not be effective (Cortés-Salas et al. 1995).

The measures outlined above should be accompanied by activities to increase land tenure security, particularly for traditional inhabitants and producers (see Chapter 7). This would benefit long-term investment in sustainable management. The first step in land tenure regulation would be to collect information on land use and property registries (World Bank 1993c). Properties with titles, occupied lands, and areas claimed by indigenous communities should be demarcated. Rural development proposals should take into account an area's carrying capacity, population growth, and the potential for generating economic opportunities off the farm, such as agro-industry or rural forest industries, among others.

Forest Concessions. Traditional forest concessions have in many cases failed to prevent the degradation of forests associated with productive uses, while permitting legal and illegal colonizers to penetrate these areas. To function appropriately, forest concessions should operate under the conditions discussed below (see also Chapter 10):

- Facilitate broad access to bids on forest concessions and offer guaranteed space and time allotments to users who adequately manage the resource (TFAP-CA 1992). Historically, concessions have been granted to timber companies and not to rural communities. The concession system should encourage community activities and collaborative efforts that bring together different resource users.
- Base calculations of fees on a system with a high degree of vertical integration in order to favor greater economic efficiency. Vertical integration can be encouraged with policies that favor value-added activities. Concession fees should not be based exclusively on volume harvested, but also on the area under concession. This combination would provide the state with both a fixed and a variable source of income.
- Allow concession holders to receive their share of income derived from the sale of environmental services produced by the forest, once these are negotiated in national and international markets.
- Establish requirements for certification of sustainable forest management in forest concessions. Such certification should be carried out, for example, by entities accredited by the Forest Stewardship Council based in Oaxaca, Mexico (see Chapter 10).
- Tie failure to comply with sustainability criteria and indicators to an immediate revocation of concession licenses without recourse to indemnity. Elements of these indicators should be included in national forestry legislation (CCAD/CCAB-AP 1996).
- Consider transferring ownership of areas under concession to concession holders that demonstrate good forest management practices under international certification (Razetto 1995).

Possible Use of Incentives. The use of incentives may be justified to compensate land owners for environmental externalities (see Chapter 4). Incentives may take various forms, such as, timely information about available technologies providing access to extension services and credit and possible direct financial subsidies in support of particular activities. If an incentive system is to encourage sustainable development in the sector, it should incorporate certain elements. The system's purpose should be clearly defined in order to prevent these resources from promoting undesired activities. The potential benefits for sustainable development through economic, social and environmental analyses should be demonstrated. A possible use of new incentives within the forest sector should be accompanied by a reduction or elimination of incentives in other sectors that encourage conversion of forests to pasture and cultivated lands. These measures will increase the value of forest conservation and management relative to competing land uses. Incentives should be kept in line with the value society assigns to the goods and services from the forests. They should be just high enough to cover the marginal cost of adopting other socially and environmentally undesired land uses for forested areas. Incentives to particular actors should be tailored in such a way as to ensure that the investment of resources is effective and efficient. Rentseeking behavior should be minimized.

Financing Environmental Services. The value of environmental services supplied by natural forests must be recognized, particularly in areas with unique biodiversity or fragile ecosystems (Castilleja 1993). Land use policy makers should recognize all alternative uses and the associated opportunities and restrictions they may impose on owners. Possible restrictions should be accompanied by a valuation of the environmental services and forest owners should be duly compensated for them. There is little possibility of preserving forest land where environmental benefits are great, but where maintaining a natural forest is financially unprofitable. When the forest owner or occupant does not value the forest it is highly probable that it will be cleared.

Just as concessions are granted for extractable uses of the forest, they may also be created for conservation and protection of the forest. Ecotourism and parks or reserves with user fees can generate revenue for concession holders. These operations may be run by the private commercial sector, local communities, or traditional inhabitants. National and international conservation groups can co-manage these operations or simply provide technical support. Private commercial firms may be willing to finance conservation in order to obtain a good "green" image. For example, a timber company might contribute to a protected area in exchange for being allowed to promote itself within the park as an ecologically friendly business.

Other ways to provide funding for protected areas are using economic instruments to internalize the positive environmental benefits provided by these areas, through fees paid by local beneficiaries, refundable deposits or performance bonds to guarantee specific actions; payments by the international community based on carbon stored or maintained (Pascó-Font 1994); and payment by commercial companies for bioprospecting rights, among others. If a government or a regional entity has, or can develop, adequate institutional support and information dissemination, it can then make these environmental services tradeable on the market. The market will set the price for such services, and begin to internalize environmental factors in the wider economy.

International efforts to obtain compensation for global environmental services resulting from forest conservation are critically important. Countries will demonstrate greater interest in preserving biologically important areas if such preservation provides concrete benefits. In some cases, however, creating a market for these services may weaken national management and control over these areas, so countries must decide what degree of external economic interference they are willing to tolerate (Adger et al. 1995).

Conclusion

Latin American forests have global importance due to their size: one fourth of the world's total forests and one half of the tropical forests lie in the region. These vast expanses provide important global and national environmental services and could have significant economic potential in many countries. Deforestation in Latin America can be curbed by improving forest policies and practices that could, in turn, generate income and ensure sustainability.

These changes can be achieved only through the active participation of the various stakeholders: conservationists, traditional inhabitants, forest producers, and those who want to convert forest lands to other uses. The forest sector is notorious for lack of consensus among the affected interest groups. Despite heightened awareness about the need to manage forest resources in a sustainable and equitable way, many stakeholders still see no reason to stop their destructive practices and come to the bargaining table, unless forced to do so by law or by economic or ecological necessity. Given Latin America's long history of opportunistic exploitation of its resources, there has been little incentive for users to cooperate for the sake of other interest groups. Nevertheless, most actors currently involved in forest exploitation are becoming aware of the limitations of the ecosystems they depend on and may be more willing to negotiate with other users for their future stake in the resources. In addition, increasing democratization in the region has encouraged dialogue among various sectors of civil society, and may also facilitate the consensus-building process needed for sustainable forestry development.

Governments should support the conservation and management of forests for the ecological services and natural products they generate. The creation of new extractive reserves and adjacent protected areas should be encouraged. In addition, joint ventures between private companies and rural and indigenous owners of forests need to be facilitated. Through such ventures, sustainable harvesting and extractivist activities may become commonplace. The possible vertical integration of these production processes may then increase the income of rural communities. Furthermore, accords must be established between indigenous groups and other user groups to guarantee appropriate land use rights and practices.

Specific national objectives could include, among others, increasing land tenure security, adjustments in forest concession procedures, adequate use of incentives in response to the present trend toward transferring forests to the private sector, and support to green labeling to promote environmentally responsible forest production. Agricultural and macroeconomic policies should be analyzed and constraints to sustainable forest development should be identified and removed.

Policy changes will require the participation of both public authorities and affected interest groups. Stakeholders' active role in formulating and implementing new policies needs to be vigorously promoted. In addition, the costs associated with reforms and services should be assumed by those who receive the benefits. On the other hand, important parties traditionally with little voice in the reforms (such as indigenous groups) must be included in the policymaking and implementation processes. The preservation and sustainable management of the region's forests will ultimately depend on a satisfactory sharing of the wealth of benefits among all the interest groups.

CHAPTER 7

Deforestation and Property Rights

Carlos Felipe Jaramillo and Thomas Kelly

Introduction

There is increasing support for the notion that current rates of deforestation in Latin America are excessive. There is less agreement about the role that property rights over land play in the processes that lead to excessive deforestation. In some interpretations, ill-defined rights are largely accountable for poor resource management in the region. In others, property rights issues have a secondary influence on the rapid pace of deforestation.

To consider how individual property rights are linked to deforestation in Latin America, we review two areas where tenure issues have an effect on land-clearing pressures. The first deals with the security of established agricultural lands and how that affects agricultural production and employment. The second involves tenurial arrangements on forested areas and their impact on the sustainable management of resources.

The analysis concludes that strengthening property rights should be an important part of a strategy to reduce deforestation rates in the region. However, it also suggests that tenurial reforms are not a solution by themselves to prevent excessive land clearing. Property rights measures must be accompanied by complementary actions, including the elimination of ill-conceived government policies (macroeconomic and sectoral) that encourage extensive agricultural growth and subsidize the settlement of forested areas.

The first part of the chapter discusses deforestation trends in Latin America and their relationship to property rights issues. The second explores the linkage between deforestation pressures and the strengthening of individual land tenure on established agricultural areas. The third part analyzes property rights issues on forested areas, and the fourth presents some policy recommendations.

The causes of the rapid pace of deforestation in Latin America are complex. While demographic pressures, road building, income growth and agricultural yields seem to be the critical variables in explaining aggregate deforestation rates, differences in land-clearing processes have been detected in different areas of Latin America. At least two general patterns can be discerned. On the one hand, a pattern has been identified in Central America where the bulk of forest clearing over the last three decades has been motivated by the expansion of pastures for large commercial livestock operations (Kaimowitz 1995b). On the other hand, deforestation in a large share of the Amazon frontier seems to be driven by demographic pressures spearheaded by low-income, shifting cultivators (Barbier 1997; Kaimowitz 1995a). This pattern is most obvious in countries like Colombia, Ecuador and Peru where migrants from rural areas are responsible for the bulk of forest clearing. In Brazil, the pattern is mixed. Most areas have been cleared by rural migrants searching for livelihoods on the frontier. However, a substantial share sell cleared plots to ranchers and move on to clear new lands further into the frontier (Mueller 1997; Alston et al. 1995; Schneider 1995).

A number of government policies are also often cited as contributing to accelerating deforestation. In particular, policies that increase the profitability of agricultural activities in the frontier are frequently blamed for inducing inefficient land use. These cleared areas typically have soils incapable of sustaining agricultural exploitation for extended periods. Generally, the government policies include credit, input and marketing subsidies, road construction and other transport subsidies, tax incentives, and price supports through tariff and nontariff protection for selected crops (Binswanger 1991; Barbier 1997).

Less attention has been given to the link between deforestation and government policies that affect the exploitation of long established agricultural lands. For some analysts, the key to reducing pressure on natural forests lies in promoting the intensification of crop and livestock production away from the frontier (Southgate and Whitaker 1992; de Janvry and García 1992; Barbier 1997).

In most countries in Latin America, development strategies have altered the relative prices of crops and inputs in an attempt to favor a pattern of agricultural modernization that emphasizes large mechanized production (Grindle 1986). Protected crops have usually been those produced on large-scale mechanized farms, and they receive the bulk of the benefits from government-funded research and extension efforts (de Janvry et al. 1997). Credit subsidies, low tariffs and overvalued exchange rates have lowered the relative price of farm machinery and induced early replacement of traditional labor-intensive methods in the past. Agricultural growth patterns in most Latin American countries have not been friendly to the interests of the smallholder sector, despite the fact that smallholders account for the bulk of agricultural employment.

Deforestation and Property Rights

Recent advances in the study of tenure issues suggest that property rights evolve in response to complex demographic and social trends. In the early stages of development, when agricultural lands are abundant and productivity is low, shifting cultivation is the predominant mode of production (Boserup 1965). Diffuse property rights prevail, due to the low value of land resources (Feder and Feeney 1991). However, as the population grows relative to the surrounding natural resources and agriculture becomes a more profitable activity, communities increasingly formalize rules of access to such resources. These rules resolve competing claims and facilitate the investments required to intensify production (Demsetz 1967). Failure to develop successful property rights institutions and higher productivity levels may lead to land degradation through mining the soil fertility and organic matter, and through encroachment of cropping onto steep hillsides, forest margins and other fragile areas. The prevailing regime in developed countries illustrates the successful development of property rights institutions in the face of high population pressure, technological change and greater opportunities for agricultural commercialization (Barbier 1997).

While appropriate property rights institutions may develop naturally in some societies, it is not clear that this is true in all cases (Otsuka et al. 1996). Anthropological evidence suggests that customary resource management institutions may be an effective means of managing common resources, including forests (Ostrom 1990). However, these institutions may collapse under pressure from outside forces (i.e., strong migratory flows), leading to open access and rapid degradation of common resources (Binswanger et al.

1995; Rudel 1995; Southgate 1990a). In such cases, the difficulties in organizing sufficient collective action to manage common property, policy failures, and legal restrictions may all inhibit the necessary institutional responses (Otsuka et al. 1996). Thus, policy interventions may be needed to prevent wasteful environmental use.

Many analysts have argued that tenurial problems and, in particular, the absence of well-defined property rights are among the key causes of rapid deforestation in Latin America. Analytically, it is useful to distinguish the effects of tenure problems in long established agricultural lands from those faced in forested frontier areas (although in reality it is more of a continuum than a clear-cut distinction). In the former, the insecurity of property rights prevents farmers from increasing their land use intensity. Investment, output and employment levels are lower than with full property rights. In addition, property markets do not effectively transfer land to the most efficient users. The risks of expropriation associated with land reform laws make labor hiring and tenancy contracts risky. These factors depress employment generation in agriculture and accentuate the effects of other policies which favor labor-saving large-scale agricultural activities. This trend inevitably results in greater outflows of labor from agriculture into urban and frontier areas (Heath and Binswanger 1996).

In frontier areas, where lands not suitable for sustained agriculture prevail, tenurial uncertainty also promotes deforestation. The key tenure problem in these areas is the open access character of public forested lands. For the most part, the governments of Latin American countries do not have the ability to enforce their property rights since the costs of enforcing them have been prohibitive due to the sheer size of available public lands in relation to the funds available to governments. Further, colonization of public lands has provided an escape valve to brewing social tensions in other areas, particularly in the face of strong migratory flows of laborers without employment opportunities in traditional rural or urban settings. In many cases, geopolitical interests have often encouraged the colonization of previously unoccupied areas, as in the Brazilian Amazon and Guatemala's Petén.

These migrants are attracted to the frontier because they can gain access to land and establish their rights by clearing the forest. In these areas, deforestation is a practical method to increase tenure security (Southgate 1990a; Kaimowitz 1995b). Forest clearing followed by attempts at cropping or livestock production increases the likelihood of rudimentary commerce flows and further migration, which may eventually attract a government presence and a significant increase in the price of land (Mueller et al. 1994).

Aside from the open access of public lands, Latin American governments typically induce deforestation in the frontier with other tenure-related policies. On public lands, removal of the forest cover has traditionally been a requirement for titling. This has been documented to be a major factor in frontier agricultural conversion in Costa Rica, Ecuador, Honduras, Panama and other Latin American countries (Kaimowitz 1995b; Peuker 1992; Mahar and Schneider 1994; Southgate and Whitaker 1992). In recent years, a greater awareness of the deleterious effects of the land-clearing requirement has led to its elimination in several countries of the region. However, even where it has been formally removed, it continues to be required in practice, possibly reflecting the absence of alternative, low-cost methods to assign individual rights in newly settled areas.

On lands with formal property rights held by individuals, some deforestation has been shown to be encouraged by a variety of government policies. In some cases, forest removal is promoted by laws which threaten "idle" lands with expropriation or with higher land taxes. The rapid removal of forests in Paraguay in recent years has been attributed to this phenomenon (López and Ocaña 1994). In other cases, legal provisions that require payment for land "improvements" (i.e., removal of trees) have motivated squatters to clear forests in private lands. Such inducements have been at work recently in Nicaragua (Kaimowitz 1995b). In some countries, deforestation is encouraged by policies that separate ownership of land from forest resources (known as *vuelo*), particularly when trees are legally owned by governments. In such cases, lack of enforcement capacity makes forests on private lands an open access resource.

In summary, tenure problems are among the key causes of rapid deforestation in Latin America. Tenure insecurity in agricultural lands prevents a more rational and labor-intensive use of lands that could reduce migratory pressures to the frontier. In frontier areas, the inability of governments to enforce their property rights, and other misguided policies, promote removing the forest cover.

Property Rights to Agricultural Lands

Recent advances in the study of the evolution of tenure systems suggest that the establishment of formal individual rights is a critical step on the road to agricultural intensification (Binswanger et al. 1995; Otsuka et al. 1996; Feder and Feeney 1991). While most countries in Latin America have cadastral and registry institutions designed to fulfill these needs, informal and uncertain property rights are still prevalent in many areas of the region (Jaramillo 1997). It is estimated that less than 50 percent of farmers in the region have legal title over their lands (López and Valdés 1997).

This part argues that a well functioning system for assigning and enforcing formal property rights in settled agricultural lands is a critical element in any strategy to reduce deforestation pressures in Latin America. Simply put, if farmers have access to secure property, this should facilitate agricultural intensification and employment generation in settled areas which will then reduce demographic pressures on forest resources as well as reduce the demand for additional agricultural output.

This analysis looks at the expected effects of extending secure property rights to farmers who lack them. It proposes that a greater security of ownership should increase productivity, labor use, and the efficiency of land market transactions. Secure property rights are therefore a necessary element in a strategy of agricultural intensification and employment generation. These should also be complemented with measures to spur labor demand in rural areas and urban demand in other sectors. However, increased tenure security must be preceded by removing policy biases to forestall further land concentration and the under-utilization of productive lands.

Productivity
Generally, secure individual property rights over land induces an exertion of higher levels of labor and management effort and higher levels of investment to protect or enhance land fertility (Feder and Feeney 1991). Theoretical models developed by Feder et al. (1988) illustrate that increased security of tenure is expected to enhance the productivity of farmers through at least two channels. One is the "intensification effect," which reflects the effects of land tenure security on the incentives to invest, particularly in capital goods attached to land. If there is a positive probability that the current operator may not be allowed to reap the long-term benefits of current investments, investments levels are reduced in comparison with a situation of secure property. Although intensification in established agricultural areas can reduce deforestation by tying up labor and/or capital,

similar intensification in frontier areas may have the opposite effect as it will make agriculture more profitable on new lands and thus promote further agricultural expansion.

The second way to increase farming productivity through tenure is to increase allocative efficiency by relaxing of the credit constraints typically faced by farmers without title. With limited access to credit, farmers allocate inputs under quantitative constraints. With secure title as collateral, these constraints are eliminated and farmers can borrow freely to increase their application of inputs to profit-maximizing levels.

Productivity may also increase through more indirect channels. Secure rights will induce a more rational use of the natural resources associated with the land—such as water and trees—as farmers take into account their long-term benefits. Of course, this does not mean that no tree removal will occur since there may be alternative activities that yield a higher private return. Greater tenure security also reduces the costs of defending uncertain rights, allowing more time and resources for productive activities.

Despite the prevalence of tenure insecurity in many areas of the Latin American countryside, few studies have looked empirically into the actual consequences of increasing the security of property rights for farmers. An early study by Strasma and Barbosa (1984) concluded that farmers with title in the Brazilian state of Maranhão earned significantly higher income than squatters. A more detailed empirical study was carried out by Feder et al. (1988) for Thailand, and found that a secure title increased productivity mainly through greater access to credit. However, studies by Seligson and Nesman (1989) and Stanfield and Nesman (1990) about the effects of USAID-financed land titling projects in Honduras yielded ambiguous results; they provided no clear support for a relationship between land title and productivity or farm income.

Recent studies in Paraguay by Carter and Olinto (1996), in Honduras by López (1996) and in Brazil by Alston, Libecap and Schneider (1996) confirm that land tenure security is an important factor affecting farmers' use of variable purchased inputs and their level of land-attached investments (see Box 7.1). These studies also make a valuable methodological contribution by recognizing that simple correlations between tenure status and production are likely to exaggerate titling effects, since other household characteristics (e.g., education, income, assets, soil quality) may be responsible for the greater productivity of certain segments of farmers. Results from the three countries confirm that the productivity/titling link is strong enough to correct for other possible causes of higher productivity. However, the studies for Honduras and Paraguay find that only a minority of farmers can take effective advantage of the effects of greater tenure security through credit access, since most poor smallholders do not have access to formal credit regardless of tenure status.

Aside from the constraints imposed by a limited access to credit, assigning formal property rights to farmers may not lead to increased productivity in some Latin American contexts. Formal title may not actually increase tenure security when the institutions that guarantee and enforce property rights—i.e., the cadastre, registry, judicial and police systems—do not work effectively. This is particularly true in remote areas where there is little presence from government agencies. Furthermore, many titling efforts exhibit design flaws that reduce their effectiveness. A key issue has been the high cost of the titling procedures. When these costs are borne by the beneficiaries, many small farmers are excluded from the process. Even when governments have subsidized the majority of expenses, net costs per title tend to be high, calling into question the wisdom of the investment from a social standpoint (Wachter and English 1992). In some large titling projects, formal title has been granted to farmers without their inscription in public registries. In

Box 7.1 The Effects of Land Titling in Honduras and Paraguay

Economic theory suggests that land tenure security should enhance the productivity and income of farmers, but this hypothesis has been difficult to prove in the Latin American context. The few studies available until recently looked at differences in means, or simple correlations that tend to overestimate the relationship, since the effect of omitted household characteristics (e.g., education, income, or assets) may be responsible both for greater tenure security and higher levels of productivity among certain segments of farmers.

Researchers have taken advantage of the availability of large farm household surveys in Honduras (López 1996) and Paraguay (Carter and Olinto 1996). Findings from both countries confirm that land title appears to significantly affect farming productivity. A pattern is revealed in which land title both enhances the demand for investment in capital goods attached to land and improves access to credit. In both Honduras and Paraguay, most of the income effect is derived from the greater access to credit. The investment demand effect is weaker and concentrated in land-attached capital goods.

In Honduras, the average household income of farmers that received titles increased by about $100 per year, reflecting an increase in per capita income of 5 percent. As a result, it appears that investing public funds to provide land titles, even without targeting populations most likely to obtain credit, can yield a high rate of return of at least 17 percent (López 1996).

However, in both countries title only enhances a formal credit supply for those farmers that satisfy a minimum level of education and a minimum land area (about 20 hectares). Only this group benefits from titling. Consequently, governments need to adopt complementary policies broadening access to capital markets, to avoid an inegalitarian distribution of the benefits from titling.

some particular cases, pre-existing informal institutions—such as common property schemes of close-knit communities—may have already granted sufficient tenure security, so that issuing formal titles has little effect on behavior patterns.[1]

Labor

Establishing firm and secure tenure rights to land in most Latin American countries would require eliminating legal provisions that threaten farmers with expropriation when they have tenants on their land. Tenants have benefited in the past from "land to the tiller" provisions that attempted to redistribute land away from large hacienda owners. However, traditional haciendas have mostly disappeared while these provisions have remained on the books. This situation has subsequently resulted in denying a means of access to land for many of the rural poor, promoting an under-utilization of lands, and fostering an adoption of productive technologies favoring non-labor inputs. Eliminating these provisions would reduce the perceived risks from renting out land and alter production activities in favor of labor. Naturally, these effects would be greatest well within the agricultural frontier, since at the frontier labor is scarce and more labor extensive practices may be justified.

---

[1] More discussion and some examples of tenure security and customary institutions appear in Rudel (1995) and Ostrom (1990).

Many Latin American countries facing high rural population growth need to adopt a strategy to promote labor-intensive growth in agriculture. The suppression of tenure-related risks to hiring labor and renting land could be an important ingredient of such a strategy. In addition, generating more rural jobs may be possible with complementary policies that focus on developing smallholder agriculture. This would include reforming the minimum wage and social security regulations that exert perverse employment effects. In the absence of effective land reform policies, access to land could be provided through rental agreements to segments of the rural landless population, a mechanism which has been shown to offer opportunities for social ascent in some East Asian countries (Otsuka 1993) as well as in the Brazilian Amazon (Lena 1991).

Land Markets

A well-functioning land market should facilitate transactions between land owners with high marginal productivity and those with low marginal productivity (Feder and Feeney 1991). This requires property rights that are universally recognized and fully tradable. However, with few exceptions, land markets across Latin America display serious inefficiencies (Jaramillo 1997). Land markets in the region tend to be informal, reflecting the widespread absence of formal property documents and institutions. Markets also tend to reflect transactions between members of limited communities, as informality aggravates problems of unequal information between seller and buyer. In this setting, theory suggests that the price of land often does not reflect its true social value and the extent of land transactions is thus less than optimal (Feder and Feeney 1991). The inadequate functioning of land markets contributes to explaining the persistence of underutilized agricultural lands in many Latin American countries (Jaramillo 1997).

Developing an effective system for assigning and enforcing secure property rights to land would aid in formalizing land market transactions and reduce inefficiencies and transaction costs. Most importantly, by facilitating the exit of low productivity farmers and the entry of potentially higher productivity farmers, it would promote a more intensive use of land and labor resources in settled areas which could lower incentives for deforestation in the frontier. The best example of a dynamic formal land market in the region is Chile. Strong institutions in that country guarantee land tenure rights and the result is a dynamic sales and rental market for agricultural land that has led to an intense use of land resources and the absorption of rural labor surpluses (Muñoz 1993).

Increasing the effectiveness of property rights systems to encourage formal land markets poses some inherent risks. Under the still prevalent regime of selective government support for certain influential farming groups, increased transactions may lead to greater land and income concentration (de Janvry et al. 1997). Also, if tax exemptions, high inflation and other nonproductive benefits of holding land continue to prevail, more land transactions could actually lead to a greater share of agricultural land devoted to low productivity activities. Thus, it seems essential to remove policy biases and reduce benefits for holding unproductive lands. This would be the only way to ensure that a more active and formal land market can induce more effective land usage, greater employment generation and diminished pressure on natural forests.

Despite the benefits described above, policies that guarantee a more efficient and neutral operation of land markets may face substantial barriers. More dynamic and formal land markets still confront many natural and government-induced costs relating to the search and registration of transactions (Jaramillo 1997). In addition, policies that favor medium and large-scale mechanized farmers have proven difficult to eliminate, even after the implementation of liberal reforms since the late 1980s (de Janvry et al. 1997). Most difficult may be the elimination of benefits for holding unproductive lands, since strong political interests will oppose the removal of favorable tax and credit programs.

Complementary Policies

Increased tenure security can be an important element in any strategy to promote a more intensive and sustainable pattern of agricultural development. However, other measures are also important in such a strategy. Most importantly, policy biases which have served in the past to promote patterns of growth based on labor-saving technologies must be eliminated. These include selective protection and tax measures, research and extension, credit and marketing subsidies and artificially low prices for inputs, including machinery. These policies have traditionally benefited only large mechanized farmers. In a new strategy, the removal of these policies must be complemented with promoting smallholding sectors to encourage a pattern of agricultural growth with intensive labor. Policies should include the promotion of credit sources for small farmers, the suppression of labor market regulations that artificially increase the cost of hiring rural labor, and the redirection of public investment into infrastructure, research and extension for the benefit of smallholders.

A more difficult issue to deal with is whether substantial resources should be used to promote farming at or near the frontier by populations of recent migrants. There are several reasons why this is likely to be an inappropriate use of public resources. First, scant public funds for research, extension and other services should be oriented towards those areas with high population density where they are likely to have a greater impact. Second, investment in recently settled lands tends to increase land values and attract more migrants to the forest (López 1997). Third, frontier areas are characterized by a low labor-to-land ratio that requires technologies that are less labor intensive than in other areas. Finally, development of technologies appropriate for marginal agricultural lands is likely to induce deforestation in areas more apt for forest uses. Therefore, research and extension efforts should have a greater social payoff if they are directed at developing technologies that improve the profitability of more intensive production systems. Such efforts should reduce deforestation pressures (Kaimowitz and Angelsen 1997).

Conclusion

Stronger individual property rights in settled agricultural areas are a necessary element in a strategy to intensify agriculture and reduce pressures on forest resources in Latin America. Increased productivity, lower costs of hiring labor and an increased efficiency of land markets should promote employment opportunities and reduce demand for additional agricultural lands.

However, policymakers should note that land tenure policies are not likely to be enough in achieving these results. To ensure favorable effects, increased tenure security must be preceded by the removal of policy biases that facilitate land concentration and under-utilization. Furthermore, measures should be adopted to spur employment generation in both urban and rural settings in nonagricultural activities. Governments must take care to avoid promoting labor-saving (mechanized) agricultural intensification, as this may displace laborers and encourage out-migration into forested areas.

Property Rights to Forested Lands

The analysis of property rights to forested lands with little potential for sustained agriculture is more complex than in settled agricultural areas. In these areas, private and social values about removing forest cover may differ greatly and some of the damages caused may be irreversible.[2] Agents responsible for forest clearing do not perceive the bulk of the negative effects caused by deforestation, such as, for example, diminished carbon sequestration and downstream sedimentation effects. In the absence of any first best interventions to enable settlers to internalize these values, granting individual property rights to forested lands may not be the most appropriate way to maximize social welfare.

The complexity of property rights issues on the frontier is compounded by the lack of empirical evidence on how settlers behave under different tenure regimes on forested areas. This is partially explained by the high costs of reaching target populations in remote areas. Many of the critical research questions require expensive studies to determine how forest clearing patterns of settlers respond over time to different tenurial regimes as well as to other variables. Until more definitive research is conducted, conclusions about the impact of property rights on natural resource use must be treated as tentative.

Despite the above reservations, this section argues that tenure issues loom large in motivating forest clearing in frontier areas. However, the available evidence suggests that unrestricted individual property rights seem ineffective in preventing massive clearing of forests at the frontier. Hence, a policy of indiscriminate privatization of forests is unlikely to arrest deforestation trends. Keeping forests under alternative property regimes, including state, common property and restricted individual private property, may be better options for governments in the region. However, effective methods to prevent forest destruction on lands held under these property regimes must be devised.

Unrestricted Individual Property Rights

Proponents of individual property rights in forested frontier areas argue that secure tenure arrangements should induce a more rational rate of exploitation of natural resources and a reduction in deforestation rates.[3] According to this viewpoint, there are several reasons that justify this conclusion. First, individual property rights to lands of differing agricultural potential should lead settlers to concentrate productive efforts where they are most likely to be most profitable and sustainable in the long term. Second, settlers with secure long-term rights should be more likely to keep standing forests because they are certain to capture future income streams derived from the exploitation of forest products and services. They will also bear the costs of local long-term damages from forest clearing. Third, once they obtain secure formal title, settlers do not need to continue to clear land to enforce their informal property claims. These arguments have been formalized in a model by Mendelsohn (1994), according to which increasing certainty about property rights should reduce deforestation rates.[4]

---

[2] Farming activities can also occasion substantial external damages, such as siltation and leakage of harmful chemicals.

[3] See, for example, Southgate and Whitaker (1992).

[4] A recent model by Otsuki (1997) demonstrates that increasing tenure security on forested lands may *not* reduce deforestation, if there are strong migratory pressures and weak land rights institutions.

There are various reasons why these motivations are likely to be insufficient to significantly slow down deforestation in the Latin American context.[5] First, migratory flows to the frontiers continue to be large and, in many areas, demand for land far surpasses the amount suitable for long-term agricultural exploitation. This is reflected in the growing share of deforestation that is taking place in areas with easily degradable soils. In addition, prior knowledge by settlers or government officials about the quality of soils and their long-term potential for agriculture is often incomplete.

Second, the bulk of the settlers in frontier areas are usually poor and exhibit high discount rates. Therefore, they are not likely to value the long-term private benefits of keeping forests intact. Even the local long-term costs of removing trees is likely to be of little concern to people with high discount rates.

Third, the available evidence suggests that the timber and nontimber values of the standing forest yields low private profitability compared to alternatives associated with removing the forest cover (Southgate 1997). A detailed comparison of alternative land uses in Costa Rica showed that under most realistic scenarios, clearing forests for agriculture and livestock activities is more profitable for private farmers (Kishor and Constantino 1993). This conclusion seems to be also valid in most frontier areas of the Amazon basin. A corollary to this point is that settlers may be more likely to deforest their land in favor of cattle pasture if they are secure in their ownership and can count on making a livelihood through livestock in the long-term. Conversely, an insecure tenure situation may actually prevent deforestation, since most settlers would not convert forest to pasture if they thought they would lose access to the land in a relatively short time period.

Fourth, while removing the forest cover does play an important role in strengthening a settler's claim over a given land area, it also achieves other important goals. Demonstrating that the land can be used in the short run for agricultural and livestock activities increases the likelihood that other settlers will populate the region. This, in turn, promotes greater commercial flows that will reduce marketing costs and justify public and private investments in transport infrastructure. Roads are often followed by the presence of government institutions, including those dedicated to securing property rights to land, as well as a larger pool of potential investors interested in land investments (Schneider 1995).

This cycle of increasing integration of remote areas into the formal economy offers the potential for land price appreciation and significant capital gains for initial settlers (Mueller et al. 1994; Mueller 1997). Sales of land can occur at different stages of this cycle (Lena 1991; Alston et al. 1996). Revenues from these sales can be used by settlers as starting capital for new migration ventures, to intensify agricultural production in remaining lands, or to purchase livestock (Lena 1991; Schneider 1995). Hence, the purpose of forest clearing usually goes beyond increasing tenure security.

Finally, even if secure property rights could reduce deforestation incentives, it is not clear that in most forested frontier areas of Latin America, governments have the capacity to assign and enforce these rights at a reasonable cost. It is likely that in many forested areas the costs of titling programs and establishing enforcement institutions would be large in relation to the social benefits. These investments become profitable only when population densities and the economic activity in a zone reach a certain level that can justify establishing a government presence and initiating formal tenure security measures.

---

[5] The discussion of some of these arguments is drawn from Kelly (1996).

Existing accounts of the deforestation/colonization cycle in the Brazilian Amazon do not indicate that deforestation rates fall when government agencies move in to clarify and establish definitive property rights (Alston et al. 1996; Schneider 1995; Mueller et al. 1994; Mueller 1997; Lena 1991). Typically, forests are gradually removed to plant food crops and sell valuable timber products. Eventually, falling fertility leads to converting crop land to pastures for livestock. Whether property rights are secure from the beginning of the cycle, as in government-sponsored colonization schemes, or only in the later stages, when most of the land has been converted to pasture, incentives for removing the tree cover seem to continue even after the issue of land title.

At least three reasons explain this phenomenon. First, the income-generating possibilities offered by standing forests are usually limited, especially once the most valuable logs are removed. Second, cleared land in frontier areas is almost always worth more than forested land (Mueller et al. 1994; Paveri 1997). Third, activities like establishing pastures and raising cattle are often more attractive to settlers (de Janvry and García 1992). As market links are developed, demand for grazing lands increases and offers settlers the possibility of obtaining large capital gains. Further, in areas with limited access to capital markets, investing in livestock is a practical method of accumulating savings and providing insurance for future emergencies. Among the production alternatives at the frontier, cattle are attractive because their sale price tends to be more stable than that of other crops, and ranching reduces the agronomic risks of production. Besides, livestock can "transport itself" to market, an important advantage in areas with poor infrastructure. Compared to most other income-earning alternatives, cattle raising requires little labor and keeps the land "occupied," and safe from expropriation or payment of high land taxes. In addition, government policies in several countries—including Brazil, Ecuador and some Central American nations—have often supported cattle raising with cheap credit and other fiscal incentives (Binswanger 1991).

There is little empirical evidence linking deforestation to individual property rights and other variables at the microlevel in Latin American countries. One of the few empirical clues to the influence of property rights on deforestation patterns at the frontier is offered by an ongoing research project managed by members of the International Food Policy Research Institute (IFPRI) in the Brazilian Amazon. The project administered a detailed survey in 1994 and 1996 to 150 small to medium-scale households in two colonization projects in two states of the western Brazilian Amazon (Acre and Rondonia).[6] Sites were selected so as to include areas of varying soil quality, access to infrastructure, and time since initial settlement of the plots.

Preliminary results suggest that greater tenure security is not associated with diminished deforestation activities. On the contrary, the data indicate that definitive title holders removed significantly more forest than did those without title (Witcover and Vosti 1997).[7] It is still unclear whether the results can be extended to other areas.[8] However, they confirm recent findings from an alternative source in six sites in the state of Pará (Brazil), where no significant effect of land title on clearing was detected.[9]

---

[6] The questionnaire of the 1994 survey appears in Witcover and Vosti (1996) and the preliminary results in Witcover et al. (1996).

[7] Holders of definitive titles also tended to place more of their already cleared land into pasture, at the expense of annual and perennial crops (Witcover and Vosti 1997).

[8] IFPRI researchers are still refining the analysis of tenure categories and attempting to obtain price and soil quality information, which could also be important determinants of deforestation patterns.

[9] Findings of research conducted by Lee Alston, Gary Libecap and Robert Schneider, as reported in Pfaff (1997).

Box 7.2 Determinants of Deforestation by Indigenous Communities in Honduras

A recent study among the Tawahka, an indigenous community of the Honduran rainforest, examines the household determinants of decisions to cut old-growth forest. The Tawahka live in five settlements along the Patuca river in eastern Honduras, living by slash-and-burn cultivation and intensive agriculture along river banks. They plant a variety of products, including cacao, beans, bananas, plantains, maize and rice.

   A Tobit model was employed to explain the area of old-growth rain forest removed per household. Results indicated that residence duration (an indicator of more longstanding rights of property to land) lowers forest clearance. The longer households have lived in a village, the less likely they are to clear forest, probably because they have more secure usufruct rights to their land (although lack of information about formal ownership of plots precludes drawing conclusions about the relationship between property rights and deforestation).

The evidence from Brazil is contradicted by a recent study among Tawahka communities of eastern Honduras by Godoy et al. (1997) (see Box 7.2). This study uses econometric methods to explain clearing of old-growth rainforest in 1995. The authors use residence duration as a proxy for strength of property rights. The results show that the longer households have lived in a village, the less likely they are to clear old-growth forest, in part because they have more secure rights to their land. By contrast, new residents have to clear more land to open up farming areas and establish land rights. In addition, households that were able to borrow—usually a sign of access to formal title to land—cut less primary forest than households that did not obtain credit. Unfortunately, the results of the study are not conclusive due to the absence of explicit tenure information.

A recent study of land management issues in Guatemala qualitatively reviews the effects of property rights institutions on resource use (World Bank 1995a). It concludes that excessive forest clearing is a problem found in all tenure types, including public, private and cooperative. The study finds that economic and social pressures yield stronger incentives for forest exploitation and conversion than incentives induced by tenure. In an environment where short-term returns to agriculture are high, strong individual property rights do not seem to affect the rate of destruction of natural forests.

In addition to the evidence reviewed, studies from across the region suggest that public policies have contributed to weakening the effects of formal private property on sustainable forest use. Traditional policies that required land clearing to obtain title have been strong promoters of deforestation. For owners holding titles, land and income taxes have promoted productive uses and discouraged forest protection. In addition, providing cheap credit, marketing subsidies and road construction have all increased the profitability of agriculture and ranching activities. To make matters worse, policies establishing that trees are public resources standing on private lands have encouraged excessive forest exploitation. Such policies have artificially reduced private efforts to manage forests sustainably while inducing rapid conversion to uses that are often less valuable from a social standpoint.

More empirical research needs to be conducted before the deforestation/property rights linkage is properly understood. However, preliminary findings suggest that assigning individual property rights does not seem to provide an easy solution to the problem of excessive deforestation.

Public Property of Forest Lands

If privatizing forest lands is not the best strategy to reduce the rate of forest cover removal, alternative tenure regimes to individual private property need to be explored. An obvious alternative is to keep forested lands under public control. Examples of public forests that are well managed can be found in countries such as Canada, where 90 percent of forested lands are publicly owned, and in Europe, where at least 40 percent is public. What these countries have done is privatize the silvicultural activities in their forests rather than the land ownership. Thus, forest management and exploitation is contracted out by the state to private companies, NGOs or community groups and supervised by state institutions. Although the past performance of Latin American states in protecting their property interests in forests has not been encouraging, there is some progress in this direction, as witnessed by the new Forestry Law in Mexico that grants forest protection to private concessions (Paveri 1997).

Forests under public ownership have been traditionally managed under two broad regimes. First, governments have designated protected areas, banning all private use of forest resources. Second, limited and temporary user rights have been assigned to other agents. This is the case of timber concessions, where grants are made to private parties for the primary purpose of extracting logging resources. This is also the case of extractive reserves, in which user rights are granted to specific communities to primarily use the nontimber products of the standing forest. Another alternative has been implementation of forest management projects involving NGOs, local communities and public agencies.

Protected Areas. Parks, natural reserves and other protected areas are usually managed by government agencies. Theoretically, establishing a protected forest area is the most secure way to arrest deforestation where social and biological values are high. In practice, however, the success rate of Latin American governments in safeguarding protected areas is poor. Encroachment of parks and reserves has been documented in many countries (Chapter 3) and the continued invasion of many protected areas has been fueled by the lack of alternative sources of livelihood for migrating families. Often, parks and reserves occupy vast territories that cannot be adequately guarded by agencies with inadequate human and financial resources. The absence of effective enforcement for protected areas may be leading to perverse results, since illegal settlers who have no possibility of acquiring legal title have greater incentives to mine natural resources.

Recent experience suggests that protected forests can best be managed when agencies limit protected areas to those that can actually be policed with available funds. While a case can be made for expanding the funds dedicated for protection of sensitive areas, most Latin American governments face severe fiscal pressures that make it unlikely that substantial increases will be forthcoming in the short term.

Nevertheless, some success in increasing the effectiveness of protection efforts has been found in developing buffer zones around parks. These zones can be used by local communities to obtain nontimber products and services. In some cases, enforcement costs have been reduced by sharing responsibilities with governments and organizations at the local level. However, involvement of local populations in management of protected areas is not appropriate in all cases. A recent World Bank evaluation concluded that successful involvement of local interests in forestry and conservation management can be difficult when (a) conflicts over forest resources are particularly intense, (b) forest resources are abundant relative to a small dispersed population in the forest vicinity, (c) powerful interests at the national level are opposed to policy reform or to decentralization of authority, and (d) extreme social inequalities at the local level reinforce the control of forest benefits by local elites (Banerjee et al. 1995).

Logging Concessions. An alternative method to managing forest lands is to grant leases to private concessionaires for the exploitation of logging and other resources during a specified period of time. It is frequently argued that if leases are given for a sufficiently long period of time, then the management of forest resources should incorporate long-term considerations and promote a more rational use of timber and nontimber products and services (Panayotou 1989). In addition, where they have been implemented, logging concessions have usually been granted along with a management plan to exploit the forest in a sustainable fashion, allowing for forest regeneration. However, these plans have been criticized because they focus too narrowly on promoting the growth of timber products, while ignoring the intricate interrelationships between flora, fauna and other resources that govern the growth of tropical forests (Berry 1995).

The experience with large-scale logging concessions in Latin America is mixed. Many cases of destructive logging have been documented, as concession holders have found little resistance to ignoring management plans. Poor results are attributed to short-term leases, poor government supervision, corruption and lack of technical knowledge about the best possible logging practices (Panayotou 1989; Berry 1995; Motta 1992). Even in those countries where long-term concessions have been granted, institutional instability and the fear that logging permits may be revoked have led to a short-sighted mode of exploitation (World Bank 1995b).

In most instances, regeneration activities and sustainable practices are ignored because they impose short-term costs to logging concerns while promising uncertain private benefits. The political power of the logging industry has often thwarted attempts at enforcing strict regulations, as illustrated in the cases of Guatemala (World Bank 1995a) and Bolivia (see Chapter 9). In countries where strict requirements have been imposed, as in Colombia, loggers have opted to evade excessive costs by exploiting forests illegally (Berry 1995). In some cases, concessions have been granted without consulting the traditional forest-dwelling communities living in those areas and some lands have even been doubly titled to both the local dwellers and the concessionaires, causing severe conflicts (Paveri 1997).

Logging concessions have been blamed for accelerating deforestation. In most cases, access roads built by the logging companies have facilitated the penetration of slash and burn farmers into previously unreachable areas. Concession holders often do not have the capacity and/or the interest to stem the flow of settlers (World Bank 1995b).

New approaches to logging concessions are needed to eliminate their deleterious effects on forest resources. In many countries, this may require declaring a moratorium on issuing new concessions until institutions are strengthened and a better understanding is gained of the complex dynamics of tropical forest growth. A new concessions strategy should also include a greater involvement by local dwellers. They are often more effective managers and protectors of the forests, as has been shown in the case of concessions run by Pizano S.A. in Colombia (see Chapter 9).

Extractive Reserves. In recent years, the establishment of extractive reserves has received support from NGOs and governments interested in promoting sustainable forestry. The idea that local communities can obtain significant income-earning opportunities was bolstered by estimates of the value of nontimber products in the Peruvian Amazon (Peters et al. 1989) as well as growing interest in ecotourism. As a result, public forest lands in Latin America have increasingly been managed by specific communities who are granted user rights.[10] Extractive rights have been also allowed in buffer zones around protected areas in Integrated Conservation and Development Projects (ICDPs) (Wells and Brandon 1993). Proponents of these schemes argue that they involve local communities in managing the forest for the long term, thus increasing their incentives to stave off outsiders.

Yet reviews of the experience with extractive reserves reveal a number of problems. These arrangements have often failed because of the continued low value of virtually all nontimber forest products and services. This is not surprising, given that the optimistic valuation of nontimber products and services by Peter et al. (1989) did not reckon with the price impacts of a major increase in extractive activity (Southgate and Clark 1993). In addition, few sites offer any real potential for tourism development. For example, the extractive reserves created by the Seringueiros of Brazil, and carried on by the Pilot Program for the Protection of Brazil's Tropical Forests in 1992, have faced difficulties because of the diminishing market value of traditional forest products such as latex and Brazil nuts, as well as difficulties in organizing a dispersed population with little cooperation experience (Chapter 9). A further problem is that the users' rights are limited to extracting nontimber products, which are generally of lower value in the marketplace. If these rights were extended to extracting timber products (under a good forestry management plan), such reserves might be more successful (Paveri 1997).

Placing a value on the region's forest products and services is a much needed endeavor that has only recently gained the attention it deserves. Social and environmental values are extremely important but it is generally the economic incentives that will determine whether an area is deforested or not. When a standing forest can compete economically with agricultural or grazing uses, it is more likely to be preserved because it will be equally or higher valued. Whether its products are timber, nontimber, aesthetic, biological, social or environmental, a recognized value assigned to these would encourage forest preservation. There need to be strategies, policies and instruments that promote such valuation and support those who recognize it on their properties, be they public, private or communal. Owners would be less likely to deforest their properties if their forest products had a recognized economic value that could compete with other potential uses (Paveri 1997).

Sustainable Forest Management. Joint attempts to sustainably manage forests for wood and other products by NGOs, local communities and governments have often fallen short of their stated goals. Marc Dourojeanni (see Chapter 5) has reviewed a sample of attempts at forest management for wood production in Latin America, and concludes that the majority have failed. These failures seem primarily to be a result of a lack of economic profitability, pressures by settlers for land, and poor administrative management in state-run forests.

Alternative Tenure Arrangements

Frustration with the disappointing results of managing forest lands as public property suggests that governments should explore alternative tenurial arrangements. Possible alternatives include securing common property rights as well as establishing the legal

---

[10] However, transferring legal use rights to forest dwellers and local communities simply recognizes the rights of these de facto users.

framework to allow for restricted individual rights. New tenure regimes should be designed for specific situations and adapted to changing conditions (Foster and Stanfield 1993).

Common Property. Neoclassical economists have long opposed arrangements that give groups communal property rights to agricultural lands. The argument goes that without clear individual rights, production and work incentives are diffuse and individuals tend to exert a less than optimal work effort. However, recent research suggests that these arguments do not extend to managing common resources—such as forest lands—where conservation motives are also important.

Evidence on the success of traditional and indigenous arrangements for the management of natural resources has demonstrated that individual rights are not always superior to common property rights[11] (Quiggin 1993). Common property rights are efficient when they allow members to capture economies of scale or scope that would not be possible with individual rights (Quiggin 1993; Chopra and Gulati 1997). López (1997) argues that in certain circumstances, a shift from common property to private property may lead to large environmental and efficiency losses. Chopra and Gulati (1997) have recently found in India that a decrease in land under common property regimes accelerates environmental degradation and causes a migration from rural to urban areas.

Recent research efforts have focused on determining under what circumstances common property rights can be an efficient institutional arrangement. According to Ostrom (1990), conditions are best in small and stable communities, where individuals interact repeatedly to pursue the collective interest. In these settings, cooperation in the management of common resources is likely, particularly if individuals exhibit a strong concern for the future and possess the autonomy to create and enforce their own rules. Quiggin (1993) argues that common property management is efficient when performed by cohesive groups, characterized by family ties, traditions of mutual assistance, and an absence of sharp disparities in wealth.

Common property regimes have been shown to work well in preserving forests and other common resources in some long-established communities in Latin America (Foster and Stanfield 1993). This may partly reflect the greater knowledge and awareness researchers have of the importance to indigenous groups of forest land for environmental maintenance (Rudel and Horowitz 1993). A well known case is that of the Kuna Yala indigenous reserve in Panama. A strong political organization and favorable legal treatment have kept about 80 percent of the territory in largely undisturbed primary forest (IUCN 1996). In eastern Ecuador, between 70 and 90 percent of the primary forest cover has been kept intact in lands held under traditional customary rights without legal titles, mostly because of the success of community management regimes and the absence of settler pressure (Rudel 1995).

Despite the success of some communities in managing forests as common resources, these regimes have been shown to be fragile to disturbances from outside (de Janvry and García 1992). Rapid population growth, greater integration into the market economy and technological changes may weaken common property institutions and lead to open-access regimes. This is illustrated by the case of the Amerindian reserves created in Northwestern Brazil in the 1980s under the Polonoroeste projects. Protection against

---

[11] Common property is defined as the exclusive joint ownership and use of resources, and the prevention of outsiders from using those resources.

squatters and illegal logging and mining has failed because of the high profits that outsiders can obtain from these activities and the difficulties associated with guarding vast areas (Wachter 1992).

Common property regimes for managing forest resources seem to work best in areas facing low migratory pressures and where such an administration reaffirms the long-standing customary rights of access and forest use by local communities. In such areas, governments should strengthen these regimes by providing formal rights, assisting with border demarcation, and preventing encroachment from outsiders. In many countries, this requires recognizing land claims of indigenous and other ethnic communities. Governments must also realize that "formal" tenure rights may be less secure than already established informal tenure rights in traditional communities. In other words, titling programs that promote "formal" tenure may actually increase insecurity by undermining the security provided by existing informal systems. In addition, it should be recognized that such institutional arrangements may not be best suited to the conditions of an active frontier.

Restricted Individual Rights. Recent proposals designed to address unsustainable resource use have included the development of new tenure modes that allow restrictions on private property (Bowles et al.1996; Atmella 1995). Restrictions usually refer to how the natural resources in the titled area can be managed. Restricted individual rights may be useful to protect forests in lands both currently held by private parties and those still under state control.

In lands currently held by the private sector, new legal instruments are being designed to promote a more sustainable use of natural resources. These instruments include easements and conservation agreements. Easements facilitate the establishment of permanent restrictions on resource use on private lands. Such restrictions are often recorded in a public registry. However, easements still allow proprietors to retain ownership of their land and the right to use it for certain purposes. In Costa Rica, easements have been used in recent years to preserve patches of forest on private lands (Atmella 1995). Nevertheless, despite their effectiveness, establishing easements requires certain conditions that are not always easy to meet.

Conservation agreements are temporary binding agreements that restrict the use of resources. Usually, such an agreement commits the owner to managing his land according to specific terms in exchange for periodic payments. It should also be recognized that some legal instruments, like easements, are derived from the common law system, and may not necessarily be possible under civil law applications without modifications in the national legislation (Bowles et al. 1996). As with easements, conservation agreements require effective monitoring and enforcement mechanisms, in addition to the funding necessary to make payments to owners.

In forest lands held by the state, deforestation is, to a great extent, a result of the race by many competitors—such as poor migrants, ranchers, loggers, and land speculators—for rights of access (see Chapter 3). On such lands, a strategy of granting restricted private rights may help to halt this race and allow a more sustainable use of forests. Such a strategy could involve a preemptive privatization of public forest lands. This would establish certain restrictions on resource use as well as create strong legal provisions to prevent encroachers from obtaining rights to these lands.

In order to implement a process of privatizing public forest lands, governments would need to classify such areas into at least two broad groups. The first would comprise lands with agricultural potential—these would be transferred to farmers without resource use restrictions. The second group should include forested lands without agricultural potential, and would be transferred to private agents with restrictions to safeguard the forests. Governments should keep under public management some tracts that exhibit particularly high social or biological values.

Public lands with agricultural potential could be auctioned off in large tracts to the highest bidder. Such a measure would maximize government revenues from privatization, although it may exert a negative impact on the poor by effectively barring access to new lands for migrants. On the other hand, distributing such lands to poor settlers may have a positive equity effect and diminish pressure on remaining forest lands. In either case, the agricultural potential of land that has already been cleared should be maximized before committing new lands to deforestation, whether in public or private hands.

Lands without agricultural potential may be transferred to private interests under new property arrangements to ensure that the forests will be protected. However, legal instruments must be in place to guarantee that holders of restricted property rights can be made liable if they renege on their promise to manage forests or sell off to logging, ranching or mining interests. A promising possibility is to favor agents that are interested in keeping standing forests, such as NGOs or communities that live off of forest resources. Transferring restricted property rights to such organizations may work better than public ownership in cases where community associations or NGOs can more efficiently police forest borders. However, in many cases it is likely that they will need to seek funding from national and international sources to enforce their rights.

The success of private efforts to sustainably manage forests would hinge to a great extent on the strength of migration pressures. If the latter remain unabated, it is unlikely that even the most committed NGOs can keep settlers off their land. Therefore, measures to transfer rights to private and nonprofit interests need to be complemented with policies that create income and employment opportunities elsewhere. This may be partly achieved by transferring to poor populations those remaining public lands that have agricultural potential.

Finally, governments have within their power to legislate how rural and forested lands are to be used. For example, Brazil has a law that obligates rural land owners to maintain 20 to 80 percent of their land in natural vegetation, with the percentage varying according to the region (see Chapter 5). Most if not all of the region's current forestry laws include restrictions on tree cutting and require permits for any type of forest use. These laws apply to both public and private owners. However, despite such restrictions, the laws have not inhibited (and in many cases appear to be the cause of) more deforestation (Paveri 1997).

Complementary Tax Measures. A variety of tax-related measures may be used as a complement to promote sustainable resource use. Alternative land uses may be promoted or discouraged with a scheme of land taxes favoring forests. For example, areas under natural forests could be subjected to low land taxes while those used for pasture or agricultural uses could be taxed at higher rates. In addition, easements and conservation agreements could be promoted by granting lower tax rates or land valuations to any areas committed to these regimes.

There are several practical difficulties with proposals to diminish deforestation incentives based on land tax policies. First, in order to be implemented they require the operation of an effective land tax, a feature that is still absent in most Latin American countries. The development of land taxes in the region has been hampered by both political opposition from landed interests and by high administrative costs (Jaramillo 1997). Second, varying tax rates according to land use require strong monitoring institutions which are generally lacking in the region. Third, application of such taxes require a fundamental change in the philosophy and legal framework of traditional land use policy in Latin America, which has favored productive activities and discourages "unproductive" use.

Other tax policies that may be used to discourage deforestation are income tax deductions for donations of land for conservation uses (Bowles et al. 1996). Tax deductions can also be implemented for expenses incurred in protecting forests from destruction. Furthermore, income derived from sustainable forest use could be exempted from taxation. Central governments should also consider increasing the allocation of fiscal budgets to municipalities that make significant efforts to directly protect forests or by enacting local incentives for the private sector.

Conclusion

The experience reviewed in this part suggest that establishing unrestricted individual property rights in frontier areas does not guarantee a better use of forest resources nor an end to deforestation pressures. The empirical evidence currently available does not allow solid generalizations about the link between deforestation and property rights, but micro evidence from Brazil and Guatemala indicates that establishing clear rights does not reduce land-clearing activities. This seems to be fundamentally explained by the superior private profitability of alternative productive activities. Hence, alternative property regimes in forested areas seem to be necessary to discourage excessive removal of trees.

For the most part, Latin American governments do not, at present, have the means to enforce property rights to public forest lands. In long-established areas with a low population density and cohesive communities, common property regimes may be an efficient method of managing forest resources. However, these are not appropriate for active frontier areas, where new tenure regimes must be designed to discourage the expansion of settlements. One possibility is to transfer restricted property rights to private agents or NGOs. Selection of these agents may be made on the basis of their capacity to preserve forest resources, including access to funding for safeguarding forest resources. Lower land taxes and favorable income tax treatment can also help induce more sustainable forest use.

Property rights policies alone cannot be the central element of a strategy to reduce deforestation pressures. Regardless of tenure policies, forest clearing is likely to persist if settled areas do not offer sufficient employment opportunities to potential migrants. Furthermore, deforestation trends will endure if government policies continue supporting land clearing by granting *ex post* property rights to settlers and increasing the private profitability of alternative, unsustainable land uses.

Policy Recommendations

The arguments developed in this document indicate that efforts to provide secure property rights should be an important part of any policies designed to reduce the pace of deforestation in Latin America. Granting more secure property rights should (a) increase the intensity of use of current agricultural land and generate more employment opportunities in settled areas, and (b) contribute to a more economically rational use of forest resources in frontier areas. The analysis presented here suggests that securing individual property rights is likely to be more important in settled agricultural areas. In forested areas, common property regimes and the design of restricted property rights institutions should facilitate sustainable management of forest resources by private parties.

The success of new tenure regimes in forested areas will hinge on reducing migratory flows from established rural and urban areas. Hence, tenure reforms alone are not likely to be sufficient to deal with deforestation problems in Latin America. Measures to strengthen property rights need to be accompanied by complementary policies. Most importantly, traditional macroeconomic and sectoral policies that have encouraged an extensive, unsustainable pattern of agricultural growth must be eliminated. In addition, policies that induce the settlement of areas better left under forest cover must be revised. Such policies have generally facilitated colonization (as in the case with road building) or encouraged unsustainable settlement (as in *ex post* titling, credit and marketing subsidies).

The following section presents policy recommendations about property rights regimes aimed at reducing deforestation pressures. The recommendations are grouped into three categories. The first category presents more general policies that would affect all forested areas. The second group includes policies only dealing with land in established agricultural areas. The third category addresses policy recommendations just for forested and frontier lands.

Policies for All Lands

Latin American governments must establish clear zoning and land use planning policies designed to establish which lands are suitable for agricultural use and which are better left under forests or other uses (Chapter 3). This requires completing comprehensive mapping and soil quality studies. In those countries where such soil and land use plans have already been drawn up, these need to be activated and used in decisionmaking about land use. Making zoning and land quality information widely available may also serve to shift deforestation to undeveloped areas that have greater agricultural potential or to forests of lesser biological and social value. Land use conflicts may be reduced if planning precedes colonization and resource use activities. Zoning efforts may also facilitate planning decisions about the property right regimes allowed on each type of land. However, to be effective, zoning policies must be accompanied by effective instruments to implement them.

Most countries in Latin America must undertake efforts to strengthen government institutions that support property rights. In particular, technical strengthening of cadastral and registry agencies is urgently needed. Each country will have to adopt new regulations according to whether its political system is federal or unitary, but the end result will be the same. After these institutions are functioning sufficiently, property rights will start to have practical results.

Policies for Agricultural Areas

In settled agricultural areas, two types of policies are important for reducing deforestation pressures elsewhere. First, tenurial policies are critical to strengthening individual property rights and stimulating agricultural intensification. Second, complementary policies are required to promote a more efficient pattern of land use and greater employment in agricultural activities. However, removing policy biases should precede efforts to strengthen property rights in order to increase the likelihood that property rights measures have their intended effect. The following tenure policies could contribute to reducing excessive land clearing:

Promote the establishment of individual property rights over untitled agricultural lands. Efforts should focus on two fronts: established agricultural areas and undeveloped areas with productive potential. In the latter, transferring land titles to poor migrants may be justified with equity arguments and should reduce pressure on valuable forest lands. However, every effort needs to be made to prioritize giving title to those lands already cleared of forest rather than promoting further cutting of untouched forests, even if they are on potentially productive lands. In established agricultural areas, the poor success rate of many prior titling efforts must be overcome through strengthening titling institutions, implementing lower cost methods and other measures. Titling efforts need to be preceded by macroeconomic and sectoral reforms that promote a labor-intensive pattern of agricultural development. Such projects must be included in long-term plans to increase the security of property rights in rural areas, including institutional strengthening of cadastral and registry agencies. To reduce titling costs, private sector services may be specially contracted for surveying and mapping. Subsidies that make titles affordable for poor farmers may prevent undesirable income distribution effects.

Eliminate barriers to land sales and land rentals. Many countries still restrict the sale or rental of farms given by governments in colonization or land reform programs. These restrictions produce informalities in land markets and have been shown to reduce the price of land. Most importantly, they limit the efficiency of land markets in ensuring that lands are owned by those who can use them most intensely and obtain the highest returns. In order for such transactions to function properly, however, government agencies and policies must be in place to monitor sales and rentals. Otherwise, land buyers will continue to purchase cleared areas from poor migrant settlers, who will in turn invade virgin forests (or indigenous lands or parks), clear the forests, and then sell their plots once again to legitimate land buyers in a form of land speculation. Thus, a legal and technical capacity must exist to control land sales and rentals and their subsequent titling.

Remove tenurial policies that introduce risks to hiring rural labor. The outdated legal provisions that grant tenurial advantages to farm workers, squatters or sharecroppers reduce the security of property rights and increase perceived labor costs. Removal of these provisions should increase labor utilization in farming activities. In addition, they may reduce obstacles to renting underutilized lands.

To ensure the success of the favorable effects of the tenure policies listed above, complementary policies must accompany any strengthening of individual property rights. This can be accomplished by the following five steps:

- Modify macroeconomic and sectoral policies that stimulate inefficient uses of land, particularly those that generate little employment in areas with labor surpluses, such as cattle raising and mechanized agriculture. This implies maintaining the current policies that are not in favor of overvalued exchange rates nor credit subsidies. Favorable tax and tariff treatment for farmers growing mechanized crops should be eliminated.

- Reform current labor market provisions to stimulate a more intensive use of labor in agriculture, including regulations that artificially increase the cost of hiring rural labor in farm activities.

- Promote the development of appropriate credit sources for the smallholder sector in order to improve its response to increased tenure security.
- Redirect public investment in infrastructure, research and extension for the benefit of smallholders to promote a pattern of agricultural growth that is labor intensive. These investments must be concentrated in areas where they are likely to have a greater effect on employment generation and on reducing deforestation pressures. Providing more infrastructure and technologies in frontier areas should be limited to prevent further increases in land values and continued migration flows.
- Adopt complementary measures to increase employment generation in nonagricultural activities in both urban and rural settings.

Policies for Forested Areas

Tenure policies in forested areas also have an important role to play in reducing deforestation pressures. The policy agenda for this sector should include the following recommendations.

Eliminate requiring proof of land clearing in order to obtain legal title or credit in forested lands. Where legal norms still require land clearing to obtain title, these must be suppressed.

End support of formal and informal colonization efforts in areas without agricultural potential. This requires refusing to grant *ex post* legal title to settlers and stopping the practice of promising "agricultural" lands in forested areas to landless farmers. It also entails eliminating programs that support agricultural uses and road construction in such areas.

Defend and enforce protected areas. This may imply adjusting the size of protected areas to what may be effectively protected with available resources. In some cases, valuable biological resources may be safeguarded only by a substantial increase in park policing efforts. Where feasible, local communities should be involved in managing protected areas, including designating sections of the forest as extractive areas and promoting ecotourism activities (but only when an area's protection category allows it).

Design new tenure arrangements to preserve forest lands, with three principles:

- Long-term concessions for commercial logging should be subject to the availability of proven technologies for managing the forest, effective government supervision of management plans, and the protection of forest-dweller rights. Concessions to local forest dwellers should be promoted for reasons of equity and sustainability.
- Common property rights to forested lands can be an effective method of preserving forest resources where the population density is low and where the tenure regimes reaffirm local communities' long-standing customary rights of access and forest use. Governments should strengthen customary rights by granting title to indigenous communities and other traditional communities, and assist these groups in demarcating their borders and enforcing their rights against squatters.
- Property rights to the remaining public forest areas should be transferred to nonpublic interests in order to preempt the race for those rights. Such transfers should put in practice new legal instruments that permit restricted property rights. They must also be complemented with strong legal provisions to prevent encroachers from obtaining rights to these lands. Transfers should favor those landowners who display the capacity to protect the forests, including NGOs or communities that live off forest resources. These transfers may be carried out through long-term leases that include strict forest

management provisions. Long contract periods would ensure that leaseholders would care about long-term benefits and use the forests sustainably.

Promote pilot efforts to enact local land taxes, with higher rates for pasture and croplands than for forest uses.

Support further case studies regarding tenure issues as a factor in the excessive clearing of forests in Latin America.

The effects of securing property rights are better understood in agricultural areas, where empirical studies have found a strong effect of tenure security on agricultural output and income. However, the complexity of frontier dynamics does not allow for simple generalizations between property rights and tenure security in the remaining forest areas of the region. Thus further research and analysis of case studies is needed to improve understanding of the complex relationship between tenure status and land clearing, particularly in frontier areas.

CHAPTER 8

Rights of Indigenous Peoples over Tropical Forest Resources

Julio C. Tresierra

Introduction

Latin America's tropical rainforest is being exploited and deforested by agents who had little or no contact with indigenous communities 50 years ago. As a result, the native communities of the tropical rainforest must make continual adjustments if they are to survive. Over the last 40 years, loss of biological diversity has eroded their material base for survival and loss of their traditional culture has undermined their values and social structures.

The first section of this chapter describes the exogenous and endogenous changes that affect the aboriginal groups of the Latin American rainforest and their environment. Possible strategies are suggested for the economic development of native communities, without negating the value of their traditional usage of natural resources. Changes in legislation concerning indigenous groups and natural resources are described in the chapter's second section, which also describes difficulties in enforcing the legislation. The chapter appendix outlines the evolution of national laws and international conventions bearing on these groups, their territories, and their access to and use of natural resources.

Indigenous Groups and Their Changing Environment

Although it is difficult to exhaustively catalog the native groups of Latin America, each country's legislation defines particular indigenous groups as possessing certain rights and obligations. These are tribal communities who have traditionally lived in the rainforests—termed "indigenous peoples," "indigenous communities," or "native communities" in the legislation of Ecuador, Colombia, and Peru, respectively (Mertins 1996).[1] They live in small kinship-based groups dispersed in immense forests, particularly in the tropical lowland of the Amazon. With low population densities, they have obtained or lay claim to land tenure systems that are consistent with their management systems. Traditionally they have followed a vision and moral order allowing the sustainable use of natural resources. These societies have great cultural and linguistic diversity, mirroring the rich variety of their physical context and their highly scattered small settlements, which limit the power of each tribal group to dominate others (see Smith 1996).

For these traditional societies, the production of goods has an essentially social purpose, to maintain and reproduce ties between local societies. Historically they have

---

[1] This chapter does not cover indigenous settlers who came originally from the highlands, such as the Aymara in the Chapare of Bolivia, or the Kekchi in Petén of Guatemala. These and other groups like the rural Andean indigenous and mestizo populations, sometimes referred to as *campesinos*, use agricultural techniques very different from the tribal communities' methods of managing natural resources.

Table 8.1 Amazon Basin: Territorial Distribution and Indigenous Population, 1973–97

Country	No. of ethnic groups	Estimated indigenous population	Total population	Area in km²	Percent of land in Amazon	Land set aside for ethnic groups (km²)
Bolivia	31	171,827	344,000	824,000	75.00	20,530
Brazil	200	213,352	17,000,000	4,982,000	58.50	744,661
Colombia	52	70,000	450,000	406,000	36.00	185,077
Ecuador	6	94,700	410,000	123,000	45.00	19,187
Guyana	9	40,000	798,000	5,870	2.73	N.D.
Peru	60	300,000	2,400,000	956,751	74.44	38,223
Suriname	5	7,400	352,000	142,800	100.00	N.D.
Venezuela	16	38,670	9,000	53,000	5.78	N.D.
TOTAL	**379**	**935,949**	**21,763,000**	**7,493,421**		**N.D.**

Source: Author's research.

not sought to amass wealth or to improve individual standards of living, unlike the Portu-guese-Hispanic world. The traditional native economic structure is based on subsistence activities to meet basic needs and maintain their way of life. Their trade activity is based on sharing all material goods, within a moral framework that establishes values, norms and kinship-based group solidarity.

This study focuses on indigenous groups that live in the Amazon basin and in certain strategic zones in Central America. Eight countries have territory in the Amazon and Guyana shield: Brazil, Peru, Colombia, Ecuador, Bolivia, Venezuela, Suriname, and Guyana. The indigenous population in this extended Amazon basin is estimated to be approximately 1 million (4.2 percent of the total population in the Amazon and 0.3 per-cent of the total population of the eight countries), and this population is divided into some 400 ethnic groups. Table 8.1 gives population data for the Amazon, and Box 8.1 gives additional information on native groups in Nicaragua and Panama.

The indigenous groups of the countries or nation-states[2] mentioned in this study represent a minority of the total population (0.4 percent). In Panama they occupy one-third of the country, and in Nicaragua slightly less than one-half. Peru's estimated indig-enous Amazon lowland population is the highest in the Amazon region, followed by Brazil and Bolivia. Indigenous peoples occupy territory larger than half the combined area of the eight countries that share the basin. Some 15 percent of the Amazon area is legally set aside for ethnic groups. Brazil, with some 67 percent of the Amazon basin, has set aside approximately 15 percent of that area for ethnic groups. Of the Amazon countries, Colom-bia has assigned the highest percentage of its area for indigenous groups.

Living in small isolated settlements scattered over a large area, the indigenous population developed great ethnological diversity, which has steadily diminished since the start of colonization. Today's total native population in Colombia is estimated to num-ber some 450,000. When colonization began, they may have numbered between 6 million

---

[2] Native groups view themselves as nations, since their members share an ethnic-cultural identity, but they do not form sovereign countries. The terms "country" and "nation-state" refer to a political-administrative entity that includes groups with ethnic and cultural identity, living in a territory accepted by the international commu-nity as a sovereign state.

> ### Box 8.1 Indigenous Populations in Tropical Rainforests of Nicaragua and Panama
>
> **Nicaragua.** Indigenous groups live in the Atlantic macroregion, covering some 57,000 km² (43 percent of the country) in two autonomous regions—the North Atlantic Autonomous Region and the South Atlantic Autonomous Region. Four indigenous people groups have been identified on Nicaragua's Atlantic coast: Miskitos (estimated number of inhabitants: 92,800); Sumo or Mayanga (8,075); Rama (1,404); and Garifona (3,068). Criollos (36,419) and Mestizos (104,217) also live on the coast. In effect, Nicaragua's Constitution recognizes the autonomy of native peoples in areas that cover almost half the national territory.
>
> **Panama.** Estimates place the native population at about 195,000, grouped into six peoples. Most live in the provinces of Bocas del Toro, Veraguas, Chiriquí (Gnobe with 123,085 people, Teribe with 2,194, Bokota with 3,804), Darién (Emberá with 14,657, Wounáan with 2,605), and the San Blas Reserve (Kunas with 47,700) (1990 National Census).

and 10 million. The overall native population of the hemisphere declined from an estimated 100 million to some 10 million within a century after the arrival of Europeans.

Logging and mining activities in the Amazon began in colonial times. Missions and slave trade were important factors that determined the location of many modern Amazon societies. However, compared to other forested parts of Latin America, the Amazon tribes have remained relatively isolated from Western society for a long time (Selverston 1993). Penetration into their territories has accelerated in the last 30 years (Smith 1996), and at times is genocidal in magnitude. The average size of a native settlement in the Brazilian Amazon now is believed to be 65 people, while the figure for Peru is estimated to be 95. In Brazil approximately 90 native groups (nearly 300 existed at the start of the century) have become extinct. In the Amazon some ethnic groups have a total population of 20 or fewer individuals.

Traditional Uses of Forest Resources

The survival strategies of aboriginal communities reflect a complex web of biophysical, cultural, historical, and economic factors. However, microenvironmental classification gives a good idea of potential and limitations on forest resource use (summarized for the Brazilian Amazon by Moran 1993, 1996). Traditional survival strategies focus on the application of succession (rotating uses) for obtaining diverse products. Western systems divide the land into areas for forests, agriculture, and conservation. In contrast, indigenous groups typically combine these activities in time and space. Their most important tools are fire and diversity of species. Through careful use of these tools, they have been able to increase the productive yield of desired species while conserving key functions of the ecosystem. Traditional indigenous horticulturists require conservation of biodiversity as a condition for survival. The ecological implications of the indigenous slash-and-burn system and horticulture practices have been studied in detail by Holling (1986) and Holling et al. (1994).

Soil quality determines how long annual crops can be cultivated after the land has been burned off. Perennial crops such as yucca and bananas can be grown in combination with them. When the annual crop declines due to soil fatigue, succession manage-

Box 8.2 Common Property in the Traditional Cultures of Indigenous Groups

For traditional indigenous societies in tropical rainforest environments, common property is the most suitable approach to managing natural resources, given the following considerations:

1. Nontangible public goods such as biodiversity and watershed protection benefits are especially abundant in intact forests.

2. The yield of certain products in a forest can vary from place to place in a given year, depending on environmental factors and varying states of succession in the slash-and-burn and horticulture systems. Many tribal groups allow the entire group to use these products in an extensive area, and facilitate their equitable distribution.

3. If the activities of one group of resource users entail a cost for another group, a solution is normally enforced under the common property system, thereby internalizing externalities. A typical case might be a potential conflict between gatherers and hunters, where the gatherers take away plants that would otherwise attract animals the hunters depend on.

Source: Adapted from McKean (1996).

ment is practiced. A myriad of species arises during the successive stages, springing from seed that survives in the soil or from trees retained on cleared plots, or carried by the wind or animals. Many species are used locally for food, fiber, medicine and trade before the forest ecosystem begins the process of natural succession. As a result, biodiversity is conserved fairly well, and in some cases forested areas have even expanded (Alcorn 1989; Irvine 1989).

Collective ownership and kinship form an integral part of traditional survival strategies. Box 8.2 explains the advantages of a system of common property for the use of the natural resources of tropical forests. Common property management has been most efficient when performed by cohesive groups, characterized by family ties, traditions of mutual assistance, and no sharp disparities in wealth (Quiggin 1993). As this forest management regime is especially fragile to outside disturbances (de Janvry and García 1992), it seems to work best in areas facing low migratory pressures, with longstanding customary rights of access and use of forests by local communities (Chapter 7). If forest users are unable to demarcate private areas or if a regional government cannot enforce property rights legislation, common property systems can provide solutions for management by establishing rules within and between groups of users.

Values, beliefs, and rituals are key to traditional survival strategies of forest people groups. A set of rules and a common ethic for use of natural resources (Alcorn 1989; Anderson 1990; Anderson and Posey 1989; Posey 1985) are based on the idea that the biophysical environment and human beings are linked together in a chain of relationships (Berkes et al. 1993). Because use and conservation affect the relationship between humans and other beings, discipline must be exercised by the humans in tapping natural resources. Ritual procedures are a core component for mediating perceived conflicts between humans and other creatures.

These traditional rules and sanctions are part of a system of beliefs and values, including the idea of sharing and restricting the accumulation of goods. Autonomy of small groups is another key factor that guarantees free access to forest resources. In each indigenous society, relations with other communities and with nature is the responsibility of small kinship groups.

Exogenous Factors Causing Change

In the last 40 years, the main exogenous factors causing change are related to deforestation, which destroys the base of the traditional survival strategies of tribal groups. Some 85 percent of deforestation in Latin America occurs in the Amazon basin, but the highest deforestation rates are reached in Mexico and Central America.

Road Infrastructure and Expanding Agricultural Frontiers. Building roads often leads to large settlements by nonindigenous colonizers and the advance of livestock farming. The expansion of pastures for large commercial livestock operations has caused most forest clearing in Central America in the last three decades (Kaimowitz 1995b), whereas in much of the Amazon frontier, deforestation seems to be driven by low-income shifting cultivators (Barbier 1997; Kaimowitz 1995b) with Brazil showing a mixed picture. Logging and mining concessions are other major factors for change (Smith 1996).

The trans-Amazon highway led to ecological disruption in the habitat of tribal groups as well as sociopolitical disruption. This induced the Brazilian government to pass laws to limit the advance of the market economy and to respect the rights of aboriginal communities, including rights of access to their traditional habitats. Although highways are an essential factor for development, in Latin America they have led without exception to deforestation and degradation, which makes them the main threat to biodiversity, according to Dourojeanni (Chapter 5). This notion is supported by studies that confirm the strong link between deforestation and road construction (Chomitz and Gray 1996; Alston et al. 1995; Mahar and Schneider 1994).

Mining, Petroleum, Logging, and Tourism Concessions. In Amazon countries such as Colombia, Ecuador, and Peru, fossil fuel exploration and production (and in Panama, mining) takes place on concessions that either border on indigenous territories or lie within them. In many cases, ambiguous legislation on use of the subsoil allows exploration to proceed without suitable consultations with the affected native groups. Indigenous organizations complain that neither cultural nor environmental impact studies have been performed, and that the projects lack mechanisms to compensate the people affected. The predicament arises from two types of opposing interests: those of national development through mining, and those of native groups who see their potential for survival shrink, due to the impact on the environment and on their traditional resources (see Box 8.3).

Logging continues at high rates in many Latin American countries. For example, in the Darién forests of Panama, the cativo (*Prioria copaifera*), which has formed large, homogenous forests, is on the verge of extinction, as it is also now logged inside the Darién National Park. Indigenous groups themselves are often responsible for deforestation, since they use the forest as a source of quick income to respond to market demands. In some cases they take advantage of legislation intended to assist them in obtaining ownership of forest by selling logging rights to third parties.

Ecotourism has recently become an attraction in the forested areas of Latin America and the Caribbean. Some indigenous groups have successfully managed tourism in their territories, such as the Kunas in Kuna-Yala, who act as ecotourism guides in the San Blas Reserve. In other cases, such as the Yaguas in Iquitos, tourism operators have ignored

> **Box 8.3 Conflicts between Mining and Petroleum Industry and Indigenous Groups**
>
> Often no mechanisms for conciliation are in place to permit parties to negotiate their positions. So conflict prevails, and translates into legal litigation or, in extreme cases, into physical confrontation. Some examples include the following:
>
> *Ecuador.* Legal litigation against Texaco by environmental NGOs and indigenous organizations has continued for several years in the Amazon with no settlement in sight.
>
> *Colombia.* Many confrontations have taken place in aeas where gold and oil are exploited by international companies. For example, guerrillas have frequently bombed the oil pipeline between Arauca and the Caribbean coast, causing spills of over 1.5 million barrels along 115 km of fragile ecosystems.
>
> *Panama.* Sixty-seven concessions for metal mining and 38 applications for nonmetal mining are reported in Darién alone. The Mineral Resources Branch of the Ministry of Trade and Industry continues to promote private investment in mining. The Ngobe-Bugle communities affected by copper mining in Cerro Colorado have protested vigorously against these government practices.

indigenous rights. Properly managed, ecotourism could undoubtedly be a source of income for native groups if they had official government support, trained personnel, and the capital to develop the necessary infrastructure.

Conservation and Indigenous Groups: Conflicts and Common Interests. The goal of establishing strictly protected areas contravenes the traditional values of many indigenous groups, whose objective is the harmonious coexistence of humans and forests, based on sustainable use of the resources. As protected areas have expanded, native organizations have protested that the viability of their traditional forest use strategies has declined owing to their loss of access to resources.

Most conservation units today permit the presence of humans and the sustainable use of natural resources. The approach to biodiversity conservation has also shifted from individual species to large continuous habitats. Conservation organizations and international lending agencies have been working together with native groups to ensure land tenure and promote systems for the sustainable use of resources. In other cases, in Brazil and Peru, indigenous groups are allowed to remain and national parks may not be located on indigenous reserves. However, the establishment of protected areas—in the Brazilian Amazon, for example—can restrict the lifestyles and traditional extensive uses of natural resources by native groups (Kohlhepp 1991; Mertins 1996).

Endogenous Factors Causing Change

Population Growth and Settlement. The regions with the fastest population growth in Latin America are inhabited by indigenous groups. This growth appears to reflect the arrival of nonindigenous people, rather than natural growth in aboriginal communities. Nonetheless, the birth rate in indigenous communities is considerably higher than the national average, and despite high infant mortality, the growth rate is relatively fast. The overall fertility rate in the Peruvian Amazon is an estimated 7.9 children, more than double the national average of 3.4. However, growth in the indigenous population is offset by heavy migration away from the communities.

The settlement of some nomadic groups in permanent communities, in areas such as Darién, Petén, Mosquitia, and the Atlantic coast of Nicaragua, has placed pressure on land around the villages. Population growth and the permanent settlement of native groups that turn to farming can outstrip the productive capacity of the soil in tropical rainforests. Attempts are often made to overcome low productivity through the use of agro-chemicals and "modern" agricultural techniques. These only increase yield temporarily, and have created a serious medium-term problem of lack of sustainability. After being absorbed into the money economy, indigenous people are often forced into unsustainable use of forest resources, worsening their environmental and economic situation. In many cases they leave farming and natural resource management and go to work as laborers for logging or mining companies, living outside their native groups. They therefore become part of the problem, since apart from contributing to the loss of biodiversity through their new activities, they abandon their traditional way of life and cultural identity, a process which ultimately leads to a loss of ethnodiversity.

Low Educational Levels. Historically, education for indigenous groups in Latin America has involved acculturation and has ignored their traditions and own culture. Education in the Peruvian Amazon, for example, has not been a government priority despite its legal obligation, and most schools have been run by religious missions. Regardless of the agents involved, it is unfortunate that the values of native groups have not been included in the education systems, and a number of authors believe that this has contributed to the gradual loss of their culture (Jiménez Turón 1984).

It is estimated that the indigenous population of the Peruvian Amazon has an illiteracy rate of 55 percent, more than four times the national average. High illiteracy rates in other Latin American native communities affect their potential for institutional and organizational development. Negotiating and consolidating their rights and promoting economic alternatives will require higher levels of education, because it involves interaction with government, national society, and other agents such as private companies and development agencies.

Scant education limits indigenous people's options for work other than farming, unless they emigrate to cities, where they usually join the ranks of urban poor. They are typically limited to farming, with low income levels due to low agricultural productivity. Natives often lack the technological capacity to produce the quality demanded by the market and are subject to exploitation by middlemen due to deficient education.

Organizational Weakness. Kinship is an important factor in many indigenous survival strategies, since the extended family is the forum for decisionmaking and the production unit. Natural areas are often allocated to distinct family groups. Political and administrative authorities and institutions imposed relatively recently are expressions of government policies. The assumption that native communities or their regional organizations, rather than families, are able to make decisions regarding natural resources, has led to the failure of many development projects, particularly in forest management.

In general, indigenous forest dwellers have organizational structures that group the vast majority of their members together. In the Amazon, these organizations probably cover about 70 percent of the native population. Organizations also abound in the countries of Central America with significant native populations. In Panama, the main groups live on reservations (*comarcas*) where they act as local authorities and defend their rights through local, national, regional, and international associations. From the grass-roots native groups to the international community, there are a host of indigenous organizations that respond to the needs of their respective members. The myriad of organizations on different levels and their broad-based membership have not, however, translated into successful defense of indigenous interests. Although they have achieved some legal and political recognition of their demands, with few exceptions they owe their successes to strategic alliances with nonindigenous groups (mainly NGOs), rather than to their independent efforts.

Part of this weakness is explained by the lack of linkage between the higher level organizations, such as the Indigenous Coordination Association of the Amazon (COICA), and the grass roots. This absence of organizational continuity has caused a crisis in the World Council of Indigenous Peoples, which has been hobbled and unable to realize its potential. Indigenous organizations are at a crossroads. To be effective in defending their rights, leaders have to leave their forest communities and go to the capital cities. Physical distance means that the organizations (or their leaders) generate their own dynamics, which are more in accordance with the demands of urban centers and government bureaucracies than with the needs of their members. Distance undermines representativeness.

The legitimacy of the leaders themselves is sometimes questioned. Traditionally there were no democratic mechanisms for the election of leaders of kinship. The transformation of these structures to a genuine representative community organization is a difficult process. As a consequence, it has been argued that external agents in governments and international organizations should train academics who will act on behalf of the communities without claiming to represent them. However, these agents may widen the gap between grass roots and higher echelon entities by allocating cooperation funding to the organizations at the apex, rather than to the local communities they are supposed to work for. In the past, stiff competition for funds among native organizations has widened the gap between organizations and their base, and has even led to the demise of some organizations.

Native groups and their entities have participated in international arenas: for example, in the UN negotiations on the rights of indigenous populations, in the International Labor Organization (ILO) Convention concerning Indigenous and Tribal Peoples in Independent Countries (Convention No. 169), in the Rio Earth Summit in 1992 (UNCED), in the Intergovernmental Panel on Forests, in the Convention on Biological Diversity, and in the Special Session of the United Nations General Assembly on Environmental and Sustainable Development. Despite the international recognition obtained as a result of these negotiations, many natives emphasize the importance of working at the grass roots level and prefer to use any available funds for local projects (European Commission 1997).

Another element to be considered in the organizational weakness of native communities is the lack of technical capacity for their leaders who are at a disadvantage in negotiating with oil or mineral companies with respect to the use of natural resources in their territories. Often there is no division of functions inside the organizations and the political leaders are responsible for administering resources in addition to negotiating. This amalgamation of technical, financial, and political aspects, and the concentration of power has led to many problems regarding the transparency of the organizations' financial operations. Last, there are few native lawyers to advise their organizations and even fewer qualified nonnative lawyers willing to donate their legal services. Given the current defects in legislation and unsatisfactory enforcement of the law, legal advisory services

Box 8.4 Rubber Bosses in the Amazon

In the last 30 years, the Amazon has been gradually incorporated into the economic and political life of the nations that encompass it. The population of the Amazon basin has risen from an estimated 9.7 million in 1960 to approximately 29.3 million in 1990. While concentrated in urban areas, this growth frequently spills over into rural areas. Until the early 1960s most native Amazon groups were isolated from nonindigenous society, interrupted only by sporadic contacts with the market economy (Smith 1996). Two institutions important in their lives were the "bosses" and the "missionaries." The former exploited native labor or acted as middlemen between the regional market and the indigenous groups, and the second proselytised. There was no formal education, and dominant languages continued to be local. Politically, the Indians had no concept of being citizens of a country, nor did civil society view them as such. Therefore no value was attached to indigenous rights or to their condition as citizens of a nation state.

The main rubber era came to an end after the Second World War. Rubber tapping became less profitable, and the "bosses" left in search of better financial prospects. The Amazon Indians who had depended on rubber to buy market goods were forced to seek other means of raising their income. Almost all native groups in the Amazon have acquired direct relations with the market economy. They now depend on links with government structures to satisfy their basic needs. The contact has been also necessary for the formal recognition of their rights. The language of the colonizers now dominates and native languages are used only in the homes.

As a result of massive investments by governments and private companies in the development and settlement of the Amazon starting in the 1960s, change has become and continues to be inevitable for indigenous groups. But in the Amazon, changes that had taken centuries to complete elsewhere, occurred from one generation to the next.

Source: Smith 1996.

are very necessary. Also owing to the lack of training, indigenous organizations often cannot benefit from investments in tropical rainforests through government projects, international cooperation, or government concessions to foreign companies.

Vulnerability to Market Forces

What real possibilities exist for indigenous peoples to establish sustainable relations with the market economy, without sacrificing their economic security and the resource base for future generations? Confronted with rapid changes like those in the Amazon (see Box 8.4), forest-dwelling indigenous communities move from almost complete isolation to conflictive contact with the dominant society. In Darién, up to the end of the 1960s the Emberá and Wounáan communities lived in relative isolation from the rest of Panamanian society. Until the early 1970s a significant part of the Emberá-Wounáan population continued to live a nomadic life. They only began to establish contact with the urban market after construction of the latest section of the Pan-American Highway to Yaviza.

In the last three decades, international cooperation has contributed significantly to the development of indigenous groups through funding for projects of different kinds. National and international legislation has been passed, in theory, to protect the rights of these peoples, including their territorial rights and the right to autonomous development. Despite these efforts, the most impoverished areas of Latin America today are those inhabited by indigenous groups (Deruyttere 1997). This leads to the question: How can national legal initiatives and international financial cooperation be improved, to make indigenous communities less vulnerable?

When native groups who have been incorporated into the market economy become wasteful of resources like any other external player, their subsistence activities become even more restricted. Hunting, fishing, and controlled slash-and-burn farming are no longer possible on a large enough scale to generate the desired income. As the income requirements increase and the bases for survival decrease, solidarity among the members of the native groups also declines, and in many cases the values on which this life style was built disappear. The moral base itself erodes, often leading to high alcoholism and suicide rates.

Contact with modern civilization through television, advertising, and consumerism changes values, replacing traditional ones with the aspirations of modern society. In many cases the aboriginals cannot match these new aspirations, given the absence of viable economic options owing to the lack of infrastructure in the forest and low levels of education. The result is often the feeling of economic and cultural inferiority when compared to the industrial society. Coupled with ever increasing restrictions in the access to the natural resources of the forest, the situation aggravates the change in values and the gradual loss of traditional knowledge.

The employment pattern where the indigenous population are frequently integrated as labor in development and conservation projects (affecting them, instead of them having control of these projects) usually leads to consumerism. A range of different reasons accounts for the widespread phenomenon of consumerism among aboriginal people. First, in the economic and cultural context of the rainforest, money serves mainly as a vehicle for consumerism. Second, the flow of money often is not linked to the absorption capacity of indigenous groups. Many indigenous people are unaccustomed to handling modern market economy tools. As beneficiaries of international cooperation, living in the context of their traditions and native economic rules, they are frequently unable to manage the funds adequately. Even in successful productive projects, earnings are often not reinvested. Moreover, native groups in remote rural areas have no access to banks and their savings are not institutionalized.

Weak indigenous organizational capacity often counts for the inability of community organizations to successfully deal with market or government agents foreign to the local culture. Natives often do not have enough money to be competitive. Economic disruption and lack of access to natural resources have frequently made it impossible for them to continue their subsistence economy while not permitting them to enter the market economy. In this socioeconomic vacuum, many native groups have sought options to permit them to continue enjoying access to their resources and to use them in ways consistent with their culture. When indigenous groups acquire territorial rights, often their declared aim is to establish development models connecting their productive activities with the national market economy in terms that are profitable, sustainable, and environmentally suitable, while also preserving native values.

The aboriginal tradition of common ownership has been identified as an additional reason for the failure of some economic cooperation projects. As individuals and families become successful in their new projects, social pressure is brought to bear on them to share their profits. Since most of their activities require some capital accumulation in order to have reserves for investments, it becomes difficult to manage a business successfully under the system.

Box 8.5 Peruvian Amazon: The Bora-Huitoto and the "Entrepreneur's Dilemma"

AIDESEP (Inter-Ethnic Association for the Development of the Peruvian Jungle) realized early that the key production unit of newly established microenterprises was a home or a family. One Bora family operating a microenterprise wanted to produce blocks of sugar processed from sugarcane juice. The family knew the production process through the experience of older family members who had worked for larger producers. A small loan permitted it to buy the basic equipment necessary to produce sugar. In a few years the family was producing and selling it in the departmental capital and in its opinion, it was making satisfactory returns. As the family became more successful, rumors began to spread about it. After two deaths in the family attributed to spells cast by other community members, the family halted the business.

This is a common feature of businesses undertaken in native kinship-based groups where well-established social rules exist for sharing, distributing surpluses, and reciprocity. The "entrepreneur's dilemma" was named after this family. Unless sociocultural rules change in the community, families and individuals must find a way of harmonizing the rules with commercial achievement if they are to operate successful microenterprises.

Source: AIDESEP microenterprise project.

Pressures of this kind have historically existed whenever native groups trade surpluses with other groups. In the past, one solution was a separation of people who engaged in trade from the rest of the community. Alternatives have been sought to solve the problem, and the challenge is to find a solution acceptable to the majority of the community. Box 8.5 gives an example of the so-called "entrepreneur's dilemma."

Changes in Legislation Concerning Indigenous Groups and Natural Resources

The globalization of communications, recognition of the value of ecosystems in vast geographic zones such as the Amazon or the Chocó, and the increase in international trade have a significant impact on the process of internationalizing social, economic, and political relations. These trends have led to a growing body of national legislation and international conventions, and indigenous groups are aware of them. They have established alliances and confederations that go beyond national boundaries, and have even organized groups to advise international development agencies on projects, such as a program for sustainable development in Darién, Panama.

The international community recognizes the historical presence of native groups and attempts to support government efforts to protect and promote their rights. Extensive legislation on indigenous communities and their rights has been promulgated in recent years (see chapter appendix). The last 30 years have seen significant progress in formal and legal recognition of certain native rights, but the laws still contain many ambiguities and contradictions. In many cases, recognition is simply a formality and the spirit of the law has not translated into tangible achievements.

Mertins (1996) notes two trends in land-use rights for native communities. In countries with large indigenous populations such as Bolivia, Ecuador and Peru, acceptance of the rights of lowland Indians is growing, despite the lack of a legal framework for those rights. However, in countries where indigenous groups are relatively small (Brazil and Colombia) and other strong pressure groups are claiming land, compliance with land use rights tends to be poor (Mertins 1996; Gawora and Moser, 1993).

Land Ownership

Government legislation concerning indigenous groups focuses in particular on defining their territories and their right to use resources within those territories. With respect to the size of indigenous territories, legislation is often contrary to the world view and traditional practices of these people. As hunters, gatherers, and traditional shifting cultivators they have to cover significant tracts of land. They have developed patterns that adapt to natural cycles and to the resources available. Traditional indigenous horticulturers lead a lifestyle that includes conservation of biodiversity as a condition for survival. Therefore it is often superfluous to work out minimum land allotments as a way of determining the amount of land required by a traditional indigenous group. In general, forest dwellers claim a territory as their own based on myths rooted in a rich tradition of customary law. This customary law is functional from the standpoint of the traditional indigenous economy, which under original conditions includes conservation practices.

Regarding the right to use natural resources, in the best cases there is a contradiction between the spirit and the letter of the law. A relatively solid legal base supports the right of native peoples to the use of renewable natural resources on their land and to active participation in resource administration and protection (see chapter appendix). This legislation (relatively recent in some countries) includes powers and rights over renewable natural resources, rights that are novel in the Amazon and in Latin America itself. They include the exclusive right by native communities to use the resources of rivers and lakes in their territories, contrary to the earlier situation where these resources were public domain by law. However, even comprehensive legislation concerning the claims of native communities and their organizations has not halted the destruction of natural resources in their territories by external agents.

Recognition by national governments of the culturally distinct nature of indigenous groups has led them to recognize the right to the land by natives, giving them different degrees of autonomy over it. In the Amazon, the legal right of ownership of some 500,000 km^2 has been transferred from the state to indigenous people in recent years. This figure includes 90,000 km^2 transferred by the Brazilian government to the Yanomami, 27,000 km^2 to indigenous groups in Ecuador's Amazon, and 180,000 km^2 to Colombian Amazon groups.

In Ecuador the six main indigenous groups in the Amazon comprise an estimated total of 94,700 individuals. As of March 1991, 20,092 km^2 had been confirmed to belong to 13,305 families in 316 native communities (66,525 people or 70.2 percent of the indigenous population) (CEREC 1993).

The 1973 Indian Statute of Brazil confirms the protection and legal integrity of indigenous lands. Brazil's 1988 Constitution recognizes the original rights of Indians to the land they have traditionally occupy (article 231). These lands are to be held by them permanently and they are given exclusive use rights. It should be stressed, however, that the law does not give them ownership of the subsoil, or the rivers and lakes on the land, and that the land is considered an asset of the federal government (article 20).

The Constitution established a period of five years (to 1993) for demarcating the boundaries of those lands (article 67). However, by 1993 just 196 (37 percent) of indigenous territories had been legally recognized, 93 (18 percent) had been investigated, and 147 (28 percent) were in the analysis stage. Even this modest progress was mainly due to

Box 8.6 Legislation Governing Indigenous Property in Peru

Peru's Constitution of 1993 gives broad recognition to the rights of forest-dwelling tribes to land ownership. It contains principles with respect to the cultural identity of rural and native communities. The earlier Constitutions of 1933 and 1979 had already recognized native communities in the forest as "autonomous juridical persons in their organization, communal labor and land use, and in economic and administrative aspects, within the framework established by law." In the Constitution of 1979 the indigenous lands were "imprescriptible and inalienable." The current Constitution indicates that land ownership is inalienable except in the event of abandonment (Art. 89).

It is estimated that only 673 of the 1,000 native communities in Peru have had their land demarcated and titled in ownership (22,488 km^2), with another 8,403 km^2 ceded in use. However, it is estimated that some 80 percent of those 673 communities, with a total of 21,578 families, do not have sufficient land for sustainable use of the forest and subsistence farming. Each family has 104 ha on average.

national and international pressures and protests against slow legislative procedures (Mertins 1996; Gawora and Moser 1993).

In Venezuela, the native population of the Amazon and the Orinoco lowlands was an estimated 78,160 in 1991. Of those, approximately 8,500 people (10.9 percent) held a titled area of 819,117 ha. Bolivia's native population in the Amazon was an estimated 158,000 in 1991. Of this population, some 13,500 people (8.5 percent) had a titled area of approximately 1,927,000 ha (CEREC 1993). Box 8.6 explains the situation in Peru.

Based on Aztec systems, the 1917 land reform in Mexico established the cooperative farming system (*ejidos*), which determined land ownership and use for indigenous and nonindigenous people. In general, less fertile areas are used communally for grazing and logging of the forest, while the more productive land is inherited by family members, but may not be divided or expropriated (Scheiwgert 1989; Mertins 1996).

In summary, considerable progress has been made in the relationship between states and indigenous groups. The multiethnic and multicultural nature of Latin American societies has been enshrined in constitutions and regulated in laws. Ideological and legal recognition has translated into territorial recognition. Extensive areas have been transferred legally to native communities who have traditionally occupied and used them.

In countries such as Bolivia, Brazil, Colombia, Ecuador, Nicaragua, Panama, and Peru, geographic areas under indigenous jurisdiction have been set aside as reserves, native communities, autonomous regions, or territorial units. The written laws might suggest that land claims of native groups have been recognized as legitimate and governments have responded to such claims decisively. However, that conclusion is premature, since not all the lands claimed have been recognized, and not all the land that has been granted can be used freely by its indigenous occupants.

Minerals and Fossil Fuels

Legislation on the resources of the subsoil is one of the most difficult legal areas with respect to interpretation and enforcement. On one hand, in all Latin American countries the government retains the right to use resources such as minerals and fossil fuels, above

Box 8.7 Legislation on Subsoil Resources in Colombia, Panama and Peru

Colombia. Subsoil mineral resources belong to the state. Colombia's Constitution of 1992 establishes that "The State is the owner of the subsoil and of nonrenewable natural resources, without detriment to rights acquired and developed under preexisting laws." Still, the Mining Code gives native communities broad powers to control future mining operations on their land. Natives can conclude agreements with third parties for exploration and production and their authorities have the right to designate which parts of their land may not be used owing to its social or religious significance.

Panama. The constitution declares that the subsoil resources belong to the state. Most mineral reserves of Panama are found on indigenous land; based on the constitution, the Mineral Resource Code does not contain any provisions relating to native groups. In recent years mining concessions on indigenous land have been applied for by a total of 21 companies, over an area of some 140,000 km². However, the legislation governing the Emberá and Wounáan peoples' reserves establishes that subsoil resources are the collective property of the communities. A provision is made for community participation in negotiating contracts and in profits. The percentage of benefits to which the reserve is entitled (under contracts signed by the government) is classified in the charter by type of mineral, and ranges from 40 to 80 percent. Even if the charter establishes that the mineral rights are a collective property of the Emberá and Wounáan peoples, the constitution holds that they are subject to state authority, and therefore the mineral rights are state property.

Peru. According to the constitution of 1993, all mineral resources belong to the state under its inalienable and absolute ownership. Mineral resources are tapped under concessions, and promotion of investments in mining is deemed to be in the national interest. Fossil fuels in the ground also belong to the state. PETROPERU has rights and ownership over them after extraction, and enters into contracts with licensees for exploration and production. The Peruvian government has discretionary powers to utilize subsoil resources in the manner it considers most useful and convenient. There are, however, other regulations that require landowners to be consulted and compensated for the use of subsoil resources by the state, as seen in the text below. Notwithstanding, very few regulations exist on how to deal with eventualities affecting land occupied by indigenous groups, with or without title. In Peru, as in many other Latin American countries, indigenous groups argue that ownership of their territory is ancestral and prior to any other arrangement by colonial powers and modern states, and that the underground resources in their territories belong to them.

Sources: Roldán 1997; Madrigal 1997.

the rights of any other social actor. However, in the case of native groups, legislation has been passed that places certain limits on absolute ownership by the state. The cases of Colombia, Panama, and Peru illustrate the complexity of the issue (Box 8.7).

Legal gaps and internal contradictions weaken much of the legislation concerning nonrenewable resources. A significant portion of those resources are found in indigenous territories, and governments are under heavy pressure to finance their development programs through concessions to the private sector to tap them. The ecological balance in forested regions is being severely affected by the exploitation of nonrenewable resources and especially by the indirect negative environmental impacts, generally on account of improved access and the expansion of the agricultural frontier irrespective of legal ownership of the land. The survival of indigenous communities is jeopardized when they are deprived of their traditional territories and when their use of natural resources is restricted.

Current national development models are in marked conflict with the survival of native groups, and legislation should seek ways of alleviating that conflict. For example, Peruvian law requires agreement with a landowner regarding mining and fossil fuel production. In the event that rights-of-way are granted, the owner must be paid compensation.[3] This legislation allows room for negotiation, backed by international conventions that establish the responsibility of governments to consult the groups of people affected.[4]

Biological and Water Resources

Most Amazon countries have legislation that guarantees native communities the right to ownership, use, and autonomous or joint community and state management of renewable natural resources such as wildlife, plants, and water. There is no similar legislation for communities in Central America except for the native reserves in Panama.

There are significant differences between South and Central America with respect to the management of renewable natural resources in native territories. In Colombia, for example, with the creation of native territorial entities as political and administrative bodies whose functions include "overseeing the preservation of natural resources," the communities assume the direct and primary function of administering their own resources. This does not mean that the function is no longer public in nature, since the new entities now form part of the political and administrative structure of the state. At the same time, it can be assumed that indigenous communities have the same options and limitations on the use of renewable natural resources in their territories as any other owner of private property. In Central America the management of forested areas is often regulated by biosphere reserves and other large protected areas. These spaces, often inhabited by native groups, are generally located in border areas and contain a wealth of biodiversity. On many occasions they are subject to growing pressure from agricultural colonization. The legal framework governing protected areas and the indigenous peoples' rights on natural resources in Central America is often inadequate.

Genetic Resources. The protection of genetic resources is one of the most complex issues from the standpoint of legal treatment, especially with respect to rights over traditional native knowledge. National legislation does not normally regulate biodiversity as such, and is often limited to forestry and wildlife laws. If native groups are legally recognized as the owners of their territories, then they also own the biological resources (flora and fauna) within them, according to most legal experts.[5] For lands that have traditionally been occu-

---

[3]   The Peruvian Land Act states that: "The use of land for mining and fossil fuel production requires that an agreement be reached in advance with the owner or a completed process of obtaining rights-of-way exist. [...] For rights-of-way for mining and fossil fuel production, the owner must be compensated in advance in cash" (law 26505).

[4]   Article 15 of ILO Convention 169 of 1989, ratified by Peru in 1993, clearly establishes the responsibility acquired by the Peruvian government, given its status as legal owner of minerals and subsoil resources, to "establish or maintain procedures through which it shall consult these groups, with a view to ascertaining whether and to what degree their interests would be prejudiced, before undertaking or permitting any programs for the exploration or exploitation of such resources pertaining to their lands."

[5]   Under civil legislation, anyone who owns land also owns the plant and animal resources on it. Since indigenous communities and people have been recognized as full owners of the territories they occupy, either under formal titles or even under traditional possession, they also have full ownership over forest resources.

pied without legal recognition, ownership of those resources should also be recognized under the ILO Convention (Art. 14).

Bioprospecting involves exploration and extraction of biological resources in search of commercial value for the manufacture of medications, agricultural products, or cosmetics. Over the last decade the interest of pharmaceutical and biotechnology companies and middlemen in new commercial products has focused on tropical rainforests. Making use of native knowledge can be decisive in search for economic benefits from bioprospecting (RAFI 1997). On many occasions cooperation of native groups has been sought in bioprospecting without informing them of the intended use of the discoveries, thus depriving them of fair economic returns for their knowledge. It has often been the case as well that bioprospecting has been carried out on indigenous land without obtaining consent of the communities in advance.

A suitable legal framework to govern the biodiversity of tropical forests is required to regulate access to genetic resources, distribution of the profits from that use, and adequate protection for traditional knowledge. The Brazilian government guarantees the rights to maintain the secrecy of traditional knowledge and to refuse access to this knowledge through the Indigenous Societies Act. There is a right to apply for protection of intellectual property rights and the right to prior informed consent for access to, use of and application of traditional knowledge. It also establishes the right for co-ownership of research data, patents and products derived from the research, and enables indigenous communities to nullify patents derived from their knowledge (Simpson 1997).

To apply the Convention on Biological Diversity (already ratified by most Latin American countries; see chapter appendix), a major gap must be bridged, and adequate protection provided for the traditional knowledge of native communities. Apart from this legislative gap, a number of other practical obstacles make it difficult to achieve this aim. Securing intellectual property rights is expensive (ITTO 1997). Even if grants were provided for the initial registration, rights have to be perpetuated by paying maintenance fees. The investment is long-term, and it will take time to obtain significant income from these rights. Most native groups will not be able to afford the expenditure.[6]

Water Resources. Water legislation in Peru is typical of the situation in Latin America: the state is the owner of water resources although the water rights of native communities are also recognized. There, the government is the chief allocator and regulator of water use and there is "no private property or acquired rights over water."[7] According to this legislation, native communities in the Peruvian Amazon have no special rights over any of the water in their territories (navigable and nonnavigable rivers, streams, lakes, lagoons, etc.). However, the Native Communities Act guarantees the integrity of the communities' territory, and it can be inferred that water also forms part of that territory.[8] Ecuador's Agrarian Development Act of 1994 states that concessions and management plans for water

---

[6] An attorney's professional costs for preparing and prosecuting an individual patent application may reach several thousand dollars. While rights in a single country might cost $5,000 to $10,000, securing protection for a reasonable number of countries is likely to cost $30,000 to $50,000 or more.

[7] The Peruvian Water Act declares that the State has ownership of all the country's waters, that the ownership is "inalienable and imprescriptible," and that there is no "private ownership or acquired rights" over water. The act was drawn up in 1969 and adopted in the 1979 constitution.

[8] Article 10 of the Peruvian Native Communities Act declares that "The State guarantees the integrity of the territory of native communities." It can be argued that water also forms part of indigenous territorial space.

sources and watersheds must give consideration to cultural aspects of the indigenous and local populations.

The Brazilian Constitution specifies that the traditionally occupied lands are owned permanently by indigenous groups and should provide for the subsistence needs of the communities. Access to water is a basic need and the rights to the sources and uses of this resource are guaranteed by the Brazilian legislation (Solanes and Getches 1998). In Colombia, decree 2164/95 establishes strong communal property rights for the indigenous communities. However, it also establishes that the legislation on reservations does not change the regulations on water resources of public domain. It is not clear what the total implication of this statement is. However, it appears that the establishment of indigenous reservations would not include indiscriminate rights to water for the communities (Solanes and Getches 1998).

Pitfalls of Legislation Concerning Indigenous Groups

This brief overview of legislation concerning indigenous groups indicates that the large majority of countries in the region formally recognize the distinctive character of native communities and their territorial and sociocultural rights. Then how can we explain the neglect and lack of protection of most of these peoples when they try to exercise those rights? Five possible answers are suggested below.

First, the history of national legislation concerning native groups fails to take their traditions and true situation into account. Customary laws by the indigenous peoples were not generally recognized by the European settlers in Latin America. Only this century there have been attempts to incorporate them into the constitutional or civil laws in the region. This lack of attention has been significant since in cases such as patents for traditional knowledge of genetic resources, natives have not found due protection in legal instruments since collective patents or community property have not been recognized.

Second, legislation on indigenous peoples has been based on the general objective of their assimilation into national society. The trend toward assimilation has slackened, but has been replaced with another that implies the incorporation of native groups into modern society in general and into the market economy in particular. This focus prevails in Latin American legislation and the legal frameworks that regulate forms of ownership and management of resources that are antithetical to indigenous economic and cultural traditions. For example, certain legislation promotes cooperativism in forms that are not traditional in the native groups, as well as individual ownership, which often is completely contrary to the tradition of property held collectively by indigenous kinship-based groups.

Third, even when legislation is adequate, it is often not enforced. In all countries, private interests with sufficient resources and influence manage to promote legal interpretations that weaken the political power of native communities. Environmental and cultural impact studies on energy projects or road infrastructure are often produced by legal experts who take great pains to comply with legal technicalities, but not with the law's respect for native rights. And while consultations are usually limited to obtaining "informed consent," there is no participation of native communities regarding energy projects in their territories.

Fourth, there are still many areas of legislation that need to be clarified. The advance of globalization and the changes in international trade, the gradual establishment of monetary values to environmental services and to the ecological preservation of forests, and new forms of applying intellectual property rights to genetic resources are all areas that require legislation and are closely linked to native groups. In some cases legislation is promulgated recognizing indigenous rights to a resource, while other legislation gives the state full ownership of such resources. As a result of these contradictions, legislation is sometimes legally used as an excuse for sidestepping indigenous rights.

Fifth, native communities and their organizations rarely have full access to the law. They do not have information systems to keep abreast of progress in legislation on their behalf, or qualified personnel to compile laws, interpret them, and apply them in the service of the communities. There is no access to the judiciary. Rarely have they been able to participate in the design of legislation affecting indigenous groups.

In short, legal, civil, and constitutional rules have not always been sufficient to guarantee the ownership by indigenous communities of their traditional territories and the natural resources they contain. In general, the criteria used by governments reflect state priorities rather than native realities. In a time of change in native groups and in their environment, the legislation frequently contains defects, gaps, contradictions, and ambiguities. The challenge for the governments is to eliminate legal contradictions and for public institutions to apply the legal rules properly. Only an ongoing analysis of legislation by indigenous organizations and the capacity to negotiate with governments can overcome these contradictions. It will be necessary to move from a situation of confrontation between native groups and external agents to one of constructive cooperation.

Finding Solutions for Complex Situations

Latin America's forest dwellers have sustained their traditional way of life for thousands of years, while not destroying the fragile ecosystems of the tropical rainforest. Indigenous organizations argue that their practices, such as low-impact slash-and-burn, hunting, fishing, and other traditional forms of use, can guarantee their communities' survival and sustainable use of the resources only when the territory is large enough to support the population. Opposing groups criticize granting tropical forest use rights only to a relatively sparse indigenous population. They believe that with a growing population, and increasing levels of consumption, neither native communities nor anyone else can live today without having an impact on tropical forests.

In economic and political terms, tropical forest dwellers continue to be at a disadvantage. Apart from the gaps and ambiguities in domestic legislation, they find legal processes difficult to comprehend from the standpoint of their traditional ways. Lack of legal training and of formal education heighten their vulnerability. Based on these and other adverse factors, a number of recommendations are made below. The recommendations require a critical evaluation of particular contexts in each country: cultural, social, environmental, economic, political, and legislative. The goal is sustainable development and the preservation of biodiversity and ethnodiversity, based on close cooperation among all the stakeholders involved.

Regularization of Land Tenure
Land zoning plans should be prepared for the areas inhabited by indigenous groups. Government agencies, indigenous representatives, and international agencies should be involved in this process. The plans should include identification of current and potential land tenure conflicts, such as overlapping zones between protected areas and native communities, newly settled lands, and indigenous lands. Legal advisory services should be included for parties in conflict to find negotiated solutions. The plans should also include demarcation, delimitation, and titling for indigenous land.

In many cases, native groups' interests are affected by constitutional reforms to modernize the state, such as Article 27 of the Mexican Constitution, or Peru's recent Land Act. Particular attention should be paid to the nature, scope, and consequences of privatization that compromise indigenous territories and their natural resources, land that is no longer "inalienable." Stress should be placed on the processes of titling and demarcation of indigenous land. Access to resources without control over them is a calamity. Nothing encourages people more to depredate forests, land, and water than the fear of losing access to these resources in the short term (World Bank 1987; Chambers 1987).

Investment Programs

Native groups should participate in all stages of programs, from the project identification stage to its execution and evaluation. Government agencies responsible for the use of conservation of natural resources should include native people in their work teams. Indigenous communities are often best qualified to perform activities such as the demarcation of parks, surveillance boundaries, and data-gathering for natural resource inventories, as well as monitoring.

The recommended strategy advocates sustainable economic activities, which accord with the cultural foundations of native groups who would manage the natural resources. For example, small industries producing indigenous food and other goods for regional consumption can be promoted, as can traditional medicine, and ecotourism services that are supported by the cultural philosophy of native groups. Such activities should offer a comparative advantage to indigenous people, especially if they are based on traditional knowledge of the use of natural resources. Optimally they should support the sustainable use of resources in fragile ecosystems, and the native people should act as managers and the prime beneficiaries of the newly emerging products and services. Where native communities do not enjoy any such comparative advantage and the market is dominated by external agents, indigenous people remain in a subordinate position. On the other hand, experience has shown that favorable conditions can be established and considerable value added can be obtained for indigenous production when technologies are adequate and production and marketing approaches are culturally attuned to indigenous views.

As most native groups already participate in the market, their bargaining position needs to be improved. Conditions should be created to improve their knowledge of marketing techniques through training and pilot investment projects that require marketing. Economic interlocutors should be identified within the native groups themselves. The approach should be gradual and requires training for producers, identification of products, market studies, financial resource management, the development of infrastructure, and so on.

Building Indigenous Capacity

Negotiating Capacity. Since there are contradictions between indigenist legislation and legislation on the use of natural resources and the management of protected areas, native organizations should be strengthened to enable them to participate in preparing and negotiating proposals, revising domestic legislation, and applying international conventions in their countries. A systematic legal inventory could be the stepping stone for integrating native issues and affairs in a logical and clear fashion in future legislation.

Because native communities in fact make very limited use of legislation on their rights owing to their lack of knowledge and/or access to the law, it is recommended that support be provided for indigenous legal advisory services to be used to steer community claims and to compile and systemize legislation on indigenous affairs. Legal documentation centers should be established, and legal aides from among the native population will have to be trained. Legal advisory services and documentation centers could operate as specialized offices in national indigenous organizations such as AIDESEP in Peru, ONIC in Colombia, or CONAIE in Ecuador. The concepts of land occupation and use, usufruct rights, and administration of natural resources by native groups and third parties should be clarified. "Land possession" and "ownership" in each country are to be defined.

The main external agents include oil, mineral and logging companies, ecotourism operators, ranchers and farmers. In some cases, government agencies intervene to such an extent that they too become external agents. Outside agents often have the will to reach negotiated solutions, but national governments fail to create suitable spaces for negotiation and natives do not have expert advisory services to defend their legitimate interests. International cooperation and development lending agencies could facilitate advisory services for the parties on the one hand, and on the other, could introduce conditionalities requiring the state to ensure the necessary clarity and participation in negotiations through consultations with indigenous organizations. Support for negotiation between native groups and governments is also required in different development projects having impact on the survival and well-being of indigenous people, such as road construction and other infrastructure projects and the granting of concessions to third parties for activities such as ecotourism or logging.

In the context of the the many privatization initiatives and current modernization of the state in Latin America, regulatory frameworks must be designed to position native groups in the new institutional framework and to plan their development. Accordingly, it is critical to improve the capacity of indigenous organizations to negotiate with governments and private agents on these initiatives.

Technical Training. The international community has earmarked funds to improve the living conditions of native groups in Latin American tropical rainforests. Nonetheless, in most cases the quality of life of those groups continues to deteriorate. One reason has been the lack of real participation by the beneficiaries in projects designed to "assist" them. One of the stumbling blocks for constructive participation by native groups or their representatives has been their lack of technical capacity. If projects are to be successful, more effective participation, basic education and technical training for native groups must be promoted.

Training should be geared to the emerging relations between native groups and the market, the government, and national and international financing. Diversified training should place less stress on technical agricultural production, and include areas such as receptive ecotourism, marketing local products such as handcrafts and indigenous food, business management, negotiating techniques, and conflict resolution. Indigenous people should also be made aware of intellectual property and the commercial potential of biological and genetic resources.

Training methods should ensure that the knowledge imparted serves the native groups as a whole rather than separate individuals. Training should be included in programs to support indigenous groups as an integral part of every project. This avoids the flight of talent that might be facilitated by training programs offered outside the native group, or separate from the activities of a specific community program. The entire indigenous group should benefit from new technological know-how, with specific training based on the features of each natural or cultural environment.

Culturally Compatible Financing

When money intrudes into the natural economy of indigenous communities, it becomes primarily an instrument for consumption. Most native people have not developed an interest in saving, and relations with financial institutions are only beginning. Financing mechanisms must be gradually introduced to native groups, combining economic components of the market with indigenous culture. The elements to be considered include the following:

- A significant reduction in donations in productive projects. The culture of reciprocity in most Latin American indigenous kinship based groups requires that goods are circulated and are not channeled unilaterally with no expectation of return, as in the case of grants.
- Loans for production could be based on revolving funds, with indigenous groups sharing the returns, and could initially be interest-free.
- Nonreimbursable financing should only be used for social and community projects.
- Cofinancing should be required for all investments. Diversification of the sources of money would eliminate dependency on a single source and reduce risks relating to the availability of development funds.
- Native groups should be involved from the outset in designing projects for which financing is sought. Responsibilities for the administration of financial resources should be shared, so that indigenous people can gain a full understanding of money management, its uses, and benefits.

Conclusions

A growing body of national legislation and international law on indigenous groups and their rights to the use of natural resources has been promulgated in the last 30 years. The legislation on indigenous peoples' rights in the region is complex. Most Latin American countries have laws to guarantee native populations the right to ownership and use of renewable natural and water resources. Many countries have legally recognized their rights to large land areas. Despite the advances in legislation, in practice the laws are not properly enforced, and the destruction of natural resources in indigenous territories has not ceased. In most cases this destruction has been caused by external agents, but at times it is caused by the needs of native peoples themselves. The myriad of reasons include lack of knowledge of the law and weak negotiating capacity on their part, ambiguities in the law used by legal experts on behalf on nonindigenous external agents, poor enforcement of legislation, and institutional weaknesses of both governments and native communities.

The dynamics of change and the complexity of potential conflicts do not allow for across-the-board solutions. Before initiating development activities, the factors leading to nonsustainable uses of tropical forests should be analyzed on a case-by-case basis. Development activities should be geared to gradually combine market economies with native cultural elements. Due to cultural characteristics, donations should be cut back significantly; instead, loans for productive projects should be granted with interest rates (although minimal), right from the beginning. Indigenous groups should be encouraged to participate in investment projects, and trained to handle market economy tools. The sustainable use of forest resources based on ethnobiology and the participation of indigenous communities in conservation projects are promising examples of culturally compatible cooperation programs.

International cooperation agencies should assist indigenous organizations to gain a better understanding of existing and proposed legislation regarding native peoples, and by providing legal advisory services for parties in conflict. Land tenure conflicts in particular should be solved through coordinated action by governments, indigenous organizations, and international agencies. Finally, there is a need to monitor the effects of constitutional reforms and privatization processes on the land use of indigenous territories.

Appendix 8
National Legislation and International Conventions on Indigenous Peoples

Development of Indigenous Legislation in Latin America, 1920-1996

1920   Articles 41 and 58 of the Peruvian Constitution recognize the legal existence and inalienability of indigenous property.

1933   The Peruvian Constitution recognizes indigenous peoples' identity and culture, and their rights to self-government and land.

1934   The Brazilian Constitution speaks of "the incorporation of forest dwellers into the national community" (article 5). It adds that the possession of land in which they are permanently located shall be respected and prohibits the transfer of ownership of such lands to others (articles 129 and 154 of the Constitution of 1937).

1940   The Inter-American Indigenist Institute is created in Pátzcuaro, Mexico, under the auspices of the Organization of American States.

1944   Colombia creates the Colombian Indigenist Institute.

1946   The Brazilian Constitution ratifies the will of the state to incorporate indigenous groups into national life and to respect their possession of land.

1961   The Colombian Agrarian Reform Act (Law 135) creates reservations for native groups in unoccupied land.

1965   Brazil's Law 4771 (Forest Code) establishes that the forest heritage of native groups is subject to permanent protection.

1967   The Brazilian Constitution recognizes the right of native groups to use of the natural resources on their territories.

1967   Brazil establishes the National Indian Foundation (FUNAI), which replaces the National Council for the Protection of Indians and the Indian Protection Service.

1967   In Brazil, the constitution of the military government defines indigenous land as "goods belonging to the Federal Union," declaring them "inalienable" and recognizing the right to "exclusive use and enjoyment of natural resources" (articles 186 and 198), thereby permitting the use, but not the ownership, of natural resources by indigenous groups.

1973   The Indian Statute is promulgated in Brazil.

1974   In Peru, the military government of Velazco Alvarado issues the first comprehensive legislation in response to the claims and proposals of native groups. It promulgates the Native Communities Act (legislative decree 20653), which recognizes the legal existence and status, territorial rights, and autonomy of native forest-dwelling communities. Many of these communities were created under the Act. Instead of recognizing the traditional territories of natives, the government recognized small settlements around schools or certain trading posts.

1979 The Peruvian Constitution recognizes the native forest-dwelling communities of the forest as "legal entities that are autonomous" in their organization, use of community labor, land use and economic aspects.

1980 Colombia launches the Indigenous Development Program (PDI). This ambitious plan for socioeconomic development fails because of the absence of mechanisms for indigenous participation.

1981 Article 30 of Nicaragua's Agrarian Law contains a special reference to indigenous groups: "The State may set aside land to be worked by the Miskito, Sumo, and Rama communities ... and they may benefit from its natural resources."

1983 In Panama, Law 22 creates the Emberá-Wounáan Reserve and establishes that it is necessary to obtain authorization from chiefs (band and regional) to use renewable resources (article 19) and community participation in the use of nonrenewable and water resources (article 20).

1983– The constitutions of the Americas begin to recognize the distinctive nature of in-
1994 digenous groups, including Ecuador and Panama (1983), Guatemala (1985), Nicaragua (1987), Brazil (1988), Colombia (1991), Mexico and Paraguay (1992), Peru (1993), and Bolivia (1994).

1984 In Colombia, the National Indigenous Development Program (PRODEIN) replaces the PDI.

1987 The Nicaraguan legislature passes the Statute on the Autonomy of Atlantic Coast Regions.

1987 The Brazilian constituent assembly, responding to the lobbying of the UNI (an indigenous organization) and the CIMI (a Catholic organization), declares in article 231 that the land occupied permanently by native groups, and used by them for production for their physical and cultural survival in accordance with their uses and customs, is inalienable.

1988 In Colombia, Law 30/1988 reiterates that land occupied by native peoples cannot become the property of third parties.

1990 In Supreme Decree 2407, Bolivia proclaims an "historical ecological pause," suspending new logging concessions for five years to give native peoples time to regularize their land claims.

1991 The Mexican Constitution is amended. The new article 4 recognizes the multicultural composition of the Mexican nation, based originally on its native groups. Reforms to article 27 open up the possibility of privatizing the land belonging to the *ejidos*.

1992   The Colombian Constitution states that the reserves and communal land of ethnic groups are inalienable and imprescriptible (articles 63 and 326).

1992   Bolivia promulgates the General Environment Act, which authorizes established traditional communities to participate in managing protected areas, and adds that setting aside protected areas is compatible with the existence of traditional communities and native peoples (article 64).

1993   The Peruvian Constitution is reformed. Article 88 guarantees communal property and article 89 maintains recognition of the legal existence and status of native communities. It adds that the communities are free to dispose of their land, contrary to the previous position that the land was inalienable and imprescriptible.

1994   Ecuador promulgates the Agrarian Development Act, which guarantees collective land ownership. Article 41 states that concessions and management plans for water sources and watersheds must give consideration to cultural aspects of the indigenous and local population. It also declares that the state will enter into agreements with indigenous and rural communities that maintain ancestral production systems to develop, register, and transmit their traditional techniques and customs (article 5).

1995   On March 31, the Guatemalan government and the URNG (Guatemalan guerrilla movement) sign an agreement on the identity and rights of native peoples, which elaborates on the need to promote indigenous participation in national society.

1996   In Brazil, President Cardoso signs Decree 1885, permitting third parties such as logging and mining companies, ranchers and settlers to claim "contrary" rights; in other words, they can challenge unregistered indigenous land within certain deadlines. Approximately 140 native areas that have not been demarcated now run the risk of being contested under the decree.

International Conventions

Convention on Indigenous People. The International Labor Organization established this convention in 1957. In 1976 a committee of experts reviewed it. The International Labor Conference of June 1989 adopted Convention 169, concerning Indigenous and Tribal Peoples in Independent Countries, currently in force. It focuses on aspects such as territorial rights, ownership, and use of resources on the lands of indigenous people. To date, countries that have ratified the Convention include Argentina, Bolivia, Colombia, Costa Rica, Guatemala, Honduras, Mexico, Paraguay and Peru.

Convention on Biological Diversity. This convention was presented and approved at the United Nations Conference on Environment and Development held in Rio de Janeiro, Brazil. It was signed on June 5, 1992, and has been ratified by virtually all the countries of Latin America and the Caribbean. Its recognition of the value of traditional knowledge is particularly relevant for indigenous peoples. Articles 8(j), 10(c), 17.2 and 18.4 refer to this point.

Declarations and Bodies to Support Indigenous Peoples

United Nations. The Economic and Social Council has a Working Group on Indigenous Populations. The U.N. Human Rights Commission has established a working group to draw up the final text of the Declaration of the Rights of Indigenous Peoples.

Agenda 21. This document from the UN Conference on Environment and Development (Rio de Janeiro, June 1992) contains a special chapter on indigenous groups and sustainable development.

Declaration of the Rights of Indigenous Peoples. The General Assembly of the Organization of American States requested the Inter-American Human Rights Commission to prepare a legal instrument on the rights of indigenous peoples in 1989. The Commission proposed this project, which should be approved by the General Assembly in 1998.

Leticia Declaration. This declaration stems from the international meeting of indigenous peoples and other forest dwellers on Management, Conservation, and Sustainable Development of Forests, held in Leticia, Colombia, December 9 to 13, 1996.

Indigenous Fund. Established in 1992 with headquarters in Bolivia and initial support from the IDB, IFAD, the UNDP, and the ILO, the fund is intended to respond to indigenous initiatives.

International Year of Indigenous Peoples, 1993. Declared by the UN as a preparatory phase to the International Decade of the World's Indigenous Peoples from 1994 to 2004.

<table>
| CHAPTER **9** |
</table>

Rethinking Forest Concession Policies

Jared J. Hardner and Richard Rice

Introduction

Radical rethinking of forest resource contracts is now imperative for Latin American countries. In advancing the region's economic development, it has become increasingly difficult to conserve forest resources. The major constraints include financial incentives that strongly favor selective logging rather than management in tropical forests; the lack of a technical basis for silviculture in neotropical forests; weak administrative capacity and political will to impose management; and cultural and social norms that do not recognize local users of forest resources.

Forestry is generally viewed as an important activity in rural development. If conducted in a "sustainable" manner, it is widely embraced as a means to maintain forest cover and thereby provide various environmental services such as biodiversity conservation, watershed protection, carbon sequestration, soil conservation, and habitat preservation. Given the constraints outlined in this chapter, it seems unlikely that the dual objectives of economic development and conservation will be achieved via current forest resource use contracts.

Examples of the current constraints and future opportunities for improving forest resource contract practices are illustrated here in four case studies, as follows. In *Bolivia*, the Bosque Chimanes case study illustrates that extensive forest management can be both efficient and of relatively low impact without regulatory oversight. Past efforts to mandate "sustainable" management through regulatory force have failed in Chimanes due to financial, silvicultural, and administrative constraints. In *Colombia*, an industry/ community collaborative effort at intensive forest management provides an example of resolving the issues of multiple-use and local user rights that plague many forest resource use contracts in Latin America. In *Brazil*, the creation and development of extractive reserves offers insight into the viability of nontimber forest products as economic alternatives to timber production. And in *Chile*, to reduce the burden on state agencies and improve forest management, the government is experimenting with the transfer of forest concessions to private enterprises for ecotourism development.

Description of Contracts and Other Arrangements

In general, a forest utilization contract gives a nonpublic entity the right to harvest and/ or manage given resources under general conditions related to maintaining the health and productive potential of the forest. It also defines the payment for using those resources. The Food and Agriculture Organization of the United Nations (FAO 1977) defines a forest utilization contract for woods as follows: "... formal permission of the government or a public agency, which entitles an individual, a private company or a public or semi-public corporation, under clearly defined conditions, to the exclusive rights to explore the forest potential, to harvest wood, and/or to manage a specified area of public forest land. Such a contract combines public ownership of land with private or semi-private utilization of the raw material thereon. This kind of arrangement may lead to a partial or complete integration of the production process of forestry and the industrial utilization of wood without affecting the ownership of the land."

This definition could be broadened to encompass nonexclusive rights to forest resources, and could explicitly include nontimber forest resource uses as well. Under these terms, the grantor of the utilization contract is responsible for enforcing forest policies. These can include regulating any management requirements, legally protecting the contractee from encroachment on the granted forest land and/or from poaching the resources under contract, and, in some cases, installing and maintaining the necessary infrastructure (such as public roads) used to transport the products extracted from the forest.

Forest utilization contracts are based on the legal status of the property. In much of Latin America, forested land is the property of the government and is generally composed of two types of legal property: the forest itself and the land on which it grows. In those countries where the forest does not have a separate legal identity from the land, extracted forest resources may be defined separately. The property regime, therefore, affects directly the type and scope of a utilization contract for forest resources.

The property rights for land and natural resources comprise a legal property relation that is enforceable by the state. Such rights define the specific set of uses for the land and its resources to which the property holder is entitled. In much of Latin America, the government holds the formal property rights over forest resources, although local populations often exercise customary property rights over those same resources. In such cases, any contractual use of shared forest resources must consider how the rights of customary users may be affected by contracts between the government and other private entities.

Forest utilization contracts differ in their length in time, the size of forest area to be exploited, and the required forest management practices. Generally speaking, the larger an area under contract, the longer the contract period and the greater the management requirements. The terms and conditions of contracts in Latin America vary greatly from one situation to another.

A contract may be between the government and a private firm, a community, a corporation of private entities, or other groups. There are several elements to be considered in a forest use contract. First, the contract may cover a variety of resources, each with its own utilization and management characteristics. Second, the government's objectives may vary according to social, environmental, economic, geographical or other factors. Third, the profits from resource utilization may be shared between the government and the contractee through use of revenue systems. A government may choose to privatize public forest resources, to reduce its administrative burden, or to increase the efficiency of resource allocation and use.

Forest Revenue Systems. Forest revenue systems are designed to capture the funds generated by the use of public forest resources. These funds are then redistributed through public agencies and may be used for forest regulation and management. The following list of taxes and fees includes the most commonly used ones in the forestry sector of many developing countries.

- *License fee.* This fee is determined administratively and is generally paid as a fixed fee prior to issuing a license for use. The license fee is very easy to administer and offers little opportunity for evasion.
- *Area tax.* Area taxes are similar to license fees but are generally paid on an annual basis and are proportional to the area of land under contract. This fee is administratively simple, with little opportunity for evasion.
- *Standing timber volume tax.* This tax is based on an inventory of the commercial trees in the area under contract and requires an extensive appraisal of the forest resources if it is to be properly applied.
- *Per-tree harvest charge.* Charges per tree are paid prior to harvest and are generally set as a uniform charge that is undifferentiated by species value. Furthermore, revenue collection is negatively affected by the failure to reflect stumpage value. This, however, could be corrected by a more sophisticated administration process for collecting the charge.
- *Volume charge* on extracted timber and nontimber products. This charge is applied after scaling and grading extracted timber. Although it demands more administrative work, this charge when properly implemented can reflect more accurate values for the extracted resources than the other taxes.
- *Charge for direct services.* The most common charge for a direct service is a reforestation tax. Although such taxes should be based on the cost of reforestation services, they are more often based on production. If properly applied, a reforestation tax could fund large-scale nurseries that would supply various forest contractors with the seedlings and technical guidance needed for reforestation. In reality, however, reforestation is rarely implemented in the context of natural forest management in the humid tropics and applying a reforestation tax is generally viewed by loggers as an unnecessary burden.
- *Charges on producers and nonextractive users.* Producers and nonextractive users can be charged on their profits by calculations derived from either their income taxes or from their profit-based royalties. A user's income tax cannot be considered a substitute for other forest utilization charges. Using an income tax in developing countries as a basis for user charges has the disadvantage of having to rely on accurate record-keeping for auditing. In contrast, profit-based royalties are derived from the per-unit profitability of forest resource production and can be calculated from a business' profits. Both systems can be used for nonextractive uses as, for example, in ecotourism. Ecotourism operations that have contracts for using a forest can be charged based on the income tax on their revenues, or on the per-unit royalty for services provided.

Privatization. A forest utilization contract is only one of several possible resource use arrangements for public lands. The government or public agency responsible for forest resources may choose among several options: to utilize and manage the forests itself; to capitalize on the experience and efficiency of the private sector through forest resource utilization contracts; or to transfer the property to private entities through privatization.

Privatization occurs when public forests or forest lands are sold to private entities. In an efficient market, the sale price of private lands should reflect the net present value[1] of the forest's productive capacity or services in perpetuity. Naturally, markets

---

[1] The net present value of a forest's future productive capacity is the maximum amount one is willing to pay for the sum of financial returns from the forest expected over its lifetime. Such returns are "discounted" according to inflation and risk, reflecting estimated change in currency values.

can affect land prices via speculation and other behavior associated with uncertain information regarding the future value of forest land. Privatization can generate revenue from the one-time sale of the property, but it only reflects the current assessment of the long-term value of the forested land. In addition, the government receives income from annual taxes on production and volume harvested. The income flows resulting from these taxes rely largely upon the property regime of the country. It is imperative to acknowledge that a private owner may have no incentive to manage the forest and may choose to liquidate it instead.

Interest in privatization of forest resources in countries such as Peru has been driven primarily by a desire to improve the efficiency of domestic industries. Following the logic of Coase (1960), private property rights are fundamental to market economies since they facilitate the efficient allocation of resources. A growing amount of literature focuses on the role of property rights in natural resource management in developing countries. The common themes in this literature are the relationship between land rights and investment, and the mitigation of possible negative environmental effects.

If forest management is profitable for the private sector, privatization of forests may result in the long-term management of those resources by private entities. However, there are serious financial and silvicultural constraints to long-term forest management in Latin America. Specifically, the nonmarket environmental benefits of privatization (with the objective of promoting long-term forest management) are not realized if the owner clears away the forest. As a result, provisions in the privatization agreement that restrict activities on privatized forest lands will most likely be necessary, especially those that regulate the conversion of forest land to agriculture.

Forest lands can be privatized for uses other than timber extraction. Ecotourism, hunting and fishing, and nontimber forest products (NTFP) are all possible uses for such lands. For example, land designated as permanent forest may be privatized, with the provision that the new owners only use the land for forest resource management. If such management no longer makes sense for the responsible entity, it may exercise the option to sell the land to another private entity or to the state. Use restrictions on privatized forest should be made in conjunction with land-use planning and zoning.

Protection of Permanent Forests. Whether through contractual utilization or privatization, mechanisms must be established to prevent forest degradation. Three currently used mechanisms are contract renewal provisions, performance bonds, and other liability insurances.

- *Renewal provisions* apply to contractual use only. The provisions may include an assessment of the contractee's performance as a forest manager (in terms of forest damage caused during extraction), payment of taxes, reforestation, forest health, and productivity resulting from silvicultural treatments, etc.
- *Performance bonds* may be used under both forest utilization contracts and privatization. A performance bond is paid by the private entity that wishes to manage a specified area of forest land. The value of the bond reflects the expected renewable resource value of the forest that could be lost if the forest were improperly managed. This bond remains in public hands until the contractee ceases using the forest and demonstrates that the forest remains in a healthy and productive condition, at which point the bond is returned to the contractee.

- *Other liability insurance.* Although the performance bond is the most straightforward liability insurance, more sophisticated systems may be developed. These could include a forestry insurance industry and tort standards for compensating affected stakeholders.

Contract Objectives

There are two general objectives of a forest use contract for public land: economic development and conservation of forest resources. The success of a forest resource use contract is measured by how well these objectives are fulfilled.

Economic Development. The measurement of economic development is widely disputed, but the most common objectives of economic development are the efficient use of resources for economic growth and equitable access to those resources. The goal of the policies is to promote a multiplicity of competitive economic activities that contribute to a country's overall growth. The standard measure of success for achieving an efficient use of forest resources is the maximization of the net present value (NPV). It is important to note, however, that rarely do estimates of NPV include comprehensive valuation of positive and negative ecological externalities. Admittedly, even incomplete measures of NPV are helpful in determining efficient allocation of resources. In Latin America, where land reform has defined economic history, equitable access to resources begins with land use rights.

The primary constraint to maximizing profits is enforced regulations. Regulations are intended to protect forest resources, but they frequently cause unnecessary economic distortions in the forestry sector. Significant opportunities for maximizing economic efficiency generally exist in areas where the conditions do not require intensive regulation to protect the forest's health.

Equal access to forest resources is often constrained by several factors: the lack of access of local communities to bidding documents and inability to profitably manage commercial forest concessions; political corruption in the contract allocation process; and the implementation of norms for exclusive rather than integrated forest resource management. Nevertheless, opportunities exist for alternative forest use contracts that allow local users to benefit from public forest resources, such as NTFP contracts and integrated commercial/community forest management plans.

Conservation. The measurement of success in forest conservation ranges from the maintenance of forest cover, erosion control, watershed protection, and habitat preservation, to the conservation of biological diversity. The primary constraints to achieving conservation via forest resource use contracts are the lack of regulatory enforcement and scientific knowledge needed to design regulations that are environmentally sound. Forest use contracts need to include conservation set-asides. Other essential elements are the creation of conservation and ecotourism concessions, and the promotion of other environmentally friendly economic activities—specifically those that complement conservation goals.

Sustainable Forest Management. At present there is a great deal of confusion regarding the objectives of forest resource use contracts. The various definitions of sustainable forestry treat economic development and conservation of forest resources as complementary. While the larger objectives of economic development and environmental quality are strongly related, at the level of a managed forest, conservation and economic development may often be at odds. As a result, forestry regulations that are designed under the rubric of "sustainability" often fail to accomplish the goals of either economic development or conservation.

Sustainable forestry plans often focus on the continuous yield of timber from a forest, ad infinitum. In many cases, this approach fails to maximize the net present value of forest resource use. Indeed, continuous yield forestry often results in economic loss in the neotropics. Economic development might best be served by maximizing the net present value from selective species harvesting in production forests with minimal environmental impact and subsequent forest protection, followed by an allocation of public forest revenues to infrastructure, education, health care, and private sector investment in growing sectors of the economy. Failure to understand this concept will result in a continued misdirection of forest resource use policy and in economic failure of many forest use contracts.

Conclusions

In order to evaluate forest resource use contracts, the objectives of the contracts must be clearly defined. The ability to achieve these objectives must be evaluated considering the economic, ecological, political, geographical, and cultural constraints and opportunities. By tailoring the objectives to fit the context of forest use contracts, the potential for their success increases.

Achieving the objectives of conservation through forest resource use contracts is an uphill battle. Both the contracts that suffer economic failure due to the regulations imposed by sustainable forestry and those that succeed due to the evasion of such requirements may result in significant harm to forest health. It is a misconception that economic behavior does not necessarily correspond with forest resource conservation. Conservation must often be addressed as a separate objective.

Constraints to Achieving Contract Objectives

Forest resource use contracts are hindered by four factors in particular:

- Financial incentives that strongly favor selective logging, rather than long-term management in tropical forests and investment in regeneration;
- Lack of a technical basis for adequate silviculture in neotropical forests;
- Governments that lack administrative capacity and political will to impose sound management; and
- Cultural and social norms that fail to recognize the local users of forest resources.

The failure of resource use contracts to achieve economic and conservation objectives can largely be attributed to one or more of these constraints.

Financial Context of Forest Management in the Humid Tropics

Fundamental to the economics of renewable resources is the *productivity* of the natural resource. Foresters understand productivity to be the volume of timber that grows in a forest. Foresters also understand that productivity can be increased by the use of silvicultural techniques designed to improve the growing conditions for commercial trees and to otherwise manage the health of the forest environment. Such treatments incur costs and are thus viewed as investments whose return will be realized upon the eventual harvest of the trees.

Interest Rates versus Growth and Price Appreciation. Latin American countries tend to have high interest rates due to public economic policies and to a strong preference for capital in the present (rather than the future) by members of those economies. This combination makes the discount rate a crucial consideration for long-term investments in land use in the region (Schneider et al. 1993). Recently, annual real interest rates in many Latin American countries have exceeded 10 percent for periods of years. As a consequence, long-term investments in natural resource management are discouraged (Costanza and Daly 1990).

Reid and Rice (1997) estimate that annual growth rates of nontemperate natural forests in Latin America range between 0 m^3 and 4 m^3 per hectare, with most between .5 m^3 to 2 m^3 per hectare. The range of annual growth rates is approximately 0.5 to 4 percent. Empirical data from Bajo Calima in western Colombia indicate that many species of trees may require substantially more than 30 years to recover from harvesting, indicating that previously anticipated rotation periods of 30 years or less for natural forest management are unrealistic (Faber-Langendoen 1992).

Price appreciation for tropical timber is equally discouraging. Real annual price appreciation for tropical timber from 1950 to 1992 was 1.2 percent (Varangis 1992). According to the FAO (1994), nonconiferous sawnwood prices from Latin America showed a depreciation of 3.74 percent from 1981 to 1992. It is generally believed that the supply of non-specialty woods is abundant on the global market and shows little or no demand pressure (Vincent and Binkley 1992; Sedjo and Lyon 1990).

A series of studies demonstrates this point with empirical evidence and simulation models. Reid and Howard (1994) compared non-managed timber extraction with two alternative management systems for a humid tropical forest in Guatemala. They found that without management the NPV of forest production was 21 to 55 percent more profitable than that of the management alternatives. Hardner and Rice (1994) used a simulation model to test various parameters, such as rotation length, interest rates, growth and mortality rates, and management expenditures. They found that, under normal growth and mortality rates for a managed forest in the Eastern Amazon, the opportunity cost of postponing the harvest of all commercial trees in a stand resulted in a negative return on management investments. Howard et al. (1996) simulated four alternative management systems for the Chimanes forest in Bolivia and found that current unregulated logging is two to four and a half times more profitable for the logger than the potential returns from management. This analysis, however, does not include in its accounting the rents forgone by the government, nor the value of the negative externalities caused by the unregulated logging operation.

Timber Certification. Timber certification is one possible method to provide a financial incentive for long-term forest management (see Chapters 5 and 10). It is based on a price premium offered by "green" markets (timber harvested in an ecologically sound manner). There are two problems with this approach. First, the financial incentive required to make long-term management profitable is a guaranteed real price appreciation that matches the discount rate used by forest managers. It is unrealistic to assume that the market price appreciation could match the extremely high discount rates affecting forest management in Latin America (Hardner and Rice 1994).

Secondly, the global market for ecologically harvested tropical timber is currently estimated to be less than .2 percent of the total tropical timber market (Varangis et al. 1995). Even if all tropical timber imported by the United States and Europe were certified, it would only represent .75 percent of the total production of tropical timber (ITTO 1995). The bulk of tropical timber demand comes from producing countries whose domestic markets cannot, or are not inclined to, absorb the green market premium.

Economics of Nontimber Forest Products. Despite bold assertions of the relative economic potential of NTFPs over alternative land uses (Peters et al. 1989; Fearnside 1989; Schwartzman 1989; Allegretti 1990; Grimes et al. 1994), formal efforts to harness these benefits have been disappointing (Browder 1990; Pinedo-Vásquez et al. 1990). Multiple problems plague NTFPs, including production irregularities, inadequate market demand, production and transportation costs, and lack of management experience at the local production level (Flynn 1995). The most significant constraint to relying on NTFPs as a land use option is the pressure from alternative land use activities.

Three examples illustrate this point. Among the most advanced multiple-use inte-grated forest management programs in Latin America is the Maya Biosphere Reserve (MBR) in Guatemala. The core of the MBR is a protected area, surrounded by a forested buffer zone and multiple-use zone. Among the variety of services and products that the MBR generates, NTFP production is a centerpiece; but due to the low profitability of these activities, NTFP production alone is not a suitable alternative (Salafsky et al. 1991).

On the Pacific coast of Ecuador, *tagua* nuts are collected and sold to button manu-facturers in Europe and the United States. Collection of the nuts typically takes place in unoccupied and unmanaged forests and its sale supplements local families' income. *Tagua* is not an especially lucrative product (Southgate 1997), but it is a viable option for income generation among the very few in the area, given the isolation of the producing region from markets and roads. Hardner (1995a) interviewed *tagua* producers in this region and found that they chose *tagua* as a second-best activity to clearing forest for more intensive uses that were not possible due to capital constraints.

Natural latex production, or rubber-tapping, is widely held as a sustainable forest activity in the Brazilian Amazon. This activity has also fallen prey to market forces, as national price supports for this product become increasingly important for its viability. The inability of latex producers to compete in the global rubber market is understandable considering the transportation costs, production techniques, and the production limits of the forest to produce natural latex.

Summary. Natural forest management is rarely economically viable for the private man-ager under the conditions prevailing in the neotropics. This is not to say that forest man-agement will never be economically viable, but rather that forest utilization contracts must take economic constraints into account.

Silvicultural Context

Silviculture is the application of scientific principles of forest ecology to increase the utility of a forest. The utility of a forest can be ascertained from its role in watershed protection, wildlife habitat, recreation, and most commonly, for timber production. Silvi-culture involves the control of forest structure, process, composition, and regeneration. The basis of silviculture is *silvics,* or the principles underlying the growth and develop-ment of individual trees and of the forest as a whole ecological unit. The management of a forest, especially when the objective is to produce timber, requires knowledge of the regeneration mechanisms and growth characteristics of the constituent species in the forest. It also requires an understanding of the dynamics of the whole forest that play out as a result of the interactions between species within the ecological parameters of the forest.

In the neotropics, very little is known of the silvics of even the most common native commercial species. What is known about neotropical forest ecology is that these forests are generally composed of a stratified mixture of species, are highly diverse and dynamic, and they depend on disturbances for regeneration. In addition, many species may not exhibit "density dependence," an important regeneration characteristic that determines the resilience of that species to harvesting. All of these factors in combination result in a level of ecosystem complexity that makes the controlled and systematic management methods used in more simple temperate forests extremely difficult to transfer.

Current Forest Management in the Neotropics. Silvicultural methods remain to be developed for the long-term management of commercial species in humid neotropical forests (see Boot and Gullison 1997). Current forest management in much of Latin America can be categorized as multi-cyclic selective harvesting systems with no basis in silvicultural principles. The result of this type of management is a progressive "high-grading" of the forests that begins with first extracting the very highly valued species such as mahogany *(Swietenia macrophylla)* and Spanish cedar *(Cedrela odorata, mexicana)*, then eventually turning to lesser-known hardwood species or even "secondary," early successional species. The latter are easily regenerated to produce lower quality wood for such uses as construction (Brown and Lugo 1990). Once the selective harvesting of the small number of high-valued species is finished and the demand for the lower-valued wood does not support production and transportation costs, commercial logging stops.

Examples of selective high-grading can be found in the Proyecto Chimanes, an ITTO-sponsored experimental forestry program in Beni, Bolivia (Synnott and Cassells 1991; Gullison 1995), and the Quintana Roo Pilot Program in Mexico (Snook 1991). In both of these projects, the standing populations of mahogany and cedar were systematically harvested without any suitable silvicultural treatments to ensure their regeneration or the release of established seedlings in the understory. As a result, the commercial populations of these two species in those areas may never recover. Logging equipment and sawmills have been devoted increasingly to extracting and producing lesser-known and lower-valued species, again with no silvicultural treatment.

Other acclaimed forestry experiments in Latin America have succeeded in minimizing damage during harvest and have increased the growth rates of existing commercial trees, but they are still a far way from managing the regeneration and stand dynamics of specific species. Perhaps the most often cited programs are the CELOS Management System in Suriname, the Tapajos National Forest and the experiments of the Instituto do Homem e Meio Ambiente da Amazônia (IMAZON) in the Eastern Amazon. All of these programs have done an excellent job of systematically reducing logging damages and controlling harvests. The CELOS and Tapajos projects demonstrated significant increases in the growth rates of commercial species through thinning operations (DeGraaf 1990; DeGraaf and Rompaey 1986; Silva et al. 1995), and the IMAZON project may soon conduct similar experiments. However, none of these programs has been financially attractive enough for commercial management, and therefore are yet to be implemented by the private sector.

Much attention was drawn to the operation of Cartón de Colombia's concession in Bajo Calima, Colombia, where a sophisticated clear-cutting technique was utilized for the production of cellulose. This project was touted as an example of sustainable forestry

(Johnson and Cabarle 1993). The concession was abandoned due to regulatory problems long before the silvicultural system could be tested, but studies by the Missouri Botanical Garden indicate that Cartón de Colombia vastly overestimated forest regeneration (Faber-Langendoen 1992). The company planned to harvest each clear-cut area every 30 years, but evidence suggests that 90 years would actually be required to replace the biomass removed by the first harvest. Furthermore, if Cartón de Colombia harvested every thirty years, many species would be eliminated from the local population due to their inability to reestablish themselves in so short a period of time.

The formal knowledge about NTFP extraction is even more sparse than that of timber. Several studies indicate that long-term management plans for many NTFPs are lacking, while many result in the decrease of commercial populations of these species (Hall and Bawa 1993). In Guatemala's Petén region, the regeneration of *xate*, an ornamental plant harvested for export to a lucrative U.S. market, does not compensate for the heavy harvesting of this plant, and formal management systems for *xate* still do not exist (Dicum and Tarifa 1994; Cabrera-Madrid et al. 1990). In contrast, the harvest of products such as natural latex, chicle, and Brazil nuts is documented as not adversely affecting the natural populations of these species. Simply put, much remains to be learned about the ecology of these species.

A recent FAO survey of natural forest management throughout Latin America concluded that ". . . notwithstanding all the numerous research and development projects undertaken here and there in Latin America, in most of the countries tropical forest management exists only in theory, and has practically never been put in practice in the field, though governments require submission of a forest management plan before issuing a logging permit" (FAO 1993).

Biodiversity Impacts. Another perspective on forest management and logging is their impact on biodiversity. Although a great deal of international attention has been focused on the conservation of biodiversity, we remain woefully ill-informed about the ecosystem dynamics that regulate diversity especially in the humid tropics and the effects of such ecosystem manipulations as timber extraction and forest management. Indeed, very little is known about the detailed species composition of most tropical forests. The discovery of new species, for example, is commonplace in virtually all taxa, including those such as primates, that have been heavily studied. In Brazil alone, six new species of monkeys have been discovered since 1990. For the bulk of species described so far in tropical forests, the abundance, population distributions, life histories, habitat requirements, and responses to natural and man-made disturbances are completely unknown. In short, there is little scientific basis for the development of management plans to ensure the conservation of biodiversity within the context of timber production in tropical forests.

What is known, in general terms, is that timber extraction can significantly impact forest ecosystems, such as the habitat composition of the forest canopy. For species dependent on the canopy for habitat, this change in forest structure can be every bit as dramatic as converting the forest to pasture. Studies in temperate forests indicate that some species dependent on old growth for a portion of their life cycle can nevertheless survive in a managed forest, provided that it is in sufficiently close proximity to a relatively undisturbed forest. How these findings relate to species conservation in the tropics is only beginning to be addressed in scientific studies. In view of our ignorance, however, the retention of significant areas of undisturbed forest in and around areas devoted to logging would appear to be prudent if conserving biodiversity is an objective of forest policy.

Summary. The scientific fundamentals of humid forest management in Latin America are currently inadequate to reliably implement silviculture there. Though some experiments in forest management have shown promising results, they are experiments nevertheless, and have a long way to go before they become useful as management models. Regulations that demand forest management plans are therefore unrealistic and are often treated as such by both private firms and regulators alike. Forest policy that aims at promoting silviculture should acknowledge that much of the information and experience necessary to make it happen are either nonexistent or nontransferable.

Political and Regulatory Constraints

The implementation of good forest policy is also constrained by governments that lack the administrative capacity and political will to enforce forestry regulations. On paper at least, Latin America has sophisticated and rigorous forest management requirements governing the design of forest management plans, the volume and diameter limits for extracted timber, reforestation practices, and tax obligations for forest resource users. In reality, however, it is often difficult to discern whether forest resource use is governed by anything other than the contract holders' business management decisions. The enforcement of forest regulations is further weakened by possible corruption among inspectors; inadequate staffing and resource allocation for enforcement; lack of technical expertise to determine whether management plans submitted by contract holders are valid, viable, or being executed properly; and a lack of political accountability to people who are affected by the misuse of forest resources.

However, despite the many advantages to forest resource contract holders that result from the lack of regulatory enforcement, these parties often suffer from the inability of the government to maintain its contractual obligations. Contracts often explicitly guarantee state-assisted reforestation programs, and implicitly guarantee infrastructure support as well as the enforcement of land-use regulations that prevent colonization on forest areas under contract with a private firm. Much to the contractee's dismay, such guarantees are often not met by the accountable government agencies.

To make matters worse, tax revenues from the contractual utilization of forest resources are essential for the provision of these services, but are often mismanaged or not collected properly. The common problems experienced with revenue systems in Latin America are: (1) fees and taxes are too low to fully capture the potential funds from forest use contracts; and (2) most of the revenue systems are administratively complex and costly to operate. For example, in Peru, the Cámara Nacional Forestal (CNF) argues that state reforestation taxes have rarely been used for reforestation (Razetto 1996). The CNF argues that if reforestation is to occur, private firms will either have to pay for it themselves, in addition to the fees already paid to the state, or eliminate the tax altogether and place reforestation into private hands. In Colombia, the large industrial concessions of Cartón de Colombia and Pizano were permanently abandoned because the government did not control colonization on the land under contract (Rodríguez 1996). Without the proper realization of basic government functions (such as enforcing regulations), it is difficult to imagine a successful forest sector in any country.

Whether such problems can be remedied is doubtful given the current level of responsibility assigned to governments and the limited resources they have to execute their duties. Recent efforts to redesign forestry bureaucracies in Bolivia and Suriname revealed that the proper management of public forest resources would require management agencies whose size far exceeded their revenue-generating capacity and could pos-

Table 9.1 Stakeholder Issues

Stakeholder	Concern
Forest industry	Security of accessing resources Acceptance of forest investment as collateral Limitations on usufruct rights of colonists Administration of a reforestation tax
Government	Utilization of forest resources Conservation obligations from UNCED Conference and international conventions (biodiversity, climate change, CITES) Protection of indigenous lands
Indigenous groups	Protection of indigenous lands
Local users	Security of accessing resources, usufruct rights
Conservation NGOs	Protection of biodiversity, sustainable forest management

sibly dwarf all other government agencies. Without an adequately staffed, technically sound, and properly equipped forest authority, the breakdown in enforcement that is witnessed in many regions of Latin America will continue to occur.

Cultural and Social Constraints

Local uses for forest resources are often overlooked in the design of national-level forest policies. Utilization contracts that protect the usufruct rights[2] of local populations are uncommon (Davis and Wali 1994). Land-use conflict most often erupts when property rights are not clearly defined. This is particularly common for indigenous groups and customary users of forest resources such as the Brazilian rubber tappers. The principal stakeholders should participate in forest resource use decisions (Table 9.1).

However, the definition of property rights is often complex. When resource use contracts provide for the exclusive use of a resource, they often neglect the nontimber and fuelwood resources that local populations use from these forests. Another example is found in small-scale agricultural clearings that unofficially occur in areas under forest concessions. Additional complications may occur when botanical resources are extracted for pharmaceutical purposes, as intellectual property rights may not be included in forest resource use contracts.

When land-use conflicts erupt as a result of poorly delineated property rights, then forest resource use contracts are placed in jeopardy. The key to resolving such con-

---

[2] The customary informal right to utilize parts of a resource.

flicts is to acknowledge that local users hold usufruct rights that must be respected if land-use conflict is to be avoided. Unfortunately, it is rarely a cultural norm for these usufruct rights to be respected or even perceived by commercial users as a formal legal property relation (Hardner 1995b).

Until this point in the discussion of forest use contracts, the emphasis on timber production has been a reflection of the proportion of timber utilization contracts versus nontimber utilization contracts that exist in Latin America today. The economics of NTFP production for national and international markets does not appear promising at present, but the potential for the production of a variety of goods in the future may warrant the allocation of NTFP contracts. Nevertheless, the obstacles are great. The Extractive Reserves Project in Brazil provides evidence that one of the greatest barriers to success is deficient organization among NTFP producers. Hunting and fishing activities may also warrant the allocation of a concession, especially where managing wildlife for local populations is necessary (TCA 1994b). Failure to acknowledge that hunting is important to local populations, or that fauna is a forest resource that demands careful management and conservation (TCA 1994b), is reflected in the absence of hunting- and fishing-oriented concessions.

Ecotourism is also not widely recognized as an alternative means of forest utilization. Unfortunately, even less is known about ecotourism as a contracted forest use. Experience to date indicates that ecotourism has a great potential for revenue generation, although informal studies have shown that the total area necessary to support an ecotourism site may be rather small. Furthermore, ecotourism sites are more selective than timber concessions, since natural characteristics and infrastructure factors contribute greatly to the merit of a tourism locale. The potential for ecotourism sites in Latin America should not be overestimated in terms of geographical extent.

Conclusions

Forest policy planning must reckon with the various constraints to achieving economic and conservation objectives through forest resource use contracts. If forest policy objectives take account of the constraints in a particular area, then forest use contracts may be more successful than otherwise. The next section presents case studies that exemplify such constraints and offer some opportunities for revising forest use contracts.

Case Studies

The following four cases illustrate the constraints and opportunities for forest use contracts in Latin America. The first case illustrates how economic efficiency and conservation are achieved in Bolivia, despite regulatory failure, and provides an opportunity for implementing this model in other regions with minimum regulatory oversight. The second case describes an innovative alternative forest use model in Colombia that integrates commercial forestry with numerous local users. This model satisfies the dual objectives of economic development for local users, as well as logging activities for the commercial timber sector. The last two case studies analyze programs for extractive reserves in Brazil and for ecotourism in Chile.

Bolivia: Industrial Forest Concessions in Bosque Chimanes

The case of Bosque Chimanes illustrates many of the difficulties encountered in the efforts to employ forest use contracts to encourage long-term management in primary tropical forests. In this case, light selective harvesting, or extensive forest management, prove

Table 9.2 Indigenous Populations in Bosque Chimanes, Bolivia

Group	Number
Mojeno	2,188
Chimanes	2,170
Yuracares	181
Movimas	28
Total	**4,567**

Source: Authors' research.

to be both efficient and of relatively low impact despite failed regulatory oversights. It is an example of both the ineffectiveness of contract regulations in a typical remote forest concession, and the relative insignificance of their absence. This case study demonstrates the opportunity for other countries with similar characteristics to achieve the objectives of economic efficiency and forest conservation in areas where government oversight is limited.

Bosque Chimanes. The Chimanes region occupies an area of 1.4 million ha in the Amazon Basin of west-central Bolivia. This region includes the 422,000-ha Chimanes Permanent Production Forest, the 81,000-ha Beni Biosphere Reserve, the 392,000-ha Chimanes Indigenous Territory, the 355,000-ha Multi-Ethnic Reserve, and the 130,000-ha Yacuma Regional Park. Bosque Chimanes is classified as a humid forest with an average precipitation of 2,180 mm and four to six dry months per year.

In 1986, two logging firms established themselves in Bosque Chimanes to extract mahogany (*Swietenia macrophylla*), a highly valued commercial species in the neotropics. In 1987, the Programa Chimanes was created to implement a model of sustainable tropical forestry for the Amazon region; and in 1988 it was chosen by the ITTO to be funded. By 1990, six major logging concessions were established in Bosque Chimanes under the guidance and regulation of the Programa Chimanes.

Fourteen indigenous sub-groups reside in Bosque Chimanes, the largest of which are shown in Table 9.2.

Failure of the Sustainable Forestry Management Plan. Forest management in Bosque Chimanes was subject to both national regulations (promoted by the former Centro de Desarrollo Forestal, or CDF), and local guidelines (designed and enforced by the Programa Chimanes). Due to the lack of silvicultural knowledge about mahogany, an approximation of silviculture was devised that preserved a minimum density of seed trees and guaranteed a second harvest by leaving smaller trees behind. The management plan for the region also required the extraction of lower-valued species to eliminate reliance on a single species (mahogany), and to generate interest in managing these forests for multiple species. The success of this management plan relied on four factors: (1) adhering to the terms of forest utilization contracts and regulations; (2) the presence of a significant population of trees of commercially valuable species below the minimum diameter cutting limit; (3) the natural regeneration of the extracted species; and (4) economic incentives to adhere to the management plan. Unfortunately, the project has failed in each factor.

Regulatory guidelines for Bosque Chimanes allowed the harvest of selected trees above 80 cm in diameter and required the maintenance of a minimum density of seed trees. The Programa Chimanes then calculated a maximum total annual area and volume of harvest for each of the six concessions to allow a 30-year rotation. In addition, all harvested trees were to be approved and marked for extraction by an officer of the Programa Chimanes prior to cutting.

Despite such careful planning, the actual harvest within these concessions resembled a maximized extraction of mahogany rather than a planned, controlled harvest of a wide variety of species. The majority of wood extracted from Bosque Chimanes is mahogany *(Swietenia macrophylla)*, followed at a distant second by cedar *(Cedrela ordorata)*. The high value of mahogany relative to other forest species encouraged firms to be highly selective in their harvesting, traveling great distances to extract a very few mahogany trees, and leaving most other species. Since the initiation of the management plan, extracted volumes and harvested areas have greatly exceeded those intended by the management plan (Synnott and Cassells 1991). The marking of harvestable trees by project technicians often included trees below the 80-cm diameter limit and failed to provide the minimum stand density of seed trees indicated by the management plan. In some cases tree marking was simply absent from the harvesting process (Gullison 1995). This lack of compliance may be explained by weak or nonexistent enforcement mechanisms combined with understaffing and possible corruption. However, the underlying cause is most likely a lack of political will on behalf of policymakers.

One year after the official beginning of the project, it appeared as if the commercial population of mahogany would be depleted in short order. By 1995, the entire harvestable population of mahogany was exhausted in at least one concession (Gullison 1995). Even had the concessionaires complied with the management plan, it is questionable that it would have corresponded to the planned silvicultural prescription for providing future harvests.

The stand structure of mahogany in Bosque Chimanes reflects its disturbance-driven regeneration characteristics, resulting in stands of even-aged trees. Statistical analysis of the stand structure in Bosque Chimanes indicates that very few mahogany trees actually exist in diameter classes below 80 cm, thereby making the 80-cm diameter limit of little use in ensuring a second rotation (Gullison 1995). In addition, the regeneration of mahogany in Bosque Chimanes relies on large hydrological disturbances, a process that does not correspond with the seed tree prescription in the management plan. Gullison (1995) found that after logging, the population density of mahogany was reduced from 0.25 trees per ha to 0.036 trees per ha and that seed trees were generally with low fertility. Gullison concludes that this reduction in the density of mahogany had dramatically reduced the probability that mahogany seedlings would become established in gaps generated by natural but infrequent hydrological disturbances.

Another inherent weakness of the management plan was its lack of financial logic. The greatest source of resistance to adopting the management plan was its impact on company profits. Given the high value of mahogany, combined with prevailing interest rates and low tree growth and price appreciation, loggers have a strong incentive to clear the standing mahogany as quickly as possible. Relative to the simulated management plan designed to promote regeneration of mahogany and extract a greater variety of species, Howard et al. (1996) found that the net present value of current practices that do not adhere to the management plan is much greater. They conclude that the voluntary adoption of long-term forest management practices by concessionaires in Bosque Chimanes is unlikely given the financial disincentives. The lack of regulatory enforcement in the area demands that private agents be motivated by other means (such as financial returns), to manage the forest. In the case of Bosque Chimanes, such incentives do not exist.

Table 9.3 Royalties and Fees for Selected Timber Species

Species	Sum of fees and royalties ($/m³)
Mahogany	21.25
Cedro	17.67
Almendrillo	17.30
Verdolago	15.46
Roble	14.70
Bibosi	13.06
Ochoo	13.06

Source: Authors' research.

Failure of the Revenue System. Concessions in Bosque Chimanes are subject to several fees. *Derechos de Monte* is a fixed fee paid per cubic meter of roundwood extracted, payable to the CDF. The volume of roundwood is back-calculated from the volume of sawnwood that leaves the sawmill. This is the CDF's primary revenue vehicle. *Plantaciones Forestales* is a fixed fee set at one-half the value of the *Derechos de Monte*, paid to the Programa Chimanes to reforest logged areas. *Regalias* is an 11 percent royalty on the profit margin, based on market prices in the capital city of the department. This tax is paid to the regional economic development agency. The total fees and royalties paid for mahogany and lesser-valued species are shown in Table 9.3.

In theory, the revenue system should capture funds generated by the extraction of timber from the natural forest. In practice, Rice and Howard (1997) found that only a small percentage of the fees were collected. Instead, the bulk of these monies accrued to companies as windfall profits. Rice and Howard calculated the profitability of mahogany extraction (with variable production and capital depreciation) to yield a profitability between 10.3 percent and 200 percent due to these imperfections.

Failure to Define Resource Rights. In 1990, hundreds of indigenous residents of Bosque Chimanes marched 650 kilometers to La Paz to protest the designation of their lands as a forest reserve, and later, the allocation of timber concessions on their lands. In response to this march the Bolivian government enacted Supreme Decree No. 22611, which limited future forest concessions in Bosque Chimanes and protected indigenous lands from third parties. With the assistance of the Amazon Cooperation Treaty (TCA 1994a), indigenous lands were demarcated and a policing system was designed that involved members of the indigenous communities and a network of short-wave radios.

Despite the decree and the assistance of the TCA and NGOs, the indigenous lands in Bosque Chimanes have been aggressively harvested for mahogany by third parties. The diminishing supply of accessible commercial mahogany on these concessions has generated a great pressure to use the indigenous lands as a supplementary source of timber. Independent loggers commonly entered the indigenous lands to cut trees for the big concessions. According to a report by the Center for Research and Documentation for the Development of Beni (CIDDEBENI) in 1995, as many as 300 chainsawers were registered in a nearby town, San Borja, presumably to work on indigenous lands. Access roads skirt the indigenous lands and skid trails enter the indigenous territories in many places as a result of harvesting trees on these lands.

In 1992, 2,800 trees illegally felled by chainsawers in the Multi-Ethnic Territory were auctioned to two of the six concessions in Bosque Chimanes. The auction served to legitimize the sale of illegally felled timber and eventually led to the sale of 3,130 additional trees in 1994 alone. Despite the prohibition of these transactions by the forest law, the CDF approved each of these sales (CIDDEBENI 1995).

This breakdown in forest utilization contracting and in regulating resource rights has resulted in great animosity between the various groups in the region. These failures are the consequence of inadequate resource rights allocation and enforcement in the Bosque Chimanes from the outset.

Conclusions. Many lessons can be learned from Bosque Chimanes. First, its regulation was more of a burden on industry and government than an aid to sustainable forest management—successive high-grading occurred despite the regulating agency's efforts to control it. Second, even if the administration had been perfect, the ecological basis of the forest management plan was inadequate. Third, the lack of property rights delineation at the outset of the contract design led to unnecessary land/resource use conflicts.

Despite these failings, the overall damage to Bosque Chimanes was rather limited. The light selective extraction of commercial species occurred at a very low density and resulted in limited damage to the forest cover (Gullison and Hardner 1994). The objective of conservation through forest management was achieved in spite of the failed designs of the regulating agency to achieve this objective. In addition, the extraction of timber was more efficient than would have occurred had loggers left abundant commercial trees in the forest for future harvest. If efficiency and conservation were the objectives for the management of Bosque Chimanes, they could have been achieved at much less cost and effort on behalf of the regulating agency through the use of limited, effective regulatory tools, such as those discussed in the following section.

Colombia: The Pizano S.A. Industrial/Community Interface

Pizano S.A. is one of Colombia's largest commercial producers of wood. This case study examines an innovative program of Pizano S.A. to integrate local populations into forest management for commercial-scale wood production. The history of forest resource use contracts in Colombia that led to Pizano's initiation of this project is characterized by conflicting commercial and local forest resource use. The Pizano model satisfies the dual objectives of economic development for local users as well as profits for the commercial timber sector. It does not address the objective of conservation of biological diversity, as forest management will result in the simplification of the forest ecosystem to produce select, fast-growing, commercial trees.

Recent History of Forest Concessions in Colombia. Forest policy in Colombia is in a transitional phase. With the establishment of a new Ministry of the Environment, a new set of guidelines for forest resource utilization on public lands is being created, and a technical staff to facilitate this transition is forming. The new forest policy will revise the current concession paradigm by the following means:

- Acknowledging corporations of small producers;
- Creating stringent concession renewal terms;
- Establishing new revenue systems;
- Devising new forest resource allocation systems;
- Setting new processing standards; and
- Developing regional parameters for forest resource management.

The Ministry of the Environment concedes that the Achilles' heel of the new forest policy is the persistent lack of knowledge regarding the silviculture and ecology of the nation's forests (Cifuentes 1996). The new forest policy will replace the forest concession system established in 1974 by Decree No. 2811. Under the 1974 forest concession system, five types of forest utilization contracts are available:

1. Extraction permits for local users limited to 20 m³/year, with no management plan required;
2. Extraction permits limited to 200 m³/year for 10 years, with no management plan required, and technical assistance available from the government;
3. Extraction permits limited to 2,000 m³/year for 10 years, with a technical extraction plan required;
4. Extraction permits limited to 10,000 m³/year for 10 years, with technical extraction and management plans required; and
5. Concessions of unlimited size requiring a sophisticated management plan.

Concessions have not been granted during the last 20 years due to the inability of applicants to provide a suitable management plan. The notable exception to this was Cartón de Colombia. Operated by Smurfit/Latin America, Cartón de Colombia was granted a 30-year concession on 61,000 ha of humid tropical forest with a projected production of 80,000 m³/year of mixed hardwoods for pulp. The concession was initiated in 1974 and rapidly became recognized for its innovative extraction and management methods, which included clear cutting and natural regeneration of mixed species for cellulose. An environmentally friendly aerial cable system was designed for removing cut timber in steep terrain.

Cartón de Colombia was cited as an example of a promising sustainable forestry initiative by Johnson and Cabarle (1993). Unfortunately, the concession was abandoned due to the cost of production and the uncontrollable occupation by colonists of production forest lands within the concession. Cartón de Colombia now relies exclusively on plantation forests of eucalyptus and pine on private lands in the Andes. The failure of Cartón de Colombia's concession is an example of the financial and regulatory difficulties that have plagued forest utilization on public lands in Colombia.

The Pizano S.A. Project. The history of Pizano S.A. is also one of a production shift to private plantations for the supply of timber. Pizano S.A. for years relied on public forest land through extraction permits, but increasingly was plagued with land conflict from colonization (Rodríguez 1996) and customary rights disputes with indigenous groups (Espinosa 1996). Pizano's shift towards plantation forestry on private lands is balanced by an innovative project aimed at organizing local users and small land holders to commercially produce timber on an industrial scale.

In the Pacific coast state of Chocó, Colombia, the population of descendants of freed African slaves holds communal property rights over forest land (law 70). Pizano S.A. believes these forests to be very productive, and contends that it has developed a viable silvicultural system for producing *ceiba roja (Bombacopsis quinata)*, *gmelina (Gmelina arborea)*, and *camajon (Sterculia apetala)* on these lands. Much like the *ejido* system of southern Mexico, industry can enter into an accord with the community in order to utilize their forest lands. Pizano S.A. is entering into such accords with the intention of integrating the local use of the forest into a timber management plan in which local users will maintain a vested interest in management. In return, Pizano S.A. will compensate the local "forest managers" by paying them on the basis of the annual growth increment of the commercial species in their management units. Pizano S.A. itself will benefit from the final harvest and use of the timber produced on this land.

What is interesting about this plan is that it directly addresses several of the traditional problems in forest utilization in Latin America in very innovative ways. For example, it avoids the exclusive use of the land for only one purpose by producing timber concurrently with many nontimber and noncommercial timber products and forest services. This integration has multiple benefits, such as increasing the economic value of the standing forest by broadening its productivity and addressing the economic equity concerns of exclusive land use. It can also serve as a model for avoiding land-use conflict, because the economic value of the forest is both increased and distributed, thereby diminishing any motivation for converting the forest to agriculture.

Pizano S.A. still has had some of the difficulties shared by other models of community forestry. The main challenges lie in organizing the communities; ensuring that forest management is more economically attractive than agriculture to local populations; and reversing the negative sentiment about commercial timber producers, especially with regards to their failure to distribute economic benefits from resource utilization to local communities.

Organizing the communities has required more than conventional "deal-making" and business arrangements. Pizano S.A. approached this problem from the rather unconventional angle of assessing the rural anthropology of the area before devising an organizational strategy. Based on its experience with cooperatives and community production in this region, Pizano S.A. concluded that the political dynamics of these groups tended to lack an effective distribution of power in decision making, leading to an eventual breakdown of business ventures caused by internal disputes.

In an effort to avoid relying on cooperatives, Pizano devised a household-level organizational strategy. Pizano representatives visited villagers in an area covering approximately 40,000 ha and explained their proposed forestry plan. Each household would manage a specified area of forest, perform minor silvicultural treatments, protect the forest from conversion to agriculture, and still be able to extract forest products. Pizano S.A. developed educational tools (such as taped dialogues with corresponding picture books) to further explain how the system would work.

Pizano S.A. ensures that forestry will be more profitable than agriculture by paying each household for the annual growth increment of commercial trees in their management area. The company is absorbing the entire risk that their projected financial and silvicultural outcomes are correct. They plan to divide the 40,000 ha area into a 20,000 ha production forest and a 20,000 ha protected area. From the production forest, Pizano S.A. expects to extract 35–75 m³/ha of *cativo (Prioria copaifera)*, and reforest with *ceiba roja, gmelina* and *camajon*. The *ceiba roja* is projected to produce 170 m³/ha every 17 years, and the *gmelina* and *camajon* are projected to produce 110 m³/ha every 6 years.

Conclusions. The Pizano S.A. plan is commendable in its efforts to manage multiple-use forestry while integrating local and commercial objectives for forest utilization. This project may serve as a model in the region for its innovative social aspects in forest management. Reversing the negative sentiment among local forest users towards industrial timber producers will be a long process, but hopefully will be speeded along by the success of this project. The annual compensation paid to local households for their forest management should facilitate the process.

This case study also illustrates the incentive for simplifying natural forests by creating stands of high-yielding species (plantations at the extreme), as opposed to the relatively low yields from selective harvesting of hardwoods from natural forests—the most commonly embraced paradigm of "sustainable" forestry. While this style of management is promising from the perspective of ensuring successful long-term management, it is at odds with maintaining biodiversity.

Brazil: Extractive Reserves

In 1992, representatives of the Group of Seven (G-7) nations agreed to support the conservation of Brazil's tropical forests and created the Pilot Program for the Protection of Brazil's Tropical Forests. Among the projects within the Pilot Program was the establishment of four extractive reserves, forest areas designated for nontimber resource use. The objective of the extractive reserves was to provide an alternative land use to logging that is environmentally and economically sustainable. The traditional producers of nontimber forest products in Brazil, already occupying the forests of the extractive reserves, were expected to execute a development strategy, with the assistance of the Brazilian government. The objective of the strategy was to provide improvements both in the quality of life of the population and conservation of the tropical forests in which they live.

Context. Commercial forest extractivism was once a major part of Brazil's economy. The rubber boom of the nineteenth century contributed greatly to the settlement of the Amazon and growth of the cities of Manaus and Belém. Rubber production in Brazil resulted in the migration of individuals and families to the interior of Brazil seeking a livelihood from rubber-tapping. The descendants of these rubber-tappers, in addition to more recent rural migrants, continue to inhabit the interior, many of them still dependent on rubber-tapping for a living.

The accelerated development of the interior of Brazil in the 1970s and 1980s led to a land use conflict between extractivists and colonists. The extractivists, battling for land tenure, allied with the growing environmental movement of the 1980s, which embraced the extractivists as sustainable users of the Amazon's forests. This alliance proved powerful and the establishment of extractive reserves was among their accomplishments.

There are now four extractive reserves in the Pilot Program: Chico Mendes and Alto Juruá in Acre; Rio Ouro Prêto in Rondônia; and Rio Cajari, located in Amapá. The creation of the Chico Mendes Reserve has been supported financially by the IDB. In each of these reserves, inhabitants produce one or more traditional nontimber forest products. With the assistance of the National Center for the Sustainable Development of Traditional Populations (CNPT–IBAMA), economic development programs are underway to diversify the nontimber forest production within the reserves, organize production, and develop education and health services. Conservation is an overarching goal of all the projects, including the restriction of forest clearing beyond the minimum required for subsistence agriculture.

Economic Plan of the Extractive Reserves. Forest production can be classified into traditional and alternative categories. Traditional products include natural latex and Brazil nuts—products originally produced in the reserves and sold in international commodity markets. Alternative products are those that have been introduced to, or developed in, the reserves since their establishment. They include fruits such as *açaí* and *cupuaçu*, the *guaraná* seed, and rattan-like forest vines. Additional products continue to be developed.

The economic plan for reserve inhabitants is to organize the production of both traditional and alternative products to the extent that losses to middlemen can be minimized and value-added activities can be developed within the reserves. One example is the creation of vegetable leather, an ecologically friendly leather substitute made by coating light fabric with natural latex. Additional opportunities for the production of a variety of other products manufactured with vegetable leather exist, such as shoes, bags, and articles of clothing.

Opportunities and Barriers. Extractive reserves present an opportunity to create a model for long-term productive management of tropical forests. Through the development of nontimber forest products, conservation goals may be achieved in tandem with economic development. In the case of the extractive reserves in Brazil, the attention to achieving these goals has resulted in the empowerment and organization of previously disenfranchised people involved in traditional forest production. With increased political and economic power, real gains in quality of life are being realized.

Many barriers stand in the way of this process, though. One problem is the difficulty of organizing a dispersed population of traditional producers who have little history and experience with mutual cooperation and local governance. Associations of producers that were formed within the reserves still suffer from incomplete membership participation and poor organizational decision making. Integration of collection and production activities has been difficult. The slow progress in efficient Brazil nut processing is an example of this.

Another large barrier to the success of the extractive reserves has been the diminishing market value of traditional forest products such as latex and Brazil nuts. At the time of this writing, latex prices had fallen to levels that no longer justified production in the reserves. Reserve inhabitants are looking more and more to alternative products that are as yet unproven sources of income.

Conclusions. The extractive reserves represent a strong endeavor to establish nontimber forest production as a long-term forest management strategy in tropical Latin America. The success of this endeavor will rely upon adequate market prices of the natural products, diversification and vertical integration of economic activities, and organization of the producers to succeed in competitive markets. Even with its weaknesses the models of extractive reserves in Brazil could serve as a example for nontimber forest extractivism throughout Latin America.

Chile: Ecotourism

Chile is currently proposing to grant concessions in national protected areas to private ecotourism enterprises. The Chilean government has two objectives: (1) generate revenue and reduce the government burden of managing protected areas; and (2) improve the quality of ecotourism sites, including the conservation of these areas. Although the implementation details remain undetermined at this time, the case warrants attention as a potential model for ecotourism concessions in other Latin American countries.

The Legal and Administrative Context. The Corporación Nacional Forestal y de Recursos Renovables (CONAF), the state forest service, would be direct beneficiary of the proposal. CONAF was created in 1973 under Law No. 18.348 and was given the mandate of coordinating Chile's forest sector. Among CONAF's designated responsibilities are regulating

Table 9.4 Selected Protected Area Locations in Chile

Region I	Lauca
Region II	Los Flamencos
Region II, III	Pan de Azúcar
Region VIII	Laguna de Laja
Region X	Vicente Pérez Rosales

forestry, managing protected areas, controlling forest fires, and managing watersheds. CONAF has an annual budget of $36 million.

CONAF administers 34 national parks, 43 reserves, and 12 natural monuments, totaling 14.4 million ha. It indicates that its current resources are insufficient to adequately protect and maintain these areas while fulfilling its other mandates. According to CONAF, only 22 percent of the protected areas under its mandate are effectively controlled by the staff, which includes only 350 guards. Given the enormity of trying to keep up with the daily maintenance and control of resource utilization in and near these areas, CONAF has chosen to look for private sources of capital to assume some of these responsibilities.

The Concession Proposal. In April 1996, the government of Chile announced that it would accept proposals for private concessions on public lands for the purposes of ecotourism. Thirty-year concessions will be granted to those private entities that present the best management plans for the five chosen protected areas, totaling 521,000 ha. The state tourism agency, SENATUR, chose the areas on the basis of their revenue-generating potential. During 1997, the best proposals will be selected and implementation of the ecotourism concessions will commence. The areas offered for concessions are shown in Table 9.4.

Advantages of Ecotourism Concessions. The expected advantages of ecotourism concessions are calculated from the development of profit-generating tourism activities in Chile's protected areas. If successful, the profitability of these activities will give private entities an incentive to maintain and conserve the areas. At the same time that sufficient revenue is being generated, profits can be shared with the state and reinvested in conservation or resource management programs. The potential for reducing the burden of CONAF's mandate will allow a greater concentration of that agency's resources on proper forest management—an area that has received criticism from domestic environmentalists. In sum, the expected advantages are as follows: improved management and conservation of protected areas; revenue generation for the government; reduced administrative burden for CONAF; and development of the private tourism sector.

Disadvantages of Ecotourism Concessions. There are specific foreseeable dangers to the allocation of ecotourism concessions on public lands. First, profit maximizing behavior by concessionaires can lead to environmental degradation as a result of road building, construction, and providing excessive amenities within the protected areas. Two controls will be required: (1) an environmental impact assessment for any proposed activity in the protected area; and (2) an insurance mechanism such as a conservation bond that will discourage the degradation of the area by means of a financial penalty.

Second, if a private enterprise fails, it may be difficult to guarantee the protection of the area. In such an instance, the concession should either be immediately contracted to another firm or returned to the management of CONAF. However, if CONAF proceeds with its plan to allocate its resources to alternative activities, it may not have ample funds available to resume its regulation of an area on short notice. Additionally, private sector management of protected areas may either fall short of expectations or be poorly implemented. Therefore, a continued, albeit less intensive, regulation of the area by CONAF is needed.

Third, as CONAF's resource allocation for protected areas diminishes, unanticipated conservation losses may occur despite private management of ecotourism concessions. Costa Rica provides a perfect example: it generates a substantial portion of its GNP from ecotourism sites and has established an international reputation for its ecotourism attractions. However, despite the enormous benefits derived from ecotourism, government support for the conservation of these protected areas continues to be relatively weak.

Conclusions. The potential benefits of granting concessions in Chile's national protected areas merits close observation over the coming years. If implemented properly, the private/public partnership for protected area management may prove a useful model for other countries.

Opportunities and New Models

Experiences to date with forest resource contracts in Latin America have shown that policy objectives must be matched with the political will to support them, and that the means to achieve those objectives must be tailored to accommodate the available capabilities. Over the last several years much hard work has been poured into the technical and policy components of sustainable forest management in Latin America. The discouraging results of these efforts can be attributed to unrealistic goals, or worse yet, to the lack of clearly defined goals altogether. Nevertheless, the specific objectives of economic development and conservation that are often blended into sustainable forestry plans can be achieved if innovative means are applied that acknowledge constraints and capitalize on opportunities. This section identifies a series of opportunities for meeting the economic and conservation objectives of forest management and presents three forest use contract models that exploit these opportunities.

There are models for forest resource use contracts that define realistic objectives and acknowledge the constraints to, and opportunities for, long-term management of humid tropical forests in Latin America. Some examples of such models are: (i) extensive timber extraction contracts, with reduced management requirements; (ii) intensive forestry with regulated adaptive management strategies; and (iii) multiple use areas. These three models are appropriate for different forest management objectives, and in each case the trade-offs implicit to achieving those objectives should be recognized. By doing so, forest policymakers will acknowledge contextual constraints and opportunities rather than continue to reinforce current models with hazy objectives of "sustainability."

Opportunities for Forest Resource Contracts

This section does not include an exhaustive list of opportunities, nor are these opportunities appropriate for all contexts, as each will be subject to its own set of constraints. In more general terms, any opportunity to simplify forest resource use contracts should be examined. The following five criteria are examples of simplified approaches to achieving many of the objectives embraced by the definitions of sustainable forest management.

Performance over Compliance. Among the most important changes in environmental policy today is the transition from the previous "command-and-control" enforcement systems to performance-based regulations. The basis of this transition is the realization that enforcing environmental regulations is too costly and administratively complex given the public resources devoted to it. Furthermore, in many cases the same level of environmental performance could be achieved by the regulated firm with greater efficiency if the firm were allowed to design its own methods for meeting environmental objectives. This principle tends to apply to a broad range of industries, from chemical manufacturers in the U.S. to loggers in Bolivia.

Regulation of company performance can be simplified to periodic audits of environmental indicators that would normally be affected by that firm's behavior. In the case of forest management, an examination of forest health would include measurements of the total disturbed area, stand composition, reforestation rates, and remediation efforts (if necessary). Such monitoring would reveal ample information about the behavior of the contracted firm to judge whether it is meeting contract obligations. If not, the management contract could be terminated, and a financial penalty could be assessed through the seizure of a performance bond.

A tremendous advantage of this system is its potential for honest evaluations. Performance audits could be conducted by third party auditors, or multiple entities, to ensure the validity of the audit, reduce opportunities for corruption, and make information available to any interested stakeholders.

An important requirement for the audit to function properly is the definition of criteria used to judge a firm's performance on its management plan. Failure to clearly define these criteria could result in disagreement after irreparable environmental damage has already occurred. Defining these criteria at the outset will also assist in clarifying management goals and in careful consideration of their feasibility.

Area Tax. Hand-in-hand with the simplification of the regulatory process is the simplification of the forest revenue system. The most straightforward means to do so is to tax forest resource use by area rather than by an estimation of the volume of resources extracted. The "area tax" is not perfect, but it is simple, and therefore more likely to be administered properly and less likely to be evaded. An additional advantage of the area tax is that it can facilitate the creation of protected areas within concessions through tax breaks for lands designated as off-limits to logging. Although it is in the firm's interest to place land with the least commercial value into tax-deferred protected areas, this also accomplishes the dual objectives of encouraging the firm's efficiency and creating protected areas with little appeal for future exploitation.

The area tax is not as economically efficient as a volume or production tax. Since the area tax is assessed on the average stumpage value of the entire forest, it lacks the accuracy of taxes that charge only for the amount of resource removed from the forest. This will likely be a point of contention between the government and the contracting firm when the area tax is established. Indexing the area tax to the commercial value of the timber would require a specific detailed agreement on the species to be considered in the index, the frequency of revising the index, and a fair mechanism for adjusting it to reflect inflation, price changes, and alteration in the composition of marketable species.

Protected Area Set-Asides for Conservation. Conservation objectives (including maintaining biological diversity, protecting watersheds, sequestering global carbon, and providing long-term sources of forest resources), have generally been determined by forest managers. In theory, sustainable natural forest management achieves these conservation objectives. However, in reality conservation objectives are often the greatest victim of forest use practices in Latin America. In contrast, protected areas and biological reserves have fared much better in Latin America over the past decades, while managed forest resources in national forests have dwindled. There are abundant problems with protected areas in Latin America, most of which correspond to local user conflicts, but the clear exclusion of commercial interests in these areas has benefited conservation greatly.

More protected areas may be established by requiring a minimum set-aside within each contracted forest as one of the contract's provisions. This approach has several advantages. First, it acknowledges that conservation objectives may not be met through normal forest management practices. Second, protected areas may serve as a genetic reserve for seeds and other biological resources and as habitat that is not provided for in a production forest. They may also provide an important control area for adaptive management research (see below) for forest managers. Third, protected zones would be established within the contracted area, and maintained by the firm as a contract renewal criterion. This would reduce the financial and regulatory burden on the government for protection of these areas. Fourth, the geographical distribution of protected areas may vary. It may be directed to maintaining a more widely distributed forested landscape. Alternatively, set-asides could be concentrated in one area to minimize the negative effects that occur when areas are preserved in fragments rather than as one larger unit.

Adaptive Management. It is clear that natural forest management in the neotropics will require more ecological knowledge than is currently available. One way to work around this deficiency is to use an "adaptive management" strategy. Adaptive management requires a constant appraisal of the effects of forestry activities, and periodic revision of management plans to accommodate this information. If executed properly, adaptive management has the advantages of buttressing the current state of knowledge on neotropical forestry, and providing an opportunity to reassess forestry activities to maximize their chances of achieving stated objectives.

Implementing adaptive management corresponds very well with the use of a periodic audit. Audit criteria should be related to the measurements used in the self-monitoring necessary for adaptive management. Audits can serve as a verification of this self-monitoring process and can provide an opportunity for outside experts, government technicians, environmental watchdogs, or other third parties to evaluate the progress of the management plan in achieving its objectives as well as provide guidance for the plan's revision.

Integrate Multiple Users. Traditionally, forest resource use contracts in Latin America have granted the exclusive use of forest resources to one contractor. The FAO's (1977) definition of a forest resource use contract cited before stresses exclusivity. There are important reasons for providing exclusive rights to a contractor, such as making it easier to administer the contract, provide security for investments in forestry, and assign accountability for the proper management of the forest resources. However, exclusive rights are not entirely possible nor desirable in areas with multiple local users with usufruct claims to forest resources. Substantial local economic development could be encouraged by integrating the commercial forestry sector with the interests of these users. The Pizano example from Colombia detailed earlier serves as an excellent illustration of the potential for cooperation in management objectives.

Rethinking the Forest Resource Use Contract

Acknowledging the constraints described in earlier sections and exploiting opportunities to overcome them will demand new models for forest resource use contracts. Three generalized models for forest resource use contracts are presented here, each addressing specific objectives. In the first model, a contractual use scheme is recommended that accommodates remote forest areas where transportation costs or the lack of a developed value-added wood processing industry often eliminates the demand for lower-valued products. This is the predominant case in the Western Amazon basin as well as in the forests of Suriname, Guyana, and French Guiana. This model corresponds with the objectives of maintaining forest cover, conserving biodiversity, maximizing profitability of the forest industry, and minimizing overall forest damage from logging and colonization.

In the second model, a contractual use scheme is recommended for highly populated areas where extreme pressure is put on the forest for timber of various species and qualities. This context better describes some areas of Central America and the Eastern Amazon (though *public* forest contracts are uncommon in this region). In this model, vigilance is required to prevent serious environmental harm where the conservation of forest cover is a primary objective.

In the third model, alternative modes of forest resource use are contemplated, including NTFP production, ecotourism concessions, and the integration of commercial resource management with local users in areas where land use conflict between commercial and local users is prevalent (as was the case in Colombia). The objective of this model is economic equity and the maintenance of forest cover through multiple-use management.

For each model the use of a highly simplified forest revenue system based on an area tax is recommended. Forest revenue systems in Latin America most often break down when their administrative complexity exceeds the institutional capacity. An area tax remedies this problem by virtue of its simplicity, the low cost of its administration, the lack of opportunities for corruption, and the difficulty in evading it. Areas that are under contract for harvesting are paid for on an annual basis by the contractor. The charge is uniform across an entire area, and payment compliance is easily monitored.

Model 1: Extensive Extraction of Timber without Management. This model recognizes that light selective logging as it occurs throughout the humid tropics of Latin America can be both economically efficient and of relatively low impact without intensive regulatory oversight. The regulatory focus in this option is to establish and enforce protected forest areas. The success of this model relies on a limited demand for species of lesser value by virtue of the remoteness of the forest (high transportation costs) and/or the lack of development of value-added forest industries (plywood, furniture and cabinet making, etc.). In this model, forest utilization contracts should:

- Require minimum silvicultural treatments in reforestation;
- Provide no diameter limits or volume constraints;
- Require a carefully designated system of protected area set-asides;

- Be of short (five-year) duration with renewal contingent upon satisfactory performance;
- Charge an area tax; and
- Require a performance bond.

The behavior of contractors under this model will not differ greatly from the effective behavior of contractors under more sophisticated forest management regulations that are *not* enforced. At present, in areas with low densities of commercial trees, the selective extraction of timber without management or reforestation causes relatively little damage to the forest, as indicated earlier in this section (Gullison and Hardner 1994). Indeed, less damage may occur under this model if contractors are allowed to conclude their forestry activities when profitability diminishes, rather than be held responsible for unprofitable management activities that would require maintaining and/or reopening the road infrastructure in the forest. In those regions where a large demand for many species of wood exists, and consequently results in larger harvests, this system would not be appropriate.

The advantages to this model are its minimization of forest damage from light selective harvesting and the efficiency it gains by eliminating unscientific and unenforced regulations. The limited resources allotted to forest sector regulation should be directed to the more manageable task of periodic performance audits. Satisfactory results from these periodic audits should be a prerequisite for periodic contract renewal.

Model 2: Intensive Forestry and Redirecting Regulatory Activities. As indicated in the preceding sections, it is unlikely that the long-term management of natural forests for selective harvesting in the humid tropics of Latin America will prove a feasible land-use option. It is more likely that in areas with a substantial commercial demand for lower-valued species, intensive forestry will take one of two forms: intensive extraction with heavily enriched natural forests and plantations of fast growing species. The reality today is almost exclusively one of intensive extraction without management, but it is possible that enriched natural forests through reforestation and plantations will take over forest lands in these areas.

In such a context, this model for contractual use aims to protect an area as much as possible from severe environmental harm caused by intensive extraction without management. It also intends to regulate enriched and plantation forests in such a way as to promote the maintenance of forest cover in these areas that might otherwise be entirely converted to agriculture or pasture. If such styles of forest management are the only timber utilization schemes that can compete with alternative, nonforest land uses, it would be wise to encourage them and regulate them properly. In either case, conservation of biological diversity must be accomplished through the use of protected area set-asides.

In this model, forest utilization contracts should:

- Require a management plan that outlines the best management practices for reducing forest and environmental damage;
- Use periodic audits of forest conditions, with the specific criteria for judgement stated in the contract;
- Make contract renewal contingent upon satisfactory audits;
- Require adaptive management plans and periodic modification or rewriting to be based on self-monitoring;
- Provide resource access (prevent colonization in the contracted area) to allow investment by the contractor;

- Reinvest public forest revenues into forestry research and technical assistance;
- Require the provision and protection of conservation set-asides by the contractor;
- Charge an area tax; and
- Require a performance bond.

The basic idea of this option is to minimize damage as much as possible given the existing regulatory capacity, and provide an opportunity for intensive management if it becomes viable. In theory, the risk in this model is that management will never occur, and the environmental harm of intensive forest extraction will not be mitigated by regulations because of institutional weakness. In practice, the adoption of this model incurs little risk, as intensive extraction without management is already the status quo in many areas with high commercial demand for lower-valued species.

This model relies upon the open-ended innovation of adaptive management. If management plans are rewritten periodically to integrate new knowledge about neotropical silviculture and the responses of the site itself to forest management, there is a greater chance that such plans will adapt to the constraints and opportunities present at the time. Specific criteria for rewriting the management plans would correspond directly with the criteria from the audits.

The regulatory emphasis in this model is on the periodic audit of the health of the production forest and the maintenance of conservation set-asides. The audit results, as in the first model, can be used as a criterion for continuing the forest use contract. If the stake in achieving a satisfactory audit is backed by a performance bond, a substantial incentive will be created for the contractor to maintain the forest's health. The periodic audit of forest health has the advantage of requiring fewer regulatory resources and personnel than constant monitoring, and *emphasizes performance rather than process*. Regulatory resources would thus be reallocated from command-and-control methods that enforce nonviable natural forest management activities, to the encouragement of best management practices that reduce damage and provide the opportunity for innovative adaptive management methods.

Model 3: Multiple-Use Areas. There is merit in exploring contracts for alternative methods of forest resource use, though very little experience exists from which to draw lessons on their implementation. Three compelling ideas are NTFP contracts; ecotourism concessions; and integrated commercial and community resource management. The objectives of these alternative forest use models are economic equity (derived from involving local users in the economic activity of public forest resource use), and maintenance of forest cover (as encouraged by multiple resource management).

A number of lessons have been learned from NTFP development projects, especially from the Extractive Reserves Program in Brazil. First, NTFP production may not be profitable enough by itself as an economic activity to support local populations. If production is inadequate to support local populations, restrictions on land use must be made, especially for clearing forest for agriculture. Beyond this, if NTFP production is to be combined with timber extraction, resource rights must be clearly defined, and timber activities must be planned in order to minimize unnecessary damage to the NTFPs.

In fact, NTFP-use contracts are almost never made between the government and one private entity. Associations of producers are generally the contracting entity, and therefore may have characteristics that require special contract requirements. Formal management systems for long-term management of NTFPs have been rare.

Based on these limited experiences, the following criteria for establishing NTFP and hunting and fishing contracts should be considered:

- Ensure that NTFP production is financially viable and is the most suitable activity for that area;
- Control forest clearing in the contracted area;
- Ensure that the contracted entity is capable of managing the operation, is representative of the producers, and demonstrates presence in the area; and
- Look for opportunities to place NTFP production in areas where nondestructive logging has already occurred.

Probably the most promising method of nontimber forest utilization is ecotourism, which provides a service rather than a product. Revenues from ecotourism have increased dramatically in Latin America over the past decade. Two examples of national-level ecotourism planning are found in Costa Rica and Chile. Costa Rica supports the most visited tropical forests in Latin America and arguably derives a higher proportion of income from nature-based tourism than any other country in the region. Ironically, the public sector invests little in the protection or management of these areas. The protected areas of Chile also attract many tourists. Currently the majority of forests visited are managed by the government, but Chile plans to grant ecotourism concessions on these lands in the near future. The privatization of these services represents a significant change in natural resource management: one that, if successful, could expand the government's supervisory capacity to currently unattended areas, while simultaneously reducing its overall workload. The implementation of this plan may serve as a model for future forest utilization plans for ecotourism.

Policy Recommendations

The governments of Latin America will need to acknowledge the various constraints to forest resource use contracts and exploit any opportunities to overcome them. To begin this process, clear management objectives must be defined and rational means to achieve them should be developed. Policy recommendations are offered here in four general categories, as follows: to strategically strengthen institutional capacity; to work *with* and not *against* financial forces; to promote political participation; and to increase technical knowledge.

Policy Actions
Countries need to step up efforts to review rural development projects for their potential environmental and social impacts, and should mitigate or avoid projects with substantial negative impacts. Where feasible, they should work with international organizations and lending institutions to design projects that not only minimize environmental and social negative effects, but strengthen the institutional and economic conditions for improved performance.

Strategically Strengthen Institutional Capacity. Governments must simplify their regulations and revenue systems. Regulatory agencies tend to have too few resources to fulfill their mandates and are vulnerable to corruption. Two means to overcome these constraints are to redesign the regulatory scheme to emphasize performance rather than command-and-control compliance, and to replace complex revenue systems with an area tax.

The distinction between performance and compliance-based regulations is that performance-based regulations rely upon ecological indicators, where compliance-based regulations rely upon the satisfaction of procedural requirements. For example, a common compliance-based regulation is the diameter cutting limit for timber harvesting. This forest management requirement is only reasonable for certain species and is difficult and costly to control. A performance-based regulation would monitor the actual regeneration and recruitment of managed species to ensure that the management plan and harvesting techniques correspond with the management objectives for the forest, as well as monitoring overall forest health. This shift in regulatory focus places more emphasis on site-specific methods and technologies appropriate for the area, determined by the forest managers themselves. Monitoring is periodic for such a performance-based system, rather than daily—as is the case for a compliance-based system. Success is measured by the health of the managed forest instead of compliance with other regulations that may be largely irrelevant.

Performance-based regulations may require substantially fewer regulators, as monitoring is less frequent and not as intensive. If performance reviews are public, and allow multiple auditors, the process should be less susceptible to corruption. When hinged directly with adaptive management, performance audits should lead to appropriate changes in the forest management plan. When all factors are considered, performance-based regulation of forest management should result in a lighter regulatory burden for the public sector, cost savings for the private sector through reduced regulatory compliance requirements, and above all, better forest health.

Specifically, performance-based forest resource use contracts should include the following:

- Regulation and enforcement of environmental performance using defined standards, rather than current regulations based on command-and-control techniques;
- Straightforward monitoring of forest use contracts, including mechanisms for adaptive management, as well as public sector performance audits and independent review; and
- Simplified forest revenue systems, like an area tax.

Work with and Not against Financial Forces. Forcing the implementation of management plans that are not financially viable will always result in failure. Forest policymakers must recognize that incentives leading to improved financial performance do not necessarily correspond with conservation objectives. They should seek opportunities to implement profit-maximizing logging in ways that do not cause substantial, irreversible harm to forest health. Where conservation objectives are not clearly achieved by forest management contracts, provisions should be made to meet them through alternative methods such as conservation set-asides.

A classic error to be avoided is the financing of infrastructure for value-added forest resource processing in areas where long-term management is not financially viable. Value-added processing may generate more profitability from forest resources, but it does not change the economics of forest management. From the forest manager's perspective, timber appreciation must exceed the discount rate in order to justify its management, and value-added processing does not alter this relationship. Furthermore, many regions of Latin America do not have a comparative advantage in value-added timber processing and have substantial difficulty penetrating markets for processed wood products.

Promote Public Participation in the Political Process. Political participation by the various groups affected by forest resource use contracts is important for the integrity and success of forest policy. Political support for forest resource management is weak in many regions. This may be the result of government representatives defining policy priorities without the input of the affected constituencies. One means of encouraging participation by these groups is to empower them with information and to facilitate the exchange of ideas with NGOs. Where forest management is concerned, monitoring data should be made available to the public, and collected or verified by independent parties. The public availability of data related to management performance provides citizens and NGOs with a source of evidence that can be used to endorse or criticize forest policies and the politicians who support them. This process, in turn, provides politicians with incentives to design accountable forest policies. In cases where multiple use conflicts arise, forest policy should anticipate mechanisms for integrating new management schemes.

Increase Technical Knowledge. The ecological knowledge upon which forest management plans and regulations are based is insufficient in many areas of Latin America. Discussions with the region's forest managers often reveal claims that silvicultural systems for their particular forests have been developed. Though some systems are in place, especially for temperate forests, knowledge is still lacking about many tropical forest ecosystems in the region. Two conclusions can be drawn from this situation: first, knowledge of neotropical silviculture must be increased; and second, management plans must be adaptable to new knowledge as it becomes available.

Adaptive management accompanied by monitoring can accomplish these two goals. Adaptive management (as described in the previous section), is a management system that allows the management plan to be revised to respond to observed results from current practices and new knowledge. It also has the additional advantage of systematic data collection, which is useful for both the forest manager and the general field of forest management.

It is highly recommended that policies be adopted demanding adaptive management plans that include specific criteria and periodic revisions. Such policies will integrate well with simplified regulatory schemes and with candid and reliable performance information.

Conclusions

The recommendations of this chapter should be accompanied by technical and institutional support measures. For example, performance audits depend on the establishment of well-defined, appropriate indicators to accurately reflect a forest's ecological health. Developing such indicators requires adequate scientific research and information sharing. Equally important is a credible enforcement mechanism that is able to detect violations and impose penalties.

Forest development and concessions should be preceded by careful, evaluative financial analysis. Although that may seem obvious, numerous forestry projects have failed due to financial insolvency. Policymakers should thus try to design structural incentives to coincide with prevailing financial forces, rather than forcing projects such as value-added industry that, although viable in certain circumstances, may be unsustainable for longer time horizons. Such prior analyses again depend on adequate funding, research capacity, and information networking.

Finally, public involvement is key to the success of a responsible forest concession policy. An informed and participatory public will support responsible politicians and businesses, and be more critical of those whose profit-seeking comes at the expense of national resources. Public involvement in this sense, of course, depends on ample opportunity for public participation, as well as transparency of policy objectives and implementation.

Forest policy reform must be based on three points: clearly defined objectives, methods of measuring progress towards those objectives, and means to achieve those objectives, given the constraints and opportunities of the regulatory context. This chapter proposes guidelines for more realistic and effective forest policies, which can be used by policy analysts, nongovernmental organizations and multilateral lending institutions interested in facilitating this process. Substantial opportunities exist for improving forest resource contracts, which could benefit all those who rely on the economic development and conservation of forests in Latin America.

Appendix 9.1 Forest Area in 17 Countries of Central and South America

(In thousands of hectares)

Country	Forest area	Public forest contracts
Argentina	34,436	N.D.
Belize	1,998	N.D.
Bolivia	49,345	22,500
Brazil	566,007	none
Chile	8,033	none
Colombia	54,190	no official estimate
Costa Rica	1,456	N.D.
Ecuador	12,007	none
El Salvador	127	N.D.
Guatemala	4,253	168
Guyana	18,424	5,500
Mexico	48,695	N.D.
Panama	3,123	18
Paraguay	12,868	none
Peru	68,090	1,220
Suriname	14,776	2,415
Venezuela	45,943	N.D.

Sources: WRI (1990-97); ITTO (1995).

<table>
<tr><td>CHAPTER
10</td><td># Trade and Environmental Issues in Forest Production</td></tr>
</table>

Markku Simula

Trade has both direct and indirect influences on environment. Conversely, environmental policies and regulations influence the competitiveness of individual producers, thereby influencing trade flows. Trade liberalization and macroeconomic policy reforms have led to expanded exports by developing countries, particularly in commodities. The environmental impacts on natural resources of such policies are not yet fully assessed, but evidence is mounting that negative impacts do exist.

The assessment presented here of the trade and sustainable management of renewable natural resources draws on the case of forests—the most complex sector from the viewpoint of land use policy. Forest resources occupy a large share of the world's land area, and their future existence is threatened by conversion of forest land to other uses and by inappropriate harvesting practices. Forests are essential to maintaining biological systems, but often this is understood only after forests disappear.

Forest Production and Sustainability

Because the origins of the deforestation problem lie outside the sector proper, intersectoral coordination in policies is necessary. Forests provide habitat for the bulk of the world's biodiversity. Forest products are traded extensively in the world and represent a major source of foreign exchange earnings to many developing countries. Necessary investment in resource management and utilization could be financed largely through revenues generated by the sector itself. However, the sector is notorious for policy failures and, in particular, rent capture in developing countries is low. Current public concern for future management and conservation of the world's forests acknowledges this problem, and the issue is now under intense public debate in many countries.

Environment and Trade Policy Linkages

Environmental issues now influence the international trade agenda, partly because the environment is recognized as a global common good. International trade policy has increasingly reflected public concern. Environmental issues were part of the Uruguay Round negotiations of the GATT, and as a result the WTO established a working program on trade and environment. The environment was also an essential ingredient when NAFTA was negotiated. Recent reductions in traditional barriers to imports have resulted in greater exposure of national economies to foreign competition. This drew attention to domestic policies, including cost-raising environmental standards that continue to influence the international competitiveness of firms and industries. This is especially true when new players with lower standards enter the scene (Anderson 1995).

The question of standards is also relevant in forest management. Deforestation and forest degeneration are in part related to management rules, regulations and their enforcement. International public concern focused first on tropical forests, where biodiversity is highest and deforestation rates are also high. In the boreal and temperate forests, clear-cutting, intensive silviculture and the violation of indigenous peoples' rights have lately been the main reasons for concern. The simplistic view is that sustainable forest management can be achieved through normative action using forest regulations and their enforcement. But that overlooks fundamental issues that impede forest management, such as policy failures outside the sector, independent of the legal framework in forestry.

Environmental standards in forestry are typically related more to production processes than to product standards. In the long run, the focus will shift from the production process to sustainable consumption patterns, and emphasis on trade as a channel for necessary policy changes. In designing such changes, WTO rules and multilateral environmental agreements must be taken into account in order to avoid discriminatory and protectionist practices (Andrew 1995).

In evaluating trade-related policy instruments, three aspects need to be considered: (i) effectiveness in achieving their specific goals and whether the measures proposed are sufficient; (ii) tradeoffs between environmental effects and economic development; and (iii) efficiency. These typical elements of policy analysis are frequently overlooked in the promotion of a particular instrument (e.g., log export ban, certification of forest management). Another complexity arises from the fact that both international and national impacts should be included in the analysis.

The theory of comparative advantage has been expanded to incorporate environmental aspects. With growing per capita income and industrial output, the value the public places on the environment increases. The location of industries is assumed to be influenced by national differences in pollution standards. Relocation of a pollution-intensive industry from one country to another may in turn affect the environment in a third country. This generalization may not be fully relevant in forestry because of the immobility of natural resources and long gestation periods of investments. For example, the recent interest of Asian logging firms in Latin America and the Caribbean (LAC) countries is probably guided by shortage of raw material supplies in their own region rather than avoiding national environmental standards. In pulp and paper production clean technology tends to be an international standard, as it is also the most efficient one. In solid wood products, pollution clearly plays a smaller role in industrial decisions than in resource endowment.

Objectives and Scope of the Analysis

This chapter analyzes some of the key issues on trade and environment in the forestry sector. In the international trade of forest products from the LAC region, two primary issues are: (i) implications of the removal of trade barriers for the economic contribution and sustainability of production of the forest sector; and (ii) prospects for "green" markets and ecolabeling of forest products based on improved management and harvesting practices. Increasing the value of forest resources and the environmental sustainability of forest lands through greater production of nonwood forest products (NWFP) will also be considered.

Recent trends and patterns of forest products trade are first identified to establish the importance of trade in the LAC forestry sector. A broad perspective on trade-related policy instruments is adopted to provide an adequate framework for analyzing different options.

Four main areas of policy influence can be identified: production, consumption, trade, and environment. Many individual instruments straddle these areas, and thus their specific impacts are difficult to identify. Only those instruments that have direct implications for trade are reviewed, covering various types of trade barriers, national policy strategies and multilateral environmental and other agreements. Assessment criteria are efficiency and environmental sustainability. In the discussion on trade barriers, their beneficial and harmful secondary effects on forest management and conservation are identified. Trade policy reforms are viewed with regard to their environmental priority and possible action needed to mitigate negative impacts on the environment.

Special attention is given to certification of forest management and ecolabeling in view of their expected potential to contribute to sustainable forest management due to their current importance in various national and international initiatives, including the LAC region. This chapter focuses on the environmental impacts of forestry sector policies, as well as the impact of environmental policies on forest management (see also Chapter 2 of this book).

Forest-based Products: Trade Trends and Environmental Impacts

Forest-based products are divided into (i) wood and wood-based products and (ii) nonwood products. Their value in global trade is estimated at $128 billion/year,[1] of which nonwood products account for about 7 percent. The figure does not include the value of traded services such as forest-based ecotourism, a significant revenue source in many countries.

Trade Patterns
Wood-based products have the best-known trade patterns. They are traded as: (a) roundwood or chips, (b) primary processed products (sawnwood, wood-based panels, pulp and paper), or (c) further processed, value-added products (builders' woodwork, wooden furniture, converted paper and paperboard products, etc.). Out of the total industrial roundwood production,[2] about 6 to 7 percent enters international trade (Barbier 1995). This share varies by product and region, and tends to increase as a function of product unit value. Trade has changed over the past few decades as exports of roundwood diminished, mainly due to physical supply limitations, bans and restrictions of exporting countries. In contrast, the trade share of processed products has been increasing.

The total value (FOB) of the world trade in wood and wood-based products is about $99 billion per year (1993). The main categories of products are paper and paperboard, 43 percent; sawnwood, 24 percent; wood-based panels, 13 percent; woodpulp, 11 percent; and roundwood, 10 percent. The LAC region accounts for about 4 percent of the world trade of wood-based forest products. The regional exports generated foreign exchange worth $4.3 billion in 1993. There was a significant trade surplus of $0.5 billion, as the respective imports were valued only at $3.8 billion. Regional exports are rather evenly distributed, with woodpulp (28 percent of the total), paper and paperboard (20 percent), and sawnwood (18 percent) being the main export items, followed by wood-based panels (13 percent) and industrial roundwood (10 percent). More than half (52 percent) of the regional exports comes from Brazil. Chile is the second largest exporter, accounting for 29

---

[1] FAO (1993). This estimate excludes converted paper and paperboard products. All dollar figures are in US dollars.

[2] Fuelwood is not included in these figures, because it is traded in limited volumes internationally.

percent of the regional total, followed by Mexico (7 percent) and Argentina (4 percent). The rest is distributed over a number of countries, none of whose share exceeds 2 percent (Appendix 10.1).

The regional import pattern is dominated by paper and paperboard (60 percent) followed by sawnwood (14 percent), woodpulp (12 percent) and panels (8 percent). Mexico is leading the imports with 33 percent of the regional total, followed by Argentina (13 percent), Brazil (9 percent) and Venezuela (6 percent). The four countries with positive trade balances in wood-based forest products were Brazil, Chile, Bolivia and Paraguay.

The LAC producers depend extensively on trade in plywood and wood pulp. In 1993, about 45 percent of plywood and 43 percent of wood pulp products were exported. About 14 percent of sawn softwood, paper and paperboard was exported, while in other wood products exports amounted to less than 10 percent of production. The share of imports in consumption is highest in plywood (38 percent), paper and paperboard (27 percent) and woodpulp (19 percent) (Appendix 10.2).

The main trading area in tropical wood-based products is Asia, which accounts for two-thirds of the total imports of developing countries. That region's share of the respective exports is even higher, roughly 70 percent. Asian trade is mostly intraregional, but Asia dominates the world exports of wood panels. The second largest region for exports of tropical wood-based products is Latin America and the Caribbean, due mostly to trade from Chile and Brazil. Poor competitiveness and limited purchasing power make Africa a minor contributor to trade in this sector, despite its physical potential.

Except for Brazil and Chile, most LAC forest products exports have been based on natural forests. The two main factors forcing an evolution towards plantation forestry are (i) increasingly limited raw material resources for wood, and (ii) environmental pressures related to tropical timber products. The reduction in natural forest-based production has been compensated for through increasing investment in plantations. The characteristics of wood output for these natural forests and plantations are different, resulting in structural changes in timber production patterns. The earlier emphasis on large-sized logs of indigenous species enabled the development of plywood for wood panels and sawmilling industries, while the homogenous plantation wood (often exotic species) has been traditionally targeted at the production of pulp, paper, reconstituted panels and low-grade sawnwood. Substitution possibilities between the two types of raw material are now being explored by the industry, but the change has so far been relatively slow, suggesting traditional attitudes in trade. Nevertheless, when the physical availability of natural species becomes scarce, the industry takes action.

Market Shares and Environmental Pressures

To what extent have developing countries, and the LAC region in particular, suffered from environmental pressures in international markets? Globally, their market shares in forest products have varied in the short run, but no declining trend can be observed between developed and developing countries. The LAC share in the world trade of forest products has increased slightly in the period from 1980 to 1993 (Appendix 10.3).

Sawn hardwood and plywood have been most vulnerable in markets where species and tropical origin are identified to the consumer. Since the mid-1980s there has been a decline in developing countries' share of the world market for sawn hardwoods, while in plywood the trend is reversed. These trends are also observed in LAC exports. The extent to which tropical sawnwood trade has suffered from environmental pressures should be explored in more detail in individual major markets.

Environmental groups in Belgium, Denmark, Germany, the Netherlands, and the United Kingdom have pressured tropical timber importers to be environmentally responsible. Pressures have also been felt in other European countries and North America, which are particularly important markets for Latin American and African suppliers of sawn hardwoods and plywood. The Asian exporters principally depend on their regional markets and are therefore much less vulnerable. In fact, Latin America and Africa combined account for no more than 13 percent and 4 percent of world exports in sawn hardwoods and plywood, respectively. However, in key European markets the Latin American exporters have increased their market share from 4.3 percent in 1990 to 6.1 percent in 1994 in sawnwood products, and from 4.5 percent to 13.2 percent in plywood in the same period despite environmental pressures.

International Competitiveness of Wood Products

Price factors are more important in products with homogenous characteristics, while nonprice factors limit substitution possibilities in differentiated products. Sawnwood, veneer and plywood are examples of products where the inherent quality of natural tropical timber (visual characteristics, strength, etc.) has led export trade to concentrate on end-use sectors (high-value furniture and joinery, parquet flooring, etc.) where quality factors have enabled effective product differentiation. However, even for these products substitutes are available (e.g., hardwoods from temperate regions), and are used when price disparities are large enough.

Pulp, paper, and reconstituted panels are examples of relatively homogenous products where price factors influence purchasing decisions, once quality requirements are met. Latin American countries like Brazil and Chile are the least-cost producers in the world, due to low-cost wood raw material and labor. Those advantages may be partly offset, however, by lower productivity and higher capital costs, the latter due to the relatively high investment risks associated with developing countries in general.

In an intermediate group of forest products, both price and nonprice factors define the competitive position of individual suppliers. Sawnwood is such an example, as the origin (species and growing conditions) is related to many inherent parameters that establish product quality patterns in processing. On the other hand, consumption patterns of import markets by species are mainly influenced by local traditions, which are also reflected in building regulations. This leads to somewhat limited substitution possibilities. If supply availability becomes an enduring constraint, the market patterns tend to change. To assess how trade and environmental policies affect competitiveness in wood-based products, both price and nonprice factors need to be considered. Substitution elasticities between sources and products are therefore important.

The trade in further processed products offers an important development potential to LAC exporters, particularly in furniture. The trade in converted paper and paperboard products is limited and mostly intraregional, as technology is readily available and not very capital-intensive. International trade in further processed wood products was estimated at $20 billion in 1993, of which $4.3 billion came from developing countries. The LAC region generated export earnings of some $760 million, corresponding to about 4 percent of the world trade (Appendix 10.4).

As the processing of these products tends to be labor-intensive, export growth from the developing countries has been faster than in primary processed products during the last few years, and this trend is expected to continue. The principal exporters of wooden furniture and builders' woodwork are found in Southeast Asia (Malaysia, Thailand, Indonesia, and the Philippines). Latin American exporters have not been able to fully tap this potential, despite an increase in their world market share. Thus the promotion of further processing of wood products is a policy priority in many Latin American countries.

Nonwood Forest Products

These products cover a wide range of items from medicinal and aromatic plants and their extracts to nuts, fruits, resins, tannins, waxes and artisan products. The FAO (1995b) has identified 116 commercial NWFPs. Markets have traditionally been local or regional, but many products also enter international trade.

The development of this subsector has experienced various obstacles, starting with lack of awareness of the development potential. From the trade point of view, production is labor-intensive, but products have low value in the forest due to the role of intermediaries in the value chain of NWFPs. Substitutes may be available either in the form of cultivated or synthetic products. Other problems include lack of market transparency and insufficient quality standards (Chandrasekharan 1995). It is common for a plant to be developed for cultivation if it has more market potential than can be met by extractive production.

The data on NWFP trade are not reliable, but suggest that these products are more important than previously assumed. Globally, the value of international trade was estimated at $7.5 billion to $9 billion per year (1993), but that figure does not include medicines from plants. The world trade in such plants has been estimated at $24 billion per year (1990), while the trade of medicines based on these plants could amount to $84 billion (Pearce 1995). The above estimates exclude forest-based ecotourism, which is a growing subsector, particularly in the LAC region.

In economic terms, wood and wood-based products continue to be the main output of forests at the global level. NWFPs offer important possibilities for developing multiple objective forest management methods and for generating socioeconomic benefits, thereby contributing to sustainability of natural tropical forests (Pérez et al. 1993). NWFPs are particularly important at local levels, where other economic options may be limited.

Environmental Impacts of Trade Barriers and Other Policies

Trade Barriers on Imports

Logs and rough-sawn timber have had low or nonexistent tariff levels in most markets (Bourke 1988). Tariff rates have also been declining in processed products, but tariff escalation on the higher value-added products continues. Examples are speciality plywoods, builders' woodwork, furniture and some converted paper and paperboard products. Intraregional trade is important for many forest products that are bulky or have a low unit value. Tariff rates are generally higher in developing countries than in industrialized countries (Bourke 1992).

The impact of the Uruguay Round of the GATT on forest products was limited, due to relatively low starting tariff rates. The tariff differential between Most Favored Nation and Generalized System of Preferences (GSP) rates was also reduced significantly, due mostly to reductions in the former, while the GSP rate (often zero) remained largely unchanged. Although complete elimination of tariffs on forest products was not achieved, the Uruguay Round reduces overall tariff rates and prevents their escalation. In relative terms, the tariff reduction of the Uruguay Round was strongest (65 percent) in industrialized countries, while developing countries continue to maintain higher tariffs (Appendix 10.5).

In fact, 84 percent of the industrialized country imports in wood, pulp, paper and furniture is currently duty free (de Paiva 1995). In addition, the establishment of bound rates (ceiling limits on tariff rates) will reduce market risk. Furthermore, major industrialized-country importers committed themselves to completely phase out remaining tariffs on pulp and paper products (Barbier 1995). These changes should foster exports of forest products from developing countries and encourage plantation-based production.

Nevertheless, the remaining tariffs on high-value products will bias development of the export-oriented forestry sector toward unprocessed products. *Ceteris paribus*, there is risk that the relative burden on the environment will increase when the focus is on exploitation, rather than integration of wood production with processing industries. Sustainable management of natural forests is easier to achieve with a diversified industrial pattern than in cases where the best logs are sold directly to export markets without further processing. Local conditions vary extensively (structure of the forest, domestic market patterns, labor availability and skills, unit costs of production, etc.) and therefore, environmental preconditions for industrial development and respective impacts also vary, suggesting the need to analyze each case separately.

A classical example of tariffs and quotas for imports has been the case of plywood. The tariff applied in the European Union (EU) for more than 20 years was all but eliminated in 1995 (although it continues to limit imports in Japan). The elimination of the system will benefit tropical plywood exporters in Indonesia, Malaysia, Brazil, and to a lesser extent, African countries. Most of the plywood industry in these areas is based on natural forests, and expanded exports could lead to their more extensive use.

Forest products are subject to a range of nontariff barriers which have been resistant to change. It is difficult to determine how severely these barriers have affected trade, and if they have been used primarily to restrict imports or as legitimate restrictions with important economic functions (Bourke 1992). An additional effect of the Uruguay Round's reductions in tariffs has been to lessen some of the nontariff import restrictions.

The EU prohibits all imports of green coniferous sawnwood typically used for construction purpose unless certain standards[3] are met, such as kiln drying or a phytosanitary certification. The restrictions have mostly affected North American exporters, but have also influenced Chilean exporters of plantation-based coniferous sawnwood. The Agreement of Sanitary and Phytosanitary Measures of the Uruguay Round could result in a relaxation of certain inspection criteria, deemed excessive for simply protecting wood supplies from pests and disease.

Practices and product characteristics vary by countries, and are reflected in their technical standards. Of particular importance are building codes, where differences stem from traditional user preferences and established practices. Furthermore, different sheet sizes of wood-based panels in the North American, Western European and Japanese markets act as effective trade barriers to exporters who can only afford to specialize in one market area.

The EU has taken major steps towards harmonizing building codes and standards that would facilitate foreign exporter access to several national markets. Further harmonization would contribute to the gradual elimination of technical barriers. However, harmonization at a regional level often favors local producers, thereby presenting an obstacle for other suppliers (Bourke 1992). In forest products the problem has occurred most with sawn softwood.

---

[3] Restrictions on wood imports designed to prevent the spread of wood pathogens from foreign countries.

Many governments have used subsidies in their export markets to allow their producers to flood the market with large quantities of low-priced goods, a practice called dumping. Anti-dumping penalties have been used by importing countries as a type of trade barrier, but are now less frequent, except in the United States (Bourke 1992). In forest products these investigations have so far focused on developed countries. An interesting precedent is the ruling of the U.S. International Trade Commission in 1992 which set a countervailing duty of 4.6 percent for imports from Canada because of alleged subsidies from artificially low government stumpage and log export restrictions. This dispute has simmered for nearly a decade and remains unsettled, although in 1995 the U.S. returned $590 million to traders in special duties collected since 1992.

In conclusion, it appears that various nontariff trade barriers have been established with little or no consideration of their impacts on forest management. Indirect impacts should be expected if the market access of a particular product is impeded. All barriers that influence competitiveness tend to bias towards inefficiency, which is often linked with negative environmental effects. In forest products such measures tend to reduce the revenue received by forest managers, thereby reducing the possibilities for improved management practices.

Eco-taxes on Imports

The purpose of environmental product taxes and charges (eco-taxes) may have two objectives: (i) to raise revenue; and (ii) to discourage the production and consumption on which the tax is levied (UNCTAD 1995b). Eco-taxes have been considered as a potential instrument for importing countries to use to limit imports of products, such as tropical timber or paper that does not contain recycled fiber. Such initiatives have been strongly opposed by exporters as discriminatory policies.

In the case of tropical timber it has been demonstrated that a special tax or levy would not be an effective instrument to reduce trade-related deforestation. Furthermore, such a measure could reduce incentives for sustainable forest management and risk encouraging unsustainable conversion of forest lands to other uses (London Environmental Economics Centre [LEEC] 1992).

In 1993 Belgium issued a decree for an eco-tax on paper lacking a minimum content of recycled fiber. The intention was to promote recycling and reduce timber harvesting in the countries that Belgium depends on for its virgin fiber supply. Such a tax, however, disregards the fact that recycled fiber always requires an input of virgin fiber, as fibers increasingly disintegrate with each successive round of recycling. Furthermore, the tax acts as a trade barrier for external suppliers, penalizing their competitiveness, rather than encouraging sustainable resource management. The tax also favors local paper producers who rely mainly on recycled fiber for raw material. For these reasons the decree has been postponed, while the Belgian government studies other options.

Initiatives to introduce environmentally targeted taxes and levies on forest products present a number of problems, such as unequal treatment of like products. There is an obvious risk that such measures will lead to protectionism. Eco-taxation is not proposed here as a feasible instrument unless it can be targeted correctly and designed to accord with WTO rules (equal treatment of similar domestic and imported products). The same holds for trade subsidies in exporting countries which can risk becoming a disguised means of trade promotion. Instead of direct trade subsidies, other national-level measures to correct policy and market failures should be preferred (LEEC 1992).

Box 10.1 Export Ban in Costa Rica

Log exports were prohibited in 1986, and sawnwood exports in 1987. As a result, domestic log prices dropped and in 1989–91 were only 18 to 52 percent of what they would have been without the ban. Winners of the ban have included the processing industry enterprises and their employees. Losers have been forest owners, forest workers and the government. In the long run, the industry is also a loser, as investment in plantations is lagging.

The welfare gains are likely to be negative, due to reduced supply and lower prices of unprocessed wood and limited value-added gains. Environmental net benefits from the ban can be assumed to be negative, due to reduced forest revenue available for sustainable management and logging plantation development.

Sources: Stewart 1992; Stewart and Arias 1995; Kishor and Constantino 1994.

Quantitative Restrictions and Taxation of Exports

Latin American countries have applied log export bans with the dual purpose to curb deforestation and encourage local processing. Some other countries have used various quantitative restrictions tied to the volume of wood produced (sometimes specified by tree species). More recently, similar regulations for exports of rough sawnwood have also been applied. The policy objective has been the promotion of local processing to create value added and employment by ensuring low-cost raw material for the industry.

The economic effects of these measures are, however, varied as, even though the industrialization has taken place, efficiency and distributive effects have often been negative. The inevitable result of isolating a country from international trade is the lowering of the price of roundwood, which often leads to waste in raw material processing (e.g., Constantino 1990). Forest owners or holders of cutting rights have been obvious losers, as their political weight is less than that of industry and labor lobby groups (Box 10.1).

Log prices in Ecuador and Bolivia have been only 15 percent to 40 percent of what they would have been without export bans (Stewart and Arias 1995). This has led to substantially reduced competitiveness of forestry as a land use, both in terms of management of natural forest and of plantation forests, contributing in turn to the conversion of forest land to other uses. Export-grade logs represent a small share of the total harvest because of limitations related to log quality and species. Whereas the best grades of high value species can capture prices as high as $500/m³ or more, the local industry structure is rarely geared towards maximizing the value of such logs due to constraints in marketing, technology and skills. When such raw materials are processed into plywood or standard sawnwood, an economic loss of $320 to $380/m³ may occur under Bolivian and Ecuadoran conditions. In addition, low log prices act as a disincentive to improve processing efficiency, thus working against the objective of reducing the harvesting volume in the forest.

Similar effects can be expected from export taxation of forest products occurring in many developing countries (Gillis 1990). As the taxes are generally scaled according to species, they have been targeted at preventing excessive harvesting of primary species and promoting low-value, lesser-used species. The same efficiency and distributive problems associated with quantitative restrictions have, however, been experienced.

The environmental objectives of these types of measures are of recent origin. In particular, log export bans have been proposed as a measure to control deforestation. If the hypotheses that assigning a correct value to natural resources leads to improved conservation is accepted, export bans are not likely to be effective in reaching environmental objectives. An appropriate measure would be adjustment of concession terms and royalty fees so that the price of timber corresponds to its economic value.

Export bans and quantitative restrictions appear to work against internalization of environmental effects by distorting the economic value of the resource and its output. However, if such restrictions are removed as isolated measures, there is a risk that increased wood demand would lead to excessive utilization in the short run. Therefore, a broader policy package would be necessary to ensure that increased wood demand could be met from sustainably managed natural forests or new plantations in deforested lands. Through such measures, removing internal trade barriers could lead to improved economic efficiency, environmental net gains, and possibly even to distributional benefits. However, each case has to be analyzed separately, not only to consider market and environmental impacts, but also to seek a politically feasible way to implement policy reform. In such an analysis countrywide reforms should be considered for legal and illegal trade implications.

Production Subsidies

Many countries provide incentives for forest conservation to rural communities, farmers and forest dwellers. Such incentives may be direct or indirect, varying from access to resources (secured tenure) to the provision of inputs. Incentives become controversial, especially when they are financial. The justification of subsidies is usually based on market failures resulting in differences between private and public benefits. The environmental and social benefits of forests for society as a whole are not reflected in the price of forest products, and cannot be captured by the private landowner. This notable difference in public and private benefits can be diminished by the use of subsidies.

Although financial incentives may encourage environmental conservation, they become controversial when used to promote industrial forestry, particularly commercial plantations. When using subsidies, the value of the nonmarket externalities should guide the use of incentives. If financial incentives are justified, they should be targeted and, if possible, temporary. Priority should be given to activities where subsidies cover only the marginal cost of adopting improved practices (IDB 1995c). Whereas a country is mainly interested in the generation of benefits at the national and local levels, the willingness of international financing institutions to provide funding also depends on global benefits such as carbon sequestration (Keipi 1995a). Pooling international resources for comprehensive incentive schemes should be preferred to the development of individual projects with separate management structures (Oksanen et al. 1994). A careful analysis of the distribution of benefits could be useful to determine how much local input should be used, given that a portion of the benefits may be strictly local.

From the trade point of view, incentives such as financial subsidies influence competitiveness of individual producers. Fiscal incentive schemes have enabled such countries as Brazil and Chile to develop large-scale export-oriented industries. In Brazil's case, however, the supported activity (tree planting) collapsed when fiscal incentives were removed.

The trade dispute between the United States and Canada on forest subsidies and tariffs shows that the issue can be raised in trade negotiations even though forest policies have largely been perceived as a national issue. The United States claimed that Canada subsidized wood production through low royalty fees of forest concessions and that production costs are lower than economically justified. At the same time Canada claimed that production in U.S. forests was also subsidized by Congressional appropriations (Repetto et al. 1992). Subsidies expand the export supply of forest products from the United States and Canada. There is a risk that such subsidies are encouraging excess harvesting, resulting in negative environmental impacts (e.g., deforestation and increased CO_2 emissions) (cf. Repetto 1993).

Subsidies in related sectors sometimes have adverse environmental impacts on forests. Agricultural subsidies make certain land uses, such as crop production or grazing, artificially attractive, and lead to deforestation (Chapter 2). Such a conversion has proved to be unsustainable on land with poor soils or where nutrient leaching from soils is a problem.

Subsidies that make domestic prices differ from border prices risk generating external environmental costs. In forestry, subsidies are typically used to mitigate policy failures, rather than to address fundamental issues such as underpricing. It has been easier politically to establish subsidies than to increase stumpage prices on government lands. Subsidies are not considered to be environmental policy instruments, but they significantly affect the use and management of land resources with environmental consequences.

Trading of Global Environmental Benefits

Recognition of the global environmental values of forests could make trade a potential instrument for conservation financing. Such benefits can be derived from carbon sequestration, and biodiversity conservation (existence and option values), but hydrological benefits or other local externalities can also be significant. To complement public sector mechanisms for international transfer of funds for environmental conservation, new arrangements have been made to tap the resources of the private sector. This is necessary as it has become obvious that the public sector can only meet a fraction of the needs in developing countries.

In carbon offset agreements, carbon emissions in one country are exchanged for carbon sequestration in another country. The potential for such an activity is huge in view of both the current level of CO_2 emissions, and the need to expand tree cover through planting or to sustainably manage existing forests in developing countries. The number of existing carbon offset deals is still limited, and accumulated experience will be needed to improve the design for worldwide promotion (Chapter 3). Several issues will have to be addressed, such as a finalized international agreement on the use of forests as carbon sinks, in the Clean Development Mechanism (CDM) of the Climate Change Convention. In other mechanisms to provide funding for environmental services, such issues as local land-use conflicts, possible restrictions of the use of forests created through the mechanism, and organizational and institutional arrangements will have to be addressed.

International contracts on the commercial use of biodiversity is another recent trade-related instrument. The first example of these has been the contract established between the INBio (the National Biodiversity Institute) in Costa Rica and the pharmaceutical company Merck. INBio is in charge of classifying and studying the existing species in the country for their possible sustainable utilization. Costa Rica does not have funds to carry out this huge task, and therefore Merck will provide funds in exchange for the exclusive commercial rights to the information generated by INBio. The initial outlay of $1.1 million may be increased later (Chapter 9).

This example of an international biodiversity deal is likely to be one of many. Several issues still need to be addressed to make these deals attractive to local governments and foreign investors such as provisions for biodiversity conservation in perpetuity, and duration, exclusivity and limits of rights.

In addition to trading global environmental benefits, there is also potential and need for regional and local arrangements, particularly in watershed management. The current approaches in critical watersheds are mostly based on strict regulation which typically suffers from weak enforcement. Equitable sharing of costs and benefits of the hydrological functions of forests is a complex task, particularly if countrywide impacts are involved (Hueth 1995).

Multilateral Agreements Influencing Forest Management

Multilateral environmental agreements can be important instruments for environmental management and sustainable development. With few exceptions (e.g., the Montreal Protocol), however, their effects on trade and environment are not clearly established (UNCTAD 1995a). Out of the 180 agreements negotiated, several have indirect or direct influence on forest management and competitiveness. The most important of these are the Conventions on Climate Change and Biological Diversity, and CITES. Among the commodity agreements, the International Tropical Timber Agreement (ITTA) deals only with forestry. Under the U.N. Commission on Sustainable Development (CSD) an International Panel on Forests has been studying possibilities for an international convention on forests which could integrate most of the sector-specific issues under a single agreement.

The main multilateral environmental agreements influencing forest management have had limited impact on trade flows and competitiveness in part because they are relatively recent. The conventions on climate change and biological diversity are likely to result in the provision of additional resources for conservation activities. In forestry, like in other natural resource sectors, it is difficult to separate development and environmental conservation. The implementation guidelines of the agreements must ensure that (i) win–win situations between global and local direct and indirect benefits can be maximized, and (ii) effectiveness and efficiency in the use of available funds are enhanced.

Ultimately, the parties involved in these agreements will determine their effectiveness. The experience of the ITTA implementation shows that much can be done to develop suitable recommendations based on an international consensus. Enforcement mechanisms are, however, weak. In the case of tropical timber, the problem is related more to the time frame than to the actual principle of sustainable forest management. A broader framework with equal treatment of all types of forests is therefore necessary to ensure improved forest management on a global scale.

Conventions on Climate Change and Biological Diversity
Forests play an important role in the global carbon cycle and serve as a major carbon sink. Forests also provide a major habitat for biodiversity. Therefore, deforestation and excessive exploitation are serious global concerns. The Convention on Biological Diversity (CBD) establishes a framework for sustainable management and utilization of biodiversity with a strong economic dimension.

The Global Environmental Facility (GEF) provides the financing for the two conventions. Financing is based on the rule of incremental costs induced by necessary action to achieve global environmental benefits. The incremental cost principle of GEF, however, represents a constraint for financing biodiversity conservation, as the application of the principle is loaded with ambiguities. It is difficult to separate global benefits from the local ones. Win–win situations are being sought, and the role of the private sector is emphasized. As a spinoff of the two conventions, a number of new financing instruments have emerged where the purpose is often either to support biodiversity conservation or to increase biomass through reforestation.

From the trade point of view GEF's problem is that direct or indirect subsidies provided to selected producers may increase their competitiveness at the expense of others. Reforested areas for carbon sequestration need to be managed and harvested at the end of the rotation period to increase wood supply in the market. The policy implications of these subsidies have not been analyzed in full, but as long as their main objective is environmental, they may be considered justified (e.g. IDB 1995c).

The global environmental values of forests offer possibilities for trade through international transactions. Financing schemes for carbon sequestration and tradeable pollution permits are typical examples, but they may lead to single-objective investments when benefits could be maximized using multiple objective frameworks (e.g., including biodiversity conservation). The forthcoming international convention on forests should be seen as an instrument that could provide the necessary framework for efficiency improvement in a field whose present arrangements (climate change, biodiversity) tend to lead to suboptimization.

The Convention on International Trade of Endangered Species

The Convention on International Trade of Endangered Species (CITES) directly regulates commercial trade. Three levels of species vulnerability are recognized:

- Species threatened with extinction and possibly affected by trade (in practice, commercial trade of these species is prohibited);
- Species that are not necessarily threatened now, but may become so unless trade is strictly regulated; and
- Species for which trade is subject to regulation to prevent exploitation, and where cooperation between trade partners is needed to control trade.

In practice, trade of species listed in the second group requires import and export permits by the competent authorities in respective countries.

A review of the CITES lists reveals that the tree species are mostly of tropical origin. Therefore, developing countries have viewed CITES as a trade barrier instrument to reduce their competitiveness in export markets. Having failed to turn the International Tropical Timber Organization (ITTO) into an instrument for restricting trade in timber from poorly managed tropical forests, some conservation groups are focusing their attention on CITES to achieve that goal. Several tree species have recently been nominated for listing in the second group, even though none of these is in direct danger of biological extinction (IUCN 1993). As an example, there has recently been an intensive debate on restricting trade in some of the most valuable tropical timber species, e.g., mahogany (*Swietenia spp.*), on the initiative of some developed countries. Several species of mahogany occur in about 20 countries in the LAC region. The issue is complicated by the fact that mahogany resources vary by country. The trade impacts also vary: in some countries mahogany is a major source of revenue, while in others it plays only a marginal role. In 1994, *Swietenia humilis* and *S. mahogani* were included in CITES, while *S. macrophylla*, the main export species, was excluded. This is a good example of how CITES can vary depending on the species and country.

It appears from the above discussion that the original objectives of CITES could be expanded to restrict forest harvesting and alter management practices. The earlier success in controlling clearly identifiable wildlife products in trade may be difficult to achieve in the trade of timber: where identification of species requires specialized skills; where final products are not necessarily specifically related to the raw material used; and where imitations are easy to produce.

To properly address the type of problems faced in the case of mahogany, CITES lists should be expanded to include the origin—with appropriate verification and labeling systems established to effectively monitor trade from different locations. Such an effort was tried for tropical wildlife, such as elephants, but the CITES parties were unable to reach an agreement (UNCTAD 1995a).

Although CITES can be considered an effective convention, its regulatory approach in forest products does not encourage sustainable management of forests. Economic incentives are not provided to those countries that succeed in increasing the stock of the endangered species to a level that allows sustainable utilization, thereby providing further motivation for conservation efforts. Experience has shown that forests with no value to local people tend to be destroyed or converted into other land uses. CITES should therefore be regarded as a protection measure of last resort to be applied for a minimum necessary period, rather than a major instrument for sustainable development. The unintended effects of CITES on trade and competitiveness should be duly assessed. An increasing shortage of a species tends to be reflected in its price and encourages a search for substitutes. For instance, the emergence of rubberwood as a major raw material for wood industries in Southeast Asia partly derives from the fact that it can, to some extent, replace certain rare or endangered species (cf. ITC 1993). Many of the problems inherent to CITES could be partly eliminated through a credible timber certification and labeling system.

International Tropical Timber Agreement

The International Tropical Timber Agreement (ITTA), renewed in 1994, was not conceived of as an environmental pact, rather it is a commodity agreement. However, it does affect both development and the environment. It also provides a framework for sustainable management of tropical forests through three areas of intervention: forest management and reforestation; forest industries; and improved market transparency through the provision of economic and market information. Various guidelines have been developed for sustainable management to provide a common general framework for national action (ITTO 1995). A goal to have tropical timber trade entirely based on sustainably managed forests by year 2000 has been promoted in both producing and consuming countries. Project financing is a major instrument, but the available resources have been grossly insufficient to meet the respective requirements.

ITTA has been valuable in bringing consumers and producers together, both in policy work and development. Common positions have been established on the sustainable development of forests, and the clear targets set have been instrumental in focusing efforts both at international and national levels. Due to different perceived interests and priorities, however, progress in the field has not met the expectations of the parties. Key problems have been related to (i) the limitation of the Agreement to tropical timber only, as regards policy development, and (ii) insufficient financial resources for field activities. Largely for these reasons, the international environmental community has reduced its support of the ITTA. The focus of the environmental movement has turned to other approaches, notably timber certification and CITES. However, ITTA's achievements are significant and, if the parties wish to commit themselves to ratifying the Agreement there is a potential for substantial contributions to the sustainable development of forests.

Certification of Forest Management and Ecolabeling of Forest Products

Certification combined with ecolabeling is a potentially powerful information-based instrument that could make trade contribute to the sustainable management of natural resources. Use of this instrument in the forestry sector is primarily concerned with improving the production process, i.e., the quality of forest management. For this to work, information has to be transferred through the chain-of-custody from the forest to the end use. The producer countries often conceive the requirements to be designed to generate global and not necessarily national environmental benefits (Andrew 1995).

For a producer country there are two objectives to consider: improving forest management and ensuring market access. Certification alone may not be sufficient to achieve these objectives (Baharuddin and Simula 1994). Rather, it should complement other tools such as external auditing to monitor the compliance of forest management. With secured market access, it is expected that the incremental costs can be paid for with the anticipated additional revenue ("green premium").

A set of ancillary objectives can also be attached to timber certification which may be achieved by improving the transparency of forestry activities. Such objectives can be set by the government (e.g., better control of forestry operations and land use change, higher recovery of collection of forest fees and taxes) or by firms (e.g., improved total productivity). Some of these ancillary objectives may be particularly important in tropical countries where the present arrangements of law enforcement, supervision and control are inadequate due to insufficient resources of public forest agencies.

Forest Products in Existing Labeling Schemes

Parallel to timber certification initiatives, paper and wood products have been included in various national or regional ecolabeling schemes, such as in the European Union. Because the processing of these products does not require a life-cycle perspective of the resource, the quality of the raw material source is often ignored. Moreover, the industry has not differentiated among raw material species used for this production, nor has it considered the inherent environmental characteristics of different materials, such as their renewability.

On the other hand, attention has focused on less critical environmental aspects that are more noticeable and easier to measure. The recycled fiber content in paper and board products is a typical example. In particular, the draft criteria of the EU eco-label on tissue paper products have been subject to criticism by such pulp exporters as Brazil for whom this market segment is important (UNCTAD 1995c). Brazilian exporters have alleged that the emphasis on recycling as a criterion for determining renewable resource use discriminates against Brazilian producers who use wood from plantations and not from natural forests. They also allege that the criteria related to SO_2 emissions in the production process are of little or no relevance since acid rain was not a concern in the location of production in Brazil (although it can be in Europe). They also claim that the criteria used to determine production process compliance with renewable energy standards discriminate against Brazilian producers, who depend largely on hydroelectricity (UNCTAD 1995d).

Box 10.2 Ecolabeling for Paper Products in Argentina, Brazil, and Chile

Due to favorable conditions of both climate and soil, the productivity of forests in Argentina, Brazil and Chile is very high for both pines (long fibers) and eucalyptus (short fibers). The environmental effects of plantation forests depend on whether the plantations replace natural forests or are established on degraded lands, and whether native or exotic species are used. In all these countries, plantation forests have been mainly established on marginal agricultural land, and most of the pulpwood processed or exported comes from them.

Argentina's leading exporter of paper competes internationally and, according to a case study, is using best environmental practices. For example, the firm has reduced the environmental impacts of its effluent and improved its forest management in response to concerns expressed by foreign clients. Based on a technology developed within the firm, the bleaching process has been modified and the firm is now producing paper that is totally free of chlorine, a potential contaminant.

Brazil's pulp industry has achieved a high level of vertical integration, which is exemplified by several larger firms that possess their own plantations. Fast-growing eucalyptus plantations and mastery of forest management technologies provide Brazilian industry with important comparative advantages. The supply of renewable energy resources and economies of scale also constitute comparative advantages.

A study undertaken by the German Development Institute (GDI) indicates that the pulp industry in **Chile** meets stringent international standards and exceeds domestic regulations, in particular with regard to chlorine-free bleaching, effluent treatment, water consumption, energy use and sustainable forest management. The GDI study notes that the Chilean pulp industry has nevertheless opted for a low-profile policy in its public relations, rather than trying to take advantage of its achievements in terms of environmental management.

Source: Adapted from UNCTAD (1995d).

It is apparent that the existing ecolabeling schemes will not be adequate to address all environmental concerns of environmental NGOs and the public at large. The schemes are mostly national and have been developed with little consideration for how they influence the environmental situation or competitiveness of foreign producers. Some developmental issues from the Latin American perspective are discussed in Box 10.2.

Criteria for Sustainable Forest Management

At a national level, forest legislation, rules and regulations provide the normative framework for assessing forest management performance. Certification is a response to two problems in particular: (i) existing standards that may not be sufficient to promote sustainability; and (ii) supervision and control that are ineffective in preventing inappropriate harvesting practices.

There is an extensive, ongoing international attempt to define the principles and criteria of sustainable forest management, both in the tropics and elsewhere. This effort, which gained momentum after the 1992 UNCED Conference, has a total of about 20 organizations or processes working to this end. The effort is intended to lead to a worldwide agreement and form part of an international convention on forests sponsored by the CSD Intergovernmental Panel on Forests.

Box 10.3 International Criteria for Forest Management

ITTO (Tropical Forests Worldwide)	Montreal Process (Temperate Forests in Western Hemisphere)	Tarapoto (Amazon Countries)
1. Secured forest resource base	1. Conservation of biological diversity	1. Local and national socio-economic benefits
2. Continuity of forest production	2. Maintenance of productive capacity of forests	2. Policies and legal-institutional framework
3. Level of environmental control and acceptable impact	3. Maintenance of ecosystem vitality	3. Sustainability of forest production
4. Conservation of flora and fauna	4. Conservation and maintenance of soil and water resources	4. Conservation of forest cover and biological diversity
5. Socio-economic benefits	5. Maintenance of forests' contribution to global carbon cycles	5. Conservation of integrated management of water and soil resources
6. Institutional framework	6. Maintenance and enhancement of long-term multiple socio-economic benefits	6. Science and technology
7. Flexibility in applying criteria according to experience	7. Legal, institutional and economic framework for forest conservation and sustainable management	7. Institutional capacity
		8. Global economic, social and environmental benefits from Amazon forests

In 1990, the ITTO drew up guidelines for the sustainable management of natural tropical forests and plantations. These guidelines were followed up with definitions of criteria, and indicators for biodiversity conservation (ITTO 1990, 1992, 1993). The LAC member countries and other ITTO members have agreed to the ITTO initiative. However, the guidelines are not legally binding, and they do not adequately cover the ecological and social aspects of tropical forest management geared toward sustainability.

In February 1995 in Tarapoto, Peru, the countries of the Amazon Cooperation Treaty agreed on a proposal that set criteria and indicators for sustainability of Amazonian forests to be adopted by the respective governments. The Tarapoto Proposal attempts to promote the sustainable development of the Amazonian forests—to make use of their environmental, economic, cultural and social potential, while recognizing the national sovereignty of the member states. The criteria were established at three levels: local forest management unit, national, and global (see Appendix 10.6). It is the only proposal where the global benefits have been considered explicitly. The proposal includes provisions for broad participation and consultation, especially at the local level. It forms a useful subregional instrument for harmonizing the normative framework in the forestry sector. Its effectiveness, however, will depend on adoption and application in the member states.

The various initiatives relevant to the LAC region have a number of common features (Box 10.3). They broaden the traditional concept of sustainable forest management to include biodiversity, environmental services and socioeconomic aspects. Although these initiatives have not been designed for certification purposes, they do provide a common basis for normative framework. They also suggest different actions at the local, national and global levels.

The underlying principle in the existing forest certification schemes (not necessarily always explicit) has been to use forest estate or management unit as the entity of assessment. In small management entities, which are common in LAC countries where private forest ownership dominates, only a limited number of criteria and indicators may be relevant at a given point of time, depending on the prevailing structural characteristics of the management unit. CIFOR's ongoing work on testing of alternative certification criteria and indicators is therefore necessary to establish the feasibility of practical assessment.

On the other hand, certification should be based on criteria and indicators which are relevant to improved forest management and thereby sustainability in a given country. A country may be divided into biogeographical vegetation zones, each having its own biological characteristics which also define the specific features of forest types occurring in these zones. At the international level, the Forest Stewardship Council (FSC) has provided a certification framework that has been adapted to local conditions by accredited certifiers. The FSC principles were developed through a consultative process and approved by the council assembly (see section below). Site-specific forest management standards should be developed based on similar consultative processes to be applied in the assessment of individual management units.

Concerns have been expressed about the human resource requirements for carrying out qualified assessments of the compliance at forest management with the criteria to be established. Forest management is often a complex exercise where understanding of local environmental and social conditions is essential. It can be questioned whether external auditors largely basing their assessment on documentation are able to measure or evaluate a large number of different indicators that may be in conflict with each other.

Harmonizing Certification Criteria

International harmonization and mutual recognition of certification criteria and indicators are essential for smooth trade in international markets. The intergovernmental processes described above, together with national-level follow-up work, are intended to provide a common framework within which forest management certification can take place. It has to be emphasized that forest management practices depend on many location-specific factors (species composition, ecosystem, dynamics, socioeconomic situation, etc.). It is therefore unlikely, for example, that an importing country's specific forest management standards would be directly applicable in an exporting country. For this reason, some importing countries or large buyers of forest products have developed their standards for foreign suppliers (e.g., Initiative Tropenwald in Germany). While these types of initiatives are convenient for specific trading partners, they have structural limitations if they cannot be attached to an appropriate international framework. At present, ISO and FSC offer the only broad-based, widely applied international standards.

International Standardization Organization. The ISO's ongoing work on the environmental management systems standards (14,000 series) provides a basis for international certification of enterprise-level management systems related to environmental issues. Because of the broad participation base and the organization's mandate to assess management processes, the ISO is seen as a potential instrument to provide the necessary common framework for certification of forest management as well. In 1995 the Canadian Standards Association (CSA) made a proposal to ISO to start the development of an international standard for sustainable forest management systems. The proposal did not pass, as it would have established a sector-specific precedent for general management systems. In addition it was opposed by NGOs that saw it as a countermeasure for the FSC where economic interests play a minor role in decision making. The issue is being pursued within ISO through an informal study group with a mandate to develop a method for assessing forest management.

Forest Stewardship Council. The FSC, headquartered in Oaxaca, Mexico, was established to promote voluntary, independent certification of forest management. Its highest decisionmaking body, the general assembly, is divided into two voting chambers: the first, with 75 percent of the vote, represents social and environmental interests; and the second, with 25 percent of the vote, represents economic interests. The imbalance has made industry hesitant to participate in the FSC, yet experience from other ecolabeling programs shows that industry participation is needed to make such schemes successful.

FSC is an accreditation organization for independent certifiers. The Council has a set of principles and criteria for forest management, and a draft manual with rigorous and clearly defined procedures for evaluation and accreditation bodies. The FSC is also actively promoting the establishment of national working groups to develop forest management standards. The World Wildlife Fund has been the driving force in setting up and promoting the FSC. With rigorous and transparent procedures, the FSC is the only existing international framework with principles and criteria for forest management certification. It has accredited four certifiers, of whom three operate in the LAC region: the Smart Wood scheme of the Rainforest Alliance (U.S.A.); and two commercial enterprises, Scientific Certification Systems Inc. (U.S.A.) and SGS Forestry Ltd. (U.K.) (see Baharaddin and Simula 1994).

FSC principles and criteria should apply to all types of forests (tropical, temperate and boreal), all ownership categories, different sizes of forest management units, and various socioeconomic conditions. This presents a number of problems, however, due to the way the principles and criteria have been drafted. The FSC-accredited certifiers should also develop their own homogeneous assessment criteria and procedures. At least four factors are involved in FSC-accredited certifications: (i) global principles and criteria; (ii) national forest management standards; (iii) the general criteria for selecting certifying organizations; and (iv) site-specific criteria developed by the certifier for the field assessment. All four must be compatible. According to some critics, FSC standards are too demanding on environmental and social factors and weak on economic viability.

Certification Schemes and Initiatives in the LAC Region

As indicated earlier, certification programs are in their nascent stages. While estimates of the current number of certified managed forests vary, at least 17 independently certified forests existed in June 1995. Seven of them were located in the LAC region covering a total area of 676,000 ha (Box 10.4). The aggregate volume of wood affected by the schemes was estimated at less than 100,000 m^3. This represents 0.1 percent of the regional production of industrial roundwood. The two driving forces in the LAC initiatives are (i) foreign and local NGOs subscribing to the FSC and receiving donor support, and (ii) industry initiatives as a counter measure to market pressures. There is a clear need for a coherent approach to ensure a wide impact and broad support from all stakeholders.

As part of the USAID-funded project on Bolivia Sustainable Forest Management (BOLFOR), a feasibility study was carried out in 1994 with a recommendation to embark on the development of a national certification scheme in the country. The target is

Box 10.4 Certified Forests in the LAC Region, June 1995

Name	Area (ha)	Wood production (m³/year)
Amcol Ltd. Portel, Pará, Brazil	50,000	25,000
Broadleaf Forest Development Project, Honduras	25,000	1,650
Demerara Timber Ltd., Guyana	500,000	39,000
Plan Piloto Forestal, Quintana Roo, Mexico	95,000	11,000
Portico S.A., Costa Rica	5,000	7,700
Tropical American Tree Farms, Costa Rica	1,336	—
Total	676,336	84,350

Source: Bianchi et al. 1993.

to have 25 percent of all the Bolivia forests certifiable within seven years (Crossley 1995).

In 1994, Sociedade Brasileira de Silvicultura started to develop a national scheme for certification (see Box 10.5). Through an extensive process, the assessment criteria and a methodology for the certification process have been developed. CERFLOR has two supporting bodies and a secretariat, but has received only limited support from NGOs. Its credibility may also be challenged because of limited transparency and industry dominance.

Another scheme in Brazil has recently been initiated by the Instituto de Manejo e Certificação Florestal e Agrícola (IMAFLORA) as part of the Smart Wood network. IMAFLORA is apparently the first scheme intending to certify nonwood products, notably Brazil nuts and natural rubber.

In response to the certification used also in other countries, the FSC is laying the groundwork for national certification programs in Peru, Ecuador, and Venezuela. Mexico is reportedly developing its own national certification program in conjunction with a nongovernmental council (Consejo Civil Mexicano para la Silvicultura Sostenible) directed primarily at the domestic market (Crossley 1995). In addition, Central America has created the Regional Council on Forests and Protected Areas (CCB-AP) and the regional Chamber of Forest Industry, which could support the creation of certification schemes in the subregion. Lastly, there is the Latin America Forest Network, comprised of one hundred NGO members, which is trying to coordinate a regionwide, FSC-based certification system (Crossley 1995).

Demand and Price Premiums for Labeled Products

Several comprehensive studies are underway to determine the demand for "green" forest products, which undoubtedly varies by country and timber product. Varangis et al. (1995) concluded that certification is likely to affect 10 to 20 percent of the European market for tropical timber, and 5 to 10 percent of the U.S. market. A team of specialists of the Economic Commission for Europe (1995) proposed two tentative scenarios for the market shares of certified forest products. By the year 2000, a minimum of 10 percent could be

Box 10.5 Brazilian Initiatives in Certification

CERFLOR

Since 1992, the Brazilian forestry sector had been developing a methodology for a certification program that would identify the origin of raw materials used by the forest industry of Brazil. This work resulted in CERFLOR (Certificate of Origin of Forest Raw Material). The CERFLOR regulations are based on the assumption of self-regulation transparency, adaptation to Brazilian conditions, non-discrimination, voluntary application, flexibility and compatibility with international standards.

CERFLOR's five guidelines for planted and natural forests are as follows:
- Care of biodiversity;
- Sustainability of natural resources and their rational use in the short and long term;
- Protection of water, soil and air;
- Environmental protection combined with sustained economic and social development in areas affected by forestry activities; and
- Compliance with national legislation.

CERFLOR will grant certification only if there is compliance with all five principles and the related criteria, which take account of regional variations in forestry.

IMAFLORA

Recently, IMAFLORA, a Brazilian institute specializing in the eco-labeling of agricultural commodities, has ventured into the certification of forest products in association with the Rainforest Alliance (U.S.A.). Its strategy is to develop criteria and indicators on a local basis, compatible with FSC principles and criteria. At present they are working on two projects: one related to the certification of wooden boxes in the Atlantic forest, and the other concerning Brazil nut and rubber production in the Amazon Basin. With the assistance of FSC, IMAFLORA intends next to develop criteria for the certification of plantations.

Source: Dubois et al. 1995.

achieved. A decade later, by 2010, a maximum of 60 to 80 percent of the market might consist of certified products. These scenarios imply different levels of demand and different objectives and implementation strategies for certification. The high scenario assumes that certification will become a basic requirement for market access. Institutional factors may also play an important role in demand. As an example, a current Dutch legislative proposal allows only the imports of tropical forest products that are certified by FSC-accredited certifiers. At present in Europe, the demand for certified forest products cannot be met—constrained by limited certification capacity and industry reluctance to participate in a program that lacks clearly defined rules.

In view of the export destinations of Latin American wood-based products and the demand pressures, the following trade flows could be vulnerable, or could benefit from improved market access through certification: (i) Brazilian mahogany and other tropical hardwood exports to the U.K.; (ii) exports of Brazilian and Chilean pulp and paper to sensitive European markets; and (iii) exports of further processed tropical hardwood-based furniture and joinery to the U.S. and European markets. Exports of wood panels, mainly from Brazil, Chile and Argentina, and softwood lumber, mainly from Chile, are not assumed to be particularly sensitive.

The estimates of the "green premium" are still tentative and vary by product, country of destination, market and phase of the economic cycle. Industry should be cautioned not to count on excessive price benefits, particularly for roundwood until there is evidence to the contrary (Baharuddin and Simula 1994). If certification becomes a basic requirement in the market (high scenario above), the price differential is likely to disappear.

Costs and Net Benefits

Certification is a policy instrument designed to promote sustainability of forest management and market access (Baharuddin and Simula 1994). To make certification practical, all phases of the production and distribution chain should obtain net benefits. Experience in certifying forest products is still limited and the procedures are evolving, so that a rigorous economic analysis is not yet possible. This section therefore focuses on identifying relevant issues and the possible benefits and costs involved (see Simula 1995b).

Economic Issues Related to Certification Criteria and Indicators. The criteria and indicators used in the assessment of forest management may be expressed in terms of standards that determine the costs of certification. From the economic point of view it is important that the criteria and indicators are goal-oriented and lead to efficiency in implementation. International standards for different types of forests are general by nature. Each country has particular conditions to consider in developing national-level criteria and indicators.

The incremental costs of "sustainable" forest management depend on the difference between the standards applied in assessment and the current status of forest management. It is important to distinguish between the certification standards and those defined in the laws and regulations of the country in question. Compliance costs for government laws and regulations are unavoidable production costs. In contrast, certification is a voluntary activity for which the standards are generally set above those defined by the government. However, sustainability in the broad sense of economic and social benefits and maintenance of ecological functions has already been given political recognition by many LAC governments (cf., UNCED forest principles, ITTO guidelines of sustainable forest management). In the long run, government norms and certification criteria may converge, and incremental costs due to certification may gradually lose their importance. Nevertheless, in the short and medium term, the question of incremental costs remains.

Figure 10.1 shows how the marginal costs may increase disproportionately with higher forest management standards. This hypothetical curve demonstrates how raising the level of criteria (e.g., from S_1 to S_2) may result in a very high increase in costs (from C_1 to C_2). If information on biodiversity is inadequate, one must take a precautionary approach to management. Especially in the LAC region, the reported levels of biodiversity are high but knowledge thereof in many ecosystems is still very limited. The more information becomes available, the more closely targeted criteria can be applied. This is likely to lead to lower input requirements and justify investment in biodiversity research.

If certification assessment criteria and indicators are set on the level of bio-geographic zones or other relevant regional units, they are likely to be economically more efficient than national-level standards or even broader international standards. Such indicators can be based on specific local conditions and related to specific objectives in biodiversity conservation or social development. Nevertheless, location-specific criteria have to be compatible with the general set of forest management standards that provide a basis for national and international harmonization.

Another issue related to criteria is whether they should be prescriptive. There appears to be a strong preference for a flexible, nonprescriptive approach to promoting the continuous improvement of forest management operations without specifying perma-

Figure 10.1 Marginal Costs of Applying Forest Management Standards

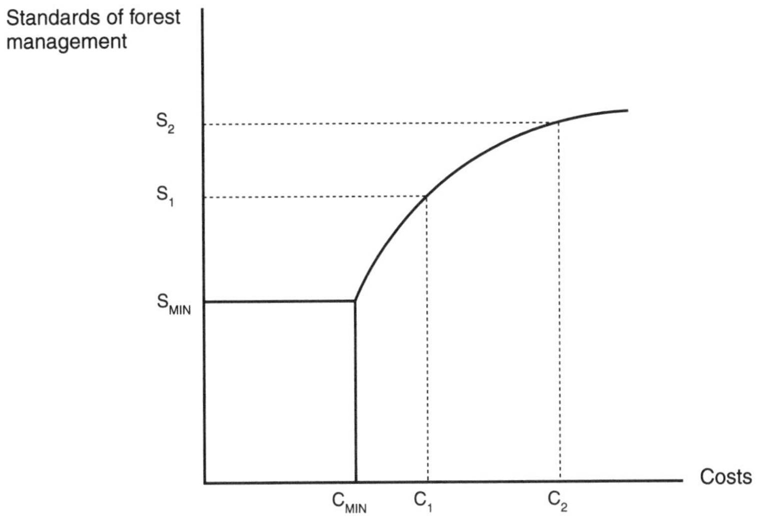

Note: S_{MIN} = the minimum level of government standards.

S_1 and S_2 = alternatives for certification standards.

nent standards. From the economic point of view, this would mean that incremental costs are likely to change over time in response to assessment criteria.

Costs Related to Certification. Direct costs cover the actual certification operation and are paid to the certifying organization. Indirect costs of certification refer to covering incremental expenses of forest management, and foregone benefits from activities without certification.

Setting up certification schemes generally requires significant prior investments in the establishment of institutional framework for the accreditation and certification, definition of criteria and indicators, human resource development, development of administrative procedures, etc. These costs can vary extensively depending on local conditions. The existing certification systems are self-financing and profit-seeking, operated by commercial certifiers.

Reliable data on the *direct costs* of certification are limited: only a few certifiers are willing to release such information, considered commercial confidential data. The current rates may not be representative for the future if certification becomes a major business activity subject to competition between certifiers. Pricing policies will also be influenced by long-term considerations, particularly if the same company provides services in both certification and consulting to assist clients in implementing the recommendations of the assessment exercises.

The costs of the certification inspection depend on the information available and the kind of team (number of persons, expatriate or local) involved. The existing certifiers are located principally in the United States and the United Kingdom, so fielding of assessment teams outside these countries represents a major cost element. To eliminate this disadvantage at least one certifier, Rainforest Alliance (1993), relies on local specialists as much as possible. The size of holding also influences the unit costs of inspection, and can be a major obstacle for small holdings. To reduce costs, these lands could be certified using sampling based on a regional unit, such as a cooperative, an association, a municipality or a district.

The theoretical unit cost functions are depicted in Figure 10.2. It has been estimated that large-scale forest producers in tropical forests, with annual extractions of 1,000 ha or more might face increased costs of .5 percent over net harvesting costs due to certification, if the standards meet FSC requirement (Palmer 1995). This may correspond to $0.24 per ha for areas of 100,000 ha and $1.30 per ha for areas of 5,000 ha.

According to a commercial certification body, preliminary evaluation typically costs from $700 to $4,500 (excluding expenses) and full forest management assessment from $2,250 to 18,000 (excluding expenses). The following average figures on inspection costs are available:

Donovan (1994):	$5,000–$75,000 per assessment, depending on consultant time and travel
SGS Silviconsult (1994):	$31,000 annually for a large overseas operation (500,000 ha)
Upton and Bass (1995):	$500 for a small farm near the assessor's office, and $130,000 for a 100,000-ha natural forest concession in the tropics over six years
Soil Association:	In large forest operations, 1 percent of sales value; in smaller operations, annual fee varies from $225 upwards per estate, depending on forest products sales value.

These costs may change considerably if certification becomes a major activity. This is due to several factors: (i) there are few experienced certifiers in the world, and the areas and volumes have been more experimental than routine operations, for the most part; (ii) several issues still lack definition, as many schemes are still in the planning or initial implementation phase; and (iii) competition between certifiers has not been a major factor influencing costs. Future participation in certification schemes may possibly be priced in the same way as the existing ecolabeling programs—application and annual fees, supplemented by a royalty on the value of sales (with a possible ceiling).

Incremental Costs of Forest Management. The incremental costs (including foregone benefits) of forest management can generally be derived from five different sources: (i) costs of planning and monitoring; (ii) additional silviculture and harvesting costs; (iii) lower yields and thus higher per-unit costs in harvesting areas; (iv) setting aside areas for protection; and (v) changes in the distribution of costs and benefits in time that alter the net present value of the investment. Assessing the above costs and benefits foregone would require analyses of current government regulations and the certification criteria applied. The difference between the two could then be attributed to the incremental costs of forest management due to certification.

The additional *costs of planning and monitoring* can be significant, particularly in the initial stage. They typically include mapping, inventory, logging preparation, road and trail planning, sample plot establishment, post-harvest inventory, and environmental impact studies. In plantation forests, costs are substantially lower. In any case, improved planning usually reduces operational costs.

Figure 10.2 Operational Costs of Certification and Forest Unit Size

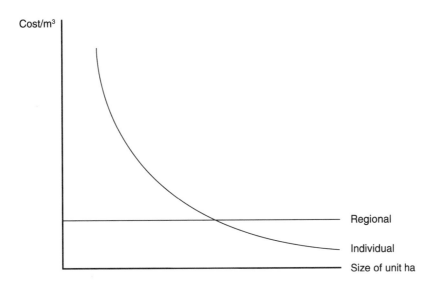

Silviculture and harvesting costs increase when nontimber resources are managed, but there are also savings associated with this type of management. Hendrisson (1989) found that costs did not increase substantially when controlled harvesting was introduced as part of the management system in Suriname. Nevertheless, existing market conditions provide few short-term incentives for management of environmental quality and natural resources.

Lower harvesting yield per unit area in natural tropical forests may be due to "low-impact logging" to reduce damage on the remaining vegetation. The short-term economic sacrifice could be partially compensated for by higher overall yields of timber in the long run and reduced damage of nontimber resources (Bach and Gram 1993).

The need for protected areas of key biotopes or landscape depends mostly on local conditions. The amount of land allocated to nonproductive use is subject to debate and ranges from 5 to 50 percent of the contract area. Among the existing certifiers, Rainforest Alliance (1993) proposes that 10 percent of the total area under forest management (excluding stream and roadside buffers) be designated as a "conservation zone." In Brazil the forest law requires that 20 percent of the plantation area be set aside as legal reserves of natural vegetation.

In their assessment of incremental forest management costs, Bach and Gram (1993) conclude that changes in the timing of costs and benefits associated with sustainable management can be an economic constraint, especially for low-income forest owners. Foregone benefits through alternative, noncertified management may be high in the initial years of sustainable forest management. The problem is aggravated by the fact that part of the additional costs come during the initial period. Longer time horizons required for sustainable forest management cause many managers to consider it a risky endeavor.

In conclusion, incremental costs usually occur when forest management is improved. The main reason is foregone initial benefits and longer investment periods. The prevailing levels of forest management, infrastructure, human resources and information systems vary greatly by country and forest owner, so incremental costs also vary. The incremental costs of certification cannot be estimated from the existing studies, because they are not related to the achievement of specific standards.

Economic Benefits. In the long run, improved management should result in higher yields for forest products. In assessing costs and benefits, the choice of discount rate decisively influences the result. The marginal impact of certification on the yield will also depend on how national standards and certification criteria vary. The marginal contribution of certification is again due to the fact that the improved management systems would be adopted faster when induced by certification.

A potentially important source of economic benefits is the possible elimination of trade intermediaries between producers and final consumers of forest products. While such cases are reported, one cannot yet assess in broad terms the potential economic benefits of shortened distribution channels. In countries where illegal practices are common, efficiency gains can also be expected from better control of wood flows through certification.

In conclusion, it is still too early to assess whether certification will improve forest management and market access. Certification will undoubtedly increase costs, varying by countries and local conditions. There is a risk that the main benefits will be found in the market access and that the benefits for forest management alone will be marginal.

Possible Impacts of Certification on Trade and Production

Because producing and exporting countries differ in their exposure to trade and dependence on environmentally sensitive markets, how certification affects them will also vary. This could influence trade flows and accelerate substitution of materials. Consumption patterns may also change: for example, plywood substituted for solid wood, as the latter's price increases. Although how certification might change the production structure is not clear (Baharuddin and Simula 1994), small- and medium-sized enterprises are poorly equipped for a certification-based market (Box 10.6).

How can small forest owners be effectively certified without excessive costs? In some cases, ecolabeling in conjunction with technical assistance and other support measures could help establish a niche in the market for environmentally friendly, nonwood products. However, certification is not a prerequisite for using environmental and developmental marketing strategies for nonwood forest products. Public interest in environmentally friendly markets has so far been minimal within the LAC region.

Certification of forest management will be applied as an instrument to provide necessary information on the environmental friendliness of forest products. To focus only on forest production might effectively penalize these products, by favoring commercial substitutes that do not involve similar complexities in raw material supply. Therefore, certification assessments should occur at all levels of production in order to lead to sustainable consumption patterns. Certification of forest management is therefore only a partial solution and should be accompanied by a broad, integrated package of policy instruments to correct market and other imperfections.

Policy reforms are likely to have a greater impact on the sustainable development of forests than forest management certification and labeling. Of particular importance will be further development of international harmonization of forest sector policies with full support of all the involved stakeholders. Confrontation between parties may be an appropriate mechanism to spark reform, but it cannot form a basis for the systematic, comprehensive measures that are needed to improve forestry practices on a global scale.

Box 10.6 Small Firms and Certification

Small and medium-sized enterprises may find it difficult to comply with certification and eco-labeling requirements, for the following reasons:
- Lack of access to information, technology and capital;
- Economy-of-scale factors that render investments unprofitable;
- Inability to ensure that raw materials are actually coming from certified forests if producers lack their own procurement organization;
- Lack of economic power to transfer criteria compliance costs to customers and suppliers;
- Higher relative costs of verification, including plant inspection.

Source: Adapted from UNCTAD (1995d).

Directions for the Future

Countries in Latin America and the Caribbean are experiencing difficulties in consolidating environmental and trade issues in their national policies. The multilateral processes have provided common goals and objectives, but implementation strategies have to come from within the countries themselves and the region.

Policy Support

In spite of significant progress in policy development, notably through the Tropical Forest Action Programs supported by the FAO and other international entities, most countries need capacity building in policy design. In addition, few countries have effectively addressed the implications of international obligations and nonbinding commitments in their national policies.

On the other hand, regional interests should be promoted in the implementation of multilateral environmental and other forest-related agreements. There has been inadequate coordination in this respect (e.g., *Swietenia*-mahogany listing in CITES). In spite of the sometimes conflicting national interests, regional and subregional consultations could assist in promoting consensus.

Trade in forest products in the LAC region is poorly researched, and the readily available data refer to primary wood products. Therefore, more study and analysis of the effects of trade liberalization on forest trade is needed, especially of nonwood forest products. The development of the nonwood exports is particularly constrained by lack of market transparency.

Improvement in forest management and more aggressive reforestation programs will require adequate policy framework for private sector investment. When important environmental externalities are present, incentives may be necessary to compensate for the lower rates of return associated with conservation forests (which are offset by improvements in environmental quality). Under certain conditions incentives could be provided in the form of subsidies, but such subsidies might then become a trade issue. This could also negatively influence the concessional financing of forest conservation through new emerging financing instruments. Any trade implications should be clarified before implementing new financial incentives for forest production.

National policies related to restricting and promoting trade in forest products are in need of review. Log export bans should be seriously reconsidered in view of their often negative environmental and developmental impacts.

In the LAC region, national forest policies sometimes have contradictory goals and are often poorly implemented. Inconsistent enforcement leads to ineffectiveness and even negative impacts. Integrated policy design approaches should be promoted, and there is a particular need to introduce comprehensive policy packages that address relevant extrasectoral issues affecting forests.

Multilateral lending institutions, international organizations and conventions, industrialized country development assistance and NGOs could work together to provide the following assistance to LAC country efforts in this field:

(i)   Support the trade liberalization process with adequate consideration of possible environmental impacts. National-level monitoring mechanisms should be devised to consider such impacts, as present arrangements do not emphasize environmental policy linkages. Further analysis on the environmental impacts of structural adjustment programs on forest management would be useful for the design of specific adjustment instruments.

(ii) Improve and update trade data on forest products to facilitate policy design and export development. Specific information is needed on: (a) direction of trade flows, (b) trade figures of processed industrial forest products, and (c) data on nonwood forest products with a particular emphasis on intraregional trade. Data collection and processing could be arranged in cooperation with international organizations such as the FAO, ITTO, and UNCTAD.

(iii) Expand national capacities for policy analysis, design and implementation. This would alleviate a fundamental bottleneck in the effectiveness and efficiency of public forest administrations and would strengthen broad-based participatory processes.

(iv) Support the design of comprehensive policy packages through case studies and workshops. Regional and subregional workshops on selected policy issues and specific initiatives would contribute to the transfer of knowledge and policy harmonization, particularly at a subregional level.

(v)   Give priority to the promotion of nonwood forest products and further processed wood products, emphasizing the environmental and developmental benefits to be obtained from their increased trade. Support the removal of unnecessary or harmful trade barriers such as export bans. Make adequate provisions for transition periods to soften any short-term adverse impacts of such measures.

(vi) Contribute to policy development and coordination in the LAC region by participating in regional and international policy processes, major policy-oriented conferences, seminars and workshops.

Development of Certification and Ecolabeling

Certification of forest management and ecolabeling of forest products combine to form an instrument that can potentially promote forest conservation through trade, and increase financing by the private sector. Several fundamental issues related to these activities still need definition. At present, certification is in its initial stage worldwide. In the LAC region, interest has been channeled through NGO-supported initiatives and emerging national schemes in response to external market pressures.

The demand for certified products is still limited and should be promoted to ensure marketability. In some cases, certification has led to increased prices to compensate for higher costs. Certification can have negative impacts, especially on small-scale producers or communities that lack resources and technical knowledge to implement the required forest management. Similarly, the lower unit costs of certification for large forest areas can inadvertently favor big producers. Finally, the problem of local capacity-building needs to be addressed, to enable the countries themselves to implement their certification schemes in a cost-effective manner.

Strategies in this field could consist of the following elements:

(i)   When production is aimed at export markets, certification alternatives and requirements should be analyzed, and necessary measures to implement certification should be included for improving market access and competitiveness of LAC producers. With the goal of standardizing certification, regional consultations and background studies should be carried out to identify areas of conflict and common interest.

(ii)   Certification and ecolabeling schemes should be equitable, to avoid possible adverse impacts on small-scale and community producers.

(iii) Support the development of credible subregional and national certification schemes meeting the international harmonization requirements.

(iv)   Support the building of local capacity in: (a) improving forest management by producers in order to meet certification requirements, and (b) establishing a pool of local certifiers through training and institutional development.

(v)   Assess possibilities for financial support to national and subregional schemes in their initial phases, avoiding mechanisms that are not likely to be self-sustaining.

(vi)   Improve awareness among countries about the positive and negative aspects of forest management certification, through publications, conferences, seminars and workshops.

Financing

Emerging new financing instruments have unexplored potential. These instruments are aimed at increasing the trade of the global environmental services offered by forests. The role of the private sector should be enhanced, as public sector funding is falling short of the financing needs of forestry development and conservation.

The forestry sector's capability for self-financing is significant, but the potential is far from being reached due to the undervaluation of forest resources. Underlying policy and market failures should be corrected. Projects need to meet both public and private sector decision makers' assessment criteria and have the capacity for self-financing. A number of actions could make financing more efficient and effective:

Correct policy failures through elimination of inappropriate instruments within and outside the forestry sector. To allow smooth transition without unnecessary adverse effects, actions may be carried out in phases.

Perform detailed analyses on alternative financing instruments for forest and biodiversity conservation investments, and mitigation of climate change. Instruments such as joint venture trust funds, carbon offset deals, and biodiversity prospecting contracts should be considered.

Consider the special requirements of programs with forestry related components, namely:

- Mechanisms for trading forest environmental services at the global, subregional or local levels; as for the latter, such possibilities could be integrated, for example, in watershed management projects;
- Studies of instruments that involve the private sector (both domestic and foreign) in financing forest conservation for commercial ends (e.g., eco-tourism); and
- Careful analysis of incentives for forest conservation, forest management and reforestation to minimize the possibility of such incentives becoming a trade issue.

Include plans for building local capacity and strengthening institutions in project budgets to ensure policy implementation, and to encourage private sector organizations to develop such instruments as national certification schemes.

Appendix 10.1 Trade in Wood-based Forest Products by Country, 1993

Country	Exports	Imports	Trade balance	Share of Latin American	
				Exports	Imports
	In US$ 1000			Percent	
Argentina	148,584	463,048	–314,464	3.9	12.8
Belize	1,935	3,051	–1,116	0.1	0.1
Bolivia	54,110	19,863	34,247	1.4	0.6
Brazil	1,994,730	308,471	1,686,259	51.7	8.6
Chile	1,134,024	152,259	981,765	29.4	4.2
Colombia	18,480	182,741	–164,261	0.5	5.1
Costa Rica	2,454	111,408	–108,954	0.1	3.1
Cuba	316	8,635	–8,319	0.0	0.2
Dominican Rep.	225	106,752	–106,527	0.0	3.0
Ecuador	27,656	111,531	–83,875	0.7	3.1
El Salvador	104	45,121	–45,017	0.0	1.3
Guatemala	3,634	66,913	–63,279	0.1	1.9
Guyana	5,632	1,813	3,819	0.1	0.1
Haiti	18	5,161	–5,143	0.0	0.1
Honduras	29,306	39,913	–10,607	0.8	1.1
Jamaica	89	76,969	–76,880	0.0	2.1
Mexico	276,214	1,187,089	–910,875	7.2	32.9
Nicaragua	523	6,115	–5,592	0.0	0.2
Panama	3,658	37,514	–33,856	0.1	1.0
Paraguay	61,868	32,026	29,842	1.6	0.9
Peru	12,194	104,312	–92,118	0.3	2.9
Suriname	1,491	2,352	–861	0.0	0.1
Trinidad and Tobago	1,174	53,939	–52,765	0.0	1.5
Uruguay	30,838	48,206	–17,368	0.8	1.3
Venezuela	41,112	208,471	–167,359	1.1	5.8
Other countries	4,256	223,632	–219,376	0.1	6.2
Total	**3,854,625**	**3,607,305**	247,320	100.0	100.0
World Total	99,618,384	106,741,888	–	–	–
Share	3.9%	3.4%	–	–	–

Source: FAO Forest Products Yearbook.

Appendix 10.2 Production and Trade in Major Wood-based Forest Products in LAC, 1993

Product	Production	Exports	Imports	Trade balance	Export share of production	Imports of apparent consumption
		1000 m³			*Percent*	
Coniferous logs	37,540					
Non-coniferous logs	36,005					
Logs, total	73,545					
Pulpwood (round and split)	38,857					
Industrial roundwood	133,173	7,705	244	7,461	6	0
Coniferous sawnwood	14,884	2,043	1,644	399	14	11
Non-coniferous sawnwood	16,129	1,106	517	589	7	3
Wood-based panels	5,327	1,629	865	764	31	19
Wood pulp (1000 ton)	8,673	3,705	1,197	2,508	43	19
Paper and paperboard (1000 ton)	11,593	1,577	3,670	-2,093	14	27

Source: FAO Forest Products Yearbook.

Appendix 10.3   LAC Export Trends and Share in World Exports of Wood-based Forest Products, 1980 and 1993

Export Trends

Product/Region	1980	1993
Non-coniferous sawnwood	1000 m³	
World	13,190	16,949
Developing countries	8,486	10,323
Latin America and Caribbean	1,137	1,105
Plywood	1000 m³	
World	6,623	17,072
Developing countries	3,852	13,037
Latin America and Caribbean	232	733
Wood-based forest products	US$ million	
World	56,005	99,618
Developing countries	9,306	19,386
Latin America and Caribbean	1,609	3,854

LAC Share of Exports

(In percent)

Region/Product	1980	1993
Share of world exports		
Non-coniferous sawnwood	8.6	6.5
Plywood	3.5	4.3
Wood-based forest products	2.9	3.9
Share of developing countries' exports		
Non-coniferous sawnwood	13.4	10.7
Plywood	6.0	5.6
Wood-based forest products	17.3	19.9

Source: FAO Forest Products Yearbook.

Appendix 10.4 International Trade in Processed Forest Products and LAC Market Share, 1989 and 1993

World Exports	1989	1993
	US$ billion	
Furniture	11,855	10,826
Builders' woodwork, etc.	5,995	9,417
Total	17,850	20,243
Exports from Latin America	US$ billion	
Furniture	64	361
Builders' woodwork, etc.	162	401
Total	226	762
Share of LAC	Percent	
Furniture	0.5	3.3
Builders' woodwork, etc.	2.7	4.3

Source: United Nations International Trade Statistics Yearbook.

Appendix 10.5 Uruguay Round Tariff Reductions in Wood, Pulp, Paper, and Furniture

Trade Flow	Trade (US$ billion)	Average pre-UR tariff	Tariff post-UR	Tariff reduction
		(Percent)		
Developing country imports to industrial economies	10.3	4.3	1.5	65
Industrial economy imports to developing countries	7.8	10.8	7.8	28
Imports among developing countries	2.9	7.9	5.9	25

Source: de Paiva Abreu 1995.

Appendix 10.6 Tarapoto Proposal for Criteria and Indicators of Sustainability in Amazon Forests

CRITERIA	MAIN INDICATORS
I. NATIONAL LEVEL	
1. Socioeconomic benefits	• Income, production and consumption levels • Investment and economic growth rates in forest sector • Cultural, social and spiritual needs and values
2. Policies and legal-institutional framework	• Adequacy of political and legal framework for sustainable development planning • Demonstrated capacity to implement international instruments
3. Sustainable forest production	• Production level in forest areas • Evidence of sustainability of forest production • Percentage of forest lands managed for recreation and tourism • Diversification and number of forest product
4. Conservation of forest cover and biological diversity	• Number and area of protected areas • *In situ* species conservation and other genetic conservation indicators • Forest damage evidence • Regeneration rate • Indicators of impacts on forestry from other sectors
5. Conservation and integrated management of water and soil resources	• Soil conservation measures and erosion rate • Number and area of environmental protection areas • Indicators of wetlands and flooded forests • Indices of effects on water quality and quantity
6. Technologies for sustainable development of the forests	• Adequate and appropriate technologies • Level of investment in research, education and technology transfer • Evidence of remuneration for traditional knowledge • Indicators of access to technology and information
7. Institutional capacity to promote sustainable development in Amazon	• Indicators of institutions and their coordination • Existence and quality of management plans and their level of execution • Levels of participation

II. MANAGEMENT UNIT LEVEL

8. Legal and institutional framework	• Quality and level of execution of forest management plan • Evidence of periodic evaluations • Adequacy of legal framework to ensure investment outcome
9. Sustainable forest production	• Sustainable timber and non-timber production levels • Indicators of soil quality affected by forest alteration • Indicators of diversification of production • Existence and use of environmentally friendly technologies
10. Conservation of forest ecosystems	• Number and area of protection areas • Evidence of sustainability in the use of species • Damaged forest area • Natural regeneration rates • Soil conservation indicators • Water protection evidence
11. Local socio-economic benefits	• Quality of life indicators • Profitability measures • Indicators of efficiency • Employment and other benefits from forest management and extraction • Availability of forest for local use • Effectiveness of consultation and participation mechanisms

III. GLOBAL LEVEL

12. Economic, social and environmental services performed by Amazon forests	• Contribution to global demand for sustainably produced timber and non-timber products • Carbon sequestration levels • Measurable benefits for global water cycle • Contribution to biological diversity • Indicators for radiation balance and regulation • Effects on cultural values and diversity, indigenous knowledge • Indicators of impact on economy, health, culture, science and recreation

Source: Adapted from TCA (1995).

CHAPTER 1

Future Directions for Policy and Financing

CHAPTER

11

Kari Keipi

The forests of Latin America and the Caribbean have the potential to fuel the region's economic development, while still preserving their natural integrity and tremendous biodiversity. A central premise of this volume is that a balance can be struck between the preservation of forests and the sustainable contribution they can make to economic development. Over the past four decades, strategies for forest management have evolved significantly. Industrial forestry, the first paradigm, was widely implemented during the sixties, and became a tool in the economic takeoff of developing countries. Next came "social forestry" and rural development through small farmers. Then, starting in the mid-eighties, there was wide acceptance of environmental forestry, with emphasis on global and national ecological benefits.

These approaches to forest development and conservation programs often failed to achieve their goals, for several reasons (Byron 1997). Many programs involved top-down, often formalized, approaches, paying only nominal attention to the real needs of the population and to public participation. One-factor logic and quick-fix schemes were popular, such as the use of fast-growing "miracle trees" in plantations. Finally, those who controlled forests tended to embrace abstract goals of maintaining the forest sector as an island, independent from other sectors. In some cases, nature was considered more important than people. These failures eventually led to unmanageable encroachment on the forest estate (Frühling and Persson 1996).

Improving National and International Forest Policy

There are few uncontested forest policy successes in Latin America. Utopian ideas and grand goals have often dominated the rhetoric to save tropical forests. Some recommendations, such as proposals to stop all tropical forest harvesting, were not sufficiently flexible for the reality of a particular country. In addition, the policy environment for forestry has been characterized by many "North-South" differences. Financial transfers for forestry from governments of the industrial countries are well below target levels of commitment of the UNCED process. In fact, globally they have been declining.

If clear national policies regarding forest development and conservation investments are to succeed, a political mandate is required to develop the necessary data and implement those policies. Strong government and civil society support should provide a basis for consensus-building among different actors concerned with forests and their use.

While forest lands produce ecological and economic benefits on a global scale, the lands are subject to laws of the countries where they exist. Therefore, domestic policies and practices are of prime importance in optimizing forest use. International support will be effective only if it does not conflict with local interests. Specifically, national governments need to be cautious when creating policies that may promote settlement in forested areas, or encourage indiscriminate forest conversion for agricultural development, or open up new areas to unregulated resource extraction.

Whether landowners can obtain title to their property also affects local land use patterns. While land tenure and titling processes have long been contentious issues in Latin America, they appear to influence investment decisions on the land. By expediting access to land titling or usufruct rights of indigenous peoples, communities, or individuals, a government increases the individual or group interest in long-term responsible management of their lands.

Land titling in settled areas is not enough to encourage forest management and tree planting, however. Human capital formation—training people to provide alternatives to clearing forest lands, or using forest lands for agricultural purposes—should be the centerpiece of a strategy for rural development and conservation of the region's tropic forests.

Experience has shown that protected areas have maintained forest cover better than other categories of forest in Latin America. State ownership of protected areas is only a partial solution, however, because many Latin American governments lack the means to enforce property rights and ensure forest preservation in new areas. Governments need to work also with the private sector to develop effective incentives, regulations and best practice guidelines. The certification of products in the forest sector, grown or harvested in an environmentally responsible way, represents a major new direction in the ongoing attempts to achieve sustainable production. We must design both domestic and international policy development to support the expansion of certification, which the United Nations and the ITTO have endorsed.

Public policy in much of Latin America has been moving toward deregulation in all areas, including forest management, utilization, and trade. The choice is between public management of forests, which in principle should protect nonmarket values, but lacks the institutional capacity to do so; and private ownership, which is effective for management but deficient in defending public interests. The recent democratization process has established dialogue among various sectors of civil society and encouraged the consensus-building that is essential for sustainable forestry. As a result, coalitions have been formed between rural inhabitants and the private sector. In response to a growing trend towards privatization, a system of market-based incentives and regulatory mechanisms should be strengthened to facilitate responsible management and conservation of forests.

Finally, monitoring the impact of these activities on forest health is critical to natural resource management at all levels. The results of ecological monitoring should be the basis for determining compliance with performance standards and any enforcement actions that may be required. Data from monitoring also help in determining the effectiveness of particular programs. Finally, monitoring allows the provision of historical records and baseline data for long-term ecological analysis.

Promoting a Range of Forest Uses

The fate of much of the world's forests depends on the financial viability of alternative forms of forest resource use. Unless sustainable forest management and conservation are financially competitive with other uses, preventing deforestation and forest conversion will be very difficult. While appropriate policy support from governments is needed, diverse economic activities must establish the financial viability to secure the forest estate.

Plantations and management of secondary or degraded natural forests are likely to play an increasingly vital role in the provision of domestic timber and fuel wood. Homogeneous, large-scale plantations are frequently subject to disease and pest infestation in humid, lowland tropical forests. They may become feasible, however, when combined with set-asides of protected natural ecosystems, when mixed species composition is applied, or in combination with crops, as in agroforestry projects. Furthermore, such plantations can provide watershed protection and soil conservation, and may lessen pressure on nearby natural forests.

Natural forest management represents another important type of forest use, although ecologically more complex than plantations. The concept is relatively new in Latin America, where harvesting in natural forests has rarely been characterized by sustainable management. Many natural resource professionals are skeptical that the incentives and enforcement mechanisms will result in responsible management. Some researchers doubt that our current scientific knowledge is sufficient to manage complex natural forests in the lowland tropics on a sustainable basis. By contrast, others see natural forest management as providing great opportunity for both economic development and conservation in selected, well-studied ecosystems.

Forest concessions on government lands, if properly established, could promote sustainable uses of forests. Concessions for timber, as well as for nonwood products and ecotourism, should be granted not only to private commercial timber companies, but also to local communities and NGOs for multiple uses. Concessions for both marketable products and environmental services should be subject to broad-based public bidding. Experience suggests that policies regulating concessions must be matched with the capacity of private entities to fulfill the terms of concession agreements, and the public sector to enforce them.

Nontimber forest products, such as resins, bark, nuts, and medicinal plants, represent burgeoning and relatively noninvasive economic uses of primary and secondary forests. As long as these practices do not compromise the biodiversity of a forest, they are also consistent with bioprospecting efforts and some level of protected area status. Nontimber forest products offer economic alternatives to more intensive timber extraction, but cannot provide broad economic opportunities to a large population.

Natural forest set-asides represent opportunities for commercial industrial operations to establish "mitigation lands" to offset harmful land use elsewhere. Certain types of natural forest management are controversial, and other types provide clear benefits. Nevertheless, it will require careful experimentation and application of new technology and understanding to learn how best to manage these lands for a variety of economic outputs.

The environmental services provided by forests are receiving more and more attention. These services can be local, national or global by nature. The local national services, such as soil and water conservation, and natural disaster mitigation are considered to be relatively tangible. Other, largely global services to benefit the whole mankind, such as biodiversity, habitat protection and carbon sequestration are perhaps less tangible but are receiving increasing attention. The possibilities of forested countries to receive payments for providing these services have been studied, for example, by the Council of Environment Ministers of Latin America and the Caribbean (Forum of Ministers 1998).

Increasing Investment and Improving Financing

The countries of the region have various policy arrangements for addressing national and local environmental problems. Some plans favor private investments in ecologically beneficial activities in critical geographical areas. Other plans are based on collecting targeted taxes and payments from local beneficiaries of environmental goods and services and transferring the revenue to agents qualified to make ecologically desirable and effective investment decisions. Still others include direct use of government funds to subsidize environmentally friendly investments.

The mobilization of private sector financial resources for developing countries, especially for tree plantations, has been remarkable. It is estimated that the worldwide private forest investment flows have increased from $193 billion in 1993 to $223 billion in 1996 and continue growing (MacNeill 1996). However, the public financing in forestry has been disappointing. The FAO estimates that in Latin America, this type of financing was $316 million for 1993—about 22 percent of UNCED's estimate of the need (FAO 1996). Market-based instruments are intended to ensure that the environmental costs of a proposed action are reflected in prices (Panayotou 1995). Ecotourism user fees, watershed conservation charges, and forest production fees are all payment mechanisms for environmental services and products the forest provides. If redirected to forestry, they may provide a sustainable means for the financing of investments in the sector.

What conditions are needed to attract investments in sustainable forestry? They include political and macroeconomic stability, access to land and secure property rights, an effective and appropriate regulatory framework, a clear forest policy (defined in consultation with stakeholders), and participatory decisionmaking processes in policy execution. Multilateral and bilateral lending and development institutions can promote investment by improving the fiscal environment and reducing the uncertainties associated with investment and financing by the private sector.

Looking Ahead

Since factors outside the forest sector often cause deforestation, the solutions may involve policies that affect land use and rural development in general. As projects treating forests in isolation disappear, most forest-related investments should be incorporated into broader natural resource management, rural development and environmental programs. Increasing agricultural yields per hectare, rural education and land tenure security may be more effective means to curb deforestation than direct forest investments.

In the past, many groups have emphasized environmental losses and dangers, rather than focusing on how to ensure sustainable production and protection of forests through market-based approaches. In the future, national and international efforts must continue to raise awareness and set agendas, but must also effectively help finance the programs. Private investment should be encouraged not only for production forests, but also for protected areas, ecotourism development, and conservation set-asides.

Further research is essential in lesser-known areas, such as the development of forest valuation methods and new techniques for management of natural forests. Important methodologies are being developed already by the FAO, CIFOR, CATIE, and others (Kengen 1997). More effective regulatory frameworks are needed, as well as new methods of energy conservation that reduce the burden on forests as producers of fuelwood. The challenges of globalization to the forest business environment should be explored, as well as methods for expanding nature-based tourism; and more study is needed concerning the ecological role of forests and water resources in and around urban areas. Finally, new sources of financing can be found, based on the environmental role of forests in biodiversity and mitigating climate changes.

Inadequate recognition of the many goods and services provided by the forests has been a major reason for the failure of sustainable forest management. Placing a value on these products and services would make forest conservation and development a more integral part of public decisionmaking. It is also essential for determining the expected benefits of forest conservation and finding sources of financing outside the region. However, the issues of ownership and rights to utilize the forest resource for which environmental payments are being received will continue to be a contentious issue. With proper evaluation methodologies for measuring the benefits and costs of conservation, use of market forces for their final pricing and adequate legal and institutional framework, large scale financing for the environmental services provided by the forest may become a reality.

All the above topics are worthy of further research effort. On behalf of future generations, the authors hope that this volume will provide valuable experiences and ideas for sustaining the productivity and diversity of forests in Latin America and the Caribbean.

Bibliography

Abt Associates, Inc. 1992. *A Policy Taxonomy and Analysis of Policies Affecting Natural Resources and the Environment.* Agricultural Policy Analysis Project and Development Strategies for Fragile Lands, U.S. Agency for International Development, Regional Office for Central American Programs.

Acosta-Solis, M. 1944. *La Tagua.* Quito: Editorial Ecuador.

Adger, W., K. Brown, R. Cervigni, and D. Moran. 1995. Total Economic Value of Forests in Mexico. *Ambio* 24(5).

Agosin, Manuel R., and Ricardo Ffrench-Davis. 1993. Trade Liberalization in Latin America. *CEPAL Review* 50: 42-62.

Alcorn, J.B. 1989. Process as Resource: The Traditional Agricultural Ideology of Bora and Huastec Resource Management and its Implications for Research. *Advances in Economic Botany* 7: 63-77.

Alcorn, J.B., and V. Toledo. 1995. In *Barriers and Bridges to the Renewal of Ecosystems and Institutions,* eds. Gunderson et al. New York: Columbia University Press.

Alderman, Claudia L. 1990. *A Study of the Role of Privately Owned Lands Used for Nature Tourism, Education, and Conservation.* Washington, D.C.: Conservation International.

Alfaro, M. 1994. Intersectoral and Interregional Policies and their Impact on Forest Policy. In *Proceedings: Regional Workshop on Needs and Priorities for Forestry and Agroforestry Research in Latin America.* eds. Alfaro et al. San José, Costa Rica: CIFOR, IFPRI, GTZ, CATIE, IICA.

————. 1996. Personal communication. Director for Planning. FUNDECOR. San José, Costa Rica.

Allegretti, M.H. 1990. Extractive Reserves: An Alternative for Reconciling Development and Environmental Conservation in Amazonia. In *Alternatives to Deforestation: Steps toward Sustainable Use of the Amazonian Rain Forest.* A.B. Anderson, ed. New York: Columbia University Press, 252-264.

Alston, Lee J., Gary D. Libecap and Robert R. Schneider. 1995. Property Rights and the Preconditions for Markets: The Case of the Amazon Frontier. *Journal of Institutional and Theoretical Economics* 15: 89-107.

————. 1996. The Determinants and Impact of Property Rights: Land Titles on the Brazilian Frontier. NBER Working Paper 5405. Cambridge, Mass.

Altieri, M.A., and J. Farrell. 1984. Traditional Farming Systems of South-Central Chile, with Special Emphasis on Agroforestry. *Agroforestry Systems* 2: 3-18.

Amacher, Gregory S., Monica Brehm, Luis Constantino, and William F. Hyde. 1994. The Design of Forest Policies in Small, Open Economies: Chile's Forestry Incentives Program. Unpublished draft report. Washington, D.C.: World Bank.

Amazón Commission on Development and Environment. 1994. *Amazonia Sin Mito, Amazon Without Myths*, UNDP, BID.

Amazon Cooperation Treaty/Inter-American Development Bank/United Nations Development Programme (ACT/IDB/UNDP). 1992. *Amazonia Without Myths*. Washington, D.C.: Inter-American Development Bank.

Anderson, A. 1989. Land Use Strategies for Successful Extractive Economies. National Wildlife Federation Symposium on Extractive Economies in Tropical Forests. Washington, D.C.

————. 1990. *Alternatives to Deforestation.* "Tolerant Forest Management." New York: Columbia University Press.

Anderson, A., and E. Ioris. 1992. The Logic of Extraction: Resource Management and Income Generation by Extractive Populations in the Amazon Estuary. In *Conservation of Neotropical Forests: Working from Traditional Resource Use.* eds. K. Redford and C. Padoch. New York: Columbia University Press.

Anderson, A., and D.A. Posey. 1989. Management of a Tropical Scrub Savanna by the Gorotire Kayapo of Brazil. *Advances in Economic Botany* 7: 159-173.

Anderson, K. 1995. The Entwining of Trade Policy with Environmental and Labor Standards. World Bank Conference on the Uruguay Round and the Developing Economies. January 26–27, 1995. Washington, D.C.

Anderson, Terry L., and Donald R. Leal. 1991. *Free Market Environmentalism.* Boulder, Colorado: Westview Press.

Andrew, D. 1995. The Trade Environment Nexus: Considerations for IDB Policy and Practices. Inter-American Development Bank, Department of Strategic Planning and Budget. Washington, D.C. Mimeograph.

Arias, L. G. 1996. Personal communication. GTZ/COSEFORMA Project. San José, Costa Rica.

Arnold, J. 1992. Production of Forest Products in Agricultural and Common Land Systems: Economic and Policy Issues. In *Managing the World's Forests.* ed. Narendra Sharma. Dubuque, IA: Kendall/Hunt.

Ascher, William, and Robert Healy. 1990. *Natural Resource Policymaking in Developing Countries.* Durham, NC: Duke University Press.

Asebey, E., and J. Kempenaar. 1995. Biodiversity Prospecting: Fulfilling the Mandate of the Biodiversity Convention. *Vanderbilt Journal of Transnational Law* 28(4): 703-754.

Atmella, A. 1995. Manual de instrumentos jurídicos privados para la protección de los recursos naturales. Conservación y Manejos de Bosques Tropicales. San José, Costa Rica.

Aylward, B. 1993. The Economic Value of Pharmaceutical Prospecting and its Role in Biodiversity Conservation. Discussion paper 93-05. London Environmental Economics Centre, London.

Aylward, B., K. Allen, J. Echeverría, and J. Tosi. 1996. Sustainable Ecotourism in Costa Rica: The Monteverde Cloud Forest Preserve. *Biodiversity Conservation* 5(3): 315-343.

Bach, C.F., and S. Gram. 1993. The Tropical Timber Triangle. A Production-Related Agreement on Tropical Timber. The Royal Veterinary and Agricultural University of Denmark. Copenhagen.

Baden, John, and Richard L. Stroup, eds. 1981. *Bureaucracy vs. Environment: The Environmental Costs of Bureaucratic Governance.* Ann Arbor, Michigan: University of Michigan Press.

Baharuddin, H.G., and M. Simula. 1994. Certification Schemes of All Types of Timber. ITTO. Cartagena de Indias, Colombia.

Baldares, M., and J. Laarman. 1990. Derechos de Entrada a las Áreas Protegidas de Costa Rica. *Ciencias Económicas* 10(1): 63-82.

Banco Central del Ecuador. 1995. *Información Estadística Mensual.* Quito.

Banerjee, Ajit, Gabriel Campbell, María C. Cruz, Shelton Davis and Augusta Molnar. 1995. Participation in Forest and Conservation Management. Environment Department Dissemination Note 23. The World Bank: Washington, D.C.

Barbier, Edward B. 1995. Assessment of the Effects of the Uruguay Round Agreement on the International Trade in Forest Products. FAO Rome. Mimeographed.

———. 1997. Rural Poverty and Natural Resource Degradation. In *Rural Poverty in Latin America.* eds. Ramón López and Alberto Valdés. Washington, D.C.: The World Bank.

Barbier, E.B., and Joanne C. Burgess. 1997. The Economics of Forest Land Use. *Land Economics* 73(2): 174-195.

Barfod, A. 1991. A Monographic Study of the Subfamily Phytelephantoidae. *Opera Botánica* 105: 1-73.

Barr, Brenton M., and Kathleen E. Braden. 1988. *The Disappearing Russian Forest: A Dilemma in Soviet Resource Management.* Totowa, New Jersey: Rowman and Littlefield.

Barrau, Enrique. 1992. La problemática del sector forestal costarricense: Análisis y posibles soluciones. San José, Costa Rica: U.S. Agency for International Development.

Barros, A., and C. Uhl. 1995. Logging along the Amazon River and Estuary: Patterns, Problems, and Potential. *Forest Ecology and Management* 77: 87-105.

Barzetti, Valerie, ed. 1993. *Parques y progreso: Áreas protegidas y desarrollo económico en América Latina y el Caribe.* Washington, D.C.: International Union for the Conservation of Nature and Inter-American Development Bank.

Batista, Paulo Nogueira, Jr. 1993. The Monetary Crisis, Dollarization, and the Exchange Rate. *CEPAL Review* 50: 93-108.

Bautista, Romeo M., and Alberto Valdes, eds. 1993. *The Bias Against Agriculture: Trade and Macroeconomic Policies in Developing Countries.* San Francisco: ICS Press.

Beattie, William D. 1995. The Forestry Sector's Success in Chile. Paper presented at workshop, Use of Financial Incentives for Industrial Forest Plantations. Inter-American Development Bank Working Paper ENV-4. Washington, D.C.

Beattie, William D., and Joldes M. Ferreira. 1978. *Análise Financeira e Socio-Econômica do Reflorestamento no Brasil.* Brasilia: IBDF-COPLAN Serie, Estudos Perspectivos para o Período 1979-85.

Beghin, J., D. Roland-Holst and D. van den Mensbrugghe. 1995. Trade Liberalization and the Environment in the Pacific Basin. Coordinated Approaches to Mexican Trade and Environment Policy. *Amer J Agr Econ.* 77 (August 1995): 778–785.

Belaunde, Elvira, and Carlos Rivas. 1993. Responding to Practice and Affecting Policy: The Experience of the MADELENA-3 Project in Central America. Rural Development Forestry Network Paper 16a. London: Overseas Development Institute.

Benavides, M., and M. Pariona. 1995. The Yanesha Forestry Cooperative and Community-Based Management in the Central Peruvian Forest. In *Proceedings of Symposium on Forestry in the Americas: Community-Based Management and Sustainability.* Madison: University of Wisconsin Land Tenure Center.

Berger, Ricardo. 1980. *The Brazilian Fiscal Incentive Act's Influence on Reforestation Activity in São Paulo State.* Ph.D. dissertation, Michigan State University, East Lansing, Michigan.

Berkes, F., C. Folke and M. Gadgil. 1993. Traditional Ecological Knowledge, Biodiversity Resilience and Sustainability, Beijer Discussion Paper Series No. 31.

Bermúdez, F. 1992. Evolución del Turismo en las Áreas Silvestres, Período 1982-1991. Ministerio de Recursos Naturales, Energía, y Minas, Servicio de Parques Nacionales, San José.

———. 1995. Unpublished national parks visitation data, Ministerio de Recursos Naturales, Energía, y Minas, Servicio de Parques Nacionales, San José.

Berry, John R. 1995. Competitividad y sostenibilidad en el sector forestal. *Planeación y Desarrollo* 26: 181-201.

Bianchi-Schweron, H., J. Valerio Garita and M. Simula. 1993. Industria Forestal Sostenible. Estudio de caso sobre Portico S.A. Costa Rica. Proyecto INEFAN-ITTO PD/155/91. Indufor. San José-Helsinki.

Binswanger, Hans. 1991. Brazilian Policies that Encourage Deforestation in the Amazon. *World Development* 19: 821-29.

Binswanger, Hans, Klaus Deininger, and Gershon Feder. 1995. Power, Distortions, Revolt and Reform in Agricultural Land Relations. In *Handbook of Development Economics III-B.* eds. J. Behrman and T.N. Srinivasan. Amsterdam: Elsevier.

Biswas, Asit K., and Qu Geping, eds. 1987. *Environmental Impact Assessment for Developing Countries.* London: Tycooly Publishing.

Blain, D. 1996. Fertility factors limiting the growth of pioneer trees on upland fallow soils of the Amazon basin, Iquitos, Peru. Ph.D thesis, Graduate Department of the Faculty of Forestry, University of Toronto.

Blake, David H., and Robert E. Driscoll. 1976. *The Social and Economic Impacts of Transnational Corporations: Case Studies of the U.S. Paper Industry in Brazil.* New York: Fund for Multinational Management Education.

Boo, E. 1990. *Ecotourism: The Potentials and Pitfalls.* Washington, D.C.: World Wildlife Fund.

Booth, W. 1989. Monitoring the Fate of the Forests from Space. *Science* 243: 1428–29.

Boserup, Ester. 1965. *Conditions for Agricultural Change.* Chicago, IL: Aldine.

Bourke, I.J. 1988. Trade in Forest Products: A Study of the Barriers Faced by the Developing Countries. FAO Forestry Paper 83. Rome.

———. 1992. Comments on the Current Situation Regarding Trade Barriers Facing Forest Products. FAO. Mimeograph.

Bowles, Ian A., Dana Clark, David Downes, and Marianne Guerin-McManus. 1996. Encouraging Private Sector Support for Biodiversity Conservation: The Use of Economic Incentives and Legal Tools. Conservation International Policy Papers I. Washington, D.C.

Bradford, Colin I., Jr. 1994. *Redefining the State in Latin America.* Organization for Economic Cooperation and Development and Inter-American Development Bank.

Brandt, S. 1992. Parque nacional de Monte Pascoal: población indígena y unidades de conservación. In *Espacios sin Habitantes? Parques Nacionales de América del Sur,* eds. S.A. Amend and T. Amend, 125-135. Caracas: Ed. Nueva Sociedad/IUCN.

Brasilense, R., and W. Bento Filho. 1998. Pacote Ecológico. *Brasil* (January 27:6).

Bray, D., M. Carreón, L. Merino, and V. Santos. 1993. On the Road to Sustainable Forestry. *Cultural Survival Quarterly* 17(1): 38-41.

Brenes, C. 1995. Community Participation in the Design of Forest Policies: Central American Experience. In Cortés (1995).

Brett, E.A. 1988. States, Markets, and Private Power. In *Privatisation in Less Developed Countries*. eds. P. Cook and C. Kirkpatrick. New York: St. Martin's Press.

Bromley, Daniel W. 1989. Property Relations and Economic Development: The Other Land Reform. *World Development* 17: 867-877.

Brooke, J. 1993. Galápagos Burden: Goats, Pigs, and Now People. *New York Times*, 30 September: A4.

Browder, J.O. 1990. Extractive Reserves Will Not Save the Tropics. *BioScience* 40: 626.

———. 1992a. Extractive Reserves and the Future of the Amazon's Rainforests: Some Cautionary Observations. In *The Rainforest Harvest: Sustainable Strategies for Saving Tropical Forests*. S. Counsell and T. Rice, eds. Friends of the Earth Trust.

———. 1992b. The Limits of Extractivism: Tropical Forest Strategies beyond Extractive Reserves. *Bioscience* 42(3): 174-181.

Browder, J., E. Matricardi, and W. Abdala. 1996. Is Sustainable Tropical Timber Production Financially Viable? A Comparative Analysis of Mahogany Silviculture among Small Farmers in the Brazilian Amazon. *Ecological Economics* 16: 147-159.

Brown, Christopher L., and John Valentine. 1994. The Process and Implications of Privatization for Forestry Institutions: Focus on New Zealand. *Unasylva* 45(178):11-19.

Brown, S., and A. Lugo. 1990. Tropical Secondary Forests. *Journal of Tropical Ecology* 6: 1-32.

Bulmer-Thomas, V. 1991. A Long-Run Model of Development for Central America. Research Paper 27. University of London, Institute of Latin American Studies.

———. 1992. Life after Debt: The New Economic Trajectory in Latin America. QMW Economics Discussion Paper 255, University of London.

Burton, T. 1994. Drug Company Looks to 'Witch Doctors' to Conjure Profits. *Wall Street Journal*, 7 July: A1 and A8.

Butterfield, Rebecca P. and Richard F. Fisher. 1994. Untapped Potential: Native Species for Reforestation. *Journal of Forestry* 92(6): 37-40.

Byron, N. 1997. International Development Assistance in Forestry and Land Management: The Process and the Players. CIFOR. Bangor, Indonesia. Mimeo.

Cabrera-Madrid, M., R. Heinzman, S. López, C. Reining, and A. Solórzano. 1990. Nontimber forest products in the Maya Biosphere Reserve: Results of ecological and socioeconomic surveys and recommendations for management and investigations. Unpublished Report to Conservation International.

Calero-Hidalgo, R. 1992. The Tagua Initiative in Ecuador: A Community Approach to Tropical Rain Forest Conservation and Development. In *Sustainable Harvest and Marketing of Rain Forest Products*. eds. M. Plotkin and L. Famolare. Washington, D.C.: Island Press.

Carroll, Thomas F. 1992. *Intermediary NGOs: The Supporting Link in Grassroots Development*. West Hartford, Connecticut: Kumarian Press.

Carter, Michael R., and Pedro Olinto. 1996. Getting Institutions Right for Whom? The Wealth-Differentiated Impact of Property Rights Reform on Investment and Income in Rural Paraguay. University of Wisconsin, Madison. Unpublished mimeo.

Castilleja, Guillermo. 1993. Changing Trends in Forest Policy in Latin America: Chile, Nicaragua, and Mexico. *Unasylva* 44(175): 29-35.

Castner, James L. 1990. *Rainforests: A Guide to Research and Tourist Facilities at Selected Tropical Forest Sites in Central and South America*. Gainesville, Florida: Feline Press.

CATIE. 1994. *Plan de manejo forestal para la unidad de manejo San Miguel, Petén, Guatemala*. OLAFO Project. San José, Costa Rica.

CCAD/CCAB-AP. 1996. *Políticas forestales en Centroamérica: análisis de las restricciones para el desarrollo del sector forestal*. San José, Costa Rica: CIFOR, IICA, GTZ, FAO, IUCN, WRI, CCAD, CCAB-AP.

CCT/WRI. 1991. *Accounts Overdue: Natural Resources Depreciation in Costa Rica*. Washington, D.C: WRI, and San José, Costa Rica: CCT.

Censo nacional de Panamá. 1990. Dirección de Estadísticas y Censo, República de Panamá.

Centeno, J.C. 1990. *El desarrollo forestal de Venezuela*. Mérida, Venezuela: IFLA.

———. 1995. Certificación de productos forestales: la perspectiva de América Latina. In Cortés (1995).

Centro de Estudios de la Realidad Colombiana (CEREC). 1993. Reconocimiento y demarcación de territorios indígenas en la Amazonia. La experiencia de los países de la región. Serie Amerindia 4. Bogotá.

Chambers, R. 1987. Poverty, Environment and the World Bank: The Opportunity for a New Professionalism. IDS, Brighton, England.

Chandrasekharan, C. 1995. Desarrollo de productos no madereros de América Latina y el Caribe. In *Memoria Consulta de Expertos sobre Productos Forestales No Madereros para América Latina y el Caribe.* Santiago: FAO.

Chase, L. 1995. Capturing the Benefits of Ecotourism: The Economics of National Park Entrance Fees in Costa Rica. M.S. thesis, Department of Agricultural, Resource, and Managerial Economics, Cornell University, Ithaca.

Chomitz, K.M., and David A. Gray. 1996. Roads, Lands Use and Deforestation: A Spatial Model Applied to Belize. *World Bank Economic Review* 10(3): 487-512.

CIAT (Centro Institutional de Agricultura Tropical). 1994. Press release for activities. September 1994.

Chopra, Kanchan, and S.C. Gulati. 1997. Environmental Degradation and Population Movements: The Role of Property Rights. *Environmental and Resource Economics* 9: 383-408.

CIDDEBENI (Center for Research and Documentation for the Development of Beni). 1995. Reflections on a proposal for forest management and harvest in the multi-ethnic indigenous territory of Beni, Bolivia. in *Case Studies of Community-Based Forestry Enterprises in the Americas.* Presented at the symposium, Forestry in the Americas: Community-Based Management and Sustainability. University of Wisconsin-Madison Land Tenure Center/Institute for Environmental Studies.

Cifuentes, Maria Victoria. 1996. Personal communication. (*Coordinadora General* of the Ministry of Environment of Colombia)

Claessens, Stijn, and Sudarshan Gooptu. 1994. Can Developing Countries Keep Foreign Capital Flowing In? *Development and Finance* 31(3): 62-65.

Clawson, Marion. 1975. *Forests for Whom and for What?* Washington, D.C.: Resources for the Future.

Clay, Jason. 1988. *Indigenous Peoples and Tropical Forests: Models of Land Use and Management from Latin America.* Cambridge, Massachusetts: Cultural Survival.

Coase, R.H. 1960. The Problem of Social Cost. *Journal of Law and Economics* 3: 1-31.

COICA–OXFAM America. 1996. Amazonia: Economía indígena y mercado. Los desafíos del desarrollo autónomo. COICA, Quito.

Coles-Ritchie, M. Analysis of Nontimber Extractive Products from Tropical Forests: The Tagua Example in Ecuador. M.S. thesis, Graduate School of International Studies, Bard College, Annandale-on-Hudson.

Conservation International. 1989. *The Debt-for-Nature Exchange: A Tool for International Conservation.* Washington, D.C.: Conservation International.

Constantino, L.F. 1990. On the Efficiency of Indonesia's Sawmilling and Plymilling Industries. Ministry of Forestry, Government of Indonesia and FAO. Jakarta.

————. 1995. Financial Incentives for Industrial Plantations in Argentina: The World Bank Story. Paper presented at workshop, Use of Financial Incentives for Industrial Forest Plantations. Working Paper ENV-4, IDB. Washington, D.C.

Contreras-Hermosilla, A. 1995. Government Policies and Forest Resource Management in Latin America. In Cortés et al. (1995).

Cook, Paul, and Colin Kirkpatrick. 1988. *Privatisation in Less Developed Countries*. New York: St. Martin's Press.

Coomes, O. 1995. A Century of Rain Forest Use in Western Amazonia: Lessons for Extraction-Based Conservation of Tropical Forest Resources. *Forest and Conservation History* 39(3): 108-120.

Copeland, B.R., and M.S. Taylor. 1995. Trade and the Environment: A Partial Synthesis. *Amer J Agr Econ.* 77 (August): 765–771.

Cortés-Salas, H., R. de Camino, and A. Contreras., eds. 1995. *Readings of the Workshop on Government Policy Reform for Forestry Conservation and Development in Latin America*. CIFOR, USAID, EPAT/MURCIA, IDB, The World Bank. Costa Rica: IICA.

Costanza, R. and H. Daly. 1990. Natural Capital and Sustainable Development. *Conservation Biology* 6: 37-46.

Coxhead, Ian, and Sisira Jayasuriya. 1994. Technical Change in Agriculture and Land Degradation in Developing Countries: A General Equilibrium Analysis. *Land Economics* 70(1): 20-37.

Cropper, M., and C. Griffiths. 1994. The Interaction of Population Growth and Environmental Quality. *American Economic Review* 84: 250–254.

Crossley, R. 1995. A Review of Global Forest Management Certification Initiatives: Political and Institutional Aspects. A Background Paper Prepared for the UBC-UPM Conference on Certification. Malaysia. May 1996.

Daly, Herman E. 1990. Carrying Capacity as a Tool of Development Policy: The Ecuadorean Amazon and the Paraguayan Chaco. *Ecological Economics* 2(3): 187-195.

Davis, S.H. and A. Wali. 1994. Indigenous Land Tenure and Tropical Forest Management in Latin America. *Ambio* 23(8): 485-490.

Deacon, Robert T. 1994. Deforestation and the Rule of Law in a Cross-Section of Countries. *Land Economics* 70(4): 414-430.

de Camino, Ronnie. 1993. El papel del bosque húmedo tropical de América Central: Desafíos y posibles soluciones. *Revista Forestal Centroamericana* 6 (2). Turrialba, Costa Rica.

————. 1996. Experience monitoring forest management in Nicaragua's Northern Autonomous Region (RAAN). Mission for ASDI. Nicaragua.

de Camino, Ronnie, and Alicia Barcena. 1995. Medidas para incrementar la efectividad de la cooperación internacional para el desarrollo sostenible de América Latina: El caso forestal. In Cortés (1995).

————. 1994. Improving the Effectiveness of International Assistance for Sustainable Development in Latin America: The Case of Forestry. In Cortés (1995).

de Camino, Ronnie, and Sabine Müller. 1993. *Sostenibilidad de la agricultura y los recursos naturales: Bases para establecer indicadores.* Serie Documentos de Programas 38, Proyecto IICA/GTZ. Coronado, Costa Rica: Instituto Interamericano de Cooperación para la Agricultura.

DeGraaf, N.R. 1990. Managing natural regeneration for sustained timber production in Suriname: The CELOS silvicultural and harvesting system. *Man and Biosphere Series*, Vol 6.

DeGraaf, N.R., and R. Van Rompaey. 1986. The CELOS experiments on silviculture with natural regeneration in Suriname. Workshop on the Management of Low Fertility Acid Soil, Paramaribo.

de Groot, R. 1983. Tourism and Conservation in the Galapagos Islands. *Biological Conservation* 26(4): 291-300.

Deininger, K., and B. Minten. 1996. Poverty, Policies, and Deforestation: The Case of Mexico. Washington, D.C.: The World Bank.

de Janvry, Alain, and Raul García. 1992. Rural Poverty and Environmental Degradation in Latin America. IFAD Staff Working Paper 1. IFAD, Rome.

de Janvry, Alain, Nigel Key and Elizabeth Sadoulet. 1997. Agricultural and Rural Development Policy in Latin America: New Directions and New Challenges. Working Paper No. 815. Department of Agricultural and Resource Economics, University of California, Berkeley.

de Miras, C. 1994. Las Islas Galápagos: Un Reto Económico y Tres Contradicciones Básicas. Institut Français de Recherche Scientifique pour le Développement en Coopération, Quito.

Demsetz, Harold. 1967. Toward a Theory of Property Rights. *American Economic Review* 57: 347-359.

de Paiva Abreu, M. 1995. Trade in Manufactures: the Outcome of the Uruguay Round and Developing Country Interests. World Bank Conference on the Uruguay Round and the Developing Economies. Washington, D.C. (January 1995).

Deruyttere, A. 1997. Indigenous Peoples and Sustainable Development: The Role of the Inter-American Development Bank. No. IND97-101. Washington, D.C.

De Vylder, Stefan. 1992. *Nicaragua 1982-92 Macroeconomic Context and Relevance of the Forestry Sector Programme.* Swedish-Nicaraguan Development Cooperation in Forestry Sector, Stockholm School of Economics, Stockholm, Sweden.

DHV Consultants BV. 1992. Biodiversity Protection and Investment Needs for the Minimum Conservation System in Costa Rica. Report to World Bank, Amersfoort.

Dicum, G., and R. Tarifa. 1994. *Plan de Manejo de Xate en la Area de Carmelita, San Andres, Petén.* Report to Conservation International.

Dixon, John A., and P.B. Sherman. 1990. *Economics of Protected Areas: A New Look at Benefits and Costs.* Washington, D.C.: Island Press.

Donovan, R.Z. 1994. Strategic Options for Initiating Voluntary and International Forest Management Certification in Bolivia. Proyecto BOLFOR. Santa Cruz.

Dorner, Peter. 1992. *Latin American Land Reforms in Theory and Practice.* Madison, Wisconsin: University of Wisconsin Press.

Douglas, J. 1983. *A Re-Appraisal of Forestry Development in Developing Countries.* The Hague: Martinus Nijhoff/W. Junk.

Dourojeanni, Marc J. 1986. La calidad de la enseñanza forestal actual. *Unasylva* 154(38): 22-31.

———. 1987a. Manejo de bosques naturales en el trópico americano: Situación y perspectivas. *Revista Forestal del Perú* 14(1): 91-108.

———. 1987b. Aprovechamiento del barbecho forestal en áreas de agricultura migratoria en la Amazonia peruana. *Revista Forestal del Perú* 14(2): 15-61.

———. 1990. *Amazonia: ¿Qué Hacer?* Iquitos, Peru: Centro para Estudios Teológicos de la Amazonia.

———. 1993. *Compatibilizando desarrollo y conservación: El caso del manejo de los bosques naturales.* Working Paper No. ENV-102. Inter-American Development Bank, Environment Protection Division.

———. 1994. Some thoughts on the applicability of the Convention on Biodiversity in Latin America. Inter-American Development Bank Working Paper ENV-104. February. Washington, D.C.

———. 1995. Evaluación ambiental de proyectos de carretera en la Amazonia. Seminario Regional de Evaluación Ambiental de Proyectos de Desarrollo en la Amazonia. Tratado de Cooperación Amazónica. Tarapoto, Peru, July 9-13.

————. 1996. Condominio natural: Una nueva estrategia para establecer reservas naturales privadas. *Medio Ambiente* 11(68): 44-51. Lima, Peru.

————. 1996, 1997. Personal communications. Regional Environmental Advisor, Inter-American Development Bank. Brasilia, Brazil.

Dove, Michael R. 1993. A Revisionist View of Tropical Deforestation and Development. *Environmental Conservation* 20(1): 17-24, 56.

Dower, R.C., and M.B. Zimmerman. 1992. The right climate for carbon taxes: Creating economic incentives to protect the atmosphere. Washington, D.C.: World Resources Institute.

Downing, Theodore E., S.B. Hecht, H.A. Pearson, and C. Garcia-Downing. 1992. *Development or Destruction: The Conversion of Tropical Forest to Pasture in Latin America.* Boulder, Colorado: Westview Press.

Drake, S. 1991. Local Participation in Ecotourism Projects. In *Nature Tourism: Managing for the Environment.* ed. T. Whelan. Washington, D.C.: Island Press.

Dubois, O., N. Robins and S. Bass. 1995. Forest Certification and the European Union: A Discussion Paper. London: IIED.

During, A. 1993. Saving the Forests: What Will it Take? *World Watch Paper No. 117.* Washington, D.C.

Echeverría, J., M. Hanrahan, and R. Solórzano. 1995. Valuation of Non-Priced Amenities Provided by the Biological Resources within the Monteverde Cloud Forest Preserve, Costa Rica. *Ecological Economics* 13: 43-52.

Economic Commission for Europe (ECE). 1995. Certification of Forest Products: Report of Team of Specialists. TIM/R. 260/Add.1. Geneva, Switzerland.

Edwards, S. 1991. The Demand for Galápagos Vacations: Estimation and Application to Conservation. *Coastal Management* 19(2): 155-169.

Elgegren, J. 1993. Desarrollo sustentable y manejo de bosques naturales en la Amazonia Peruana: Un estudio económico-ambiental del sistema de manejo forestal en Fajas en el Valle del Palcazú. M.S. thesis, Facultad Latinoamericana de Ciencias Sociales, Quito.

Espinosa, Jose Oswaldo. 1996. Personal communication. (Division Chief for Environmental Planning, DNP, Colombia)

European Commission. 1997. Indigenous Peoples Participation in Sustainable Development. No. 2.—Indigenous Peoples Participation in Global Environmental Negotiations. Brussels.

Evans, B. 1995. Technical and Scientific Element of Forest Management Certification Programs. A Background Paper from the UBC-UPM Conference on Certification May 12–16, 1996. Draft.

Evans, Julian. 1992. *Plantation Forestry in the Tropics: Tree Planting for Industrial, Social, Environmental, and Agroforestry Purposes.* Oxford, England: Clarendon Press.

Eyzaguirre, N. 1993. Financial Crisis, Reform and Stabilization: The Chilean Experience. In *Financial Sector Reforms in Asian and Latin American Countries,* ed. S. Faruqi and G. Caprio. PUBL.

Faber-Langendoen, D. 1992. Ecological Constraints on Rain Forest Management at Bajo-Calima, western Colombia. *Forest Ecology and Management* 53: 213-244.

Farnsworth, N., and D. Soejarto. 1985. Potential Consequences of Plant Extinction in the United States on the Current and Future Availability of Prescription Drugs. *Economic Botany* 39(3): 231-240.

Faustman, M. 1849. On the determination of the value which forest land and immature stands possess in forestry [English translation from German]. In: *Martin Faustman and the evolution of the discounted cash flow,* ed. M. Gane. Commonwealth Forestry Institute Paper no. 42.

Fearnside, Philip M. 1988. Jari at Age 19: Lessons for Brazil's Silvicultural Plans at Carajas. *Interciencia* 13(1): 12-24.

———. 1989. Extractive Reserves in Brazilian Amazonia. *BioScience* 39(6): 387-393.

Fearnside, P.M. 1989. Extractive Reserves in Brazilian Amazonia. *BioScience* 39: 387-393.

Feder, Gershon, and D. Feeny. 1991. Land Tenure and Property Rights: Theory and Implications for Development Policy. *World Bank Economic Review* 5(1): 135-153.

Feder, Gershon, T. Onchan and T. Raparla. 1988. *Land Policies and Farm Productivity in Thailand.* Baltimore and London: John Hopkins University Press.

Fernández, R.A. 1995. Capital Markets Reforms in Latin America and Their Impact on Income Distribution. University of London, Institute of Latin American Studies and London School of Economics. Mimeo, 40 pp.

Ferreira, V., and J. Paschoalino. 1987. Pesquisa sobre Palmito no Instituto de Tecnología de Alimentos. In *Proceedings from the First National Conference of Researches on Palm Hearts.* Curitiba: Empresa Brasileira de Pesquisa Agropecuária.

Figueroa, E. 1995. Sustainable Development in the APEC Context: The Role of Regional Organizations. Paper presented at the Pacific Trade and Development Conference, September, Ottawa, Canada.

Figueroa, L. 1995. Análisis del Impacto Económico del Turismo sobre la Comunidad y sobre la Reserva Biológica Bosque Nuboso Monteverde. Report to Tropical Science Center, Servicios Corporativos Emanuel S.A., San José.

Flynn, S. 1995. Local Heritage in the Changing Tropics: Innovative Strategies for Natural Resource Management and Control. ISTF Conference at Yale University School of Forestry and Environmental Studies, New Haven, Connecticut.

Food and Agriculture Organization (FAO). 1971, 1977. *Handbook on Forest Utilization Contracts on Public Land.* Rome: FAO, United Nations Development Programme.

————. 1978. *Forestry for Local Community Development.* FAO Forestry Paper No. 7, Rome.

————. 1986. *Appropriate Forest Industries.* FAO Forestry Paper No. 68, Rome.

————. 1992a. Evaluation of Forest Resources in 1990: Tropical Countries. FAO Forest Document 112, Rome.

————. 1992b. *Peasant Participation in Community Reforestation in Peru.* FAO Community Forestry Case Study 7, Rome.

————. 1993. Agriculture—Towards 2010 (Document of the 27th FAO Conference). Forest Resources Assessment 1990: Tropical Countries. Management and Conservation of Closed Forest in Tropical America, #101. Rome: FAO.

————. 1994. *Forest Products Yearbook.* Rome: FAO.

————. 1995a. *Situación forestal de la región. Memoria consulta de expertos sobre productos forestales no madereros para América Latina y el Caribe.* Santiago, Chile: Comisión Forestal para América Latina y el Caribe.

————. 1995b. Forest Resource Assessment 1990. Forestry Paper 124. Rome, Italy.

Food and Agriculture Organization/UNDP/MARA. 1992. *Principais Indicadores Sócio-Econômicos dos Assentamentos de Reforma Agrânia,* Project BRA-87-022.

Forest Advisors Group (FAG). 1995. Common Principles for National Forestry Planning and Programme Implementation. Tropical Forestry Action Plan. Forest Advisors Group.

Förster, R. 1994. *Hacia la sostentabilidad en el uso de los recursos forestales en Quintana Roo.* Mexico-Germany Agreement. Chetumal, Mexico: IICA/GTZ Project.

Fortmann, Louise, and James Riddell. 1985. *Trees and Tenure.* Madison, Wisconsin: Land Tenure Center, University of Wisconsin.

Foster, Nancy, and David Stanfield. 1993. Tenure Regimes and Forest Management: Cases Studies in Latin America. Land Tenure Center Paper 147. University of Wisconsin, Madison.

Frühling, P., and R. Persson. 1996. Back to National Realities: Rethinking International Assistance to Forestry Development. SIDA. Stockholm.

Fundação Instituto Brasileiro de Geografia e Estatística (FIBGE). 1982. *Censo Demográfico de 1980: Acre, Amazonas, Pará, Roraima, Amapá, Rondônia.* Rio de Janeiro.

Galletti, H.A., and A. Arguelles. 1987. Planificación estratégica para el desarrollo rural: El caso del Plan Piloto Forestal de Quintana Roo. In *Proceedings of the International Conference and Workshop: Land and Resource Evaluation for National Planning in the Tropics.* Washington, D.C.: USDA Forest Service Publication GTR WO-39.

Garlipp, R.C.D. 1995. O boom da certificação: É preciso garantir a credibilidade. *Silvicultura* 16(61): 15-22. Brazil, March/April.

Gawora, D., and C. Moser. 1993. Amazonien. Die Zerstörung, die Hoffnung, unsere Verantwortung. Aachen.

Gillis, M. 1990. *Forest Incentive Policies.* Washington, D.C.: The World Bank.

Giroldo, Victor. 1987. El manejo privado de los bosques. In *Management of the Forests of Tropical America,* eds. J.C. Figueroa Colón, F.H. Wadsworth, and S. Branham. Rio Piedras, Puerto Rico: U.S. Department of Agriculture Forest Service, Institute of Tropical Forestry.

Godoy, R., et al. 1997. Household Determinants of Deforestation by Amerindians in Honduras. *World Development* 25(6): 977-987.

Goldemberg, J. 1990. A Simple Plan to Stop Global Warming. *Princeton University Technology Review.* November/December: 24-31.

Goldin, Ian, and Dominique van der Mensbrugghe. 1992. The Forgotten Story: Agriculture and Latin American Trade and Growth. In *Strategic Options for Latin America in the 1990s,* ed. Colin I. Bradford, Jr. Paris: Organization for Economic Cooperation and Development.

Goodland, Robert J. 1975. *Amazon Jungle: Green Hell to Red Desert?* Amsterdam: Elsevier Scientific Publishing Company.

Goodland, R.J.A., E. Asbey, J. Post and M. Dyson. 1990a. Sustainability of hardwood extraction from tropical moist forests. Centre for Sciences and Environment, New Delhi.

———. 1990b. Tropical Moist Forest Management: The Urgency of Transition to Sustainability. *Environmental Conservation* 17: 303-318.

Gottfried, Robert R., Charles D. Brockett, and William C. Davis. 1994. Models of Sustainable Development and Forest Resource Management in Costa Rica. *Ecological Economics* 9: 107-120.

Gradwohl, J., and R. Greenberg. 1988. *Saving the Tropical Forests.* London: Earthscan Publications.

Grainger, Alan. 1993. *Controlling Tropical Deforestation.* London: Earthscan Publications.

Gray, A.G., and W.I. Jenkins. 1982. Policy Analysis in British Central Government: The Experience of PAR. *Public Administration* 60(4): 429-450.

Gray, John. 1983. *Forest Revenue Systems in Developing Countries.* FAO Forestry Paper No. 43. Rome, Italy.

Gregersen, Hans M. 1984. Incentives for Forestation: A Comparative Assessment. In *Strategies and Designs for Afforestation, Reforestation and Tree Planting,* ed. K.F. Wiersum. The Netherlands: Wageningen.

Gregersen, H.M., B. Belcher, and J. Spears. 1994. Policies to Contain Unproductive Deforestation. Draft Policy Brief. EPAT/MUCIA/USAID. Minnesota.

Gregersen, H.M., K.N. Brooks, J. Dixon, and L. Hamilton. 1987. *Guidelines for the Economic Appraisal of Watershed Management Projects.* FAO Conservation Guide 16. Rome Italy.

Gregersen, H.M., and Arnoldo H. Contreras. 1975. *U.S. Investment in the Forest-Based Sector in Latin America.* Baltimore, Maryland: Johns Hopkins University Press.

Grimes, A., et al. 1994. Valuing the Rain Forest: The Economic Value of Nontimber Forest Products in Ecuador. *Ambio* 23: 405-410.

Grindle, Merilee S. 1986. *State and Countryside: Development Policy and Agrarian Politics in Latin America.* Baltimore: The Johns Hopkins University Press.

Guess, George M. 1991. Poverty and Profit in Central American Forest Policies. *Public Administration and Development* 11: 573-589.

Gullison, R.E. 1995. Conservation of tropical forests through the sustainable production of forest products: The case of mahogany (*Swietenia macrophylla* King) in the Chimanes Forest, Beni, Bolivia. Doctoral Dissertation, Princeton University, Princeton, N.J.

Gullison, R.E., and J.J. Hardner. 1994. The effects of road design and harvest intensity on forest damage caused by selective logging: Empirical results and a simulation model from the *Bosque Chimanes*, Bolivia. *Forest Ecology and Management* 59: 1-14.

Hall, P., and K. Bawa. 1993. Methods to assess the impact of extraction of non-timber tropical forest products on plant populations. *Economic Botany* 47: 234-247.

Halle, M., and A. Steiner. 1994. Ajuste estructural y medio ambiente. IUCN. Gland, Switzerland.

Haltia, O. 1995. Forest Investment Financing Mechanisms in Latin America: Guidelines and Recommendations. Inter-American Development Bank Environment Division. Washington, D.C. Mimeograph.

Hardner, J.J. 1995a. Report to Conservation International on the Economic Potential of the Tagua Initiative Program.

———. 1995b. Indigenous Land Rights: Local Peoples and Natural Resource Management. *Journal of Environment and Development* 4: 221-225.

Hardner, J.J., and R.E. Rice. 1994. Financial constraints to "sustainable" selective harvesting of forests in the eastern Amazon: Bioeconomic modeling of a forest stand in the state of Pará, Brazil. Development of Strategies for Fragile Lands (DESFIL) working paper. USAID, World Bank. Washington, D.C.

Hartley, Keith and David Parker. 1991. Privatization: A Conceptual Framework. In *Privatization and Economic Efficiency*, eds. A.F. Ott and K. Hartley. Hants, England: Edward Elgar Publishing.

Hartshorn, Gary. 1978. Tree Falls and Tropical Forest Dynamics. In *Tropical Trees as Living Systems*, P. Tomlinson and M. Zimmermann, eds. Cambridge University Press.

———. 1990. Natural Forest Management by the Yanesha Forestry Cooperative in Peruvian Amazonia. In A. Anderson (1990).

Hartshorn, G., R. Simeone, and J. Tosi. 1986. Manejo para el rendimiento sostenido de bosques naturales: Un sinopsis del proyecto de desarrollo del Palcazú en la selva central de la Amazonía Peruana. Tropical Science Center, San José.

Harvard Business School. 1992. INBio/Merck Agreement: Pioneers in Sustainable Development. Case study NI-593-015. Cambridge, MA.: Harvard University.

Heath, John, and Hans Binswanger. 1996. Natural Resource Degradation Effects of Poverty and Population Growth are Largely Policy-Induced: The Case of Colombia. *Environment and Development Economics* 1: 65-83.

Hecht, Susanna and Alexander Cockburn. 1990. *The Fate of the Forest: Developers, Destroyers, and Defenders of the Amazon.* New York: Harper and Row.

Hecht, Susanna B. 1992. Logics of Livestock and Deforestation: The Case of Amazonia. In *Development or Destruction: The Conversion of Tropical Forest to Pasture in Latin America*, eds. Theodore E. Downing, et al. Boulder, Colorado: Westview Press.

Hendrisson, J. 1989. Damage-Controlled Logging in Managed Tropical Rain Forest in Suriname. Wageningen Agricultural University, The Netherlands.

Hirschman, A. 1958. *The Strategy of Economic Development.* New Haven: Yale University Press.

Holling, C.S. 1986. Resilience of Ecosystems; Local Surprise and Global Change. In *Sustainable Development of the Biosphere*, eds. W.C. Clark and R.E. Munn. Cambridge University Press.

Holling, C.S., et al. 1994. Biodiversity in the Functioning of Ecosystems: An Ecological Primer and Synthesis. In *Biodiversity Loss: Ecological and Economic Issues*, eds. C. Perrings, K.G. Maler, C. Folke, C.S. Holling and B. Jansson. Cambridge University Press.

Hopkins, Raul. 1991. Heterodoxy and Agricultural Development: The Recent Peruvian Experience. In *Modernization and Stagnation: Latin American Agriculture into the 1990s,* eds. M.J. Twomey and A. Helwege. New York: Greenwood Press.

Howard, A., and J. Magretta. 1995. Surviving Success: An Interview with The Nature Conservancy's John Sawhill. *Harvard Business Review* 73(5):109-118.

Howard, A., R. Rice, R.E. Gullison. 1996. Simulated economic returns and environmental impacts from four alternative silvicultural prescriptions applied in the Neotropics: A case study of the Chimanes Forest, Bolivia. *Forest Ecology and Management* (December).

Huber, R. 1996. Case Studies Showing Costs and Benefits of Ecotourism and Cultural Heritage Protection. Sixth Caribbean Conference on Ecotourism, Point-à-Pitre, Guadeloupe.

Hueth, D.L. 1995. The Use of Subsidies to Achieve Efficient Resource Allocation in Upland Watersheds. Inter-American Development Bank Working Paper ENV-1. Washington, D.C.

Hyde, William F., and David H. Newman. 1991. *Forest Economics and Policy Analysis.* World Bank Discussion Paper 134. Washington, D.C.

Inter-American Development Bank (IDB). 1992. Consultation on the Forest Policy of the Inter-American Development Bank. IDB Project Analysis Department. Mimeo.

———. 1995a. Strategy and Policy Framework for Fulfilling Mandates of the Eighth General Increase in Resources: Medium-Term Program. Washington, D.C.: Strategic Planning and Operational Policy Department.

———. 1995b. Terms of reference. Consultancy for a document on equitable and sustainable use and management of Latin American forests (*Sistemas de propiedad y administración forestal entre los pueblos indígenas de América Latina y el Caribe*). Unpublished. Washington, D.C.

———. 1995c. Workshop on the Use of Financial Incentives for Industrial Forest Plantations. Working Paper ENV-4 (*Taller sobre el uso de incentivos financieros para plantaciones forestales industriales. Memorias.*) Environmental Division, Washington, D.C.

———. 1996a. Pocket Profiles. Washington, D.C.

———. 1996b. Socioenvironmental and Forest Development Program for Nicaragua. ENV/SDS. Mimeo.

Inter-American Institute for Agricultural Cooperation (IICA). 1994. *Lineamientos para diagnosticar el uso actual y manejo de los recursos naturales renovables en estudios sectoriales agropecuarios.* IICA/GTZ Project. San José, Costa Rica.

Instituto Costarricense de Turismo (ICT). 1994. *Encuesta Aérea de Extranjeros: Época Alta Turística, 1994.* San José.

————. 1995. *Anuario estadístico de turismo, 1994.* San José.

Instituto Nacional de Estadística y Censos (INEC). 1992. *Análisis de los resultados definitivos del V Censo de Población y IV de Vivienda, Provincia de Galápagos.* Quito.

ITC. 1993. Rubberwood: A Study of the World Development Potential. UNCTAD/GATT. Geneva.

International Tropical Timber Organization (ITTO). 1990. Guidelines for the Sustainable Management of Natural Tropical Forests. ITTO Technical Series No.5. Yokohama, Japan.

————. 1991. Incentives in Producer and Consumer Countries to Promote Sustainable Development of Tropical Forests. Report by The Oxford Forestry Institute and TRADA for ITTO. Yokohama, Japan.

————. 1992. Criteria for the Measurement of Sustainable Tropical Forest Management. ITTO Policy Development Series No.3. Yokohama, Japan.

————. 1993. Guidelines on Biodiversity Conservation of Production Tropical Forests. ITTO Policy Development Series No. 5. Yokohama, Japan.

————. 1995. *Annual Review and Assessment of the World Tropical Timber Situation 1993–1994.* Yokohama, Japan.

International Union for the Conservation of Nature (IUCN). 1995. *Arborvitae* 13 (IUCN/WWF forest conservation program newsletter). Switzerland: WWF International.

————. 1996. *Communities and Forest Management.* Washington: The World Conservation Union.

Irvine, D. 1989. Succession Management and Resource Distribution in an Amazonian Rain Forest. *Advances in Economic Botany* 7: 223-237.

Janka, H., and R. Lobato. 1995. Alternatives to Destruction of Natural Forest Resources: The Forest Pilot Plan in Quintana Roo, Mexico. In Cortés (1995).

Janzen, D.H. 1988. Tropical Dry Forests: The Most Endangered Major Tropical Ecosystem. In *Biodiversity*, eds. E.O. Wilson and F.M. Peter. Washington, D.C.: National Academy Press.

Jaramillo, Carlos Felipe. 1997. El mercado rural de tierras en América Latina: Hacia una nueva estrategia. Washington, D.C.: Inter-American Development Bank. Mimeo.

Jiménez Turón, S. 1984. Muerte cultural con anestesia. *América indígena* XLIV:1. México.

Johnson, Nels, and Bruce Cabarle. 1993. *Surviving the Cut: Natural Forest Management in the Humid Tropics.* Washington, D.C.: WRI.

Johnston, G., and H. Lorraine. 1995. Síntesis de las políticas de manejo forestal en América Central. In Cortés (1995).

Jones, D., et al. 1992. *Farming in Rondonia.* Blacksburg, Virginia: Oak Ridge National Laboratory, VPI State University.

Jones, Jeffrey R. 1989. Human Settlement of Tropical Colonization in Central America. in *The Human Ecology of Tropical Land Settlement in Latin America,* eds. D.A. Schumann and W.L. Partridge. Boulder, Colorado: Westview Press.

Kaimowitz, David. 1992. La experiencia de Centroamérica y la República Dominicana con proyectos de inversión que buscan sostenibilidad en las laderas. Washington, D.C.: IICA.

————. 1995a. Why trees are disappearing but most forests remain, in the Bolivian Amazon. CIFOR. Unpublished.

————. 1995b. The End of the Hamburger Connection? Livestock and Deforestation in Central America in the 1980s and 1990s. In Cortés (1995).

Kaimowitz, David, and Arild Angelsen. 1997. A Guide to Economic Models of Tropical Deforestation. Centre for International Forestry Research (CIFOR), Djakarta, Indonesia. Mimeo.

Kanowski, P., P. Savill et al. 1992. Plantation Forestry. In *Managing the World's Forests,* ed. Narendra Sharma. Dubuque, IA: Kendall/Hunt.

Keipi, Kari. 1991. Reducing Deforestation in Latin America: The Role of the Inter-American Development Bank. In *Economic Development and Environmental Protection in Latin America,* ed. J.S. Tulchin. Woodrow Wilson Center, Current Studies on Latin America. Boulder, Colorado: Lynne Rienner Publications.

————. 1995a. Financing Forest Plantations in Latin America: the Issue of Incentives. Proceedings of the International Union of Forest Research Organizations (IUFRO) XXth World Congress. Tampere, Finland.

————. 1995b. Inter-American Development Bank Assistance for Forest Conservation and Management in Latin America and the Caribbean. *The Forestry Chronicle* 71:4 (July-August). Ottawa, Canada.

Keipi, K., and J.C. Laarman. 1995. Evaluation of Policies Affecting Forest in Latin America: A Framework for Discussion. In *Readings of the Workshop on Government Policy Reform for Forest Conservation and Development in Latin America,* ed. H. Cortés et al. San José, Costa Rica: IICA.

Kelly, Thomas J. 1994. *The Property Rights Approach and Deforestation.* Washington, D.C.: Inter-American Development Bank, Environment Division. Draft.

————. 1996. La deforestación y la teoría de los derechos de propiedad para tratar problemas ambientales en países en desarrollo. Informe Presentado en la Conferencia de

Medio Ambiente y Desarrollo en el Trópico. Universidad Autónoma de Yucatán, Mérida, México.

Kessel, G., and R. Samaniego. 1992. Apertura comercial, productividad y desarrollo tecnológico: el caso de México. IDB Working Paper 112, Agriculture Development Division. Washington, D.C.

Kirkland, A. 1988. The Rise and Fall of Multiple-Use Forest Management in New Zealand. *New Zealand Forestry* 33(1): 35-37.

Kirmse, R.D., L.F. Constantino and G.M. Guess. 1993. Prospects for improved management of natural forests in Latin America. LATEN Dissemination Note 9, December. Washington, D.C.: The World Bank.

Kishor, Naím, and Luis F. Constantino. 1993. *Forest Management and Competing Land Uses: An Economic Analysis for Costa Rica.* LATEN Dissemination Note # 7. Washington, D.C.: The World Bank.

————. 1994. Sustainable Forestry: Can it Compete? *Finance and Development* 31(4): 36–39.

Kohlhepp, G. 1991. Umweltpolitik zum Schutz tropischer Regenwälder in Brasilien. Rahmenbedingungen und umweltpolitische Aktivitäten. *KAS-Auslandsinformationen* 7/91: 1-23.

Kreuger, Anne O. 1990. Government Failures in Development. *Journal of Economic Perspectives* 4(3): 9-23.

Kuuluvainen, J. 1989. Non-industrial Private Timber Supply and Credit Rationing—Microeconomic Foundations with Empirical Evidence from the Finnish Case. Rapport 85. Sveriges Lantbruksuniversitet, Institutionen för Skogsekonomi. Umeå, Sweden.

Laarman, Jan G. 1986. A Perspective on Private Enterprise and Development Aid for Forestry. *Commonwealth Forestry Review* 65(4): 315-320.

————. 1993. *Evaluating Environmental Impacts of Rural Development Projects.* Madison, Wisconsin: Environmental and Natural Resources Policy and Training Project (EPAT), EPAT/MUCIA.

Laarman, Jan, and Hans Gregersen. 1994. *Pricing Policy in Nature-Based Tourism.* Madison, Wisconsin: Environmental and Natural Resources Policy and Training Project (EPAT), EPAT/MUCIA.

Laird, S. 1993. Contracts for Biodiversity Prospecting. In *Biodiversity Prospecting: Using Genetic Resources for Sustainable Development*, eds. W. Reid, S. Laird, C. Meyer, R. Gámez, A. Sittenfeld, D. Jansen, M. Gollin, and C. Juma. Baltimore: WRI Publications.

Lamb, F. 1966. *Mahogany of Tropical America: Its Ecology and Management.* Ann Arbor, MI: University of Michigan Press.

Lasser, T. 1974. *Flora de Venezuela* (multiple volumes). Caracas: Instituto Botánico de la Dirección de Recursos Naturales Renovables.

Lawrence, E. 1991. Poverty and the Rate Time Preference. Evidence from Panel Data. *Journal of Political Economy* 99(1).

Ledec, George, and Robert Goodland. 1988. *Wildlands: Their Protection and Management in Economic Development.* Washington, D.C.: World Bank.

Lemonick, M. 1995. Can the Galápagos Survive? *Time Magazine,* 30 October: 80-82.

Lena, Phillippe. 1991. Ritmos e estratégias de acumulação camponesa en áreas de colonização: um exemplo em Rondônia. Boletim Mus. Para Emilio Goeldi, ser. *Antropologia* 7(1).

Leonard, H. Jeffrey. 1987. *Natural Resources and Economic Development in Central America.* Washington, D.C.: International Institute for Environment and Development.

Levin, Julia. 1991. A Comparison of Forestry Laws in the United States and Brazil, as they Promote Deforestation in Southeastern Alaska and the Amazon Basin. *Hastings International and Comparative Law Review* 14: 1017-1040.

Levingston, R. 1983. International Policy and Action for Forestation. In *Strategies and Designs for Afforestation, Reforestation and Tree Planting,* ed. K.F. Wiersum. The Netherlands: Wageningen.

Lindberg, Kreg. 1991. *Policies for Maximizing Nature Tourism's Ecological and Economic Benefits.* Washington, D.C.: WRI.

Llaurado, J. Prats and G. Speidel. 1981. *Public Forestry Administrations in Latin America.* FAO Forestry Paper No. 25. Rome, Italy.

London Environmental Economics Centre (LEEC). 1992. The Economic Linkages between the International Trade in Tropical Timber and the Sustainable Management of Tropical Forests. Yokohama, Japan: ITTO.

Loomis, Charles. 1938. The Development of Planned Rural Communities. *Rural Sociology* 3(4): 385-409.

Loomis, John B. 1993. *Integrated Lands Management.* New York: Columbia University Press.

López, Ramón. 1992. Environment Degradation and Economic Openness in LDCs: The Poverty Linkage. *American Journal of Agricultural Economics* 1138–43.

———. 1994a. The Environment as a Factor of Production: The Effects of Economic Growth and Trade Liberalization. *Journal of Environmental Economics and Management* 27: 163–84.

———. 1994b. *Financing Sustainability in Latin America and the Caribbean: Toward an Action Program.* Inter-American Development Bank, Working Paper ENV107, Washington, D.C.

———. 1995. Economic Openness and the Environment in Latin America. Paper presented at The Third Annual Conference on Financing Sustainable Development. Washington, D.C.: The World Bank.

———. 1996. Land Titles and Farm Productivity in Honduras. Department of Agricultural and Resource Economics, College Park, Maryland. Unpublished mimeo.

———. 1997. Where Development Can or Cannot Go: The Role of Poverty-Environment Linkages. Paper presented at the Annual Bank Conference on Development Economics, Washington, D.C.: The World Bank.

López, Ramón, and Claudia Ocaña. 1994. Agricultural Growth and Deforestation: The Case of Colombia. Dept. of Agricultural and Natural Resource Economics, University of Maryland, College Park. Mimeo.

López, Ramón, and Alberto Valdés, eds. 1997. *Rural Poverty in Latin America.* Washington, D.C.: The World Bank.

Lutz, Ernst, Mario Vedova W., Hector Martínez, Lorena San Román, Ricardo Vázquez L., Alfredo Alvarado, Lucia Merino, Rafael Celis, and Jeroen Huising. 1993. *Interdisciplinary Fact-Finding on Current Deforestation in Costa Rica.* Environment Working Paper No. 61. Washington, D.C.: World Bank.

MacArthur, R., and E. Wilson. 1967. *The Theory of Island Biogeography.* Princeton University Press.

Machlis, Gary E., D. Costa, and J. Cárdenas-Salazar. 1990. Estudio del Visitante a las Islas Galápagos. Fundación Charles Darwin, Quito.

Machlis, Gary E., and D.L. Tichnell. 1985. *The State of the World's Parks: An International Assessment for Resource Management, Policy, and Research.* Boulder, Colorado: Westview Press.

MacKerron, Conrad B., and Douglas G. Cogan. 1993. *Business in the Rain Forests: Corporations, Deforestation, and Sustainability.* Washington, D.C.: Investor Responsibility Research Center.

MacKinnon, D. 1990. Using the Private Sector for Sustainable Forestry Development: Forestry Private Enterprise Initiative. Working Paper No. 51. NCSU, Duke University, USDA Forestry Support Program, USAID. Washington, D.C.

MacKinnon, John, K. MacKinnon, G. Child, and J. Thorsell. 1986. *Managing Protected Areas in the Tropics.* Gland, Switzerland: IUCN.

Madrigal, P. 1997. La cuestión legal y territorial indígena en Panamá. Washington, D.C. Mimeo.

Mahar, Dennis J. 1989. *Government Policies and Deforestation in Brazil's Amazon Region.* Washington, D.C.: World Bank.

Mahar, D., and R. Schneider. 1994. Incentives for Tropical Deforestation: Some Examples from Latin America. In *The Causes of Tropical Deforestation,* eds. K. Brown and D.W. Pearce. London: University College Press.

Martínez, M.M. 1993. Financial and Industrial Policies: Colombia's Challenges and Dilemmas. In *Financial Sector Reforms in Asian and Latin American Countries,* eds. S. Faruqi and G. Caprio. Washington, D.C.: World Bank.

Mattos, M., C. Uhl, and D. Goncalvez. 1992. Economic and Ecological Perspective on Ranching in the Eastern Amazon in the 1990s. Instituto do Homem e Meio Ambiente da Amazônia, EMBRAPA Brazil.

Mayers. 1995. Draft Discussion Paper on Policy and Priorities on Tropical Forest. International Institute of Environment and Development. London. Mimeo.

McGaughey, Stephen E., and Hans M. Gregersen. 1983. *Forest-Based Development in Latin America.* Washington, D.C.: Inter-American Development Bank.

————. 1988. *Investment Policies and Financing Mechanisms for Sustainable Forestry Development.* Washington, D.C.: Inter-American Development Bank.

McKean, M.A. 1996. Common Property: What is it, what is it good for, and what makes it work? International Forestry Resources and Institutions Research Program Working Paper 24, Indiana University.

McNabb, K., J. Borges, and J. Welker. 1994. Jari at 25: An Investment in the Amazon. *Journal of Forestry* 92(2): 21-26.

McNeely, Jeffrey A. 1988. *Economics and Biological Diversity: Developing and Using Economic Incentives to Conserve Biological Resources.* Gland, Switzerland: International Union for the Conservation of Nature and Natural Resources.

Meller, P. 1992. La apertura comercial chilena: enseñanzas de política. IDB Working Paper 109. Washington, D.C.

Mendelsohn, Robert. 1994. Property Rights and Tropical Deforestation. *Oxford Economic Papers* 46(5): 750-756.

Mertins, G. 1991. Ausmaß und Verursacher der Regenwaldrodung in Amazonien. Ein vorläufiges Fazit. In *Gießener Beiträge zur Entwicklungsforschung,* Reihe 1 (Symposien) 19: 15-24. Gießen, Germany.

————— 1996. Land Tenure Regulations and Land Tenure Forms in Latin America: Structure, Problems, Trends. GTZ. Eschborn, Germany. Mimeo.

Mills, Thomas J. 1976. *Cost-Effectiveness of the 1974 Forestry Incentives Program*. Ft. Collins, CO: USDA Forest Service Research Paper RM-175.

Mittermeier, R.A., and I.A. Bowles. 1993. The Global Environment Facility and biodiversity conservation: Lessons to date and suggestions for future action. *Biodiversity and Conservation* 2: 637-655.

Moran, Emilio F. 1989a. Adaptation and Maladaptation in Newly Settled Areas.

Moran, Emilio F. 1989b. Government-Directed Settlement in the 1970s: An Assessment of Transamazon Highway Colonization. In *The Human Ecology of Tropical Land Settlement in Latin America*, eds. D.A. Schumann and W.L. Partridge. Boulder, Colorado: Westview Press.

—————. 1993. *Through Amazonian Eyes: The Human Ecology of Amazonian Populations*. Unversity of Iowa Press. Iowa City.

—————. 1996. Nurturing the Forest: Strategies of Native Amazonians. In *Redefining Nature: Ecology, Culture and Domestication*, eds. E. Rand and K. Fukui. Oxford, England: Bergamon Press.

Morell, Merilio, and M. Paveri Anziani. 1994. Evolution of Public Forestry Administration in Latin America: Lessons for an Enhanced Performance. *Unasylva* 45(178): 31-37.

Motta, María Teresa. 1992. *Régimen de Aprovechamiento del Bosque Natural y Sistema de Tasas Forestales*. Bogotá: PNUD-DNP.

Mountfort, G. 1974. The Need for Partnership: Tourism and Conservation. *Development Forum* 2(3): 6-7.

Mueller, Bernardo. 1997. Property Rights and the Evolution of a Frontier. *Land Economics* 73: 42-57.

Mueller, Bernardo, Lee Alston, Gary D. Libecap, and Robert Schneider. 1994. Land, Property Rights and Privatization in Brazil. *The Quarterly Review of Economics and Finance* 34: 261-280.

Muñoz, Jorge A. 1993. Rural land markets in Latin America: Evidence from four case studies, Bolivia, Chile, Honduras and Paraguay. Washington, D.C.: Agricultural and Rural Development Department, The World Bank. Unpublished mimeo.

Myers, N. 1984. *The Primary Source*. New York: Norton.

—————. 1988. Threatened Biotas: Hotspots in Tropical Forests. *Environmentalist* 8(3): 1-20.

Naím, M. 1994. Instituciones: El eslabón perdido en las reformas económicas de América Latina. Washington, D.C.: The Carnegie Endowment.

National Research Council. *Sustainable Agriculture and the Environment in the Humid Tropics.* Washington, D.C.: National Academy Press.

Nations, J. 1989. La Reserva del Biosfera Maya, Petén: Estudio Técnico. Consejo Nacional de Áreas Protegidas, Guatemala.

Nations, James, and D. Komer. 1987. Rainforests and the Hamburger Society. *The Ecologist* 17(14/15): 161-167.

Nelson, Michael. 1973. *The Development of Tropical Lands: Policy Issues in Latin America.* Baltimore, Maryland: Johns Hopkins University Press.

Niklitschek, M. 1995. Conceptual Considerations on Subsidies for Forest Plantations. Paper presented at workshop, Use of Financial Incentives for Industrial Forest Plantations. IDB Working Paper ENV-4. Washington, D.C.

Niskanen, A., O. Luukkanen, O. Saastamoinen and S. Bhumibhamon. 1993. Evaluation of the Profitability of Fast-Growing Tropical Trees. *Acta Forestalia Fennica* 241. Helsinki.

Nolet, Gil. 1995. An Overview of International Environmental Conventions. Working Paper ENV-2, IDB Environment Division, Washington, D.C.

Office of Technology Assessment. 1992. *Trade and the Environment: Conflicts and Opportunities.* Washington, D.C.: U.S. Government Printing Office.

Oksanen, T., J. Salmi and M. Simula. 1994. National Forestry Programs. Paper prepared for the Forestry Advisors' Group. Indufor, Helsinki, Finland.

Oldfield, Sarah. 1988. *Buffer Zone Management in Tropical Moist Forests: Case Studies and Guidelines.* Gland, Switzerland: International Union for the Conservation of Nature and Natural Resources.

Olivera, A. 1995. Forestry Project of the Indigenous Chiquitano Communities of Lomerío. In *Proceedings of Symposium on Forestry in the Americas: Community-Based Management and Sustainability.* Madison: University of Wisconsin Land Tenure Center.

Organisation for Economic Cooperation and Development (OECD). 1994. *Environmental Impact Assessment of Roads.* Paris.

———. 1995. Environmental Funds: A New Approach to Sustainable Development. Report by the Inter-agency Planning Group on the 26 April 1995 Briefing. Paris.

Organization of American States (OAS). 1984. *Integrated Regional Development Planning: Guidelines and Case Studies from OAS Experience.* Washington, D.C.

———. 1987. *Minimum Conflict: Guidelines for Planning the Use of American Humid Tropic Environments*. Washington, D.C.: OAS.

Ostrom, Ellinor. 1990. *Governing the Commons: The Evolution of Institutions for Collective Action*. Cambridge, UK: Cambridge University Press.

O'Toole, Randall. 1988. *Reforming the Forest Service*. Washington, D.C.: Island Press.

Otsuka, Keijiro, Hilary Feldstein, Peter Hazell, Jane Hopkins, Lee Ann Jackson, Ruth Meinzen-Dick, John Pender, Agnes Quisumbing, Sara Scherr and Towa Tachibana. 1996. Property Rights and Collective Action in Natural Resource Management. Multi-country Research Program MP-11, IFPRI, Washington D.C.

Otsuka, Keijiro. 1993. Land Tenure and Rural Poverty. In *Rural Poverty in Asia: Priority Issues and Policy Options*, ed. M.G. Quibria. Hong Kong: Oxford University Press.

Otsuki, Tsunerhiro. 1997. The Links Between Property Rights and Deforestation Decisions in the Frontier. Department of Agricultural and Resource Economics, University of Maryland, College Park. Mimeo.

Ottaway, M. 1995. Pick of the Bunch: Costa Rica is Central America at its Very Best. *Sunday Times* 19 November: 5.1-5.2.

Ozorio de Almeida, A. 1992. *Deforestation and Turnover in Amazon Colonization*, Discussion Paper. Washington D.C.: The World Bank.

Padua, M.T.J. 1996. Biodiversidade é conversa para sem-terra dormir. *Parabolicas* 13(2):7.

Palmer, J.R.. 1995. New Markets for Tropical Plywood Derived from Sustainable Management of the Forest. Conferencia mundial de plywood tropical en la región de América Latina y el Caribe. Quito, 2-4 mayo.

Panayotou, Theodore. 1989. The Economics of Environmental Degradation: Problems, Causes and Responses. Harvard Institute for International Development, Cambridge. Mimeo.

———. 1995. *Innovative Economic and Fiscal Instruments*. Earth Council/World Bank. Washington, D.C.

Pardo, C., H. Torres, and C. Ormazabal. 1994. South America. In *Protecting Nature: Regional Reviews of Protected Areas*, eds. J.A. McNeely, J. Harrison, and P. Dingwall. IVth World Congress on National Parks and Protected Areas, Caracas, Venezuela. IUCN.

Pascó-Font, A. 1994. Valorización de los recursos naturales y políticas para la promoción del desarrollo sostenible de la Amazonia. *Informe del taller Biodiversidad y desarrollo sostenible de la Amazonia en una economía de mercado*. Ucayali Regional Government, IVITA, INIA, CE&DAP, FUNDEAGRO and CIID. Lima, Peru.

Paveri, Manuel. FAO. 1997. Personal communication to IDB re document review.

Pearce, D.W. 1993. Valuing the environment: past practice, future prospect. Paper for the First Annual Conference on Environmentally Sustainable Development. World Bank, Washington, D.C., September 30–October 1.

————. 1994. Assessing the Social Rate of Return from Investment in Temperate Zone Forestry. In *Cost-Benefit Analysis*, eds. R. Layard and S. Glaister. Cambridge University Press.

————. 1995. *Capturing Global Environmental Value.* London: Earthscan.

Pearce, D., and S. Puroshothaman. 1995. The Economic Value of Plant-Based Pharmaceuticals. In *Intellectual Property Rights and Biodiversity Conservation: An Interdisciplinary Analysis of the Values of Medicinal Plants*, ed. T. Swanson. Cambridge University Press.

Pérez, M.R., J.A. Sayer, and S. Cohen Jehoran. 1993. *El Extractivismo en América Latina.* Gland, Switzerland: IUCN.

Peters, C. 1990. Population Ecology and Management of Forest Fruit Trees in Peruvian Amazonia. In A. Anderson (1990).

Peters, C., A. Gentry, and R. Mendelsohn. 1989. Valuation of an Amazon Rainforest. *Nature* 339: 655-666.

Peuker, Axel. 1992. *Public Policies and Deforestation: A Case Study of Costa Rica.* Latin America and the Caribbean Technical Department, Regional Studies Program Report No. 14, World Bank, Washington, D.C.

Pfaff, Alexander P.S. 1997. What Drives Deforestation in the Brazilian Amazon? Policy Research Working Paper No. 1772. The World Bank. Washington, D.C.

Pierce, D. 1993. *Economic Values and the Natural World.* Cambridge, MA.: MIT Press.

Pinedo-Vásquez, M., D. Zarin, P. Jipp and J. Chota-Inuma. 1990. Use-values of Tree Species in a Communal Forest Reserve in Northeast Peru. *Conservation Biology* 4: 405-416.

Plonczak, M. 1993. Estructura y dinámica de desarrollo de bosques naturales manejados bajo la modalidad de concesiones en los Llanos Occidentales de Venezuela. Instituto Forestal Latinoamericano. Mérida, Venezuela.

Pollak, H., M. Mattos, and C. Uhl. 1995. A Profile of Palm Heart Extraction in the Amazon Estuary. *Human Ecology* 23(3): 357-385.

Poole, P. 1989. *Developing a Partnership of Indigenous Peoples, Conservationists, and Land Use Planners in Latin America.* Policy Research Working Paper No. 245. Washington, D.C.: World Bank.

Poore, M.E.D., and C. Fries. 1985. *The Ecological Effects of Eucalyptus.* FAO Forestry Paper 59. Rome, Italy.

Posey, D.A. 1985. Indigenous Management of Tropical Forest Ecosystems: The Case of the Kayapo Indians of the Brazilian Amazon. *Agroforestry Systems* 3:139-158.

Prestmon, Jeffrey P. and Jan G. Laarman. 1989. Should Sawnwood be Produced with Chainsaws: Observations in Ecuador. *Journal of World Forest Resource Management* 4:111-126.

Principe, P. 1989. The Economic Significance of Plants and their Constituents as Drugs. In *Economic and Medicinal Plant Research III, eds.* H. Wagner, H. Hikino, and N. Farnsworth. London: Academic Press.

Quiggin, John. 1993. Common Property, Equality and Development. *World Development* 21: 1123-1138.

Rainforest Alliance. 1993. Generic Guidelines for Assessing Natural Forest Management. New York, NY.

Ramanadham, V.V. 1991. *The Economics of Public Enterprise.* London: Routledge.

Razetto, Fernando. 1994. Propiedad privada en concesiones forestales (un modelo para la subregión andina). Lima, Peru: Cámara Forestal Andina.

———. 1995. Propiedad privada en concesiones forestales: Un modelo en la región andina para la conservación de los ecosistemas y el desarrollo económico y social. In Cortés (1995).

———. 1996. Personal communication. (President of the *Camara Nacional Forestal.*)

Reardon, Thomas, and Stephen A. Vosti. 1995. Links Between Rural Poverty and the Environment in Developing Countries: Asset Categories and Investment Poverty. *World Development* 23 (9):1495-1506.

Redford, K. 1992. The Empty Forest. *Bioscience* 42:6: 412-422.

Reed, David. 1992. *Structural Adjustment and the Environment.* Boulder, Colorado: Westview Press.

Reforma. 1995. Cuando un secuestro es buena noticia. *Reforma* 2(4), June. San José, Costa Rica.

Reid, J. R., and A.F. Howard. 1994. Economic analysis of the proposed timber concession at Arroyo Colorado: Are there incentives for management? Report to USAID, Washington, D.C. Conservation International.

Reid, J.R., and R.E. Rice. 1997. Natural forest management as a tool for tropical forest conservation: Does it work? *Ambio* (in press).

Reid, W., et al. 1993. A New Lease on Life. In *Biodiversity Prospecting: Using Genetic Resources for Sustainable Development.* Baltimore: WRI Publications.

Reis, E. 1991. *Amazon Deforestation from an Economic Perspective.* IPEA. Rio de Janeiro: Universidade Rural de Rio de Janeiro.

Repetto, Robert. 1985. *The Global Possible: Resources, Development, and the New Century.* New Haven: Yale University Press.

————. 1993. Trade and Environment Policies: Achieving Complementarities and Avoiding Conflicts. *Issues and Ideas.* Washington, D.C.: WRI (July).

Repetto, R., and W. Cruz. 1992. The Environmental Effects of Stabilization and Structural Adjustment Programs: The Philippines Case Study. Washington, D.C.: World Resources Institute (WRI).

Repetto, R., R.C. Dower, R. Jankins and J. Geoghegan. 1992. Green Fees: How a Tax Shift Can Work for the Environment and the Economy. Washington, D.C.: WRI.

Repetto, R., and Malcolm Gillis, eds. 1988. *Public Policies and Misuse of Forest Resources.* Cambridge University Press.

Reserva Extrativista do Alto Juru. 1994. Informe Anual. Brazil.

Rice, R., and A. Howard. (forthcoming). Profitability in the forest sector of Bolivia: A case study of the Chimanes Forest.

Richards, E. 1991. The Forest *Ejidos* of Southeast Mexico: A Case Study of Community-Based Sustained Yield Management. *Commonwealth Forestry Review* 70:4: 290-311.

Richards, Michael. 1993. The Potential of Non-Timber Forest Products in Sustainable Natural Forest Management in Amazonia. *Commonwealth Forestry Review* 72(1):21-27.

Richardson, S.D. 1992. Sticks and Carrots in Forest Concession Management. *Commonwealth Forestry Review* 71(3/4):167-170.

Riihinen, P. 1981. Forestry and the Timber Economy in Economic Development. *Silva Fennica* 15(2): 199-202.

————. 1986. Future Challenges of Forest Policy Analysis. In *Analysis and Evaluation of Public Forest Policies: XVIII IUFRO World Congress,* ed. I. Tikkanen. *Silva Fennica* 20:4.

Rinehart, J.A. 1992. Liquidity for Non-Industrial Private Forests in California. Rinehart and Associates, San Francisco, California. Unpublished paper.

Rodríguez, Miguel. 1996. Personal communication. (Director of Natural Resources at Pizano S.A.)

Rojas, M., and C. Castano. 1991. *Áreas protegidas de la cuenca del Amazonas.* INDERENA, Bogotá, Colombia. Tratado de Cooperación Amazónica.

Roldán, R. 1993. El problema de la legalidad de la tenencia de la tierra y el manejo de los recursos en regiones de la selva tropical de Suramérica. In *Derechos territoriales indígenas y ecología en las selvas tropicales de América.* Bogotá: CEREC.

————. 1997. La cuestión legal y territorial indígena en el Perú, Brasil, Colombia, y Nicaragua. Inter-American Development Bank, Washington, D.C. Mimeo.

Romanoff, S. 1981. Análisis de las condiciones socioeconómicas para el desarrollo integral de la Amazonía Boliviana. Consulting report, Organization of American States, Washington, D.C.

Rovinski, Y. 1991. Private Reserves, Parks, and Ecotourism in Costa Rica. In *Nature Tourism: Managing for the Environment,* ed. T. Whelan. Washington, D.C.: Island Press.

Rudel, T.K. 1995. When do Property Rights Matter? Open Access, Informal Social Controls and Deforestation in the Ecuadorian Amazon. *Human Organization:* 187-194.

Rudel, T.K., and B. Horowitz. 1993. *Tropical Deforestation: Small Farmers and Land Clearing in the Ecuadorian Amazon.* New York: Columbia University Press.

Ruitenbeek, H. 1989. Social Cost-Benefit Analysis of the Korup Project, Cameroon. Consulting report, Worldwide Fund for Nature, London.

Ruiz-Pérez, M., J. Sayer, and S. Cohen. 1992. *El extractivismo en América Latina.* IUCN, Commission of the European Community. Gland, Switzerland: IUCN.

Rural Advancement Foundation International (RAFI). 1994. Conserving indigenous knowledge: integrating two systems of innovation. Ottawa, Canada.

————. 1997. RAFI Communiqué, September–October 1997. Ottawa, Canada.

Salafsky, N., B. Dugelby, and J. Terborgh 1992. Can extractive reserves save the rain forest? An ecological and socioeconomic comparison of nontimber forest product extraction systems in Petén, Guatemala and West Kalimantan, Indonesia. *Conservation Biology* 71: 39-52.

Salati, E. 1989. The climatology and hydrology of Amazonia. In *Amazonia,* ed. G.T. Prance and T. Lovejoy: 18-48. Oxford: Pergamon Press.

Sánchez, E. 1995. Los pueblos indígenas del Pacífico frente a la encrucijada del desarrollo. In *Tierra profanada. Grandes proyectos en territorios indígenas de Colombia.* Bogotá: Disloque, Editores.

Sánchez, Manuel, and Rossana Corona, eds. 1993. *Privatization in Latin America.* Washington, D.C.: Inter-American Development Bank.

Sanfuentes, Andrés. 1987. Chile: Effects of the Adjustment Policies on the Agriculture and Forestry Sector. *CEPAL Review* 33: 115-127.

Sargent, Caroline, and Stephen Bass, eds. 1992. *Plantation Politics: Forest Plantations in Development.* London: Earthscan Publications.

Sayer, Jeffrey. 1991. *Rainforest Buffer Zones: Guidelines for Protected Area Management.* Gland, Switzerland: IUCN.

Scatolin, F.D. 1995. Forestry and Agri-Business in Brazil. Economics Department, University of Paraná, Curitiba, Brazil. Unpublished paper.

Schneider, Robert R. 1993a. *Land Abandonment, Property Rights and Agricultural Sustainability in the Amazon.* LATEN Dissemination Note #3. Washington, D.C.: The World Bank.

———. 1993b. *The Potential for Trade with the Amazon in Greenhouse Reduction,* LATEN Dissemination Series. Washington, D.C.: The World Bank.

———. 1995. *Government and the Economy on the Amazon Frontier.* Latin America and the Caribbean Technical Department, Regional Studies Program Report No. 34. Washington, D.C.: World Bank.

Schumann, D.A., and W.L. Partridge, eds. 1989. *The Human Ecology of Tropical Land Settlement in Latin America.* Boulder, Colorado: Westview Press.

Schwartzman, Stephen. 1989. Extractive Reserves: The Rubber Tappers' Strategy for Sustainable Use of the Amazon Rain Forest. In *Fragile Lands of Latin America: Strategies for Sustainable Development,* ed. J.O. Browder. Boulder, Colorado: Westview Press.

Schweigert, T. 1989. Land tenure issues in agricultural development projects in Latin America. Madison, Wisc. Land Tenure Center-Paper 132. University of Wisconsin.

Scitovsky, T. 1954. Two Concepts of External Economics. *Journal of Political Economy* 62: 143-151.

Scott, C.D., and J.A. Litchfield. 1994. *Inequality, Mobility and the Determinants of Income Among the Rural Poor in Chile, 1968-1986.* DEP Series No. 53, Development Economics Research Programme, London School of Economics.

Sedjo, Roger A. 1991. Forest Resources: Resilient and Serviceable. In *America's Renewable Resources: Historical Trends and Current Challenges,* eds. K.D. Frederick and R.A. Sedjo. Washington, D.C.: Resources for the Future.

Sedjo, R.A., and K.S. Lyon. 1990. *The Long-Term Adequacy of World Timber Supply.* Washington, D.C.: Resources for the Future.

Seligson, M., and E. Nesman. 1989. Land Titling in Honduras: An Impact Study in the Comayagua Region. Land Tenure Center, University of Wisconsin, Madison.

Selverston, M.H. 1994. The Politics of Culture: Indigenous Peoples and the State in Ecuador. In: *Indigenous Peoples and Democracy in Latin America* (Ed. D.L. Van Cott). New York: St. Martin's Press, with the Inter-American Dialogue.

Sere, Carlos, and Lovell S. Jarvis. 1992. Livestock Economy and Forest Destruction. *Development or Destruction: The Conversion of Tropical Forest to Pasture in Latin America*, eds. Theodore E. Downing, et al. Boulder, Colorado: Westview Press.

SGS Silviconsult. 1994. Tropical Forest Management. Position Paper on Certification. Mimeographed. Oxford Forestry Institute.

———. 1993. Swiss Certification Program. Field Report. Oxford Forestry Institute.

Shearer, Eric B., Susana Lastarria-Cornhiel, and Dina Mesbah. 1990. *Rural Land Markets in Latin America and the Caribbean: Research, Theory, and Policy Implications*. Madison, Wisconsin: Land Tenure Center, University of Wisconsin.

Simeone, R. 1990. Land Use Planning and Forestry-Based Economy: The Case of the Amuesha Forestry Cooperative. *Tebiwa: The Journal of the Idaho Museum of Natural History* 24: 7-12.

Simpson, D., and R. Sedjo. 1996. Paying for the Conservation of Endangered Ecosystems: A Comparison of Direct and Indirect Approaches. *Environment and Development Economics* 1(2): 241-257.

Simpson, D., R. Sedjo, and J. Reid. 1996. Valuing Biodiversity: An Application to Genetic Prospecting. *Journal of Political Economy* 104:1: 163-185.

Simpson, T. 1997. Indigenous Heritage and Self-Determination. The Cultural and Intellectual Property Rights of Indigenous Peoples. IWGIA No. 86. Copenhagen.

Silva, J., J. de Carvalho, J do C.A. Lopes, B.F. de Almeida, D. Costa, L. de Oliveira, J. Vanclay and J. Skovsgaard. 1995. Growth and Yield of a Tropical Rain Forest in the Brazilian Amazon 13 Years after Logging. *Forest Ecology and Management* 71: 267-274.

Simula, M. 1991. Planning Forest Industries in Developing Countries. ITTO Technical Series 6. Yokohama, Japan.

———. 1995a. Beyond the Tropical Forests Action Program: Financing Forest Development and Conservation. Third World Bank Conference on Effective Financing of Environmentally Sustainable Development. October 4–6, 1995. Washington, D.C.

———. 1995b. Economic Aspects of Certification. In *Certification of Forest Products: Issues and Perspectives*, ed. C. Elliot et al. Washington, D.C.: Island Press.

Sizer, N. 1994. Opportunities to Save and Sustainably Use the World's Forests Through International Cooperation. *WRI Issues and Ideas* (December). Washington, D.C.: World Resources Institute.

Sizer, N., and R. Rice. 1995. *Backs to the Wall in Suriname: Forest Policy in a Country in Crisis.* Washington, D.C.: World Resources Institute.

Smith, R.C. 1994. Amazonia: Economía indígena y mercado, los desafíos del desarrollo autónomo. COICA-OXFAM América. Quito, Ecuador.

Smith, R.C. 1996. Estrategias para el desarrollo sostenible y el empleo productivo en los pueblos indígenas de la Amazonía peruana. Pueblos indígenas de la Amazonía peruana y desarrollo sostenible. OIT. Lima, Peru.

Snook, L. 1991. Opportunities and Constraints for Sustainable Tropical Forestry: Lessons from the Plan Piloto Forestal, Quintana Roo, Mexico. Presentation at the Humid Tropical Lowlands Conference on Development Strategies and Natural Resource Management, Panama City, Panama.

———. 1993. Stand Dynamics of Mahogany (*Swietenia Macrophylla* King) and Associated Species after Fire and Hurricane in the Tropical Forests of the Yucatan Peninsula, Mexico. Ph.D Dissertation, Yale School of Forestry and Environmental Studies. University of Michigan Microfilms: Ann Arbor.

Soil Association Marketing Company. 1994. *Responsible Forestry Standards.* Bristol, England.

Solanes, M., and D. Getches. 1998. Prácticas recomendables para la elaboración de leyes y regulaciones relacionadas con el recurso hídrico. CEPAL. Santiago, Chile. Mimeo.

Southgate, Douglas. 1990. The Causes of Land Degradation along Spontaneously Expanding Agricultural Frontiers in the Third World. *Land Economics* 66(1): 93-101.

Southgate, D. 1994. Tropical Deforestation and Agricultural Development in Latin America. In *The Causes of Tropical Deforestation: The Economic and Statistical Analysis of Factors Giving Rise to the Loss of Tropical Forests,* eds. K. Brown and D. Pearce. Vancouver: University of British Columbia Press.

———. 1995a. Government and the Economy on the Amazonian Frontier. Environment Paper No. 11. The World Bank. Washington, D.C.

———. 1995b. Subsidized Tree Plantations in Ecuador: Some Issues. Paper presented at the workshop, Use of Financial Incentives for Industrial Forest Plantations. IDB Working Paper ENV-4. Washington, D.C.

———. 1997. Alternatives for Habitat Protection and Rural Income Generation. IDB Working Paper ENV-107. Washington, D.C.

Southgate, Douglas, and Howard L. Clark. 1993. Can Conservation Projects Save Biodiversity in South America? *Ambio* 22(2-3): 163-166.

Southgate, D., M. Coles-Ritchie, and P. Salazar-Canelos. 1996. Can Tropical Forests Be Saved by Harvesting Nontimber Products? A Case Study for Ecuador. In *Forestry, Economics, and the Environment,* eds. W. Adamowicz et al. Wallingford: CAB International.

Southgate, Douglas, and Morris Whitaker. 1992. Promoting Resource Degradation in Latin America: Tropical Deforestation, Soil Erosion, and Coastal Ecosystem Disturbance in Ecuador. *Economic Development and Cultural Change* 40(4): 787-807.

―――. 1994. *Economic Progress and the Environment: One Developing Country's Policy Crisis.* New York: Oxford University Press.

Spears, John. 1994. Conditional Lending Experiences in World Bank Financed Forestry Projects. In *Reforma de las Políticas de Gobierno Relacionadas con la Conservación y el Manejo de los Recursos Forestales en América Latina,* World Bank, CIFOR, USAID, and IICA. Washington, D.C.: Development Strategy for Fragile Lands.

Spruce, R. 1970. *Notes of a Botanist on the Amazon and Andes, Volume II.* London: Johnson Reprint Corporation.

Stanfield, David. 1992. *Insecurity of Land Tenure in Nicaragua.* Madison, Wisconsin: Land Tenure Center, University of Wisconsin.

Stanfield, D., and E. Nesman. 1990. *The Honduras Land Titling and Registration Experience.* Land Tenure Center, University of Wisconsin, Madison.

Stanley, Denise. 1991. Demystifying the Tragedy of the Commons: The Resin Tappers of Honduras. *Grassroots Development* 15(3): 27-35.

Stewart, P.J. 1985. The Dubious Case for State Control. *Ceres* 18(2):14-19.

Stewart, R., and G. Arias. 1995. Exportación de madera en troza: ¿por qué un NO a la prohibición? *Revista Forestal Centroamericana* 4(12):16–18.

Stewart, R., and D. Gibson. 1995. Efectos de las politicas agrícolas y forestales sobre el ambiente y el desarrollo económico de América Latina: Una síntesis de estudios de caso de Costa Rica, Bolivia y Ecuador. In Cortés (1995).

Stewart, R. 1992. *An Economic Study of Costa Rica's Forest Sector.* San José, Costa Rica: Academia de Centroamérica.

Stewart, Rigoberto, and David Gibson. 1994. Environmental and Economic Development Consequences of Forest and Agricultural Sector Policies in Latin America. In Cortés (1995).

Stiglitz, J.E. 1993. The Role of the State in Financial Markets. *Annual Bank Conference on Development Economics.* Washington, D.C.: The World Bank.

―――. 1994. The Rate of Discount for Cost-Benefit Analysis and the Theory of the Second Best. In *Cost-Benefit Analysis*, eds. R. Layard and S. Glaister. Cambridge University Press.

Stone, P.H. 1992. Forecast cloudy: The limits of global warming models. *Technology Review* February/March: 32-40.

Strasma, John D., and Rafael Celis. 1992. Land Taxation, the Poor, and Sustainable Development. In *Poverty, Natural Resources, and Public Policy in Central America*, ed. Sheldon Annis. Washington, D.C.: Overseas Development Council.

Strasma, J., and Tulio Barbosa. 1984. Land Tenure and Agricultural Productivity in the State of Maranhao, Brazil: Some Empirical Evidence. Land Tenure Center, University of Wisconsin, Madison. Mimeo.

Streeten, P. 1959. Unbalanced Growth. *Oxford Economic Papers 11*. Oxford University Press.

Sugden, A. 1997. Report of the Independent Consultant on ITTO and Intellectual Property Rights. ITTO Santa Cruz de la Sierra, Bolivia. Mimeo.

Swenarski de Herrera, Lisa. 1993. Unusual Map Helps Indians of Honduras Push for Land Rights. San José, Costa Rica: Tropical Conservation Newsbureau.

Synnott, T.J., and D.S. Cassells. 1991. Evaluation Report on Project PD 34/88 Rev.1(F) Conservation, Management, Utilization and Integrated and Sustained Use of the Chimanes Region Department of Beni, Bolivia. Report to the International Tropical Timber Council of the ITTO.

Tratado de Cooperación Amazónica (TCA). 1994a. Zonificación ecológica-económica: instrumento para la conservación y el desarrollo sostenible de los recursos de la Amazonia. Lima, Peru: TCA.

————. 1995. Propuesta de Tarapoto sobre Criterios e Indicadores de Sostenibilidad del Bosque Amazónico. Lima, Peru.

————. 1994b. Uso y conservación de la fauna silvestre en la Amazonia. Lima, Peru: TCA.

TFAP-CA. 1992. Concesiones forestales a gran escala en Centroamérica: Caso de Guatemala. WWF, WRI, UNDP, FINNIDA. San José, Costa Rica.

Thiesenhusen, William C. 1991. *The Relation between Land Tenure and Deforestation in Latin America*. Madison, Wisconsin: Land Tenure Center, University of Wisconsin.

Tobias, D., and R. Mendelsohn. 1991. Valuing Ecotourism in a Tropical Rain Forest Preserve. *Ambio* 20:2: 91-93.

Toledo, Victor M. 1992. Bio-Economic Costs. In *Development or Destruction: The Conversion of Tropical Forest to Pasture in Latin America*, eds. Theodore E. Downing, et al. Boulder, Colorado: Westview Press.

Tosi, J. 1986. Natural Forest Management for the Sustained Yield of Forest Products. Tropical Science Center, San José, Costa Rica.

Trummel, Craig. 1994. Privatizing New Zealand's Forests. *Journal of Forestry* 92(9):30-32.

Tschinkel, Henry. 1987. Tree Planting by Small Farmers in Upland Watersheds: Experience in Central America. *International Tree Crops Journal* 4: 249-268.

Turner, R. Kerry, and S. Wibe. 1992. *Market and Government Failures in Environmental Management: Wetlands and Forests.* Paris: Organization for Economic Cooperation and Development.

Ugalde, L.A., and H. Gregersen. 1987. Incentives in Tree Growing in Relation to Deforestation and the Fuelwood Crisis in Central America. CATIE, Turrialba, Costa Rica. Mimeo.

Uhl, C., A. Veríssimo, M. Mattos, Z. Brandino, and I. Vieira. 1991. Social, Economic, and Ecological Consequences of Selective Logging in an Amazon Frontier: The Case of Tailandia. *Forest Ecology and Management* 46: 243-273.

Umaña, A., and K. Brandon. 1992. Inventing Institutions for Conservation: Lessons from Costa Rica. In *Poverty, Natural Resources, and Public Policy in Central America*, ed. S. Annis. New Brunswick: Transaction Publishers.

United Nations. 1995. Review of Sectoral Clusters, Second Phase: Land, Desertification, Forests and Biodiversity. Commission on Sustainable Development, Third Session. New York (April). Upton, C., and S. Bass. 1995. *The Forest Certification Handbook.* London: Earthscan.

United Nations Conference on Trade and Development (UNCTAD). 1995a. Environmental Policies, Trade and Competitiveness: Conceptual and Empirical Issues. TD/B/WG.6/6. Geneva.

———. 1995b. Newly Emerging Environmental Policies with a Possible Trade Impact: A Preliminary Discussion. TO/B/WG.6/9. Geneva.

———. 1995c. The Policy Debate on Trade, Environment and Development. TD/B/WG:6/10. Geneva.

———. 1995d. Trade, Environment and Development Aspects of Establishing and Operating Ecolabeling Programs. TD/B/WG.6/5. Geneva.

U.S. National Research Council. 1993. *Sustainable Agriculture and the Environment in the Humid Tropics.* Washington, D.C.: National Academy Press.

Uquillas, J.E., and S.H. Davis, 1992. La cuestión territorial y ecológica entre los pueblos indígenas de la selva baja del Ecuador. In *Derechos territoriales indígenas y ecología en las selvas tropicales de América.* Bogotá: Fundación Gaia.

Utting, P. 1993. *Trees, People and Power: Social Dimensions of Deforestation and Forest Protection in Central America.* London: UNRISD and EARTHSCAN.

Valdés, A. 1995. *Surveillance of Agricultural Price and Trade Policy: A Synthesis for Selected Latin American Countries.* Washington, D.C.: The World Bank, Technical Department, Latin America and the Caribbean Region.

Van Cott, D.L. 1994. *Indigenous Peoples and Democracy in Latin America*. New York: St. Martin's Press.

Van Schaik, C., R. Kramer, P. Shyamsundar, and N. Salafsky. 1992. Biodiversity of tropical rain forests: Ecology and economics of an elusive resource. Report of the Center for Tropical Conservation, Duke University.

Varangis, P. 1992. Tropical timber prices: Own trends and comparisons among them and with other timber prices. Washington, DC: The World Bank.

Varangis, P., R. Crossley and B. Braga. 1995. Is There a Commercial Case for Tropical Timber Certification? World Bank Policy Research Working Paper #1479. Washington, DC: The World Bank.

Varangis, P.N., R. Crossley and C.A. Primo Braga. 1995. Is There a Commercial Case for Tropical Timber Certification? World Bank. Policy Research Working Paper 1479. Washington, D.C.

Vásquez, R., and A. Gentry. 1989. Use and Misuse of Forest-Harvested Fruits in the Iquitos Area. *Conservation Biology* 3:4: 350-361.

Vaughan, W.J. 1995. Incentives for Watershed Management. Paper presented at the workshop, Use of Financial Incentives for Industrial Forest Plantations. IDB Working Paper ENV-4. Washington, D.C.

Veríssimo, A., P. Barreto, M. Mattos, R. Tarifa, and C. Uhl. 1992. Logging Impacts and Prospects for Sustainable Forest Management in an Old Amazonian Frontier: The Case of Paragominas. *Forest Ecology and Management* 55: 169-199.

Veríssimo, A., P. Barreto, R. Tarifa, and C. Uhl. 1995. Extraction of a High-Value Natural Resource in Amazonia: The Case of Mahogany. *Forest Ecology and Management* 72: 39-60.

Villaroel, P. 1994. Proyecto Rio Condor: Explotación forestal en el confin del mundo. *Ambiente y Desarrollo* (December): 27-38.

Vincent, J., and C. Binkley. 1992. Forest-Based Industrialization: A Dynamic Perspective. In *Managing the World's Forests*, ed. Narendra Sharma. Dubuque, IA: Kendall/Hunt.

Vogel, J. 1994. *Genes for Sale: Privatization as a Conservation Policy*. New York: Oxford University Press.

Volmer, U. 1993. Forest Policy. In *Tropical Forestry Handbook II*, ed. L. Pansel. Berlin: Springer Verlag.

Wachter, Daniel. 1992. Land Titling for Land Conservation in Developing Countries. Environment Department, Divisional Working Paper No. 1992/28. The World Bank. Washington, D.C.

Wachter, Daniel, and John English. 1992. The World Bank's Experience with Rural Land Titling. Environment Department, Divisional Working Paper No. 1992/35, The World Bank. Washington, D.C.

Wells, Michael and Katrina Brandon. 1992. *People and Parks: Linking Protected Area Management with Local Communities.* Washington, D.C.: World Bank/World Wildlife Fund/ USAID.

———. 1993. The Principles and Practice of Buffer Zones and Local Participation in Biodiversity Conservation. *Ambio:* 157-162.

Westoby, J. 1962. The Role of Forest Industries in the Attack on Economic Underdevelopment. *Unasylva* 16(4).

———. 1978. Forest Industries for Socio-economic Development. Paper presented at the Eighth World Forestry Congress, Jakarta.

Whelan, T. 1991. Ecotourism and its Role in Sustainable Development. In *Nature Tourism: Managing for the Environment,* ed. T. Whelan. Washington, D.C.: Island Press.

Wilson, E., ed. 1988. *Biodiversity.* Washington, D.C.: National Academy Press.

Winterbottom, R. 1990. The Tropical Forestry Action Plan: What Progress? *The Ecologist.* London: World Rainforest Movement/Friends of the Earth.

Witcover, Julie, et al. 1996. Alternatives to Slash-and-Burn Agriculture (ASB): A Characterization of Brazilian Benchmark Sites of Pedro Peixoto and Theobroma, August/September 1994. MP-8 Working Paper No. US 96-003. IFPRI, Washington, D.C.

Witcover, Julie, and Stephen Vosti. 1996. A Socioeconomic Characterization Questionnaire for the Brazilian Amazon: A Description and Discussion of Questionnaire Application Issues. MP-8 Working Paper No. US 96-001. IFPRI, Washington, D.C.

———. 1997. Personal communication.

World Bank. 1987. Security Helps Productivity. World Bank Research Brief. Washington, D.C.

———. 1991. Environmental Assessment Sourcebook I-III. Technical Paper No. 140. Washington, D.C.: World Bank.

———. 1992. Development Report. Washington, D.C.: World Bank.

———. 1993a. Análisis del sector forestal de Costa Rica. San José, Costa Rica: World Bank.

———. 1993b. Argentina: Agricultural Sector Memorandum. Report No. 13425-ME. Washington, D.C.

———. 1993c. Forest Policy Implementation Review. Agriculture and Natural Resources Department. Washington, D.C.

———. 1993d. Indigenous People and Development in Latin America. Proceedings from the Second Interagency Workshop on Indigenous Peoples and Development in Latin America. LATEN Dissemination Note No. 8. Washington, D.C.

———. 1994a. Belize Environmental Report. Washington D.C.: The World Bank.

———. 1994b. Mexico: Agricultural Sector Memorandum. Report No. 13425-ME. Washington, D.C.

———. 1995a. *Guatemala: Land Tenure and Natural Resources Management.* Washington, D.C.

———. 1995b. *Commodity Markets and the Developing Countries. A World Bank Quarterly.* Washington, D.C.

World Commission on Environment and Development (WCED). 1987. *Our Common Future.* Oxford, U.K.: Oxford University Press.

World Commission on Forestry and Sustainable Development (WCFSD). 1996a. Interim Report on the Outcome of an Asian Region Public Hearing. Jakarta, Indonesia.

———. 1996b. Latin America and the Caribbean Regional Hearing, 2-3 December 1996, Background Discussion Paper. Geneva, Switzerland.

World Resources Institute (WRI). 1990-97. *World Resources Guide to the Global Environment.* Washington, D.C.

———. 1991. Summary Report on the Colloquium on Sustainability in Natural Tropical Forest Management. Washington, D.C.: WRI.

Wormald, T.J. 1992. Mixed and Pure Forest Plantations in the Tropics and Subtropics. FAO Forestry Paper No. 103. Rome, Italy.

Wunder, Dieter. 1994. A Subsidy to the Forest Sector: A Quantitative Measure of its Impact, Empirical Evidence for the Chilean Case. Universidad Adolfo Ibañez, Valparaiso, Chile. Mimeo.

Wünder, Sven. 1994. Conservation Status of Native Forests in Chile. *IUCN Forest Conservation Newsletter* 19:7-8.

World Wildlife Fund (WWF). 1991. *Views from Natural Forest Management Initiatives in Latin America.* Washington, D.C.

Zador, M. 1994. Galapagos Marine Resources Reserve: A Pre-Investment Analysis for the Parks in Peril Program. The Nature Conservancy, Washington, D.C.

Zimmerman, Robert C. 1982. Environmental Impact of Forestry. FAO Conservation Guide No. 7. Rome, Italy.

Zobel, Bruce J., G. van Wyk, and P. Stahl. 1987. *Growing Exotic Forests.* New York: Wiley Interscience.

List of Authors

Ronnie de Camino is Professor of Forestry at Universidad para La Paz and President of RNT- S.A., a consulting company in natural resource management in San José, Costa Rica. He is a board member of several international organizations, including the Center of International Forestry Research (CIFOR), based in Indonesia, and the Dutch Foundation of TROPENBOS.

Marc J. Dourojeanni, formerly chief of the Environment Division at IDB headquarters, is the Principal Environmental Advisor of the Bank in Brazil. Dr. Dourojeanni was the first president of the Peruvian Foundation for Nature Conservancy, and has served as vice-president of the National Agrarian University of Peru and of the International Union for the Conservation of Nature.

Olli Haltia, an economist at the European Investment Bank, was previously with Jaakko Poyry Consulting, Ltd., U.K. He holds a Ph.D. from the London School of Economics and has studied forest sector development particularly in Brazil and Chile.

Jared J. Hardner, an associate at Industrial Economics, Inc., Cambridge, Massachusetts, holds a master's degree from Yale University's School of Forestry and Environmental Studies and has extensive experience as a natural resource economist working in Latin America.

Carlos Felipe Jaramillo is a senior research economist at the Banco de la República, Bogotá, Colombia. Dr. Jaramillo was formerly a Visiting MacArthur Professor at the Department of Agricultural and Natural Resource Economics of the University of Maryland.

Kari Keipi is Senior Forester at the Inter-American Development Bank, with project and policy experience in twenty Latin American countries. Dr. Keipi has worked as a research economist and visiting scholar with public and private sectors in several countries in Europe and the United States.

Thomas Kelly is Assistant Professor of Economics and Latin American Studies at Middlebury College in Vermont. Dr. Kelly has been a researcher with the IDB Environment Department and at the Program for Management and Conservation of Natural Tropical Resources at the University of the Yucatán, Mexico.

Jan G. Laarman, Professor of Forest Policy and Economics at North Carolina State University, has researched and taught forest economics in Brazil under the sponsorship of the Ford Foundation. Dr. Laarman is also leader of a natural resource management program in Guatemala.

Ramón López is Professor of Economics in the Department of Agricultural and Resource Economics at the University of Maryland in College Park. Dr. López has served as principal economist in the World Bank's Trade Division, as senior economist in the Canadian Department of Agriculture, and as a visiting professor at the University of Chile.

Richard E. Rice, Director of the Natural Resource Economics Program at Conservation International, holds a Ph.D. in Natural Resource Economics from the University of Michigan's School of Natural Resources and the Environment. His specialization is forest policy in Latin America.

Markku Simula, a forest economist specializing in policy formulation, financing and trade, has worked in Latin America, Asia, Europe and Africa. He is the President of Indufor Oy, a forest consultancy agency, and Adjunct Professor at the University of Helsinki, Department of Forest Economics.

Julio C. Tresierra has served as a consultant on indigenous and development issues for many international organizations in Latin America. Dr. Tresierra is Professor of Sociology and Anthropology (emeritus) at Concordia University in Montreal, and holds a Ph.D. from the University of Notre Dame (United States).